LIFE

OF

CHARLES LESLIE

LIFE AND WRITINGS

OF

CHARLES LESLIE, M.A.

NONJURING DIVINE

BY THE

REV. R. J. LESLIE, M.A.

VICAR OF HOLBEACH S† JOHN

> "Non,
> Si chartæ sileant, quod bene feceris,
> Mercedem Tuleris."
> Hor. Car. iv. 8

RIVINGTONS

WATERLOO PLACE, LONDON

MDCCCLXXXV

PREFACE.

It was intended that this biography should be preceded by one of Charles Leslie's father, the Bishop of the Isles, Raphoe, and Clogher. Its publication, however, is delayed for, it is hoped, only a short time, owing to supply of letters and other new materials, which require the work to be recast and enlarged. A very long period has been occupied in preparing this volume, beyond what the contents might seem to demand perhaps, from the difficulty experienced in consulting various books and manuscripts, often at a great distance, and verifying references, whilst engaged in the regular duties of a remote country parish. My thanks, however, are therefore more eminently due to friends, who have kindly assisted me in accomplishing a task, which I could wish to have fallen into better hands, and which I have only ventured to undertake in despair of such appearing. I gratefully record my obligation in the first place to the Very Reverend Dr. Church, the learned and admirable Dean of S. Paul's, for his encouragement and introduction to the Bodleian and Sion College Libraries. To the Reverend Dr. Sparrow Simpson, for prompt and courteous replies and information on several points of inquiry. To the Reverend Henry W. Milman, Librarian of Sion College, for similar kindness. The Very Reverend Dr. Reeves, Dean of Armagh, whose reputation stands far above any praise of mine, will permit me at least to testify the esteem and affection with which the son of an old friend still regards him. The Reverend Canon Overton, Rector of Epworth, whose friendship has been a valued privilege for many years, will recognize in these pages some memorial of many interesting conversations. Yet neither he nor any other person, except myself, must be held responsible for the statements or sentiments which this book contains. They are the result of much consideration and extensive research, although I have purposely refrained from invading my pages with authorities. Last and most of all I am indebted to a kind wife for transcribing the manuscript, and other offices of affection, without which the work would not have been completed. Such as it is now, imperfect and inferior in execution to my own conception of what is due to the memory of a great and good man, I respectfully submit it to public consideration.

R. J. LESLIE.

HOLBEACH S. JOHN,
December, 1884.

CONTENTS.

I.

Leslie's Works—Cause of Neglect—Hallam's Censures—Birth, Parentage, Contemporaries, Education—Studentship in the Temple—Ordination and Cure of Souls—Marriage—Justice of Peace—Lady Frances Keightley—Supplement—Letter to a Gentleman, abridged .... PAGE 1

II.

James II.'s Early History and Accession—Romish Proceedings—Tyrconnel in Ireland—Chancellorship of Connor—Bishop Hacket—The King and Irish Clergy—High Sheriff—Disputations—Attacks on English Universities—The Seven Bishops 31

III.

Birth of Prince of Wales—Prince of Orange's Conduct—Revolution—Coronation of William and Mary—Ejection of Nonjuring Clergy—Chancellorship of Connor—Refutation of Archbishop King's Calumny—James and William in Ireland—Sherlock—Stillingfleet—Dr. Hickes—Henry Dodwell—Nelson—Kettlewell 56

IV.

Prohibition in Parish Churches—Nonjuring Separation—Ely House Private Ministrations—Easy Methods—Conversions

—Reply to Archbishop King's Book—Prosecution—Escape—Supplements—Easy Methods with Deists and Jews, abridged 80

V.

National Debts, etc.—Bishop of Ely and Nonjuring Friends—Archbishop Sancroft—Consecrations—Characters of Prelates and Clergy in the Two Communions—" Regale and Pontificate "—Dr. Wake—Kennet—Atterbury—Massacre at Glencoe—Tillotson—Burnet—Prince of Orange—Supplements—" Gallienus Redivis "—" Regale and Pontificate," abridged 115

VI.

Order of Publications—Quakers—" Snake in the Grass "—Penn—Oliver's Porter—Crisp—Calumnies—Conspiracy—Tithes—Socinianism—Anecdotes—Supplements—Quaker and Socinian Controversies—Qualification for Administration of Sacraments 164

VII.

Convocation—Innocent XI.—King of Spain—Duke of Gloucester—King James—At S. Germain—Death—Appearance—Character—Death of William—Offer to Leslie of Preferment—Robert Leslie—Bishop Huntingdon—Queen Anne—Occasional Conformity 226

VIII.

Renewal of War—Comprehension Scheme—Theatrical Amusements, etc.—Ecclesiastical History—Mr. Parker—Mixed Marriages—Origin of De Foe—Occasional Conformity—Sacheverell—New Association—" The Shortest Way with Dissenters " discovered—Supplements—Private Judgment—Ecclesiastical History—Mixed Marriages 253

IX.

Party Nomenclature — Intimacies — Whigs and Tories — "Rehearsal" — The Church in Scotland — "Cassandra" — The Three Estates — Calves'-Head Feasts — Club — Occasional Letter Writer — Burnet's Calumnies on the Clergy — High and Low Church — Nonconformity — Dr. Davenant — "Wolf Stript" — Owen — S. Wesley — Supplement — "Cassandra" — "New Associations" — "Wolf Stript" 282

X.

Historians of Queen Anne's Reign — Scotland — Ireland — Continental Powers — "Rehearsal" — Locke, etc. — Ministers at Clackmannan — Procession at Edinburgh — Playhouse — Supplements — Extracts from "Rehearsal" 316

XI.

Catechizing in Church — Conduct of "Rehearsal" — Change of Residence — Memorial of the Church — Visit to Oxford — Weathercock at Merton — Abraham Gill — Haymarket Theatre — Literary Forgeries and Piracies — Tindal's "Rights of the Christian Church" answered — Headship of the Church — The Admiral and Alderman — Meditated Discontinuance of "Rehearsal" — Asgill's Book — Coward's — Edwards — Hoadly — "Observator's" New Editor — Mr. Dodwell's Book — False Reports — Scottish Clergy — Supplement — Extracts from "Rehearsal" 349

XII.

The Prince — Invasion — Benjamin Hoadly and Sermon of Pomp — Ill Health — Death of Prince George — Dr. Gregory — Giving Security — Sacheverell's Trial and Episcopal Appointments — "Best Answer" — "Best of All" — Mr. Higden — Tyrrel — Supplement — Extracts from "Rehearsal" 393

XIII.

Death of Lord Clarendon—Marlborough's Victories—Letter to M.P.—Commentary and Events in Ten Years' War—The Chevalier and Queen Anne—Position of Nonjurors—Mrs. Leslie's Health—Good Old Cause—Warrant—Outlawed—Mr. Cherry 432

XIV.

Lord Rochester — Jacobites at Waltham — "Truth of Christianity" — Abbé S. Real — Death of Princess Elizabeth — Illness of Chevalier—Descriptions of him—New Consecrations—Nonjurors—Mrs. Leslie's Illness and Death—Chaplaincy at Bar-le-Duc—Conversions—Supplements—"Truth of Christianity," etc. 460

XV.

Bolingbroke's Complaint—Letter to Bishop of Meaux—Bishop Bull—Letter on Usages—Other Pamphlets—Death of Queen Anne—Projected Invasion—Robert Leslie's Advice—"Church of England's Advice to her Children"—Chevalier—George I.—Jacobites — Return — An Informer — Supplement — Case between Churches of England and Rome—Letter to Bishop of Meaux concerning the Usage 490

CHAPTER I.

LESLIE'S WORKS—CAUSE OF NEGLECT—HALLAM'S CENSURES—BIRTH, PARENTAGE, CONTEMPORARIES, EDUCATION—STUDENTSHIP IN THE TEMPLE—ORDINATION AND CURE OF SOULS—MARRIAGE—JUSTICE OF PEACE—LADY FRANCES KEIGHTLEY—SUPPLEMENT—LETTER TO A GENTLEMAN, ABRIDGED.

CHARLES LESLIE, theological and political writer, was an author of great talent and learning, whose name and writings have suffered a most undeserved and unfortunate neglect during the nineteenth century. Scotland is the part of the United Kingdom where both are still held in greatest esteem; even there, however, the remembrance is on the wane, except among the old Episcopal clergy, who themselves are of a learned and orthodox school. In the country where he lived, and that in which he was born, his name and books alike now meet with scant praise, and are scarcely ever mentioned even in ecclesiastical circles or writings. Just a century ago exactly the reverse was the case. No name more frequently occurred in conversation, no author's books more frequently elicited warm approval, while yet his death was a recent event. And during his lifetime his celebrity stood unquestionably as high as that of any of his contemporaries. Two causes have operated to produce this alteration. Nonjuring and Jacobite principles with which he was eminently identified have necessarily lost all interest since the settlement of the Hanoverian dynasty, beyond revival of the question now, and extinction of the Stuart royal family. With it have died out, not only the hopes and efforts of its supporters, but the call for laboured invectives and detraction, with which their names were pursued by political writers, so long as the Hanoverian house had anything to fear from adherents to the cause of the Stuarts and hereditary right. When such persons ceased to assail eminent Nonjurors and load their memory with reproach—much of which writing under the name of history in the interest of the Whig party was paid for out of public funds—naturally a deeper oblivion overtook those men than would otherwise have befallen them. For none were longer concerned to defend any more than defame them, and the subject had become so wearisome that the public in general were glad to escape from its mention or repetition, for a season at least, among fresher and more exciting topics. Another reason for the oblivion into which Charles Leslie's name has fallen in recent times is less satisfactory—the decrease of theological learning and study among clergy as well as laity, which ensued upon the establishment of the house of Hanover upon the throne of Great Britain, and has continued down to the present day; with a very slight improvement now perhaps observable in some quarters. How very few names of divines during the last century and a half can be mentioned, who ever wrote a line worth remembrance in the communion of the Churches of England, Ireland, and Scotland! Scarcely half a dozen; and what some wrote was of very questionable orthodoxy, compared with the plain letter of their own formularies. Among Nonjurors were not a meagre half-dozen, but dozens in London, Oxford, and other places, every one of whom was confessedly thoroughly steeped in divinity, and admitted by his opponents, whether political or ecclesiastical, to be entitled to the highest respect for learning and ability in his proper calling. At the present day, incessant pastoral work and a variety of interruptions are often pleaded as an excuse for want of theological learning and study among the clergy. One would like to think the explanation satisfactory, and to extend it so far as may be obviously required. But if clergy have not time, amid the pressure of engagements of another kind, for study—which is a habit not to be acquired at a later period if neglected in youth— then they should be more chary of preaching on every possible occasion or opportunity. Competition for popularity will not be successful whilst it is conducted upon the plan of rivalling its teachers in mere empty talk, barren impoverished discourses, whether professedly extempore in delivery or otherwise, or of abusing the Church's authority to utter their unsound opinions in her name. And that both the one and the other are extensively practised, Dissenters can testify from experience as well as Church-people. If sermons were less abundant, they would not be so little esteemed; if rarer, they would be of better quality; and congregations, instead of being starved, would be fed with sound doctrine, and thus more heartily attached to the Church, than a vast majority, who go to hear but not to pray, nor to worship, but show their preference for different schools of thought-less-ness. Quite as feeble and impoverished as the sermons heard in sacred buildings are those written and reproduced under various titles in magazines and periodicals. Pens of ready writers, who would write better if they wrote more slowly, are actually hired out under sectarian auspices to give these productions currency, and of necessity contents are toned and watered down to suit the taste of the commercial undertakers. This system is doubly dishonest and unjust. For periodicals acquire popularity and circulation by the names of orthodox divines, and thus become vehicles for dissemination of opinions and statements by heterodox writers which tacitly they disapprove; but numbers of readers are unable to see the distinction. Further, instead of publishers who confine their business within the limits of conscience and authority meeting with support and encouragement for circulating only what is wholesome and sound doctrine, they find the most active opponents trying to hinder and undersell them are the Church's professed defenders for filthy lucre's sake.

If the writings of Charles Leslie have suffered neglect owing to want of study among the clergy, and the growth of a pernicious style of literature upon religious subjects, they have been as unfairly dealt with quite in another way. His arguments and statements have been pirated and plagiarized by a great many writers, without generally the slightest acknowledgment of their obligation; indeed, the silence and reserve with regard to his name is quite remarkable, as if they had never even seen his works, while borrowing wholesale, and picking his brains *ad libitum*, some of these being persons whom one would hardly have suspected of such dishonesty. Thus, while readers have often been convinced by the mode of reasoning adopted on subjects of controversy, and attributed much merit to some modern divine, they have, in fact, been reading what Charles Leslie wrote with still greater force and clearness without its new dress. His works, indeed, contain a complete armoury of defence against all opponents of the Church. There is scarcely a question between her doctrine and that of all rival and different communions which he has not treated at length. Therefore exclusion of reference to him is in itself a suspicious circumstance, which further examination of several volumes accounts for easily, if not creditably, to their authors.

To wipe off the dust of modern neglect and restore to its rightful position the name of this long-forgotten champion of the Church of England, is the aim and purpose of this work. Should the execution fall short of the design in the opinion of competent judges, yet it will be something to have endeavoured and not succeeded in default of some other pen more capable of doing justice to the subject, better than by silence seem to consent to the unmerited obscurity of a worthy and useful life. There can be no pretext for overlooking his merits any longer, because that question has been decided finally against him in which he differed from the majority of the nation, and with its now unanimous consent a Parliamentary title has been substituted for hereditary right to the throne of England. The cause for which he made tremendous sacrifices and incurred the greatest obloquy has passed beyond the region of dispute. If he were alive he would have no temptation to resuscitate it. But the principles which he laboured most industriously and powerfully to inculcate in politics remain as true as ever, applicable to other questions frequently arising for discussion. It was also in another capacity he shone conspicuously among contemporaries, as a defender of the faith against adversaries of every kind. On this account, therefore, he has a claim to remembrance by posterity. What the eminent lexicographer, Dr. Johnson, said of him has been unfairly employed to the depreciation and disparagement of other Nonjurors: "Leslie was a reasoner not to be reasoned against." Johnson's meaning was not intended by himself to be pressed too closely to their prejudice, nor had the remark any proper application to Sancroft, Hickes, and others, as has been well pointed out in the interesting biography of William Law.[1] But it was rigidly correct in respect of the persons whom the doctor mentioned by way of a distinction from a number of obtrusive advocates, whose incapacity injured the nonjuring cause which they professed to serve. The most noteworthy assailant of Leslie in modern times was Hallam the historian, who has loaded his name with abuse, and contemptuously ridiculed his arguments as mere " stuff." Dr. Johnson was, at least, equal to Hallam in capacity; and Macaulay, though writing on the same side and as prepossessed against the Church of England, has pronounced an exactly opposite verdict. But no one who has read Hallam's history carefully can doubt that his acquaintance with Leslie's writings was of the very slightest and most cursory description. He simply censured what he never took pains to read because it proceeded from an eminent representative of the religion and politics which he naturally detested and held a brief to defame. Hallam not only was laboriously unjust to Nonjurors, the Church of England, and Tories, but with amazing inconsistency has admitted the principles to be sound for which they contended, while heaping personal abuse upon the men who were no longer alive to answer him. " Bigotry," " intolerance," " scurrility," " dulness," and similar epithets, the Whig historian has lavished in profusion upon men of spotless character, exemplary piety, great learning, and shining talents, because they presumed to suffer the loss of all things rather than forswear themselves; because they refused to abandon the principle of hereditary right; because they conscientiously, against their temporal interests, declined to sanction a revolution which they deemed neither warrantable on the grounds put forth for

[1] Overton's " Life and Times of William Law," p. 60 (Longmans, 1881).

its justification, nor the best expedient for accomplishing a very necessary purpose—the control of an infatuated priest-ridden monarch within the limits of the constitution which he had solemnly pledged himself to maintain. Not a single piece of evidence has been furnished by Hallam in substantiation of any one of the accusations which with unsparing and indiscriminating fury he has hurled against Nonjurors; and yet impartiality was the one superior qualification to which he laid claim, and upon which has been based since use of his work as an authoritative standard and a text-book in educational institutions. His own pages cannot be excused from dulness even by partisans as one-sided as himself, compared with other histories quite as painstaking and much more accurate. If "bigotry," "intolerance," and "scurrility" may be ascribed to a Whig and a sceptic, then not one Nonjuror, nor Tory, nor devoted Churchman whom he has denounced ever deserved the imputation more justly than himself. Much licence is claimed by much allowance extended to controversialists who in the heat of debate deal severely with opponents. But no such licence or allowance can be pleaded for writers who, under the veil of history, endeavour to calumniate and misrepresent good and great men in the eyes of posterity, not only without proofs, but by statements contrary to facts. And of this gross injustice Hallam was deliberately guilty towards Charles Leslie and many other faithful and learned men, only because of their ardent attachment to that Church and that ancient constitution which the Whigs had sedulously laboured to destroy. When the rising generation are being inoculated and poisoned by such writings, it is a duty to protest against the system on the part of those, who have carefully examined cases for themselves, and know that characters and events have been misrepresented with a view of sapping the foundations of true religion and substituting for it a motley incongruous jumble of opinions without authority, under the specious pretence of liberality. It is a convenient method of disposing of arguments to pass them by with a sneer as "stuff," but it would have been common honesty in Hallam to state, at the same time, how many very competent critics differed from that estimate. He has involved himself in many contradictions with regard to parties and individuals at the period of the Revolution, among whom was he whose life and character are here attempted to be portrayed.

If it be shown that, amid much opposition and contention of various kinds, he maintained a reputation for integrity and piety, among honourable and pious men who even differed with him on mainly political and ecclesiastical subjects; if it be shown that he gained the admiration of eminent and learned men both at home and abroad for his talents and acquirements;—then the revilings of mercenary partisans will recoil on themselves and their party, and that justice be accorded which is desired. Leslie has been termed "the leader of the Nonjurors" and the "most distinguished man" among them. He cannot be justly entitled the latter, and he never aspired to the former position, nor was accounted to hold it. In fact, there was no such leader in his day. If there had been, by right it must have been the saintly Sancroft, by qualification George Hickes. A history of Nonjurors as a community requires yet to be written, for Lothbury's ill-digested performance can only be deemed an imperfect contribution of tracts and pamphlets towards it.

Charles Leslie was the sixth son and second surviving

of John Leslie, D.D., LL.D., successively Bishop of the Isles in Scotland, and Raphoe and Clogher in Ireland. His father had endured a siege in his palace at the second place, commonly called Raphoe Castle, first by Romanist rebels, and then by the forces of Cromwell, to whom he was compelled at length to yield, being the last to surrender to him in Ireland. This son, therefore, was born in Dublin, whither the bishop retreated for some years, till his palace could be rendered habitable again in 1658.

The event occurred upon Thursday, July 17, 1650, at seven o'clock in the morning, and he was christened by the name of Charles. Although that has become since common in the family, and generally given to the eldest son, it had not been so previously in the original branch of the Leslies settled in Scotland, from whom the bishop was descended. Probably there never had been one so named before, and the reason of its selection in this case is not far to seek. It was bestowed in honourable remembrance of the martyr-king, to whom the bishop had been both devotedly attached and greatly indebted. Well might he add in his family register to this record of loyalty a prayer for his son, "whom may God preserve," when he remembered the king's cruel murder and his own loss of children, amidst many other sufferings mainly owing to unswerving adherence to the royal cause. Some report of this devout aspiration, coupled with a vague idea of the bishop's character and principles, distorted and exaggerated in the usual manner of reports, may have suggested a foolish anecdote related in the first edition of the "Encyclopædia Britannica," to the effect that before his birth the bishop expressed a hope "that Charles should prove the greatest scourge of Covenanters ever seen." It had not a shadow of foundation in fact, for the bishop was not a man to entertain, much less to proclaim upon the housetop, silly and profane wishes of the kind for the amusement of reviewers and their readers. But because an objection was made to its repetition, a Liberal writer in the last edition has revenged himself by curtailing his account down almost to the point of exclusion; so one injustice has only been replaced by another: but, then, Charles Leslie and his father were neither Liberalists nor latitudinarians.

The year 1650 was remarkable for several important events in the history of the United Kingdom. First and most notable was the birth of the Prince of Orange, whose career so materially affected his whose life is here to be related. On May 21 the gallant Montrose was put to death in a cruel and disgraceful manner by Presbyterians at Edinburgh. Charles II. landed on a fruitless enterprise in Scotland on June 23, and on September 23 Cromwell defeated David Leslie and Alexander at Dunbar. The famous general Marlborough was born in this year also, with whom Leslie was afterwards brought into close acquaintance, though the wide diversity of their general pursuits, habits, and tastes would have prevented it ripening into friendship or intimacy had there been need of much connection. William King, Archbishop of Dublin, was not only born in the same year, but was a contemporary of Charles Leslie at Trinity College, Dublin, and the man who, in concert with Dr. Burnet, Bishop of Salisbury, first endeavoured to effect his ruin, and continued his lifelong enemy; the reason of whose antipathy will appear further on. At the age of ten years Charles was sent to school at Enniskillen; one of royal foundation then in the commencement of its useful career, and which with undiminished celebrity has continued to the present day. Grants and endowments out of forfeited estates made by James I. had been renewed by King Charles I. in 1629, and vested in the Archbishop of Armagh (then the famous James Usher) for the benefit of it and other schools in Ireland, at Armagh, Cavan, and Dungannon, the last of which, however, is the only one beside Enniskillen that has sustained a high reputation for its pupils. It used to be said for a very long time, that at entrance examinations in the University of Dublin, where high places are an object of great competition, of the first twelve seven always were gained by pupils from Enniskillen, and five by those from Dungannon. Whatever may have been the merits of his masters, no registers remain to show that Leslie exhibited any proficiency indicative of his hereditary talents or future greatness. At the early age of fourteen from thence he passed to matriculate in the University as a fellow-commoner, on August 4, 1664; but that was not unusual then as now. His tutor was Dr. Michael Ward. There is no further mention of his name in the College books till his admission to the degree of Master of Arts in 1673, not even of his becoming a Bachelor of Arts—an omission noticeable in regard to some other persons of the name of Leslie, for which no reason can be assigned. It is sufficiently evident, however, that he gained no distinctions of any kind during his University career, nor gave any promise then either of the learning or talents which subsequently he exhibited. It is the more remarkable, because he must have applied himself to books and formed a habit of study long before, or else he never could have made up for arrears of lost time so completely as to acquire that extensive range of information which he displayed when he betook himself to writing on controversial subjects. Nor had he to mourn that painful hindrance to success, worse than actual poverty, which has discouraged many a youth conscious of higher powers—domestic discouragement and neglect. Parents, brothers, and sisters have thus in pure selfishness blighted the prospects and aspirations of geniuses who could have elevated their whole families to honour and fortune. But Charles Leslie had no such injustice to complain of. What is more, his father set an example which, unfortunately, has not been followed by men of rank and station in Ireland as it ought. If any one would have been justified in sending his son for education elsewhere, it was the Bishop of Clogher, because he was not an Irishman. But he had that higher patriotism which recognized duty to the land of his adoption. Is it any wonder that the gulf of separation between the nobility and the people of Ireland has been continually widening, when the former, generation after generation, were taught to look with contempt upon the very noblest institutions of their native country? Landlords have committed many wrongs, but no graver mistake, nor more unwarrantable proof of a want of patriotism have they given than this neglect of Trinity College, Dublin.

The bishop had died in 1671, and Charles's first intention after leaving the University was to become a barrister, for which purpose he entered himself a student of the Temple in London, and continued in the profession for ten years. During this period he became conversant with the principles both of civil and ecclesiastical law, and acquired a considerable facility in dealing with the legal bearings of questions in public life, which he showed on several occasions to advantage afterwards. There does not appear much foundation for the statement, first made by Ware and Walter Harris, and frequently repeated by others since, that he grew wearied of the dryness and intricacy of the law. He never said so himself; on the contrary, he took pleasure in exercising his acquirements whenever opportunity offered. Casual expressions in conversation have been assigned a meaning they were not intended to bear. What he said was only of a general character concerning a practice of counsel trying to make the worse appear the better cause in a client's behalf. This he condemned, and to what extent it was often carried some persons can remember in a very remarkable trial on a capital charge, when the advocate solemnly assured the jury of his own conviction of the prisoner's innocence. The evil lies, not so much in the danger of an intelligent jury being misled by counsel practising it, as of suspicions of guilt being created in other cases where more conscientious men refrained from giving such assurance, if it became customary. How far counsel are tempted or required to put false glosses upon cases in general, and how far this may be justifiable *in foro conscientiæ*, is a difficult question left for others to determine.

If Leslie's scruples were not singular, yet they were not the result of any painful experience, nor had any personal and particular reference. Now, the simple truth is that, like many another clever barrister, he obtained no briefs most evidently because he had no connection among solicitors to give him a start in his profession; which did not fail to damp his expectations. It is not surprising, since his acquaintance in England was necessarily at that time limited, and no reputation of University success had accompanied his arrival at the Temple. There was another reason. Solicitors have always showed great shrewdness in discovering the young men likely to suit their purpose. They find out their characters, habits, and pursuits, as well as talents. And they would not have formed a favourable opinion of Leslie if they learned, as they easily could have done, that he was much more absorbed in the study of divinity and ecclesiastical history than the subjects in which they needed proficiency. That was the real state of the case. He had, in fact, mistaken his profession, and though no doubt he might have eventually succeeded by perseverance, nor could be said to have felt disgusted with the law, nature exerted itself at length in the conviction that his proper and more congenial sphere of employment would be the ministry of the Church. His elder brother having been set apart for that, family arrangement had settled for him to go to the Bar; as it has done in numberless other cases, without consideration of his peculiar aptitude for the calling, and before he knew his own mind. At the end of ten years the propriety of a change became apparent, and he offered himself for Holy Orders. There was no difficulty in accomplishing his wishes. His brother owned the property at Glaslough which the bishop had left, but he very gladly shared his home with him, and Charles had some means of his own; not much, but a competence. An opening also conveniently offered there to act as curate assistant of the parish church, for his brother had an incumbency in another part of the diocese. Accordingly he was ordained Deacon in 1680 by Dr. Sheridan, Bishop of Cloyne; Priest, 1681, by the Bishop of Kilmore, being at the time just thirty years of age. His first title seems to have been in Cloyne for a very short time. The parish of Donagh, in which Glaslough is situated, did not afford much field for his energies or talents. It is now a poor place, and was even more so then. The population consisted mainly of Presbyterians and Romanists; Church-people, or as they were termed, in distinction from the former as well as the latter, members of the Protestant Church, were nearly all dependents of the Castle. Thus he had the more time for pursuit of those studies to which he was devoted. His position also in society marked him out for the office of a magistrate, to which he was appointed about the same time as his ordination to the priesthood, and the ability and activity displayed in administration of justice, when the duties of that office were less simple and less of a routine character than in more recent times, soon commended him to notice and respect among other gentlemen on the Bench. His opinion began to be sought beyond his own jurisdiction and upon questions of difficulty of various kinds, so that he became the chief authority upon civil as well as ecclesiastical matters both in his own county, Monaghan, and in the adjoining ones. That he took great delight in this office is evident, not only from the zeal manifested in its work, but from a treatise written afterwards, in which at considerable length he justified the combination of clerical and magisterial functions in the same person. What can be said in its favour is there stated forcibly and clearly; but, therefore, all the more forcible are the objections which he has abstained from considering. Experience does not confirm his judgment. The practice is injurious in several respects, and tends to stamp the Church with a mark of Erastianism, however convenient it may be for State purposes, in neighbourhoods where there is a scarcity of suitable persons. The clergy most eager to become justices of the peace are not generally distinguished for their knowledge of divinity nor high estimation of the priesthood—which, however, may be a recommendation to some minds—but rather are candidates for position in society or the world's eye. There are also still more serious objections. The poor, who form the greater part of every parish, intensely dislike justice administered by a clergyman, and feel personally aggrieved by a sentence from him; which may be an erroneous sentiment, but is natural, and can never be eradicated. Besides, the two characters of priest and justice are essentially incompatible, for the confidence expected in the one case is actually forbidden, if it were not impossible, by the caution required in the other. It is a palpable contradiction that a man should upon Sunday invite his people to resort to him "for ghostly counsel and the benefit of absolution" if their "consciences be burdened with any weighty matter," and they be encouraged by the further security of secrecy, pledged in the 113th canon, that he shall "not reveal to any person an offence or crime," when that same man, no longer as a priest but a magistrate, is in duty bound to hand over to the tender mercies of the police the person who fondly ventured to confess that he had stolen a goose, or signed a wrong name, or used false weights, or sent bad meat to a distance for human food—offences not beyond the bounds of experience to be committed, or probably to be repented of and confessed.

The duty of confession is not advocated here, so Protestant readers need not be offended; but it is distinctly thus sanctioned by the Church of England, and was far more positively enjoined by the great reformer, John Knox, upon all Christian people. No answer is furnished in the treatise of Charles Leslie to these difficulties, therefore it must remain for some one else to explain and reconcile the administration of Law and Gospel by a priest under obligations both to secrecy and disclosure at the same time.

Here is a fair abstract of his reasoning on the contrary side, which clerical magistrates can quote in their own defence: "There are many prejudiced against our clergy being admitted to any share in the civil administration; they pretend that it is at least an hindrance to the office of their calling, which they would have wholly abstracted from the world, and to respect only heavenly things. . . . This is a spice of monkish superstition. I would pray these men to consider whether the practice be not as necessary to a clergyman as the preaching of good doctrine, and wherein can he show his practice more, or so beneficially, as in assisting to making good laws and preventing wickedness being established by law. . . . The young king Joash did that which was right in the sight of the Lord all the days of Jehoiada the priest. . . . God Himself made priests the chief judges even in secular affairs under the Law, and does not the reason hold the same under the Gospel, viz. that they are supposed, and ought to be most conscientious in the discharge of this duty; and consequently that it is best for the people that the clergy should have the discharge of it? Does not the apostle argue from the same topic 1 Cor. vi., and think it fit that the Church should judge of secular matters? . . . It is true Christ gave no civil authority at all to His Church; but He nowhere debarred her from it if given by the secular power. And the judging which S. Paul speaks of is plainly voluntary arbitration, not encroaching in the least upon the office of the civil magistrate. But this shows that it was no ways unfit for clergymen to concern themselves in secular matters, else it would be as unlawful to be arbitrators as judges. . . . No man but thinks it becoming the office of a clergyman to be a peacemaker, which is impossible without understanding something of worldly business. And might he not do this with more advantage if he were clothed with the civil authority? I have seen the experience of it, and the country very sensible of the benefit of a clergyman in the Commission of the Peace, where they had that dispatch, and justice and protection, which they bemoaned the want of when he was removed from them. . . . If he be a good man and understanding, no man can be a fitter magistrate, and thereby more recommend him as to his spiritual office, when they see and taste and feel his justice, prudence, beneficence, and charity, as well as hear him discourse it from the pulpit; when he can contribute and vote and act for the support of the poor, and be their remembrancer and advocate every assizes and sessions, as well as recommend it in a sermon; when he can browbeat the audacious and profane, and if not convert them, yet keep them within decency, that their infection spread not among his flock; when a debauchee dare not swear two or three rappers in his face, burlesque the holy Scriptures, or . . . without the correction of the stocks. . . . It cannot be unbecoming the character of a clergyman, that he be enabled to preserve religion and morality from insults and outrage."[1] This defence of his secular capacity, written ten years after he had ceased to exercise it, shows that time had not altered his opinion of its propriety. Nor is it hard to trace in it his own experience, for his removal on all hands was admitted a great loss to the magisterial bench.

Now it will be an agreeable diversion to view the author in his more private relations. He married Jane, daughter of the Very Reverend Richard Griffith, Dean of Ross.

One who held this same position, together with the more difficult post of Rector in a large northern town at a later date for many years, used to say that he had "never been there in his life;" but, if it were a sinecure, equally nominal was the remuneration. In Dean Griffith's day the dignity and duties were just a trifle more of a reality; but

[1] "Essay concerning Divine Right of Tithes," vol. vii. pp. 424-427, Oxford ed.

Ross itself can scarcely be said to have had much substantial existence in an ecclesiastical sense either then or since, consisting of the county of Kerry, the most remote in the south-west of Ireland, and alternately made a mere appendage to other dioceses, Cloyne, or Cork and Cloyne, without a Cathedral, and its churches during the seventeenth century nearly all in a grievous state of dilapidation. Such honorary titles are in the patronage of the Lord-lieutenant, and generally conferred upon clerical supporters of the Government, or on men of some social standing, through family interest.

Any persons concerned about the propriety of clerical marriages must be respectfully referred to what is said upon the subject in the life of his father, the Bishop of Clogher, and to Charles Leslie's own remarks in the same treatise in which their appointment to the magistracy is defended, for justification of himself in following his father's example. A more generally interesting matter will be the wife's position in her new home. What a woman is supposed to desire is a house of her own; whether a castle, a cottage, or a parsonage, to be the head and mistress of the establishment. That Mrs. Charles could not have been at Glaslough, for the bishop's wife still lived, and of course reigned supreme, at least nominally and by right. And if the Dean should marry, yet another could take precedence of the bride as only a younger son's wife.[1] How did this arrangement answer? Could not any one have predicted the consequence? Was not the very idea of its lasting preposterous? Notwithstanding any such forebodings, the arrangement did answer exceedingly well. No domestic brawls disturbed the house; no symptoms of incompatibility were ever known for some six years or more. When

[1] This occurred in 1698.

an interruption of peace and harmony did come, it came not from within, but from without; not owing to any discord among the inmates, but the political revolution which drove Charles Leslie and his family from the home and country to which he had become attached. No doubt a great deal of discretion and forbearance had to be exercised to maintain close and cordial relations at all times, and keep things in tune; but these qualities, or the want of them, would have been manifested no less under different circumstances. The more credit is due to the happy family at Glaslough, that no actual necessity hindered their separation had it been desirable at any previous period. In 1686 another event occurred out of the usual course. Lady Frances Keightley came to reside with them, sister of the Earls of Clarendon and Rochester, and wife of Mr. Thomas Keightley, a gentleman holding an office in the Civil Service, and residing at Leixlip, near Dublin; with his full consent and at her own desire. It is of importance because it explains another matter, about which much mystery and needless conjectures have been hazarded. She had been tempted to apostasy from the Christian faith by certain persons mixing in the highest classes of society. Such a step gave a terrible shock to her family, especially her husband and Lord Clarendon, who had used all efforts of dissuasion in vain. Fortunately at this time she became acquainted with Charles Leslie through a mutual friend, to whom his character and ability in controversy were well known. Her mind was in a state of great distraction, and she desired some place of retirement where she might calmly review the painful doubts which had been suggested concerning the whole truth of religion. Lord Clarendon's letter to his brother will best explain the arrangement further. "That unfortunate woman, Keightley told me a fortnight since, was offered a retreat at Mr. Leslie's house, which he agreed to. They are two brothers, clergymen who live together, and have very good women for their wives.[1] They are very worthy men, and of good esteem in their calling. Her husband knows them well. Thither she went on this day was a sennight. It is a private place in the north about 60 miles from hence, that is as far as from London to Bristol (*sic*). There she may stay as long as I will, and we will be thinking of another retreat.—Chapel Izod, Sept. 6, 1686."[2]

Now, this letter is satisfactory in two respects, when compared with one published afterwards in connection with a vindication of Leslie's "Short and Easy Method with the Deists." All sorts of ingenious speculations have been hazarded, both about the person referred to by his lordship, and the other addressed by Leslie. Mr. Gleig, in a very interesting and generous defence of him, suggested the Duke of Leeds as the latter. But it could be shown that Leslie had no communication with the duke upon any subject, nor could have held intercourse with him at that period, if ever afterwards any intimacy occurred between them. Leslie was never his chaplain, as again has been erroneously stated. The duke joined in the Church party ultimately and spoke contemptuously of the Revolution; but when that letter was originally written, he, as Earl Danby, was a decided Whig, with no concern about points of faith at all; and soon after took a foremost part in the conspiracy against King James II. His name, therefore, is out of the question. But why should the author's own positive statement be rejected, when no possible motive can be suggested for doubting it? And he distinctly asserted of his treatise upon its republication, that "it was at first

---

[1] An error. See above. [2] Clarendon's "Diary."

but two sheets of paper wrote for the satisfaction of a gentlewoman (though it is addressed as to a man) who had been staggered with the arguments of Deism even to distraction; for though she told me she had not become to be a downright Deist, yet she was not able to answer their arguments, nor to clear up the matter in her own mind. . . . She came to abstain from all prayers even in private, and she was in a most deplorable condition, owning that she was often tempted to destroy herself, which she was afraid would be the issue. I found discoursing with her had but little effect, for in that violent discomposure she could not give attention, but would fall out into terrible exclamations, and wishing herself dead, or that she had never been born. I then wrote this letter to her, free from all intricacies and suited to her capacity; and prevailed with her to copy it in her own hand, thinking that would fix her attention the more, and prevent those wandering thoughts which interrupted her consideration of what was offered to her in discourse. And by the blessing of God this had the desired effect, and at last was fully convinced, as she still remains."[1] Nothing could be more explicit than this account, tallying exactly with the facts ascertained of Lady Frances residing at Glaslough, for some reason not publicly known at the time. For want of the proper clue aspersions have been cast upon her reputation, and suggestions hazarded of her ailment without a shadow of foundation by readers of Clarendon's "Diary" and "Letters," which much more properly would apply to the eighteenth or nineteenth century habits than the seventeenth. One may well shrink from the keeping of a diary or correspondence, if private affairs are to be ruthlessly misconceived

[1] Vindication of "Short and Easy Method," vol. i. pp. 257, 258, Oxford ed.

and misrepresented in the odious light of vices belonging to a succeeding age. Instead of a stain or shade of reproach resting upon the name of the daughter of that nobleman her father, and that nobleman her brother, the two Lords Clarendon, Lady Frances Keightley stands out here distinguished as a most excellent and sensible woman, who, when subjected to that temptation of superior rather than inferior intellects, wisely resolved to seek satisfaction for her doubts by no hasty apostasy, the usual resort of weak minds. She neither flung herself into Charybdis nor upon Scylla, nor continued to flounder upon a sea of idle private conjecture, but quietly applied first to her natural and proper guides in religion, away from scenes of excitement or disturbance of her thoughts. Her conduct might afford an example worthy of imitation to many of both sexes, who often become sated and wearied with the frivolities of what is called high life, and then unreasonably for their dejection blame a religion the very elements of which they never rightly understood or cared to learn; or those with intellectual tastes, though somewhat overrating their powers, who seek notoriety and satisfaction by adopting the most fashionable craze in religion of their day. Such persons "vert"—they are none of them converted in any real sense, but perverted either to superstition or infidelity, nor add much credit to the particular system adopting or adopted by them. Lady Frances showed herself of nobler character and finer mould. The happy result was, under the Divine blessing, what had been desired and anticipated. She recovered from her painful temptation by wicked Deists, regained her lost balance of mind, and became not only, as she had been before, distinguished for honour and ability, but a faithful devoted daughter of the true Church in England. The veil of mystery properly drawn over a lady's identity would not even have been lifted here to satisfy a reasonable curiosity concerning Leslie's reference, if such delicacy had not been first dispensed with by the publishers of Lord Clarendon's "Diary," and thereby exposed his sister's name to suspicions and suggestions which are shown to be utterly unwarrantable. Her friendship continued thus cemented by the purest and holiest of obligations ever afterwards, nor did her connection and domiciliation at Glaslough terminate till Leslie himself had to remove to England. His was most truly a work of charity in affording her a pleasant home, with opportunity of meditation apart from the baneful society of infidels. At the same time, nothing could have been more judicious than his plan of putting his arguments in the shape of a letter, instead of worrying controversial discourses and conversations. Truth is seldom elicited by these, but much unwholesome agitation produced, and a combative antagonistic disposition to question, and display one's own talent in making objections. Many perverts from the Church of England have ascribed their change of faith to the mode of handling adopted by ill-qualified preachers of controversial sermons, who have only suggested doubts, and exposed their own vanity and incompetence.

An epitome of the letter is now presented, which can be skipped by readers who have no taste for such dissertations. It is hoped that ladies who may favour this work with perusal will not be among the number, but show that the author originally, in addressing his arguments to one of their sex, rightly estimated their mental capacities as on a par with the others of stronger physical powers.

The letter is here reduced to about its first dimensions, without omission of any material part of the contents as amplified and extended in publication by himself afterwards.

A Letter to a Gentleman.

I have read over your papers with great satisfaction and heartily bless God with you, and for you, that He has had mercy and opened your eyes ... given you likewise that true spirit of repentance to make what satisfaction you can for the injuries you have done to religion.

1. *Creation.*—You have laid the true foundation of God against the atheist, of His creation of the world and providence against assertors of blind chance. If all be chance then their thoughts are so too. ... Others suppose the world and all things to have been from eternity, and gone on in a constant succession. But a succession cannot be without a beginning.

2. *Providence.*—To deny providence in the First Cause, is the denying of a God. Whence had we ours, for we find we have one: "He that made the eye, does He not see?" And He who put providence into the heart of man, has He none Himself? ... The glory of His wisdom and power seems greater in providence than creation, especially in governing the actions of free agents without taking from them the freedom of their will to do as they list, and turning their very evil into good by the almightiness of His wisdom. ... This strikes us more sensibly, and is nearer to us than the making of a tree or a star. ... When the sins of men are increased, He permits their destruction of each other. And they are so free agents, that they think it their own doing; though under the unseen direction of a superior power. ... His providence is observable in private affairs. A thought sometimes darting into a man's mind to rid him of a difficulty, or show him an advantage. ... Events he thought to his utter ruin he finds afterwards

to be much for the best, and that he had been undone if that had not happened which he feared. On the other hand, things he thought for his great benefit he has found to be for his hurt. This shows a Providence, which sees further than we can, and disposes all our actions, though done in the full freedom of our own will to what He pleases.

3. *Revelation.*—Those considerations are earthly in comparison of heavenly things which God has revealed in holy Scriptures (Wisdom ix. 13-16). . . . All religions pretend to revelation for their original. The heathen and Mohammedan not only want the marks which ascertain the truth of fact, but their morals and worship are impure, and inconsistent with the attributes of God. Some philosophers spoke against revenge, but not on account of humanity and love to our brethren: and by humility they meant only dejection of mind, which is a vice; they had no notion of it as a virtue. . . . The Jewish religion has the certainty of fact, and its morals are good, but came not up to primitive purity. Perfection of morals and the true knowledge of God was reserved for the Christian religion, which has the infallible marks; and answers the objection of Jews that Christ wrought His miracles by Beelzebub; for we must alter our notion of Satan and suppose him to be good, and his kingdom be then at an end, which we see not yet done if Satan cast out Satan.

4. *The Holy Trinity.*—We acknowledge there are many things in the Divine nature far out of the reach of our reason. . . . Yet this obliges us to allow the necessary consequences of a First Cause. . . . As to the contradiction alleged in Three being One, it is none unless it be said they are so in the same respect. . . . One army may consist of thousands; there is one human nature, yet multitudes partake of it,

The three Persons are one nature, not three and one in the same respect. Again, that may be a contradiction in one nature which is not in another; *e.g.* a man may go two miles as soon as one, because two is but one and another one. Yet this is no contradiction to sight, which can reach a star as well as a chimney-top, and the sun darts his rays in one instant from heaven to earth; but more than all these is the motion of thought. ... No words can give an idea of sight or light to a man born blind, and consequently to reconcile the progress of either to him from being a contradiction. ... Therefore we cannot charge that as a contradiction in the Incomprehensible Nature, though we found it to be so in ours, of being three in one.

We find in our nature a near resemblance of the Holy Trinity, and of the different operations of each, of the Divine Persons. Understanding, the father faculty, answers to creation. From this proceeds memory, the second; the third faculty the will. These are all different, and their operations different; one is as soon in the soul as the other, yet make not three souls but one soul; none can act without the other, nor exist without the other. What we call faculties in the soul, we call Persons in the Godhead, because there are personal actions attributed to each. And we have no other words, but these are in condescension to our weak capacities. ... By the word Person when applied to God we must mean something infinitely different from personality among men. ... It was a saying among philosophers that the soul is all in all, and all in every part of the body. Is there anything in a body can bear any resemblance to this without manifest contradiction?

5. *Of Differences among Christians.*—A multiplicity of sects and divisions our Saviour foretold should come for the probation of the elect; as some Canaanites left in the

land to teach the Israelites the use of war. . . . When we are put to contend earnestly for the faith it quickens our zeal, keeps us upon guard. . . . To some this high privilege is granted "in the behalf of Christ, not only to believe in Him, but also to suffer for His sake." These go to make up the noble army of martyrs and confessors for ever triumphant in heaven. Others conquer even here on earth, that God's wonderfulness may be known to the children of men. But as he who builds a tower ought first to compute the expense, and he who goes to war to consider; so our blessed Saviour has instructed us, that he who will be His disciple must resolve beforehand to take up his cross daily.

6. *The Doctrine of Satisfaction.*—Here is the foundation of the Christian religion, that when man had sinned, and was utterly unable to make any satisfaction, God sent His own Son to take upon Him our flesh, to make full satisfaction by His perfect obedience and sacrifice upon the Cross. . . . God is not only just, but essential justice. . . . To remit is mercy, it is not justice, and the attributes of God must not oppose each other. . . . Here is justice satisfied to the least iota in the same nature that offended. Here is infinite wisdom expressed in this means found out for our salvation, and infinite mercy in affording it to us. Thus all His attributes are satisfied and filled up to the brim; they contradict not, but exalt one another.

7. *The Socinians.*—They deny the doctrine of the Holy Trinity, and the divinity of Christ. But they are confounded to give any account for His death. . . . Dying does not confirm any doctrine, only shows that he who does so believes it. If we look to the Saviour as our sacrifice, this is a rock and infallible assurance.

8. *The Church of Rome.*—She has greatly vitiated and

depressed this doctrine by her own theories of merit and satisfaction by penance—as if it were not sufficient.

9. *The Dissenters.*—They run to the contrary extreme, making good works not necessary, nor of any effect towards salvation. They damn the greatest part of the world by irreversible decrees of reprobation . . . take away free-will in man and make him a machine. They make God the author of sin . . . and His promises and threatenings of no effect.

10. *The True Notion of the Church.*—The Church must be considered not as a sect, but a society under government appointed by Christ. This power was delegated to apostles and their successors to the end of the world. Each in his own Church, and all these together, are the Catholic Church.

11. *Of an Universal Bishop.*—Christ appointed none. No such theory was known in the primitive Church, more than an universal monarch over the world. It was set up first by John, Bishop of Constantinople, then by the Bishop of Rome, in the seventh century.

If there was one universal bishop, the Church must fall if he fell. This obliged the pope to set up infallibility in his own person. And Bellarmine calls this absolute supremacy the sum and foundation of the Christian religion. Now it is generally decried by papists themselves, and sought to be placed in General Councils; but these are not always in being. Besides, they have contradicted one another. Others place this infallibility in the Church diffusive, which is indefinite.

12. *Of the Infallibility of the Church.*—There is an infallibility in the Church not personal, for millions of fallibles can never make an infallible. It consists in the nature of the evidence, which, having all the four marks,

cannot possibly be false. . . . Thus, whatever doctrine has been taught (rule of Vincentius Lirinensis) always everywhere and by all is the Christian. This was the method taken in the council at Alexandria against Arius. And thus every doctrine may be reduced to fact. A council stands as evidence of the fact, not as judge of the faith. . . . They who refuse this rule are broaching some novel doctrine.

13. *Of Episcopacy.*—The apostles did ordain bishops as governors; this was the current notion and language of antiquity. Thus it continued till John Calvin, in all which time there was not any one Church that was not episcopal. The dispute of Korah was not as to doctrine or worship, but government. And S. Jude brings down the same case to the Christian Church. . . . The Church is called "the pillar and ground of the truth," as being a society instituted by Christ for support and preservation of the faith . . . which no particular Church can attribute to itself. Heresies began by infraction upon this institution. In all Scripture there is not one instance of a schism against the priesthood which God appointed, but errors in doctrine and worship followed.

CHAPTER II.

James II.'s Early History and Accession—Romish Proceedings—Tyrconnel in Ireland—Chancellorship of Connor—Bishop Hacket—The King and Irish Clergy—High Sheriff—Disputations—Attacks on English Universities—The Seven Bishops.

THE accession of James II. to the throne of England, on February 6, 1685, was the event which brought Charles Leslie prominently into public notice. It hastened a crisis in national affairs which had long been preparing, and which not even sagacity, moderation, and high principle could have ultimately averted—qualities in which he was conspicuously deficient—though they might have delayed it or altered its course. A man, therefore, of such strong convictions and literary ability as Leslie could not have failed to come to the front, at great risk or advantage to himself, whatever direction political affairs had taken in a period so fraught with the elements of disturbance. James, Duke of York, succeeded apparently with the general good will of the nation, which had been thoroughly tired out by Charles II.'s vice, profligacy, and extravagance, however leniently many were disposed to view his faults after remembrance of the usurpation. Attempts had indeed been made to exclude James from the throne on account of his perversion to the Roman Church by a powerful party, and supported by leading ministers of State. But these had given such intense dissatisfaction to Charles, who was tenderly attached to his brother, as well as devoted to the principle of hereditary right, that sooner than listen to further discussion of the painful subject, he had for several years discontinued the practice of summoning Parliaments. It was a dangerous course, and full of inconvenience immediately to himself; but his sudden death terminated both speculation about its probable consequences, and that opposition which was its cause. At least no open signs were made, if discontent continued to work underground, till the new monarch had time to display his character. At the first it seemed as though the voices of clamour and faction had become effectually silenced by the unexpected turn of affairs, and that all people unanimously desired to give him at least a fair trial. If his private character could not be termed immaculate, yet it was not stained by the glaring vices and profligacies which had shocked and scandalized the nation ever since the Restoration on his brother's part. He had exhibited much aptitude for business, and administrative capacity in several positions; was conversant with naval and military affairs; had studied the arts of war under such a distinguished general as Turenne, and shown conspicuous bravery in expeditions by sea when commanding the fleet. His economy and prudence had contrasted remarkably with reckless prodigality and carelessness prevailing in several high places during the late reign; and, though not possessed of that easy, graceful manner which had charmed so many friends of all classes to Charles's side, he was not only dignified, but affable in demeanour, with more sincerity of meaning. A change of sovereignty then in itself from Charles to James could not be deplored, when the first emotions of regret had subsided, for an amiable profligate whom men could not help liking while they blamed. The one grave objection of an alien faith which had appeared intolerable at a distance, a majority hoped, upon being brought face to face with it, would lose its terrors by being held under proper restraint from interfering with the established religion, and liberty of his subjects. Nothing could have been more favourable to such expectation than James's first proceedings after Proclamation, nor better calculated to secure confidence and disarm suspicion. No animosity was expressed towards leading persons who had distinguished themselves by support of the Exclusion Bill, as might have naturally been apprehended. Sunderland, Rochester, and Halifax, chief ministers of State, were retained in office. And the first words spoken to the Privy Council, quickly reported throughout the kingdom, elicited a general response of confidence and satisfaction. "I have been reported," said James, "to be a man of arbitrary power, and that is not the only story told of me; but I shall make it my endeavour to preserve this Government, both in Church and State, as it is now established by law. I know the principles of the Church of England are for monarchy, and the members of it have shown themselves good and loyal subjects, therefore I shall take care always to defend and support it. I know also that the laws of England are sufficient to make the king as great a monarch as I can wish; and as I shall never depart from the just rights and prerogatives of the crown, so I shall never invade any man's property."

Grammarians were not supposed to criticize this address, but it was by no means so artless and unpremeditated as it sounded. Half the skill of well-conned sentences consisted in their air of impromptu utterance. Even that slight ring of defiance in assertion of his own rights found a welcome, because nicely balanced against a promise of respect for every one else's. A man who could thus adapt himself to the occasion, and clearly appreciate what his own peculiar position and the temper of the nation alike required, might at least have displayed some reasonable caution in trying to escape from limits acknowledged by himself to an ardent zeal for Romanism. His haste to override them was not owing to intentional duplicity and determination to violate his solemn engagement whenever opportunity should offer, but to an infatuation which saw no inconsistencies and could not wait for opportunities; engendered and inflamed by a few narrow, eager priests at his side, whose recklessness sensible members of their own communion deplored. Thus the reaction in public opinion was not long suffered to continue. Zealots, in their hurry to obtain an apparent triumph over the Church of England at some particular point, lost whatever chance there might have been to cunning and perseverance of restoring gradually and stealthily papal domination in this country—the very policy pursued at the present day by more subtle leaders. Some early proceedings little corresponded to James's assurance of respect for the Church and the law. Refusal of the Blessed Sacrament according to her rites at the coronation could hardly be blamed with justice, since reception could have been on his and the queen's part only a solemn mockery. But that they should on the next Sunday but one commence attendance at the Romish service in full state was a foolish provocation, quickly followed by another step still more alarming to the public—the constitution of a cabinet council of Roman Catholics, including the king's confessor, Father Petre, who set themselves to supersede in various posts of authority by their own religionists men of the highest probity and intelligence who were Protestants.

Next, oaths imposed under the Test Acts were dispensed with, and officers admitted to civil and military situations throughout the three kingdoms solely by virtue of the king's prerogative. Such buttresses as Test Acts and oaths were never any benefit, nor desired by the Church of England herself, but only an invention of political and nominal supporters. No just or sensible person can regret in her interest their abolition, their most obvious tendency being the multiplication of time-serving hypocrites and dissemblers with conscience. Nor is it at all clear that James did not possess such a dispensing power; much the same had frequently been exercised by his predecessors. His purpose, however, went far beyond any of theirs, and aimed palpably at a transfer of all situations of authority into the hands of Romanists. This could hardly be witnessed without signs of public indignation, which increased when monks and friars began to parade the streets in great numbers, and ostentatiously exhibit themselves in the habits of their various Orders. Then followed another bold step in revival of the exploded Ecclesiastical High Court, which inaugurated its first proceedings by prohibiting controversial sermons by the clergy, while no similar restraint was imposed upon their rivals. A sermon of Dr. Sharpe, Dean of Norwich and Rector of S. Giles, was made a pretext for essaying the new tribunal's powers; so Compton, Bishop of London, was peremptorily enjoined to suspend him, which he very properly but in most respectful terms declined to do, as beyond his powers without a regular trial and conviction. It was of no avail that Sharpe was sent by the bishop to apologize for his unintentional offence, and to promise more circumspection in future. James owed the bishop himself a grudge; therefore, Sharpe's offence being almost dropped out of sight, he was made the victim, and suspended from performance of his episcopal duties for disobedience to royal authority by this new court.

The encampment of an army on Hounslow Heath was regarded by many people as intended to over-awe the Protestant population, since there was no foreign army against whom it could be employed. The suspicion was widely strengthened by daily public celebration of mass at head-quarters, attendance at which was urgently pressed upon the soldiers by Roman missionaries.

Lying in gaol at this time for a scurrilous pamphlet, comparing the king while yet Duke of York to Julian the Apostate, was Samuel Johnson, who now managed to write and have published another of a most mutinous and inflammatory character, entitled, "An Address to English Protestants in the Army." Undoubtedly it called for condemnation from authority; but the punishment far exceeded the offence, and served to heighten popular indignation against James. Johnson was sentenced by the Ecclesiastical Commission as being a clergyman to be degraded from the priesthood, then pilloried and whipped from Newgate to Tyburn, with a fine of five hundred marks, and further imprisonment till it should be paid—cruelties rigorously inflicted, and heroically endured with a spirit worthy of a better cause. As if such things had not been enough for a twelvemonth, Lord Castlemain was dispatched as ambassador extraordinary to Rome for reconcilement of these kingdoms to the Holy See. Though coldly received there, because the reigning pontiff, Innocent XI., disapproved generally of the policy of the Jesuits, and was deeply embittered against Louis XIV., King of France, with whom James was in close alliance, none the less the fact of such a mission sank deep into the hearts of English people. The pace at which he was proceeding made sensible Romanists throughout the country very uneasy, and they would thankfully have paused to notice the effect produced already in the nation's mind. But such moderation did not suit the impatient sanguine temper of Petre and his party, who were for making hay while the sun shone, and turning present opportunities to account at any risk. This forward policy, advocated at a meeting of the most eminent Romanists in opposition to some moderate counsels, set aside as timorous and unworthy, was endorsed by the king's own special approbation; who added, for the comfort of his monastic counsellors, that he "had provided a sure retreat and sanctuary for them in Ireland, if his endeavours should be blasted in England; but as yet he had no reason to despair." Little he gauged the amount of indignation kindled in ten thousand breasts, or what a frail reed his co-religionists would find Irish support when an hour of trial should arrive. There, so far from affording encouragement, the situation was more embarrassing than in England. For affairs had proceeded since the king's accession with greater rapidity towards the restoration of papal supremacy in Ireland, in hope of obtaining a fresh lever of advantage to the work. Such hope was not without some apparent foundation, for were not the majority of inhabitants Romanists irreconcilably opposed to the Protestant Church? Had not successive confiscations, forfeitures, and evictions, from Elizabeth's to that time, alienated the greater part of the land from possession of its rightful owners to Saxon and Scotch intruders? Only the presence of a common foe kept up any semblance of unity between Presbyterians and members of the Established Church, so that its overthrow did not seem difficult. Accordingly, immediate steps were taken of a still more decided character than those as yet ventured at home, which were the means of calling into action Charles Leslie's talents and convictions.

Earl Tyrconnel was employed first as governor-general under the Earl of Clarendon, Lord-lieutenant, but with the full intention of superseding him, and under pretence of checking any support to Monmouth's rebellion, at once invested with summary powers for disarming all Protestants. No less than five hundred families among the most peaceable and industrious inhabitants of the sister kingdom were frightened away by this arbitrary and violent proceeding. No scruples of policy any more than justice interfered in the prosecution of his one set purpose to deprive Protestants of every vestige of authority, and reduce them into prostrate subjection to their enemies, who, not without some provocation, had long been thirsting for such a triumph. Even a member of the new cabinet could not refrain from exclaiming, "That fellow is mad enough to ruin ten kingdoms;" for the more reputable Roman Catholics began to entertain serious alarm at the extraordinary ferocity of his conduct. Yet he did but carry out the spirit and letter of his instructions; nor can James be justly excused on the score of ignorance, at least to the extent which Leslie afterwards pleaded, of the outrages committed by this fanatical creature, which he unreservedly condemned.[1]

In the summer of 1686, his first, last, and sole piece of ecclesiastical preferment was conferred upon Leslie. By the death of Rev. Robert Maxwell several vacancies were occasioned, mostly in the diocese of Down and Connor, amounting to no less than £900 per annum, though he never resided upon any of his benefices. For

[1] Answer to King's "State of Protestants."

one of these posts Lord Clarendon applied to the bishop of the diocese, in whose gift it was—the chancellorship of Connor. Its emoluments amounted to very little at that time; probably not £100 per annum, for the living of Rathmoram, annexed in 1603, had again been separated in 1670. It was, however, an office of some dignity, with opportunities of usefulness to the Church for which a man of legal training was specially qualified, whilst it did not involve a change of residence in order adequately to discharge its duties. At the same time, his lordship's recommendation was based upon his merits as a man of "good parts, admirable learning, an excellent preacher, and of an incomparable life," without any allusion to those private circumstances which had brought them into connection with each other. What rendered this request more honourable was the fact that the letter containing it administered also a severe rebuke to the bishop for his continuous absence from his diocese, and neglect of episcopal duties, which of course encouraged clergy to do the same. The consequence was that their cures were "left to mean and ignorant curates such as would serve cheapest, which gave great advantage to the adversaries of our religion." Equally to the bishop's credit, the favour thus solicited was immediately conferred, though how the other vacancies were filled which he was further desired "to consider well how he should dispose of," remains in obscurity. Unfortunately for himself and the Church, the serious warning failed to produce its proper effect. This prelate was Dr. Thomas Hacket, an Englishman by birth, but said to have graduated in the University of Dublin; and who must not be confounded with his namesake, a much worthier and more eminent man, Bishop of Lichfield, who spent £20,000 on the beautiful cathedral there, suffered greatly for his loyalty to King Charles, and wrote, beside several other works, a very interesting life of Archbishop Williams. He died in 1678.

The other had been a chaplain to King Charles, then Dean of Cork, Vicar of Cheshunt, in Hertfordshire, and a city rector before his elevation to the see of Down and Connor. His continued neglect, aggravated by a charge of simony, became so great a scandal that in 1693, after the Revolution, he was, upon trial by a commission of three Bishops, formally condemned and deposed. Complaints were made of tardiness in proceeding against him by authorities for two years and a half, which has been termed unaccountable.[1] It really admits of an easy explanation by remembering another circumstance. Tillotson, the archbishop concerned to move in the matter, might have felt a natural reluctance to direct such proceedings against one under whom he had commenced his ministry by serving as assistant curate at Cheshunt, in Hertfordshire.

Leslie's duties were not very arduous, as most chancellors can guess, but never or nowhere could have been less so than there at Connor. It is a poor insignificant town, without a cathedral, and the very diocese having a mere nominal existence, connected with Down, though the county of Antrim which it comprises is one of the most flourishing in the north of Ireland. Tyrconnel's proceedings, however, helped to provide work for him. Letters had been dispatched to Lord Clarendon before his removal from office, requiring him to restrain the clergy from preaching on controversial topics, with mention of some particular sermons reported to have given offence

---

[1] Mant's "History of Irish Church," vol. ii. pp. 42–45; Birch's "Life of Tillotson," p. 24; Grainger, v. 10; Clarendon's "Diary," i. 405.

to the king in this way. He wrote saying, "I made your brother (Rochester) give a severe reprimand to Dr. Sherlock, and have stopped a pension he had, and pray do you take care to do the like." Clarendon's reluctance to resign, and desire to keep on good terms with his Majesty, cannot be wondered at, considering their connection; but he might have foreseen that dismissal was only a question of time, and ought to have shown less compliance with this arbitrary attempt to muzzle the clergy. Some of them also ought to have displayed more spirit than they did, when summoned to the castle for a lecture on the subject of their preaching. Among others cautioned rather smartly for a sermon in the Vice-Royal Chapel was the Bishop of Meath, who made no remonstrance. Home Secretaries sometimes still presume beyond their province in ecclesiastical matters, but if the most exuberant should venture to dictate to a country priest the topics of discourse now, he would receive an answer which would make both his ears tingle.

Another step for the advancement of Popery was more startling than the preceding ones. A list of persons eligible for the office of High Sheriff was forwarded from England, with reflections upon individuals; and inquiries in the king's own handwriting concerning any reputed to have strong leanings in favour of the Church of England, that they might be excluded from appointment if so, upon which categorical replies were required. At the same time, Roman Catholics were to be exempted from the usual oaths on admission to office; and, accompanying this most unconstitutional and audacious order, was a recommendation to his Excellency's favour of the titular prelates Magee and Patrick Tyrrel. The latter was actually invested with the temporalities of the see of Clogher lately become vacant, where Leslie's own father had presided for ten years within the memory of the present generation. Nor did he lose time in asserting his newly devised authority. He did not venture to seize the palace at Clogher, but set up a residence for himself in the town of Monaghan, and established a large body of monks there. Then, holding a visitation at which were present some of the ablest Roman clergy from other places by special invitation, he challenged all the clergy of the English branch to a public disputation upon points of difference between them. All these were decidedly bold steps; but, coming in such rapid succession, their prudence was quite as questionable as their legality, and opened all men's eyes to the extent of change designed by James. Tyrrel's projected method of destroying heresy was a favourite hobby of James's own inherited from his grandfather, and practised upon every possible occasion in public or private, though with singular ill success in many notable instances. If a dishonourable man like Sunderland could temporarily affect conviction by his arguments, even one of so little piety as Rochester could scorn apostasy as the condition of holding place, with many more courtiers and ministers. By his own admission his champions made a poor figure in debate against divines of the Church of England. Tyrrel, however, who knew his predilection, might reasonably have presumed upon finding no such practised controversialists as London afforded among Irish heretics, and winning an easy victory. He was mistaken. With the fullest confidence and consent of his own brethren in the ministry, Leslie undertook to meet these chosen disputants single-handed; and accordingly, a great field-day for argument was arranged to take place before an assemblage of clergy and laity belonging to the rival communions.

Any one who has witnessed a similar disputation knows how thoroughly unprofitable and indecisive it has been; nor would any sensible person pin his faith to the conclusion which such a meeting might adopt. The real merits of the case in dispute can never be supposed to depend upon the ingenuity or learning of an advocate, but an easy victory might be obtained over a far superior man by some superficial but eloquent and accomplished speaker. Generally, however, no such mischief is done nor advantage gained to the cause of truth. Both sides claim to have won! Both are pleased with their favourite's performance; they have had excitement, and return more convinced than ever before that their own view is the right one. So it was at Monaghan. Protestants loudly proclaimed Leslie to be the victor. Romanists were as confident their bishop had the best of the argument. When, shortly afterwards, the discussion was resumed in the parish church of Tynan, near to Glaslough, with a change of combatants in two more acute logicians on the opposite side, the result was the same. Their supporters were satisfied the Roman Church had been proved to a demonstration the sole depository of the faith. As triumphantly members of the Church of England extolled Leslie's refutation of their errors. It was, indeed, asserted that he made one convert, a Mr. John Stewart, among his audience, who forthwith abandoned the communion to which he had belonged before, and continued steadfast to the end of his life in this attachment to his newly adopted faith. One exception only proves a rule. What remains certain, after all the clash of words and torrents of disputation, is that the subject of this biography acquitted himself creditably on both occasions. If they were drawn battles, yet he confirmed the favourable anticipations previously formed of his ability and theological learning. Nor, if manifestly worsted in the first engagement with the Popish prelate, would his party have been likely to risk another encounter against fresh assailants with the same champion. It is only fair, moreover, to remember that these discussions did not originate from any vanity or eagerness for display on his part. The challenges came from the Romanists. Any naughtiness of heart to see the battle was on their side, and theirs all the cumbrous armour of Goliath. He had but as it were a sling and a stone wherewith to meet the giants.

What seemed to show these weapons had struck home was another peremptory dispatch from James, complaining that "divers of the inferior clergy in Ireland had of late been disobedient to the injunctions of their superiors, and disturbed Roman Catholic clergymen in their functions." To which the Lord-lieutenant briefly replied, that "no application had been made to any of the magistrates concerning such disturbances." As this fresh complaint occurred in direct connection with the name of Dr. Patrick Tyrrel, there could be little doubt to what the king referred, and how foiled he felt in the result of his favourite mode of conviction; but it was rather unreasonable that even defeat should be termed disturbance, when it had issued from his own party throwing down the gauntlet.

The time came for pricking the sheriffs for the new year, and the purpose of the royal inquiries was to be made conspicuously plain in the same county of Monaghan. If argument had not availed in the mouths of ecclesiastics, force might in the hands of civilians more effectually defeat Protestantism. A Roman Catholic, William Barton, was appointed high sheriff, who, in accordance with the dispensing power claimed by the king, and fully relying upon his support, refused to take the oaths required by law.

Magistrates felt this to be a very critical matter on which to determine. It placed them in a dilemma not pleasant to contemplate, either of disobedience to the king's direct mandate, or to the law of the land which they were sworn to administer indifferently and without respect of persons. In their perplexity they resorted to Leslie at Glaslough, since a sharp attack of the gout had prevented his attendance amongst them as usual upon previous days of meeting. His advice was clear and distinct—that no one could be admitted to the office without legal qualification; nor would they be at liberty to permit a Romanist acting, even if he should venture to undertake it. They felt convinced that this argument was sound, nor could any one state it better; therefore he was requested further to be present at the next Quarter Sessions, when the claimant for office should have notice to appear. This was agreed to, and upon the appointed day Leslie took his place as chairman, at what pain and inconvenience to himself can be best appreciated by such as have suffered from the same complaint; the recurrence of which to him in after times afforded a subject of merriment to adversaries of the stamp of Burnet, Hoadley, De Foe, and Tutchin.

When the Castle nominee presented himself, he was respectfully asked by an officer of the court whether he had qualified for office upon oath; to which he replied abruptly, not because he was taken by surprise at so reasonable an inquiry, for he fully expected to encounter opposition on this ground, but with what was meant to be a tone of defiance and offended dignity—"I am of the king's religion, and am appointed to be sheriff at the king's pleasure." Under the circumstances of his position it was an ingenious reply, which had been evidently well considered beforehand. He flung the burden of responsibility adroitly from himself to the king, and hoped to quash further inquiry by the fear of his displeasure. So the more complete and happy again was Leslie's answer on behalf of his fellow-magistrates and himself—in a tone of imperturbable composure and courtesy—"We are not here to inquire into the king's religion, but only whether you have qualified yourself according to law to act as an officer of his Majesty. The law is to be deemed the king's will, and nothing else; his subjects have no other way of determining the king's will but as they find it revealed to them in the law; therefore this must be taken to continue so until the contrary shall be signified to them in the same authentic manner."

There was a neat avoidance of religious questions which might have been interpreted into offence or reflection upon the sovereign, with a denial of the claimant's plea as logical as it was appropriate. The rest of the magistrates were emboldened by this example to firmly maintain the law of the land, and resist further encroachment in the king's name. Not only was this person committed to prison for his contempt of court, but some officers of Tyrconnel's also, who presumed upon similar pretences to commit outrages and robberies in the neighbourhood. Thus, again, the advantage resulting from his early training had become apparent in the skill with which his decision had avoided the snare prepared with no little subtlety, and defeated the weak points of an opponent's case. And it ought to be further considered that at that time none but a few knew to what extent pretensions of royal authority for dispensing with the law were founded in fact. It did not appear till the publication of State secrets long afterwards that James had really given such directions, though he repudiated responsibility for much of Tyrconnel's more frantic conduct.

While thus a policy for complete subjugation of Protestants in Ireland to the Roman yoke was being pursued with headlong rapidity, it proceeded not so fast, but by no means slowly, in England. Attacks were made upon the Universities, first at Cambridge, then at Oxford, curiously enough by a mere accidental coincidence at Magdalen College in each. A person devoid of any literary qualifications was ordered to be admitted to the degree of Master of Arts in Cambridge, simply on the ground of the king's recommendation. That degrees had been often conferred upon royal mandate could not admit of any question; nor would there have been a churlish disposition among College authorities to stand upon ceremony under ordinary circumstances. But these were just what altered the case. The question was not about conferring an honorary degree; but admitting Alban Francis to the constituent body of university electors because he was a Romanist, thus opening a side door for introduction of many more of the same description, for the express purpose of subverting its character. The Senate and Vice-chancellor proved themselves equal to the occasion; and failing to obtain withdrawal of the king's candidate upon a respectful remonstrance, refused the degree. James was highly incensed; fumed and talked proudly; but did nothing, and let the matter drop. Had he but exercised a similar discretion in the case of the other University it had been well, for there he raised a spirit of resistance to himself where loyalty was wont to be carried to an extreme of enthusiasm. Already some murmurs had been provoked by bestowal of the Deanery of Christ Church upon a pervert, Massey, who had immediately set up a Chapel for celebration of the Roman mass, an example followed by a Dr. Walker, Fellow of University College. The death of Dr. Clarke had made a vacancy in the presidentship of Magdalen, and James was ill advised to assert his prerogative by proposing a stranger of blemished character, named Anthony Farmer. Very respectfully the Fellows protested, but received a curt reply that his Majesty expected to be obeyed. After a solemn celebration of the Blessed Sacrament upon the day of election, a fitting inauguration to their further proceedings, and indicative of the pious spirit which animated them, they proceeded to set aside the royal nomination, and chose for themselves John Hough, a candidate in every respect worthy of their suffrages. When James heard this he was transported with rage, which his immediate surroundings did nothing to cool; so the Ecclesiastical Commission was instructed to revenge the affront he imagined himself to have received. Its members acted with their accustomed imprudence and partiality. But Farmer's moral character rendering his appointment untenable, Dr. Parker was substituted by another royal mandate, to whom there were no such palpable objections, though he was suspected of Romeward proclivities. His position, being Bishop of Oxford, learning and piety would have entitled him to acceptance by the University without protest; but at this stage of the proceedings the Fellows felt bound to stand upon their rights. James had resolved on a royal progress through parts of the kingdom to awaken dormant or waning popularity; and when he reached Oxford, summoned the disobedient authorities before him, and scolded them in terms as undignified as offensive. But his browbeating availed no more than the threats of his Commissioners to shake their resolution. Therefore they were expelled, and their posts filled by Roman perverts. Alas! for the fatuity of the monarch whom evil counsellors were speeding to his ruin, while the approval of their own consciences was heard by those Magdalen worthies echoed in the plaudits of an admiring nation. The memory of that struggle will remain among its noblest and most cherished traditions so long as the University shall continue what it has been, a cynosure for all faithful, loving hearts in the Church of England. These events in the sister island were too nearly paralleled, or even surpassed, in unconstitutional violence by those in which Leslie himself had been compelled to interfere, for him not to feel very keenly their latent connection, and forecast the inevitable end to which they were drifting the ill-starred king. The principles involved in the contests provoked by James were identical in both countries, and among the same sort of persons, upright, honourable, intelligent, and loyal almost to excess. Leslie must have experienced even more pain than a majority of mere spectators outside Oxford, because he was already recognized there as a man of superior attainments, and on terms of personal intimacy with one or two of those immediately concerned in the Magdalen case. Among others with Bishop Parker, whose intrusion into the presidentship he afterwards severely condemned, though he did not share the suspicions erroneously entertained of his infidelity to the Church, and at that very time was in correspondence with him on literary subjects. But of course he had more sense and delicacy than to give public expression at the time to his thoughts upon that question; which many with less claim did not hesitate to do, as if a University could be better or worse for officious interference with its affairs by uninitiated strangers.

The story of the Seven Bishops has been told repeatedly by historians, who have vied with each other in depicting in glowing language their noble and intrepid defence of the Church's liberties. None have essayed more brilliantly to extol their courageous consistency of principle upon this one occasion, than writers who have laboured to decry and depreciate them individually, and load their memories with unmerited obloquy. And this alteration of tone only too truly reflects a discreditable change on the part of the nation itself, characteristic of majorities in all ages. The spirit was the same which ostracized Aristides, poisoned Socrates, assassinated Cæsar, murdered Laud and King Charles, applauded these Seven Bishops then beggared and disowned them! It is the essential spirit of the world, and if not in antagonism to the spirit of true Christianity, the Church's work and experience must in all ages have been different; whereas they have been always essentially alike.

A very brief outline of the main incidents will suffice to connect that interesting episode with this narrative. King James had issued a Declaration of Indulgence for Dissenters from the Established Church in the three kingdoms, which in Ireland produced such consequences as have been stated, owing rather to the illegal and injudicious method employed in its enforcement, than sentimental repugnance to such relief in itself. It evoked considerable dissatisfaction in Scotland, but not active opposition of a serious kind. In England it had remained for some time after its first issue a dead letter. Church-people, a vast majority, took no notice of it, and Dissenters looked askance; their leaders shrewdly divining its purport not to be for their interest, except so far as that might cover the king's own religion, which they hated as intensely as they did the Church of England. Issued, moreover, without the consent of Parliament, because that was utterly hopeless of attainment, this Declaration seemed to most people of no legal validity, either for protection claimed under it or against disobedience to it. The principle of non-recognition affirmed at Monaghan, equally applied to all sorts of cases elsewhere. Besides, Dissenters in England could see that if royal prerogative might properly secure them against law in this reign, in the next it might be exerted for their destruction without law, upon their own admission; therefore the wisest of them were very chary of accepting the proffered boon. Not discouraged by this significant silence, or misreading its meaning, James, in the spring of 1688, reissued his manifesto for tender and diseased consciences, somewhat wider in its scope and more strongly expressed. It asserted a conviction of every man's right to worship God in the manner he deemed best, and declared all laws interfering with that right to be thereby suspended, ordered prisoners on account of religion to be immediately set at liberty, and public offices of every description opened without distinction of creed or sect.

An admirable and righteous declaration, it will be almost unanimously admitted in this country at the present day, even by those who, needing it here for themselves, rigidly refuse liberty of conscience where they have ascendancy. Nor need James's sincerity be too closely scanned, for he had tasted the effects of Protestant bigotry, not at the instance of the Church of England, as sometimes most unjustly asserted, but of the Parliament, which held then in prison some three thousand persons for venturing to disagree with its self-satisfied members on one or more points of belief. Though he overlooked the inconsistency with this Indulgence of bribing or forcing to apostasy his own immediate dependents and ministers of State, he knew by his own case that intolerance and persecution rather deepened than shook conviction; therefore he might calculate upon good results of freedom in others. Nor did he deserve censure for aiming at the advancement of his own religion. Such is the desire of all earnest persons, whether one course or another be adopted for its attainment. Designing hypocritical Sunderland was the real author of this Declaration, who only wanted to ingratiate himself with his master, which he was on the eve of still further attempting by apostasy to Rome, while busily intriguing with the Prince of Orange for an invasion of the kingdom. He cared no more for one religion than another, only intending to secure for himself the unjust steward's reward under either alternative. Having observed some approachment of Dissenters towards the Church to be the result of recent proceedings, he devised this apple of discord to fling between them. For a moment his crafty purpose appeared on the point of realization; for sectarian bodies hailed the new illegal publication with enthusiasm—addresses reeking with flattery and servile adulation poured in profusion from their congregations, and deputations grovelled in the dust before the king with such nauseous extravagance, that his own soul sickened at the sight.

His Majesty went in state to a dissenting Lord Mayor's banquet at the Guildhall, with the queen; and, to complete the picture of fraternization, the pope's Nuncio sat at the same table, returning home to St. James's palace amid the shouts of the populace, which within a year would have as cheerfully tore them all three to pieces. Only the Church of England was left out in the cold, to which was now artfully attributed the blame of all penal statutes whatever. A blunder, however, upset the conspiracy, and caused Dissenters some mistrust about their ill-assorted alliance with the Church of Rome. For, appended to the new Declaration, was an Order in Council requiring it to be read in all churches, and the bishops to see the royal commands obeyed in their dioceses. After the first flutter of surprise at the directness of this assault, came the practical question, What ought to be done? As if to prevent organized resistance, scarce a fortnight had been allowed between publication of the order and the date fixed for general compliance. A few more resolute spirits among the clergy immediately avowed their intention to refuse; others counselled delay and reflection; a majority waited to see what course the bishops would adopt. Had they proved unequal to the crisis, the Church of England must have fallen for ever. What made decision on their part more difficult was the remembrance that themselves had circulated a precisely similar document in the preceding reign which Parliament had refused to sanction—conduct that now suggested an impudent menace by Father Petre couched in the language of Rabshakeh, with a strange forgetfulness how that had recoiled upon its author. Only ten Prelates were in London or within easy reach, of whom two were committed to the court interest. Seven others, after prayer and deliberation at Lambeth, drew up a memorial to his Majesty, excusing themselves from obedience to the order because Parliament had pronounced such a declaration illegal, but respectfully assuring him they were influenced neither by want of loyalty or liberality in their refusal. Sancroft, archbishop, Ken, Lake, Lloyd, Trelawney, Turner, and White signed, and carried it themselves to the king, excepting the archbishop, who had been out of favour and forbidden attendance at Court.

Misled by some of his advisers to expect no more than a show of resistance on the part of the bishops, James felt all the more angry at their uncompromising attitude, and expressed his displeasure in no measured terms. Dr. Sherlock simultaneously posted a letter to the clergy in general, pointing out how they would plunge themselves into a pit dug by enemies if they should yield compliance. The result was that only seven in London and about two hundred throughout the kingdom read the Declaration. And thus had arrived the crisis to which events had been tending long before, but more decidedly since the moment of James's accession to the throne. The most unpleasant feature consisted in this circumstance, that either to advance or recede appeared equally perilous. Two dissenting ministers were invited to assist deliberations of his Jesuit council, who only goaded him on to more desperate resolves. Legal proceedings were instituted against the bishops on the score of a seditious libel, and after tedious preliminaries their trial was arranged. Meanwhile, refusing to give bail,[1] they were committed to the Tower, on their way to which countless multitudes lined the banks of the Thames, to testify their sympathy and admiration. The very soldiers kneeled to crave a blessing from their prisoners. On the 15th of June the trial commenced in Westminster Hall and extended over a period of three weeks, but at length the jury were at liberty to consider their verdict ; nor would it have occupied a night's consultation but for the king's butcher, who could not square his conscience with his interest. He gave way at last, and upon their return into court their unanimous " Not guilty ! " was no sooner pronounced by the foreman's lips, than caught up and repeated with a joyous strength among the crowd, that made the walls of Westminster ring again. The tidings spread like wildfire through the city, till they reached the camp at Hounslow, where the king happened to be dining; so he had the mortification of learning how fully the troops sympathized with the prevailing sentiment in

[1] Leslie said Sancroft regretted this deeply afterwards.

favour of the bishops against himself. A fitting sequel to their conduct was a circular letter to the clergy, inculcating fresh earnestness in the performance of Christian duties, and tenderness in dealing with schismatics. When too late James has been represented to have pathetically confessed that "in the case of the bishops no doubt he had done better in not forcing some wheels, when he found the whole machine stop. But it was his misfortune to give too much ear to the pernicious advice of those who put him upon such dangerous courses with intent to widen the breach between him and his subjects."[1] If this were only said for him, instead of by him, it represents at least the exact state of the case. If the words were his own, it was the more lamentable that he had not the same sagacity a little sooner. Other remarks more credibly are attributed to him—that his "prepossession against the yielding temper which had proved so dangerous to his brother and fatal to his father, fixed him in a contrary method. And that he had observed failure in four reigns to force uniformity, and that it rather increased dissent." Both considerations were true enough, if he had not omitted their necessary safeguards in practice. Stubbornness is an extreme as perilous as excessive pliability, and an enforced toleration as an intolerant uniformity.

[1] Life, written by himself.

CHAPTER III.

BIRTH OF PRINCE OF WALES—PRINCE OF ORANGE'S CONDUCT—REVOLUTION—CORONATION OF WILLIAM AND MARY—EJECTION OF NONJURING CLERGY—CHANCELLORSHIP OF CONNOR—REFUTATION OF ARCHBISHOP KING'S CALUMNY—JAMES AND WILLIAM IN IRELAND—SHERLOCK—STILLINGFLEET—DR. HICKES—HENRY DODWELL—NELSON—KETTLEWELL.

THE birth of a Prince of Wales afforded excellent opportunity to the king for extricating himself from his embarrassments and restoring contentment. But James had not the good sense to avail himself of it. Instead of seizing the occasion to terminate all differences between him and his people, he left them to fester in wounded hearts, and so mismanaged affairs connected with the queen's confinement, as to afford colour to calumnies industriously circulated of a supposititious heir being palmed off upon the nation. Never was any birth more clearly attested, but the air of mystification foolishly adopted upon the occasion gave credence to cruel statements of his enemies, while the indiscreet exultation of Romanists served further to increase suspicion of foul play. For their silly stories of miraculous interposition by the blessed Virgin to defeat the Princess of Orange's succession elicited naturally counter lampoons and pasquinades which obtained a much wider circulation; all poor doggerel verses, none worthy of remembrance, and

Prince of Orange's Schemes.

some very indelicate, adapted to the most depraved taste of the populace.

At Dr. Burnet's suggestion William, Prince of Orange, husband of the Princess Mary, who had long had his eye upon the throne of England, seized upon the prevailing suspicion to make political capital for himself, by countermanding the prayers in her chapel for the Prince of Wales, which had been ordered and congratulations sent according to custom; notice also was given of an intended inquiry into the circumstances attending the birth. He had busily fomented dissatisfaction by secret emissaries to England with bribes and promises, under the guidance of Burnet with too much success among nobility and persons in public offices, including several of the highest Ministers of State for some time past. All the grievous mistakes of James's government completed by this last afforded William at length the much-desired pretext of interference for securing his wife's claim to the throne from being parried, and protecting the religion and liberties of the English people. Military and naval preparations had been carried on at the Hague, apparently intended against France; but the king there advised James of their real design, and offered assistance. He refused to believe it, returned an ungracious reply, and continued his blind confidence in William's professions of cordiality, and his traitorous minister's assurances of security, till the enemy was at his very gates. The mask was laid aside soon as those preparations were completed, and the opportunity presented itself under a combination of follies almost unparalleled in the history of self-willed sovereigns. William now openly avowed his intention of invading England; the Assembly of the Dutch States were artfully managed to support him; though hitherto a powerful party had continually opposed his government as stadtholder. Continental powers, with the exception of France, looked favourably upon the proposed expedition; even Pope Innocent XI. concurred and aided it with funds, so vainly had James jeopardized his throne for his religion; and, worst of all, Englishmen professing patriotism and to be Nobles and Gentry, were ready to welcome his enemy on the ignominious plea of the English nation being unable to protect itself from a tyrannical sovereign. James's spiritless demeanour, on being convinced that an armament had actually set sail, showed how easily he might have been brought to his senses, and compelled to confine himself in future within the limits of the constitution.

He was stunned by the announcement and perusal of a specious declaration of William's objects composed by Dr. Burnet, and corrected by other traitors resident at the Hague. All his former inflexibility and capacity seemed to desert him at the moment when most imperatively they were needed; or else the emergency, great as it was, might have been successfully encountered. For, although the nobility were false to the Altar and the Throne, yet the people were true to their hearts' core, and the Church's loyalty had not been destroyed, if both had been justly grieved and offended. Indeed, it is an amazing subject for reflection, that a plot mainly conducted by such a man as Burnet could have ever reached the point of experiment. But when secrecy no longer was required, any blunders in execution, of which there were several, proved to be more than counterbalanced by want of concert for resistance. New levies of troops were ordered, commissions freely offered to volunteers, and the king himself prepared to take the field. Sunderland also at last was dismissed from office, and penalties denounced against publishers of libels and injurious reports. But such steps fell far below what the crisis demanded. When, therefore, William landed, after some delay by bad weather, then made on for London after other delays of various kinds, which had suggested serious doubt whether he had not miscalculated the amount of support awaiting him, he found everything prepared to his hand. From that day the Revolution was complete—conquest, though Parliament afterwards chafed at this word, had been achieved, not by arms, but panic and treason—the Stuart dynasty dethroned for ever, and a foreigner seated by a parliamentary title upon the throne of England. Intervening and accompanying incidents need not be recounted in detail—such as the desertion of army officers one after another, the heartless treachery of the Princess Anne under the guidance of Bishop Compton and the Churchills, James's double flight under threats of personal violence, the illegal assumptions of a self-constituted body of lords and commons under the name of Convention, Mary's arrival and indecent levity on obtaining possession of her father's palace. These fill a page in history which even descendants of Whigs may blush to read.

How did the bishops of the Church of England act? Not very honourably as a body. A majority hedged out of sight and maintained an equivocal and suspicious silence concerning the matters which convulsed the rest of the nation. A few responded to a summons from the king for counsel, but instead of this offered him reproaches for his previous treatment of their Order. William had presumed to affirm in his Declaration that he had come by invitation of Spiritual as well as Temporal lords. This was honestly denied by those present, except Compton, who escaped under a disingenuous quibble characteristic of him, but which any man of honour would have scorned to employ. The clergy were almost unanimously in favour of hereditary right, theoretically, though late experience had not tended to enliven their zeal in the cause; and they were, as now, an unwieldy, unorganized body, without that unity of action and combination which are necessary to any powerful influence upon society. They inclined to let things drift till beyond remedy, and were bewildered for want of leadership. Erastianism had not become so prevalent or unblushing as it soon did. They, nevertheless, were generally too willing to be persuaded that duty required them to cling to their benefices if possible—that "whatever is, is right,"—and therefore the Powers that be are of Divine ordinance, whether they have come by might or right.

William and Mary were, by the authority of a Convention of nobles and commoners, entitled king and queen of England, and Bishop Compton was among the foremost to present himself before the newly patented sovereignty; though he had doffed the purple velvet uniform, jack-boots, and sword wherein he had escorted the Princess Anne in her flight to Nottinghamshire. He could not persuade the clergy of London to accompany him, so was fain to rest content with a *posse* of dissenting ministers. Other prelates had a little more self-respect than thus at once to trail their lawn in the mire, if they wanted courage to avow their convictions or resist the proposal for a Form of public Thanksgiving to be used in churches for this successful usurpation; for then before them lay a letter from the king, to whom they had sworn allegiance, complaining of the violence and threats which had driven him from the kingdom. William issued also another proclamation, attributing the Revolution to the Almighty; and the Archbishop of Canterbury's name, without his consent, was ostentatiously exhibited in a list of the new Privy Council.

So transparent an artifice did not beguile him from his integrity. He had never concurred in the invitation for the Prince of Orange's arrival, though this has been sometimes stated; now, therefore, he withheld his sanction from rebellion against his rightful sovereign.

A new Parliament, called without royal authority, and notoriously elected under an extensive system of bribery, had no more proper legality than the Convention. Nothing was said about the promised inquiry, or the purposes specified in the Declaration. If then the archbishop could have nerved himself and his brethren on the Episcopal Bench to repeat the noble part which they had lately played, there is little doubt the tide of revolution might have been rolled back on its authors, and the discrowned monarch's inheritance restored with safeguards and guarantees against fresh violation of the pledges given at the commencement of his reign.

A mitre at Salisbury falling vacant was bestowed, as was to be expected, upon Burnet. His Grace refused to consecrate him, but issued a commission empowering others to do so in his absence, which deprived his refusal of the credit of acting upon principle, and betrayed a vacillation which did not fail to encourage his enemies to bolder steps. Burnet's triumphant tone upon the occasion tempted the archbishop to another action, which with more dignity he would have omitted, if it be true that afterwards "with his own hands he destroyed the warrant for consecration."

Only two members of the House of Commons refused to take the oaths of allegiance to the new sovereignty, but in the House of Lords no less than eight bishops.[1] Accordingly a bill was introduced to compel all persons in

[1] Burnet's "History of his Own Times."

official situations to comply by a fixed date at six months' distance, March, 1689.

But again their show of resolution was shorn of half its proper influence by the fact that some of them were issuing patents to their Chancellors for the institution of Clergy into fresh cures upon condition of taking those same oaths. When the day arrived for final determination, about four hundred clergy in England and these eight prelates stood firm : sacrificed everything rather than forswear themselves, and formally transfer allegiance pledged to one king to another usurping his throne, though willing to give assurance of no active efforts to disturb his government. The requirement extended to Ireland, and therefore involved the Chancellor of Connor with a few more persons, the most distinguished being Dr. Sheridan, Bishop of Kilmore. Leslie gave no uncertain sound. Neither as deputy and agent for another, nor on his own account, could he act with duplicity. He could not conscientiously admit persons into office upon any other principle than that which himself, having sworn to observe, intended to maintain at any cost or sacrifice.

Thus vanished at a stroke the single glory which ever belonged to the Chapter of the diocese of Connor, and the one prospect it ever for a moment possessed of becoming useful or ornamental to the Irish Church. No traditional memories rescued it from oblivion in the past, and a constantly shifting succession of tenants have continued to hold the office down to the present day. A Mr. Charlton swallowed the oaths when Leslie retired, of whom no more is known, and the solitary gleam of distinction which had been associated with this post was scarcely kindled before extinction. Since then Ichabod has been legibly stamped upon Connor, where even the Roman communion, so eager generally after old titles and dignities, has not cared to establish a claim. The loss to Leslie himself of his office was very small directly and immediately. The "preferments and emoluments" spoken of by some writers must be confessed of little value or consequence in themselves, nor even had the prospects resigned been of much greater account under the Vice-royalty of Tyrconnel. What proved of serious concern was the necessary removal of himself and family from Glaslough, involving severance of family intercourse and affection which he prized most dearly, as well as of friendship and good will among poor and rich in two or three counties. He felt the prospect of such separations far beyond the loss of any gain or advancement. Even more, he declared, was the pain of being debarred from the public exercise of his Ministerial Office; and it could not be otherwise in the case of one so earnest and capable in its discharge. He had not made interest to secure a benefice when within his reach, therefore would not have deplored the loss of one very bitterly; but to be forbidden performance of sacred duties was a trial which none can adequately appreciate but sufferers under any providential circumstances. Then, moreover, the sharpest sting lay in the cause of these misfortunes, which made his no isolated case of injustice, but identified it with that of all the honourable men in England henceforth to be known as Nonjurors, and the interests of the Church at large. It was a most perilous crisis in her history, the ultimate consequences of which none on any side could predict. Ecclesiastical and civil affairs were then much more closely intertwined than now; by far the greater part of the nation professedly belonged to her communion, and the highest classes almost entirely. Though the persons who in both houses of Parliament undertook unauthorized to represent her interests were singularly ill qualified, ever since she has borne the blame of a persecuting policy which more properly should be ascribed to them, whether directed against Romanists or Dissenters. It was of no use that bishops and clergy advocated toleration, when Parliament, under pretence of defending the Church, insisted upon persecution. Again, religion was the one subject which continually occupied the attention of all classes when no great variety of other interests existed; nor had commerce, manufactures, colonial affairs, or even agriculture itself, still less public education, much place in any one's thoughts. Every political question or movement was proposed and examined in the light of its influence upon the Church, by which, however, nothing was less meant than a Spiritual kingdom, a Divine Corporation for the amelioration of mankind, only an Establishment directed by the State for domineering over conscience, and keeping the people in subjection to the Government. When, therefore, rulers themselves effaced the constitution, swept away an hereditary Monarchy, and removed the basis upon which union between Church and State had existed hitherto, none could tell how far the dissolution of that union would proceed. A disruption, which arrayed the most learned and pious of the Episcopal Bench and Clergy on one side, against a larger but less respectable body on the other, whom even the laity, while uniting with them, suspected of hypocrisy and selfish motives, and who themselves generally looked ashamed of their conduct, presented a very serious and sad consideration to Charles Leslie. Conscience afforded no loophole of escape from that decision, which he had soon to act upon; but, in boldly throwing in his lot with the little party of principle, he showed himself acutely sensible of all its perils and responsibilities. His conduct has been diligently misrepresented by contemporary partisans, who carefully concealed the authorship of their calumnies till he was no longer alive to answer them, which again have been copied and repeated in biographies, encyclopædias, and histories, without the slightest inquiry into their truth or accuracy.[1]

But these can all be clearly traced back to a single source, and that proved unworthy of credit. The modern repetitions have been taken verbatim from Noble's biography, which in the same way came from Burnet's "History of his Own Times," not published till after his death. His account, with that of his poor satellite, Bishop Lloyd, admittedly proceeded from information furnished by Archbishop King. There is the *fons et origo mali*, and his statement can be proved, beyond a possibility of doubt, both inconsistent in itself and contrary to facts.

Both parties in Ireland, Protestants and Papists, remained in deadly array against each other ever since intelligence had arrived of William's invasion, equally afraid to strike a final blow for mastery, though Tyrconnel continued to act and talk much in the same frenzied style as before. Predatory bands also roamed through the kingdom, carrying on a sort of guerilla warfare, with his contrivance if not always direct authority, against Protestants, who were left to their own protection. This was part of William's policy, that a general rebellion might seem to render his stay and services more indispensable for England. Irish clergy, who had determinately resisted James, eagerly presumed that the usurper would bid high for their support, but finding themselves mistaken, began to make overtures

[1] Evan Sherley's Monaghan, pp. 160-164.

for reconciliation to their rightful sovereign, which were very ungraciously rejected. Leslie was not among this number. The charges afterwards made against him were these: 1. That he first so far opposed James and accepted William as to take part in a public proclamation of him as king. 2. That he engaged in some conflicts against the former's adherents, and was "the first to shed blood" in Ireland at the Revolution. 3. That notwithstanding this, he in a short time turned round again to his previous standpoint. Now, no places or dates were assigned in corroboration of these statements, which ought to have been done, especially when levelled by bishops against a clergyman of high standing and character; but that was impossible, because they were utterly without foundation. 1. He never took part in, nor was present at, any proclamation of William at all. 2. Some skirmishes took place between Protestants and Romanists before and at the Revolution, in which one or two persons were killed at Glaslough and Drumbanagher, but he never participated in them. The blood shed on those occasions was in defence of houses which had been wantonly and deliberately attacked by marauders belonging to Tyrconnel's army; therefore no blame could be justly attributed to Protestants on this account. 3. Leslie, never having renounced allegiance to his rightful sovereign, however strongly he had resisted unlawful proceedings in his name, could not have changed sides a second time. The fact is, he was not in Ireland when these occurrences took place, but in the Isle of Wight with his wife and the Keightleys.[1] His brother may have been present at some proclamation of William, because he accepted the Revolution, and did very properly defend Glaslough when attacked. Such are the circum-

[1] Clarendon's Diary.

stances which have been misrepresented to Charles's prejudice, because he had been accustomed to reside there. It is not so very easy to acquit King as his brother prelates for putting the story in circulation, inasmuch as he was well acquainted with both brothers, had received kindness from their father, and professed friendship to the family. If he did not know of Charles's absence on the occasions referred to, nothing would have been easier than to ascertain the fact; and it was his plain duty to do so before committing himself, for Glaslough was only sixty miles distant from Dublin, and his very story betrayed some misgivings on the point.

But when he whispered it to Burnet and Lloyd for circulation, he was writhing under the exposure of his own tergiversation and burning for revenge, and those two men shared his animosity. The latter even wrote, twelve years after, for "an account of the matter which he might publish without saying where he got his information."[1] It is not the only instance on record of prelates combining to ruin the reputation of an opponent by a fabrication; but perhaps there never was one more discreditable to the authors and so easy to disprove from independent sources of information. Leslie had gone to the Isle of Wight partly on account of his own health, which had been much impaired, and partly for the purpose of recreation with Mr. and Lady Frances Keightley, returning with them to London, not to Ireland. Accordingly his absence explains the confusion made between him and his brother, though it does not exculpate Archbishop King. If he had remained at home, and doubtless would have endeavoured to do so had the invasion of England by the Dutch with its consequences been anticipated, it is impossible to say now how he would have acted, or what effect his influence might have pro-

[1] Ware's History and Hist. MSS. Reports, vol. ii.

duced in altering the current of affairs at Glaslough. His was the stronger mind, and he took the lead in all public affairs. John, the Dean of Dromore, was not, indeed, deficient in ability—rather above the average, and very competent in estimating the value of most things. His character was as spotless and honourable as that of his brother, and his convictions and prepossessions ran in the same direction; while a long residence together very unusual between brothers in the upper classes had strengthened the ties of affection subsisting between them. But John had tasted more of the miseries of civil war than his brother. For the first twenty years of his life he had seen little else; and burnt in upon his remembrance by painful experience was the horrible wickedness which the Church of Rome allowed to be perpetrated in her name; and now he saw a revival of similar scenes avowedly under the same authority. His own house had been attacked without any provocation; several neighbours and friends had been subjected to outrages; he seemed to know what allegiance to James meant; he did not know what William might be, and he had a large property at stake. That even a good and conscientious man under such circumstances should have given his adhesion to the cause which promised best for security and peace is at least very intelligible. Whether any alteration would have resulted if Charles had been present at that time it is almost needless to speculate, but probabilities point the other way. Men are generally much more influenced by their temporal interests than themselves are conscious of; and John, as the immediate heir and successor to the estate of Glaslough, had a vested interest at stake of the greatest importance. Moreover, no change of attitude on the part of either brother would have prevented the unfortunate loss of a few lives there, because the attack in which it occurred was directed, not against them personally, but Protestantism and property, nor had any immediate connection with the Revolution at all.

King James signalized his arrival in the Capital of Ireland with characteristic imprudence, by a series of Popish processions and pompous ceremonials in attendance at Mass, which provoked many well-disposed subjects to opposition. His next step was still further calculated to range them under William's banner—a Bill introduced into the Irish Parliament for repeal of an Act which had conferred estates forfeited at the Rebellion upon Protestants. Undoubtedly that Act had been enforced with cruelty and injustice against innocent persons, whose only offence was attachment to the Church of Rome, to whom, therefore, some compensation or redress was due. But such a mode at such a time was the last a sensible monarch would have sanctioned; and James admitted this, but had not moral courage to refuse. Even lands of temporary absentees were to be included in the new confiscation on presumption of the owners being adherents of the Prince of Orange, though closing of the ports had actually hindered some from returning who had been driven away by James's own supporters. Romanists also were authorized henceforth to transfer tithes from the clergy to the ministers of their own communion. The class upon whom these wrongs told with most severity was the one desirous of preserving their former allegiance, so that no policy ever was more suicidal. Leslie's condition was exactly analogous to that of nonjurors in England. Because he had resisted unconstitutional proceedings under James, he had incurred the hostility of the Tyrconnel party. On the other hand, because he would not therefore go further and unite with revolutionists, their animosity knew no bounds. He gave greater offence than those who had not stirred a finger in defence of the law, in proportion to the higher weight attributed to his opinion.

Such was the penalty incurred for the privilege of possessing a conscience, but it was paid with his eyes open; nor did he ever regret it, though his sufferings were lifelong and acute, and though a bishopric subsequently was dangled before him to induce him to revoke.

William went at length to Ireland to take command of his forces, and face his own father-in-law and uncle in battle, during whose absence a defeat of the English fleet by the French threw this country into a fresh panic. Nonjurors were at once the victims accused of plots against their own country. A Liturgy, containing one prayer for the discrowned monarch, which was Charles Leslie's composition, was hit upon as supporting this accusation; though Archbishop Sancroft and his brother prelates had not authorized its use. A fictitious letter to the King of France for assistance was artfully circulated for the same purpose of rendering Nonjurors odious, with the horrible suggestion of Dewitting them; that is, repeating such a murder as had been perpetrated in Holland upon unfortunate brothers who had ventured to oppose the imperious policy of William as Stadtholder there. It gave also, as Burnet said, "the king a great advantage in filling the vacant Sees." His own importunity was not wanting to this step; though, had he foreseen that his desire to be enthroned at Canterbury would not be gratified, he might not have been so eager. Directions were issued for ejection of Nonjuring prelates and clergy, who though deprived had hitherto not actually been dispossessed. Tillotson was intruded at Lambeth, a personal friend of the new sovereign who had formerly recommended himself to favour by acts of courtesy when

Dean of Canterbury, and been among the first to welcome the Revolution. He was a man of considerable popularity as a preacher, though his style would now be thought very artificial and pedantic; diligent in discharge of pastoral duties; but of no talents commensurate with his ambition, and strongly tainted with heresy. On this account he had been rejected as a candidate for the Prolocutorship of the Lower House of Convocation, when a scheme of comprehension, by which the doors of the Church were to be opened for admission of Dissenters into the Church at expense of her doctrines, was introduced, and supported by latitudinarian prelates, but happily defeated by resistance of the great body of the clergy. Dr. Sherlock was rewarded at the same time with the deanery of S. Paul's for recanting his former loyal professions under the influence of his wife, who for her masterful spirit earned the sobriquet of Xantippe. In wisdom he might be deemed a Socrates if not in integrity, far superior to the mass of beneficed brethren who followed his example from similar domestic considerations; in marked contrast to whom the learned Beveridge, though he conformed, refused a mitre. In vain Whig historians and latitudinarians have laboured to conceal the iniquity and uncanonical character of these ejections, under pretence of State necessity and false precedents. That William and Mary should resolve upon them was a matter of course—" None has ever righteously exercised a dominion acquired by infamous means." But that so little resistance should have been offered to the sacrilegious proceedings by the Church of England at large, can never be remembered without a blush of indignation, and ought to be a warning against submission to Erastian encroachment again under any pretext whatever.

Dr. Sherlock wrote in vindication of his conduct "The

case of Allegiance and Obedience to the Present Government," which called forth many severe rejoinders that were keenly felt. A single passage of one will be enough to quote here, replying to Dr. Sherlock's appeal to Overall's convocation book as the immediate cause of his conversion, but which never produced such a profound impression until William's usurpation had become an established success. " Then it was that Bishop Overall's book gave you greater freedom and liberty. Egeria appeared to you on the banks of the Boyne, and inspired you with new and freer notions; showed you how your former reasoning contradicted the general sense of mankind, and revealed unto you a divine and safer principle upon which you might swear allegiance, without the imputation of apostasy, or renouncing the doctrine of the Church of England to Will. Nass. Ang. Scot. Hibern. A Deo datus Augustus, and also swear it back again to King James, if ever he should recover the throne in a recuperative war."

The original pamphlet has been attributed to Mr. Hill, but these words recur almost verbatim in another part of Leslie's undoubted writings. In any case they clearly describe the real character of Sherlock's change. Had he and several other clergy at the first espoused the cause of Revolution, their integrity might have remained unchallenged; but perusal of an old book being urged as the ground of recantation when this suited his interests, while a plank for safe return was kept in reserve if occasion should recur, was evidently a pretext of a very flimsy and disingenuous character. Of those eminent prelates who refused the new oaths, Dr. Lake and Dr. Cartwright died in the same year, 1689. Dr. Lake, one of the seven sent to the Tower by King James, before his death made a solemn profession, that "on reviewing his conduct he had much satisfaction." Another, Dr. Thomas, of Worcester, said upon his death-bed to a fellow-sufferer, the eminent Dr. Hickes, Dean of his Cathedral, "If my heart do not deceive me, and God's grace do not fail me, I think I could suffer at a stake rather than take the oaths." The proportion who had the courage of their convictions was not inconsiderable among beneficed clergy; but Leslie appropriately remarked on this point in reply to a sermon of Sherlock at the Temple Church after his apostasy, "There is not one but knows that this comparison of numbers proves nothing at all; that truth was never tried by counting and telling of noses; that numbers were never any evidence of a good cause. At this rate the Alcoran will vie with the Gospel, and Turkism will be not only better than Popery, but even than Christianity itself. This therefore, is nothing else but cheating and deluding the people, instead of informing and instructing them. And they are hard put to it surely, when, to save their own credit and blast others, they are forced so frequently to inculcate such an argument, which themselves in their own consciences (if they have any) know to be none at all." But perhaps Nonjurors made the mistake of a too easy submission to unconstitutional deprivation, which is one never made by Puritans or Erastians. Agitation, the ordinary weapon of these parties, might have better served their cause; for, not only did many more at heart agree with this noble minority of the clergy, but their silent suffering became a pretext for conformity on the part of feeble folk. A nobler disputant than Sherlock, and whose apostasy from the nonjurors did not expose him to such obloquy, was Dr. Stillingfleet. His temporal interests coincided with, but did not so apparently suggest, recantation. In a pamphlet entitled "Unreasonableness of Separation," he put the argument in favour of compliance in a new light, making no pretence of right for the usurpation but "consent of the three Estates of the realm." Unfortunately for it, this consent had never been obtained; as Parliament had never been consulted on the matter, the House of Commons having been unconstitutionally elected, and the Spirituality notoriously overborne by Temporal peers; nor Convocation consulted at all, which is one of the three Estates. He did not improve his ground by saying, "So far as he could see that to a *de facto* king the law of England requires an allegiance, or else the whole nation was perjured in most of the reigns from the Conquest till Henry VIII." When such a man as Stillingfleet could justify revolution upon those grounds, it showed how far moral deterioration had gone, and what vile holds men were content to stay them on. This controversy continued for several years, but the original question remained exactly where Nonjurors placed it.

Another point which immediately presented itself for consideration to those who chose with them the plain unsophisticated cause of hereditary right, was, whether attendance at public services in which the names of William and Mary were substituted for those of the real king and queen, involved a sinful compliance and condition of communion. Nonjurors were not unanimous, but a majority and the highest authorities decided in the affirmative.

Foremost among these was Dr. George Hickes, the lately deprived Dean of Westminster, who received his bishop's dying confession, and whose theological treatises have won the admiration of pious and learned persons ever since. None could compare with him in research upon a variety of subjects, while his vigour and activity equalled his learning. Unfortunately his manuscripts, confided to the care of a bank, were destroyed for want of that care; but many of his best works are still extant, and a biography by a competent writer would be not only a tribute to his memory but form a very interesting volume. One remark which fell from the dean, in his apology for Nonjurors' separation, applied to none more appropriately than himself, though his habitual modesty precluded such an intention. "One Jacobite, could he turn to their Majesties upon his own principles, would be worth a hundred such subjects as you (Sherlock); and when Providence shall remove the obstacles which lie in the way of allegiance to them, they will have reason to value them as so many jewels of the Crown." This severe rebuke, with Leslie's, Sherlock denounced as libels, which elicited from the latter this retort at a later date: "These gentlemen had need talk of libels when they have taken such extraordinary pains to libel themselves. Their apostasies are libels and perpetual libels, and will remain everlasting monuments of their infamy, except they can persuade people to burn their books and forget their sermons. So that (to give these gentlemen their due), they have saved their adversaries all trouble on this point who have something else to do than be at so common and trite an argument as to trouble the world with any more libels, when they find so many made by the gentlemen themselves."

Next to Dr. Hickes among Nonjurors, and like him one of Leslie's most intimate and valued friends, was Henry Dodwell, an Irishman by birth, and Camdenian professor at Oxford. Some of his learning was unprofitably spent on strange speculations in theology; but he proved himself very capable of practically dealing with a subject when he came in contact with another antagonist of Nonjurors. This was Dr. Hody, who professed to have made a Providential discovery in the library at Oxford of an ancient manuscript, showing that intrusion of a new bishop into a See during the rightful owner's lifetime, could not justify separation from his Church, unless he were formally convicted of heresy. Dodwell pertinently pointed out that the date of the manuscript, being written in the thirteenth century, deprived it of any value as a testimony to the practice of the primitive Church. And his investigation revealed further the awkward fact that Hody, whether from oversight or intentionally, had omitted in his citation of its contents some Canons referred to which directly mitigated against the theory he advocated. However, the providential character of his discovery consisted in his own promotion speedily to high positions in the Church, and the manuscript was left to slumber again in its native dust.

Henry Dodwell was indeed "a true son of the Church, and a learned defender of it," as Leslie termed him, one of whose friendship any one might be justly proud. They had been early thrown together, long before a community of opinions and sufferings occurred to bring them into closer sympathy, and the friendship thus cemented continued to the last. Macaulay in support of an ungenerous attack upon Dodwell has made a most groundless statement. He says that "when Leslie collected his own works for publication, he omitted a discourse upon 'Marriages in Different Communities,' originally printed as an appendage to a sermon by himself, probably because he was ashamed of it." Then, in a note, Macaulay admits his knowledge of facts upon which this presumption is based to be slight and second-hand. His statement and presumption are both the very reverse of the truth, but too characteristic of a Whig historian's method of dealing with Nonjurors; though it must be gratefully acknowledged his treatment of Leslie is more honest than that of Hallam. That discourse or rather treatise of Dodwell was in form of a letter originally, and only not included in republication with the sermon because not one of Leslie's own works. But so far from being ashamed of it, in his preface Leslie spoke of it in the highest terms, and as a recommendation from his learned and judicious friend, which would help to render his own sermon "more valuable to the public."

The two productions were indeed a testimony of the long and warm attachment between them. At the period of the sermon's delivery (in substance) at Chester Cathedral, they were staying in the same house, and it was their thorough accord of sentiment upon its main subject which led Leslie to refer back to Dodwell when preparing his works for republication. Upon another occasion, when Dodwell was violently attacked by Dissenters for his treatise concerning the immortality of the soul, Leslie defended him in the warmest manner. They did not take the same view on some of the proceedings of Nonjurors at a later stage, but this difference never interrupted their personal relations of amity and esteem in the slightest degree. They sometimes were accustomed to stay together at the house of a mutual friend, Mr. Francis Cherry, of Shottesbrook, in Berkshire. He was well known for his high character, urbanity, and boundless hospitality, proffered with a special kindness to Nonjurors, so that for some months he provided Leslie shelter and support, when his zeal for King James involved him in some trouble with the Government,[1] Another pious and excellent friend, among the first with whom Leslie became acquainted early, was Robert Nelson. If he had never done more than write the "Festivals and Fasts of the Church," his name would deserve most grate-

[1] Secretary's "Life of Nelson," referred to later on.

fully to be remembered. But he did much more, being the prime mover or hearty supporter of all the best and greatest institutions in his day, and the friend and confidential adviser of more good people than perhaps any layman who has ever lived. His ample fortune and high connections afforded him that influence which piety and learning combined to turn to the most advantage on every occasion. Such influence in society was never more needed for its preservation in England than when the tide of corruption and infidelity introduced by the Revolution was at its height. Unconcealed attachment of such a person to the Nonjuring party, while not severing his connection with opponents, could not fail materially to benefit them in several ways.

John Kettlewell deserves mention among more eminent nonjurors, though his life has been well written so as to render it unnecessary to say much. He did not carry his objections so far as some on ecclesiastical grounds apart from political; but the beauty and sweetness of his character were an invaluable testimony to the excellence of any cause which he espoused. One instance of his wisdom and charity was a scheme devised for the relief of deprived clergy who had little or no private means. A vain pretence of leavening injustice with mercy had been made when the Deprivation Act was first introduced into Parliament, by allowing a portion from the livings for their support. It quickly disappeared, so soon as success of the measure seemed sure, for the clause had never been intended as a reality. Nor could adepts in the art of forswearing be expected to exhibit compassion to those whom they dispossessed. This proposal met, of course, with the cordial approbation of the true bishops of Bath and Wells, Ely, Gloucester, Norwich, and Peterborough, and a considerable amount of support among Christian people. Yet the Privy Council had the indecency to complain of it, and to hail before them the saintly Ken of Bath and Wells on a charge of "illegality and encouragement of immorality" for his assistance to Kettlewell's plan. This singular indictment was explained to consist in having given a donation to "a man who went about one day in a gown, and upon another in a blue silk waistcoat." No name was mentioned, and conjecture was left free to fix upon any Nonjuror the scantiness of whose wardrobe rendered such a change of apparel necessary. But the privy councillors omitted to remember what a much greater metamorphosis had been recently undergone in this way by one of their own chief supporters, Dr. Compton. However, the good bishop did not deem it consistent with his dignity to inquire to whom they particularly referred, and contented himself with a general remark that "to give even to an ill man knowingly was a duty, if that ill man wanted the necessaries of life," which reply caused the matter to drop.

Other names among Nonjurors eminent for their worth and attainments may occur in the further course of this narrative, but these which have been mentioned were among the first friends with whom Leslie was brought into any immediate acquaintance or connection upon his settlement in London. To have lived on terms of mutual friendship and regard with characters like these and others, is in itself no mean testimony to his own merits.

Now it is time to return to his personal history after the deprivation which, as has been seen, rendered necessary his removal from Ireland.

CHAPTER IV.

Prohibition in Parish Churches—Nonjuring Separation—Ely House Private Ministrations—Easy Methods—Conversions—Reply to Archbishop King's Book—Prosecution — Escape — Supplements — Easy Methods with Deists and Jews, abridged.

Nothing was more natural than that he should resolve upon taking up his abode in London after return from the Isle of Wight with the Keightleys, or at least residing there until some providential circumstance should direct him elsewhere. It was the centre to which his thoughts and hopes would naturally turn, because there he would have the earliest opportunities of intelligence concerning political and ecclesiastical affairs of great importance; because also there he could mix more freely in the society for which he was adapted, and find a field for employment of his abilities. On his first arrival he spent some time with Lord Clarendon at his country seat and in town, who had appointed him his private chaplain, rather in an honorary capacity than with a view of performing ecclesiastical duties. If any such intention had been entertained, it would have soon been removed by the strong measures adopted by William's government against Nonjuring clergy to hinder their officiating in churches, as well as their own scruples about the Prayers. However for a while this did not preclude him from being invited and consenting to do duty at some churches occasionally. For instance, on two successive Sundays, 8th and 15th of September, 1689, he was the preacher at the Services in Charlbury Church, when the rector was not only present, but afterwards dined with his wife at the same table, though there is no record attesting which Royalties were prayed for. And probably the same was the case at other churches. In the next year a change had taken place. Nonjuring clergy were no longer permitted to preach in parish churches, nor willing themselves or their supporters to countenance services where the king and queen's names were superseded. Tillotson, the intruding archbishop, himself admitted the propriety of this refusal with those who could not conscientiously assent; and the practice of some who were reluctant to leave their parish churches, of standing up or muttering protest against the usurpers' names, was not one to be commended upon any principle whatever. Accordingly a separation had become no longer a question for discussion in theory, but an inevitable necessity in practice. There now stood side by side two Communions, each professing to be the true Church of England, and accusing the other of schism. It was not a case of wide diversity upon fundamental points as between the Churches of England and Rome, which could not be bridged over except by abandonment of her whole position on the part of one or other, but of two sections thoroughly united still upon every material point of doctrine or discipline. There was the distressing spectacle of a house divided against itself, with rival priesthoods, altars, and sacraments, the worshippers firmly convinced for the most part that the blame of such a grievous state of things between Christians, Catholics, and Church-people lay not with themselves but with their opponents. As family quarrels generally are more bitter than any others, so Nonjurors and Jacobites (another term of reproach now brought into vogue by the necessities of political hatred, and an absurd misnomer) were more bitterly denounced than Romanists or Dissenters by professors of the same religion, and of course became in consequence embittered against them. Both declared the Rubicon had been passed, yet it was not even a new Rubric in the Prayer-book which divided them, nor a new interpretation of an old one, but the mere filling up of a blank space intended to be supplied as occasion should from time to time require. The burden of proof lay with those who demanded alteration suddenly; and since none satisfactory could be furnished, their duty and wisdom was to have devised some plan for leaving it an open question, which must have had a healing tendency in time, and helped to close the wound. Instead of which, since Christianity was not the aim of a revolutionary government, but domination, a galling seton was introduced of the most painful description. Some persons who talk blandly of the mistake Nonjurors made in separating, evidently do not realize their position in regard to principle. They did not separate from the Church of England, nor propose any alteration in terms of communion, but were violently dispossessed for adhering to engagements which they had solemnly sworn to. The real departure was on the part of those who treated these engagements as waste paper, and violated them every time they joined in public worship. The question was not at all about the doctrine of divine right to the throne; although up to that moment almost universally it had been held in the Church of England, and most of those abjuring bishops and priests had constantly proclaimed it with their own lips; but concerning the obligation of an oath which all had deliberately taken, and now claimed a liberty to revoke. Therefore the position of Nonjurors cannot be rightly estimated in the light of affairs now, when any clergy as much as laity might conscientiously renounce attachment to the House of Hanover or the Houses of Parliament, if it should be the will of the nation to get rid of them, for their only title to existence is that will. Now it is a simple question of expediency, then it was one of principle; now it is only a matter of politics, then it was an integral feature of the whole English constitution. Accordingly Nonjurors were forced to form a Communion of their own, and they did so, though the numbers were small who united with them in Public Worship; a majority who fully concurred in their principles shrinking from so open a declaration. Ely House, the residence of the Bishop of Ely, contained one of the Chapels in which service was held. The bishop, Dr. Francis Turner, had been among the Seven sent to the Tower, but he remained loyal, and was subjected to a great deal of persecution on the plea of being engaged in conspiracies against William, none of which charges could be substantiated. Macaulay, who has undertaken to repeat them, can only make out his case by putting his own construction upon language which he admits to be metaphorical in letters, which, if genuine, are quite compatible with the bishop's own asseverations. Upon the commemoration of King Charles's martyrdom, service was held at Ely House, when Charles Leslie was the preacher, and delivered "a most excellent sermon to about sixty persons, a great auditory at this time," according to the testimony of Lord Clarendon at whose desire he undertook the duty. If it be remembered that the anniversary fell upon a Thursday, when revolutionists could not for bare shame observe it, the flock was not so small in comparison of the numbers who now attend week-day services. However, such an auditory was too much for the sensibilities of men in power. And when a month more elapsed, "the king had been told of the great concourse of people" who assembled at Ely House; so it was ordered to be closed. Such was religious liberty permitted by a man who came over ostensibly to defend religion and liberty according to his own declaration. Everybody knew which of the hawk tribe had hatched this egg, and Lloyd was the cuckoo's fool who volunteered to convey the arbitrary summons. The good Bishop of Ely felt much aggrieved; and if these schemers had foreseen the obloquy to be incurred, they perhaps might hardly have thought the success of their trick repaid them. Nonjurors could not be prohibited in this manner from meeting together for divine worship. William knew better, though he had the will, than to provoke even Nonjurors to desperation and arm the multitude in their defence, who very soon began to exhibit their dislike of him. So various churches were opened in London and other places, where their little congregations could worship in peace and security. At several of these Charles Leslie often officiated as a priest, and was a favourite preacher from time to time; but he never undertook any regular cure, nor attached himself to a particular congregation.

Other ways of ministerial usefulness, which he did not fail to use, offered without giving umbrage or occasioning jealousy among the clergy of the Establishment, such as cases of conscience and sickness. One of these, which occurred in the summer of 1690, will serve as an illustration. A gentleman named Tempest was taken suddenly ill, who desired to see a clergyman; and Leslie was brought to his house. He was then in a high fever and had been raving all the night, so that the doctors objected to his being disturbed. Upon seeing Leslie he inquired if he had taken the oaths, and on being assured that he had not, expressed great satisfaction, and requested him to come again in the afternoon, which he did. The fever shortly returned, and he died early the next morning. Medical attendants are sometimes too officious thus with their patients, and take a very serious responsibility upon themselves in trying to make physical health appear of more consequence than spiritual. This instance, however, shows how strongly a conscientious objection prevailed among laity, which did not always manifest itself in public life, when a sick man felt upon his death-bed an invincible repugnance to the ministrations of a priest who had taken the oaths. Nobody, again, could hinder Leslie in holding private discussions and debates upon religious subjects, his special aptitude in which soon became extensively known, so that numbers of persons in different classes and with widely different views resorted to him for a solution of difficulties on the subject of religion, or with a view of testing his ability to meet arguments in favour of their own systems. This practice continued for several years, when not interrupted by absence on other business; and his accessibility and good humour won for him great esteem among members of various sects; though he never cultivated an unworthy popularity by the slightest concession of principle, or hesitation to speak decidedly and plainly against their errors. His particular intimacies were confined chiefly to the circle of those who agreed with him upon ecclesiastical and political matters, but he always readily acceded to the many requests made for his advice and direction in spiritual matters. Thus, happily, the base devices of Whig and unreasonable men were overruled for the benefit of the Church, and by that very attempt to silence him, an open and effectual door was provided for a ministry of mercy which he was most admirably fitted to fulfil. Clergymen are frequently said to be bad men of business, yet every conceivable business which no one else likes to undertake in a parish is by common consent shifted to the priest's shoulders. He is made a sort of parochial omnibus, so that in the multitude and variety of secular concerns thrust upon him by the laity he is sorely beset to discharge his spiritual functions. And it is observable that aggrieved parishioners and parliamentary scouts who claim to regulate ritual in public services, are those who contribute least of their time, substance, or small abilities to any useful parish work. Instead of being a reproach, it is a credit to a clergyman that he abstains from the meddlesome, fussy interference of a Burnet or a Lloyd, with affairs which belong to the laity, and confines himself to the ministry of the Word of God and to Prayer. To that his Ordination vows pledged him; and the reputation acquired by catering for public amusement, organizing lectures on all the 'ologies, presiding at bazaars, concerts, cricket matches, and various other worldly engagements, is at the expense of duty in his proper character and the study of theology.

Leslie had perceived already that discussion and controversy were ill adapted to minds much excited upon religious subjects, and that calm meditation was much more likely to have a beneficial effect. Materials for this purpose, however, were evidently wanting or inaccessible to most people. Many learned treatises had been written on almost every question, but there was a scarcity of simple and easy manuals suited to the capacities of ordinary readers, which yet should grasp the main points of each and treat them in a reverential and becoming manner. Therefore he turned his attention to a supply of this deficiency, and commenced at the very beginning; partly because the outline of an argument against the Deists lay before him which he had already used to good purpose; and partly because Deists were then most notorious and defiant in proclaiming their pernicious tenets, with very slight discouragement if not actual countenance from persons in high station, who ought to have been foremost in opposing them. His own idea was corroborated by that of many on whose judgment he could rely as to the desirability and seasonableness of such an undertaking. This was the origin of the "Short and Easy Methods," by which he entitled several treatises written in defence of the Catholic faith. It is somewhat surprising, therefore, that a modern sceptic, who has devoted himself to the task of criticizing Leslie's performances, should, in direct denial of the author's own statement, presume to ascribe this first treatise as a reply to Charles Blount's "Oracles of Reason." It was composed and published several years before that wretched man's feeble blast was heard of, arising out of those circumstances already narrated. Notice of Blount only came into Leslie's treatise incidentally upon its republication, and lest silence might be misunderstood or misrepresented in regard to Apollonius Tyanæus, set up with pretended miracles in rivalry to our blessed Saviour. Blount's work is now aptly enough styled "a collection of meagre tracts under a magniloquent title,"[1] but apparently to depreciate the value of Leslie's refutation. For the same reason Charles Gildon is sneered at as "a poor creature" whom he converted. But this is a stale and sorry device for discounting an adversary much superior to

[1] Stephen's "Hist. Eng. Thought," vol. i. 194-200.

one's self in every possible respect. Macaulay has also spoken slightingly of Gildon, though knowing nothing more of him than that he had been the subject of Pope's sneers, whose insinuation of venality was false, and who hated him much more for his religion than anything else. Pope's own quill was venal as much as his. If Gildon had been so very inferior, why should such superior men as these have so industriously laboured to depreciate him but in order to bring down the Church of England and her champion too? In truth, he was a man of fair abilities if no more, and quite undeserving of any reproach. Equally disingenuous is the covert insinuation that Gildon was a specimen of his converts. Nothing is better established than that his instrumentality was blessed to the conversion of very great numbers of persons among disbelievers and misbelievers of all sorts, and that at a period when they were far abler men than sceptics and critics of the present day. Middleton said he had spent many years in vain trying to discover an objection to the argument on which the "Short and Easy Method with Deists and Jews" is based, than whom none was more competent to judge of its weight. His testimony is supported by that of many more whose ability and impartiality are beyond question. This treatise was left upon the shelf while he proceeded to the composition of another, the "Short and Easy Method with the Jews," finished upon Good Friday, 1689. Leslie does not appear to have been brought into much personal contact with Jews, but the plan he had marked out naturally suggested dealing with them next in order, and the subjects were of a kindred nature. Indeed, he assumes perusal of the method with the Deists before that with the Jews, while in both the same rules are laid down and essentially the same line of argument adopted so far as it can apply. For none can admit the genuineness of the New Testament who deny that of the Old; and on the other hand, though Deists may not be Jews, Jews are Deists. This work was written in reply to the best and latest publications which he could find in Holland, and setting down, as the fairest way, "the defence, arguments, and objections of Jews in their own words, to get at the very heart of their cause as the likeliest method to bring matters to an issue." Grotius had written upon the same subject and been translated into English; but as this method had not been adopted by him, Leslie did not deem his own task superfluous. What effect it produced cannot be stated, as in the case of the other. Its circulation would be limited by an English dress, and the Jews in this country have not shown much interest in the study of controversy even as it concerns their own race and religion, like those in other countries. At any rate, it remains unanswered or even objected to; though, as Leslie says, "it is easier to object than to answer."

Thirteen years after the publication of the "Short Method with the Deists," appeared a treatise in reply, which he was inclined at first to dismiss with contempt, as written by some "impotent Whig or Dissenter," on account of its absurd and abusive title-page. A closer inspection could not improve his opinion of the anonymous author or his production. Therefore he thought it might fairly be left to sink under its own weight of nonsense and contradiction. Finding, however, it was boasted of among Deists as a very clever performance, he resolved to answer it. And in thinking thus over the whole subject further, he concluded that there were other marks beside the four already advanced, which might properly be added to the evidence in favour of Christianity, though not of its truth.

But he answered this treatise, the "Detection," in the first place without reference to the new marks, because the former ones were those in question by its author. The mountain had only brought forth a mouse. He attempted to parallel the books of Moses and the Gospels by other stories ancient and modern, none of which could stand on close investigation the test of the four marks, supposing for a moment their truth. They were puerile, paltry fables, indeed not deserving of serious notice, and accompanied with a torrent of personal abuse and scurrility which no person now would care to read. Nevertheless, Leslie took the trouble to refute these senseless stories *seriatim*, showing how in each instance there was a failure to satisfy some one or more of the marks, and leaving, therefore, their force unassailable as before. Previously to this a Mr. Leclerc had attacked Leslie in a haughty and contemptuous manner, charging him with writing scandalous and seditious discourses, and having opposed the revolution; political matters quite foreign to the subject. That article contained the substance of what afterwards was more lengthily stated in the "Detection." Then came another assailant, the editor of the *Observator* who charged Leslie with Popery and betrayal of his own conscience, and substituted proofs of Christianity which he deemed preferable to his. (1) Natural conscience and reason. (2) Conformity of the doctrine to the nature of God and morality. (3) Contrariety to the corruptness of human nature, etc. (4) Its independence of human philosophy or authority. (5) Its clear evidence that the pope is Antichrist. For the first it was argued that every man was sensible of conscience and reason being depraved, and the Scripture only furnishes the explanation. But the answer was obvious, that the authority of the Scriptures must be admitted before its revelation concerning the fall of Adam could be accounted a sufficient explanation. The second and third of his proofs might be equalled by the precepts of moral philosophers, or the self-mortifications of Brahmins. The fourth proof was absurd, for facts can only be proved by human testimony or revelation, so that Deists could only depend upon miracles which they denied; unless the fifth would serve every purpose of conviction, namely, the notion among some Protestants of the pope being Antichrist! To go altogether upon doctrine in neglect of facts in this manner was overlooking our Saviour's own appeal, "Believe Me for the works' sake," and "If I had not done such works, you had had no sin." The only doctrine here contended for was morality, whereas Christianity includes the doctrines of the Incarnation, Atonement, etc., which even a Presbyterian must admit.

Mr. Stephen has accused Leslie of being a "rationalist in principle,"[1] and, to give colour to the accusation, has misstated the general nature of his arguments by weaving together statements from different treatises, which were independent and unconnected with each other. Thus a show of contradiction is attempted, where there is no real inconsistency. Our author was in no proper sense a "rationalist," but, as he stated upon one occasion to some dissenting teachers who requested a conference with him upon the subject of the "Short Method," adopted the "plain principle of reason" in arguing with Deists in his day, because themselves exclusively appealed to it. He did not perhaps anticipate the new grounds to which disbelief has shifted, whether those of avowed opponents of the gospel, or of treacherous dealers. Nor if he had foreseen any of them, would it have been consistent either with his purpose or duty to have suggested them to adversaries.

[1] "English Thought," etc., vol. i. pp. 194-197.

In another place he tells us that it was always his method, in representing and discussing the opinion of any adversary, to say all he could for it as if it were really his own. All his works show that he constantly acted upon this principle most fairly; though it is an inevitable accident of controversy that unconsciously one often puts into an adversary's mouth statements easy of defeat, and which are not the strongest to be adduced for his side of the case. Men of straw are thereby put up only to be knocked down, and opponents turn about made to assail each other, so to serve as bottle-holders for the victorious party. This constitutes a vital objection to dialogues and discussions generally upon religious topics.

Plain principles of reason were all Deists would allow, therefore Leslie was compelled to adopt them, without liability to the reproach of being "a rationalist in principle." Dost thou "appeal unto Cæsar? unto Cæsar shalt thou go," was the ground on which he proceeded with scoffers who would have trampled gospel pearls under their feet.

Abuse was plentifully bestowed upon him; attempts made to answer him, though after a sufficiently long interval, to show how difficult the task was felt to be; but it never entered the imagination of any contemporaries to claim him as the "unconscious" advocate of Deists because he met them on the ground they had chosen, and fought them with their own weapons after the example of S. Paul.

Again equally groundless is the assertion that Leslie made "allegation the same thing as proof, and assumes the authenticity and contemporaneity of the records which are his, and that others are not so." It is not true. His conclusions are fairly drawn from his premises in every instance, and those premises are no more than "matters of fact," which sceptics cannot disprove. As for other records, what or where are they? There are none, unless these men who claim to a monopoly of reason mean such heathen legends and fables as have no historic basis, and which themselves repudiate. If the records are not contemporaneous, at least these sceptics ought to produce some date for the forgery, and some account of its manufacture, a task which they discreetly avoid. Their whole argument is of a negative character, which would as reasonably deny every fact in profane or modern history. The only reason for Leslie's clothing his Old Testament matters of fact in its language was evidently on account of the general familiarity with it. He has not assumed the truth of those records, but insisted on the facts, interwoven in the whole national existence, and incorporated in the legal constitution of the Jews. His appeal to the sacred books is in the way of testimony, not authority, as furnishing the only probable and possible explanation of the matters of fact which were undeniable, from which he argues step by step to an inevitable conclusion. Matters of doctrine rest on a somewhat different basis, and before a Church's authority is accepted for them, testimony must be produced for that authority; but to assert that " dogmas are not to be believed unless they stare one in the face," is tantamount to a denial of all faith whatever; for a man does not believe or hope for that which he sees.

A few further remarks seem called for in regard to the wretched man Charles Blount. He belonged to a family of some consideration, and possessed amiable qualities and sparkling conversational powers, which gave him access to the higher circles of society. He might even be termed a man of talent, if that talent had been cultivated by study and reflection, for which he was too indolent; and what he wrote, like Tindal's history, was largely borrowed, with little acknowledgment. None but a weak-minded man could have been driven to the crime of suicide because prohibited from marriage with his wife's sister, but it is almost surprising that Parliamentary champions of incest do not cite his unhappy end in support of their proposals for setting aside that prohibition of divine, ecclesiastical, and even the old Roman law.[1] Leslie gave offence to some of his friends by calling him " execrable," but rightly refused to retract or modify the expression in regard to one who had execrated and blasphemed his Saviour. The rebuke was the more needful when he could boast of being a friend and companion of Prelates. Sensitiveness about personal dignity is not an uncommon characteristic of sceptics unsparing and unscrupulous in their own expressions concerning the objects of a Christian's worship and deepest veneration.

The value of these " Methods " has not been impaired by lapse of time, they having a far wider scope than confutation of unbelievers' objections, in supplying profitable matter for study and consideration to Christians. Very far from true is the saying, that "he who has never doubted yet, has never yet believed."[2] But those who may be induced, by perusal of the sketches in the ensuing pages, to read Leslie's treatises *in extenso*, if they do not quite admit their shortness and easiness, will never regret the pains it may cost in the result of a better acquaintance with the evidences of truth and the strengthening of their own convictions in its favour.

Events which occurred in Ireland during the next two or three years after the Revolution are too generally known to require any special notice; though Protestants and Romanists there seem never to remember that the date of

---

[1] Milman's " Hist. Christ.," ii. 18.
[2] Bishop Hinds' Poem in Bacon's Essays by Whately, p. 340.

the battle of the Boyne was July 1, for they celebrate it on the anniversary of the battle of Aughrim, July 12. Leslie contented himself with the study of theological subjects and in the society of friends, who increased in number as his reputation spread. At least, there is no trace of his active engagement in political affairs during that period. One might regret that he ever suffered himself to be withdrawn from this retirement to mingle in the vortex of public life upon which he could not exercise any effective influence, whereas his services to the Church were invaluable. But he would not thus have been happy, for men cannot control their inclinations, nor put genius into fetters by considerations of expediency. Circumstances seemed to call for his active interference again on the side of hereditary right and truth. Dr. William King, Archbishop of Dublin, published a pamphlet entitled "The State of the Protestants in Ireland under King James," which consisted of violent invectives against that Sovereign, and several serious misstatements of fact, to prejudice his cause in the eyes of English people more fully than before, and exhibit himself in a favourable light. Leslie knew the exact truth of transactions which King professed to explain, and the motives of his conduct in suddenly abandoning former professions of loyalty. Therefore he undertook the task of reply and exposure in another pamphlet or book, for which purpose he paid a visit to Glaslough. Both his and King's productions are now extremely scarce; nor is this matter of much regret, for they are chiefly occupied with particular circumstances without a vestige of interest for the present day. But the books then evoked a warm controversy, occasioned Leslie some annoyance by way of reprisal, and have left an indelible stain upon King's memory. Leslie's object was not to justify King James's

Government in their general proceedings, some of which himself had resisted as unlawful, but to expose misrepresentations and denounce principles which struck at the root of all constitutional authority. He wrote under no excitement nor prompted by any personal feeling. Both pamphlets were published anonymously, nor was any actual proof adduced of authorship; so that King ventured, even in the company of other persons, to disclaim his own publication, nor ever avowed it; but the secret transpired, as such things almost invariably do; and now is put beyond question, for his posthumous manuscripts contained the heads of a reply intended against Leslie.[1] The efforts of his friends and partisans, therefore, to rescue his reputation from a sad blot have been defeated. Leslie was as well understood by the public to be the author of the reply to the archbishop, but though he never denied it, no alternative but silence was left to him; because through the secret advice of King, and at the instance of Burnet and Lloyd, the Government denounced it as a libel. Some of the more salient passages will explain the reason why such wrath was excited in the archiepiscopal breast. "It is no easy matter to know what his principles are, but those he exhibits are all the old rotten rebel commonwealth ones, the same with Bradshaw upon trial of King Charles I., viz. that all power is from the people; kings, their deputies, therefore are accountable to them, and may be deposed by them. He gives every one power to dispense with allegiance to the king, when he thinks that the king dispenses with the execution of any law. Even ecclesiastical authority shall be derived from the people. To crown all, he gives as large and loose an interpretation of that famous principle of the Church of England, of its not being

[1] Hearne's Notes, Bodleian Lib. Hist. MS. ep. ii.

lawful upon any pretence to take arms against the king, as Bradshaw, Rutherford, Bellarmine, or Mariana could desire; that private men should not take the sword or resist the king upon any pretence of private injury or wrong done to them in particular. The only true notion of abdication is a king's voluntary resignation of it to the next heir. No one will allow that every private person can determine what sort of withdrawing shall dissolve the Government, and absolve subjects from allegiance. This author's notion will do no service to Protestants in Ireland, who set up arms against King James before the convention in England declared him to have abdicated. There is another view of the case which our author takes care to conceal. Are not all revolutions carried on by making parties combinations of leading men, aspersing opponents, using all arts to bear the mob to one side? But would any member of Parliament or the State lose so much by destruction of the kingdom as the king? Therefore it is less probable that he should design its destruction than any of them. Never any charge more apparent than when Dathan and Abiram accused Moses of arbitrary government and breach of promise. ... If the people were at liberty from government they would be exposed to one another, which would be the greatest slavery in the world. ... He says, 'to lose even half the subjects of the nation in a civil war is more terrible than the loss of liberty.' Does he think Irish Protestants did not lose their liberty under King James? If they did not, his whole book is false. If they did, has not K(ing) W—— retrieved it? then if he has, his position is false. It is a terrible sort of creed to slaughter half the nation. If half be destroyed to purchase liberty to the rest, here is no good, but hurt, done to the people. And I suppose our author has not represented himself in his own mind to be one in that half which was to be destroyed. This principle opens a door to an eternal halving of the people; and we may see by experience that where it obtains, that country seldom enjoys respite from one revolution longer than to feed up and fatten for another.

"Of all pretences for rebellion, religion is the most ridiculous; because a civil war introduces greater immorality, loosens the reins of discipline, and is more contrary to the spirit of true religion than any other thing in the world. It is not propagated by the sword. It is a small still voice that cannot be heard in war. It is built, like Solomon's temple, without the noise of a hammer. War confounds and debauches it. But all is no matter so as we beat down Popery; and yet Popery was never more tolerated in Ireland than since the conclusion of our war against Popery. Another thing; God has threatened to visit the sins of fathers upon the children. And that ocean of blood spilt in one of the revolutions must lie at some door or other. . . . What will become of clergymen, what will their judgment be, who lead their flocks by their example to sin, and employ their wits and learning to find out distinctions and salvoes to keep their flocks from returning and repenting? . . . Of all things, how could the Irish who adhered to King James be made rebels to King William before they submitted to him? The Government of England being dissolved by abdication and returned back to the supposed original contract, of consequence the tie which England had upon Ireland by conquest was separated, and Ireland left as well as England, in their supposed original freedom, to choose what government and governors they pleased. The Jews were about the same time under Egypt that Ireland has been under England, but with this difference—that the English came into Ireland by conquest, whereas Israel was in Egypt by invitation of the king. And though God sent Moses to deliver them from servitude, He did not suffer their exodus till Pharaoh gave them leave to depart. The same in regard to the captivity of Babylon. The immediate and apparent cause of their destruction by the Romans was their obstinate rebellion against lawful governors. . . . Christ came to form a society independent from all others; all kings fell upon them to root them out. What were Christians to do? Were they to take up arms against their governors? No; they were totally barred from that. Damnation was preached to those who resisted their lawful governors. . . . What if the prince be indifferent and evil, and that it is evident to all men he is so? Neither is this a cause for resistance; but we are admonished to reflect that it is our sins have brought such a king to rule over us. . . . I am far from vindicating all that Tyrconnel and other of King James's ministers have done in Ireland. But after King James came in person, there was no act which could properly be called his which was not all mercy and goodness to Protestants. This author avers it was their unanimous resolution not to be the aggressors, and pleads excuse the shutting up of Derry. Was this not enough—to seize the king's forts, to enlist and array soldiers in arms against the king's forces? I never heard Protestants say but that there were many hard cases, and even unjust, in the Acts of Settlement; and they excuse this by saying it was impossible it should be otherwise. This seems to be King James's sense of that matter all along. Ought they not to be redressed, if a way can be found agreeable to reason, justice, and public good? King James did not propose, nor was inclined to the Act of Attainder, as this author slanderously reports. He has written every word with the spirit of malice against his much-inspired sovereign, to whom he had sworn fealty. He owes it to King James's mercy that he now lives to thank him for his mercy. Was he not accused of holding correspondence and giving intelligence to the rebels? King James had once so good an opinion of him that he had him frequently in private, and trusted him in his affairs till at last he found him out. This author did mightily bemoan, September, 1688, that no care was taken to make some proofs of the Prince of Wales's birth. When this was done, we hear of no more objections from him till at the battle of the Boyne he acknowledged this same prince; and yet, in his thanksgiving sermon after that, he calls it a well-contrived cheat. Oh, if this author had retained his integrity! There was a severe jest which the common people got up against the clergy, that there was but one thing which the Parliament could not do; that was, to make a man a woman! Now there is another; that is, to make an oath which the clergy will not take! There are none who have cleverly stuck to the principles they professed but the Nonjuring clergy of the Church of England. Therefore this cannot be called a defection of the Church, but only of particular individuals. At a supper, when an Irish lord began to reproach the Church for her apostasy from former principles, the king replied, 'They are the Church of England who have kept to her principles.' The lord made answer, 'But, sir, how few they are in comparison of the rest!' The king said, 'They are more than Christ had to begin with.'"

Now it has been said since in behalf of Archbishop King that "he denied *in toto* Leslie's charges."[1] This defence puts out of sight the fact that he never admitted but dis-

[1] Private letters of descendants.

claimed authorship of "The State of Protestants," etc.[1] And the charges of being in communication with the Revolutionists whilst in the confidence of James, and of praying for the Prince of Wales, and denouncing his birth as an imposition after the battle of the Boyne, may be denied, but remain as certainly established as that battle itself. That he should have been much exercised in spirit by this exposure and castigation is not surprising, and then would have been the time to avow his authorship and rebut the charges publicly. Instead of venturing upon so hopeless a task, he chose a nearer path to revenge, which at the same time relieved him of the necessity of dropping his disguise. A prosecution was ordered at his instigation, aided by Burnet and Lloyd, against the author for libel, simply because the publication was unlicensed—not that any intention was entertained of trying the question as to the truth or character of its contents. Such was the law of libel in those days; but even the Secretary of State reluctantly granted the order under pressure of Leslie's episcopal foes.

King, who could make a mistake about his presence or absence upon a former occasion, managed now to ferret out his visit to Glaslough, where the work was composed because of its seclusion from London business, and of the opportunity afforded for obtaining particular information on some points. When an officer arrived to search for proofs and arrest him, he had returned to London. It was boasted that a copy of the manuscript was found "in his study." Had the case appeared for trial this could not have served for conviction, because the house was not his, nor did he hold any legal right or responsibility over it. He was simply a guest partaking of a brother's hospitality.

[1] "Ballard's Letters." Bodleian Library.

The accusation of flight came with specially bad grace from these men, each of whom had been very ready to flee from danger themselves. However, he was pursued to London, and arrested on board of a vessel on the Thames. Returning with the officer, he upon landing offered him some wine at a public-house, which was readily accepted. Leslie laid a purse of gold upon the table, asking the officer to keep an eye upon it whilst he retired for a short time, having caught a chill on the water, and called for another bottle of claret. With such security for reappearance, it is little wonder that he consented, and made himself comfortable. His prisoner never returned, and what the officer did with the fifty pounds was never explained, as he did not report his successful capture; nor did Leslie, except in private among friends, with whom it was a favourite observation how well he told the story. No fresh or further attempts were made to arrest him, for it was deemed advisable to let the matter drop, lest the charge of anonymously replying to an anonymous pamphlet might elicit the truth of his facts and statements—which was the last thing his adversaries wished; nor had the Government inclination to push it further.

ABRIDGMENT OF "SHORT AND EASY METHOD WITH THE DEISTS."

They say that there is no greater ground to believe in Christ than in Mahomet—that all pretences to revelation are cheats of cunning and designing men upon the credulity of simple people, till, their numbers increasing, these came to be established by laws and received upon trust from foregoing ages.—What is desired is some short topic of reason without running into mazes of learning, which shall distinguish Christianity from all impostures. First, then, the truth of the doctrine of Christ will be evinced, if the matters of fact recorded of Him in the Gospels be true; for His miracles if true vouch the truth of what He delivered. The same is to be said of Moses. If he did such wonderful things as are told of him, it must follow that he was sent from God. For proof, rules are set down that where all meet, such matters of fact cannot be false; they do meet in those of Christ and Moses, but do not in any imposture whatever.

1. Such that men's outward senses can judge of them. 2. That they be done publicly. 3. That not only public monuments, but some outward actions to be performed, are kept in memory of them. 4. That such memorials commence from the time when the matters of fact were done. The two first make impossible a cheat at the time when the matter is said to be done; the two last secure against invention of them for imposing upon credulity in after ages. Moses could not have persuaded 600,000 men that he had brought them out of Egypt through the Red Sea, etc., if he had not done so, because every man's senses would have contradicted him; no more than one could persuade the people of London that they had seen the Thames divided, and been carried through on dry land, when it was not true. He could not have made them receive his five books which told of these things done before their eyes, if all were manifestly an imposture. They speak of themselves as delivered by Moses, and kept in the ark from his time. In whatever age it may be supposed they were forged, everybody must know they had never heard of them before, or that they had owned and acknowledged them all along from Moses till then, and as containing the statutes and municipal law of their nation. These books have a further demonstration of truth, for they give an historical account

of the institution of these laws, and the practice of them from that time—the Passover, etc., with yearly, monthly, weekly, daily remembrances of matters of fact. If these books of Moses were forged, and imposed upon the people in making them believe that they had kept all their observances in memory of what the books asserted, then the Jews must either have kept them in memory of nothing, or without knowing anything of their original, or the reason why they kept them. Was that possible to persuade men that they had kept observances in memory of what they had never heard of? None know the reason why Stonehenge on Salisbury Plain was set up. If I should write a book to tell these stones were set up in memory of such and such, by such and such, and say in this book it was written when they were done by actors and eye-witnesses, received as truth and quoted by authors of the greatest reputation in all ages since, well known in England, enjoined by Act of Parliament, and taught to children, could this pass upon England? Compare this with the great stones at Gilgal; which case is free from little carpings as to the passage of the Red Sea at a springtide and with a strong wind. Would not every person say we know the stonage at Gilgal, but we never heard before of this reason for it (Josh. iv. 1-18), nor of the book of Joshua. Where has it been all this while? And where and how came you after so many ages to find it? Besides, this book tells us that this passage over Jordan was ordained to be taught our children from age to age. We never were; nor have done so.

So likewise the four marks meet in the matters of fact which are recorded in the Gospel. All that is said of Moses and his book is every way applicable to Christ. His works and miracles are there said to be done publicly; then baptism and the Lord's Supper were instituted as memorials at the very time, and have been observed without interruption throughout the whole Christian world down all the way from that time to this. The Christian clergy are as notoriously a matter of fact as the tribe of Levi among the Jews, and the Gospel as much a law as the books of Moses. It being impossible there could be such things before they were invented, it is as impossible they should be received when invented in after ages. The matters of fact of Mahomet, or what are fabled of the heathen deities, all want these four marks. Mahomet pretended to no miracles, and what are commonly told of him are rejected by the learned among Mahometans. In the next place, what are told want the two first rules, being not performed before any one. The same is to be said of fables of heathen gods. They had, it is true, public institutions in memory of them, but want the fourth mark, that these should commence from the time when what they commemorate were done, appointed many ages afterwards, and by others in honour of them.

I do not say that everything wanting these marks is false, but that nothing is so which has them, and this shows that matters of fact of Moses and of Christ have come down better guarded than any others. Our very souls and bodies are concerned in the truth of what is related in the holy Scriptures, therefore men have searched into, sifted, and examined them narrowly. Some have suffered for errors which they thought to be truth, but never any for what themselves knew to be lies. And apostles must have known what they taught to be lies if it had been so, because they said they had seen and heard them, etc. More, their Master bid them expect nothing but suffering in this world, so they were not disappointed. Now, that this despised doctrine of the Cross should prevail universally against allurements of flesh and blood, of the world, and persecutions of kings and princes, must show its origin to be divine, and its protector Almighty.

There is another argument from prophecy—all which had gone before fulfilled in Christ. Deists, when not able to deny the evidence of facts, yet deny that we can be sure any wonderful thing is a true or a false miracle, because we cannot know what is the utmost extent of the power of nature. But we can certainly tell in many cases when we are not cheated. In the case of fire, though we know not its utmost extent, we do that its nature is to burn; and therefore, when three men walked in it without harm or smell, we cannot be deceived in thinking there was a stop put to the nature of fire. Deists acknowledge a God of almighty power, yet would put it out of His power to make any revelation of His will to mankind. Nay, if we know not what is nature, how do we know there is such a thing? Then all becomes supernatural till we get to downright scepticism, and doubt whether we see, hear, or feel. . . . Therefore the sum is this, that whatever matter of fact has all the four marks, could never have been invented and received but upon conviction of the outward senses. Let Deists produce their Apollonius Tyanæus,[1] or aid from Romish legends (those pious cheats, the sorest disgrace of Christianity), or the most probable fables of heathen deities, and see if they can find the four marks. If, notwithstanding, this be said to be priestcraft, they will give us an idea of priests far different from what they intend, above the condition of mortals and outdoing what has been related of infernal powers; making men believe they had practised, enacted, taught and been taught what they never had—more than God Almighty has done; for none of His miracles or the belief He has required have contradicted the

[1] Toland's book.

senses of a single man, much less of all. And since Deists (these men of sense and reason) have so mean an idea of priests, why do they not recover the world out of the government of such blockheads? They have tried their hands, and are still exploded. False religion is but a corruption of the true : the true was before it. The revelation made to Moses is older than any heathen history. If Deists say that all the world are blockheads except themselves, voted to be men of sense by themselves, this will spoil their beloved topic of appealing to the common sense of mankind. The truth is that religion is no invention of priests but of divine original, and their order a perpetual and living monument of the matters of fact. Therefore the devil has bent his greatest force in all ages against the priesthood, knowing that if that goes down all goes with it.

NOTE.—Learned men have doubted whether there ever was such a person as Apollonius. What account we have is from Philostratus, who lived a hundred years after the time in which he is pretended to have flourished. He got his knowledge, as he says, from a book of one Damis, a companion of Apollonius, and at the command of the Empress Julia he bestowed some pains in transcribing its contents, which were written in an unelegant style. He did not confine himself to Damis's book, but gathered together dispersed relations of Apollonius ; so we are only sure we have them as new dressed and vamped up by an orator to please the fancy of an oratorical lady in an age when feigned romantic stories were much in vogue, and living at court he would not be out of the fashion. All that Deists can possibly infer from their legends is that perhaps they may be true ; but they dare not bring the matters of fact to the test of the four rules.

ABRIDGMENT OF "SHORT AND EASY METHOD WITH THE JEWS."

The Jewish and Christian religions both stand upon one bottom, and only of all revelations pretended can show the four marks. So that Jews are embraced under the happy necessity either to renounce Moses or to embrace Christ. Our Messiah did not pretend to destroy the law, but to fulfil it, and did so in every circumstance; nor is there any way possible to reconcile the promises in the law but as they are fulfilled in the gospel. For instance, Gen. xlix. 10. The sceptre has long since departed, and no other Messiahs come but our Lord. Evasions of this prophecy by the rabbis carry guilt on their face, being contradictory to one another. Jer. xxxiii. 17, 22 gloriously fulfilled in our Messiah. Jews have not had since the destruction of Jerusalem any sacrifice at all. Except that of the evangelical priesthood. Some pretend the prophecy is meant of the time after the Messiah, but for this they have to add to the text, which would leave nothing certain. Isa. liii. An exact description of the death and sufferings of the Messiah, with the reason, as an expiation and satisfaction for the sins of the people. How forced and foreign the interpretation of some modern Jews, as if this were a description of the Jewish people in the name of a person, and their present dispersion with making many proselytes. If Jews keep their own ground it is the most they can expect; their proselytes are not known. The flowing in of the Gentiles has been to the Christian Church, and only so can be verified to the Jewish. Their dispersion is a punishment for their own sins, not for the conversion of the Gentiles; and the Jews shall at last be converted by them, not those by these.

What satisfaction will God accept? Even that Messiah for whom a body was prepared, described particularly in this chapter. Do the Jews make intercession for the Gentiles? Or how do they bear their sins? The "righteous servant" was not that people, but He who suffered for them. Then it is said that a real death is not meant, but great afflictions, as S. Paul says "in deaths oft." That is plainly figurative, because a man can be only once in death, though often, as the apostle meant, in danger of it. Zech. ix. 9. Modern Jews have framed to themselves two Messiahs, one Ben Joseph of the tribe of Ephraim, poor and contemptible, to undergo great indignities; the other Ben David of the tribe of Judah, to conquer all the earth, live for ever in temporal grandeur, and raise from the dead all Israelites of former ages. Thus they dream and invent Messiahs to elude the import' of prophecies concerning the true One. Dan. ix. 24. Our Messiah did come within the seventy weeks, according to the prophetical computation of a year for a day, and all spoken there of Him was punctually fulfilled. It pinches so close that modern Jews would discredit the whole Book of Daniel; though they dare not quite throw it off because indubitably received by their forefathers, and rather given preference to than excluded. So these have made a new distribution of holy Writings in the Old Testament, putting the Book of Daniel in a lower class. But if it cannot stand among those inspired in the highest degree, it must be reckoned false or blasphemous, because it speaks of itself all along as immediately inspired by God.

2 Chron. vii. 16; Haggai ii. 7, 9. Cannot be verified but as the temple was a type of the Christian Church. How was the glory of the latter house greater? Because the Desire of all nations came to give peace in the Person of Jesus Christ. Some pretend another temple yet to be built; but God spoke of only two, a former and later. Jews have several times tried to rebuild this but been defeated. Prophecies concerning the time of the Messiah were so noted, that when our Saviour appeared Jews were expecting Him. Romans had the same notion, and all the eastern

part of the world. This universal impulse cannot be made of less account than a very extraordinary apparatus of preparing of the way whereby to introduce the Son of God. Since that time have been many impostors, as He foretold. But having lost all the marks whereby they may know their Messiah, nay, willing they should be lost, and because all the marks given in the Old Testament meet in our Lord, they deny any marks at all. Or that miracles are needful. Mahomet made the like excuse; because they cannot deny those of our Saviour. Another thing—as to the time. No false Messiah set up till near the time of our Saviour foretold by Daniel and the prophets; but since then they have been perpetually setting them up. They pretend sins have hindered His coming. This is a very bare, and looks like a guilty put off! What are those sins? Jews are not so guilty as their forefathers. And the coming of the Messiah is promised to be a remedy for sin; therefore, so far from being a ground for delay, it should be an argument for hastening it. Nay, more; God expressly declared that, though He would punish their sins, He would not alter His promise. It was foretold they should not recognize their Messiah, and this is literally the case of the Jews; "the vision of all is become unto them as the word of a book that is sealed." Some Jews have set up another notion, namely, that the Messiah has come at the appointed time, but for their sins conceals Himself in various disguises. If they did not recognize Him, then, they might persecute Him as their fathers did the prophets before Him, and so fill up the measure of iniquity, for which their dispersion over the face of the earth without a king or prophet is the punishment.

The Jews again adhere obstinately to the promises made to Levi, whereas it was expressly said in the Psalms that the Messiah should be a priest, not of the order of Levi, but of Melchizedek, and to last for ever. Their great objection is, that God cannot alter what He has once ordained. It is true God is immutable, and what He ordains must answer the ends for which He ordains it; but He does not always tell us what those ends are, and therefore we cannot tell always when they are accomplished. When He pleases to make known the ends, then to think their accomplishment a breach of promise or alteration in God, is a great weakness and unhappiness on men's own part, and the very error which Samaritans committed.

Another objection much insisted upon is derived from Deut. xii. 1–3, to the effect that the Christian Messiah is not to be believed, no matter how great His miracles because He seeks to turn people after other gods. Miracles here spoken of are not true but false, mere seeming ones permitted for the trial of faith, whereas those of our Saviour were real beyond doubt. And other gods here spoken of are not true but false, against whom our Saviour was as severe as Moses, and wherever His religion has spread it has rooted out all pagan idolatry more than the law. Then the worship of Himself cannot be reckoned as false worship here forbidden, because it is paid to Him as to the Creator in human nature. Nor the worship of the Trinity; for the doctrine, whether sound or not, as some affirm, is not chargeable with polytheism, but expressly affirms the unity of the Divine nature simple and uncompounded. The Jews are preserved a visible distinct people among all the nations whither they have been scattered, because the Lord has put it out of the power of all the earth to infringe His promise to them. This is a standing miracle and a type of the Christian Church, which must struggle through many difficulties yet never be extinguished

That the Jews might not say it was through their own power they were preserved, it was necessary that the odds as to the world should be against them; and typify the Church, always greatly distressed but wonderfully preserved.

Our Messiah has fulfilled all the circumstances of the Prophecies: what hardness of heart, then, is it to expect another in whom these can never meet; and hankering after a temporal fulfilment of them to reject a better and spiritual one, yet really more literal! We carry the Law whither it was intended; we show an eternal and heavenly light shining through all and every institution of it; we look with reverence and great veneration upon it as the schoolmaster that was ordained to bring us unto Christ, as the ladder that was set to climb up into heaven. The Law and the Prophets are read every day in our churches, and their true and full import explained and fulfilled in the gospel; for the Gospel is the best comment upon the Law, and the law is the best expositor of the Gospel; they are like a pair of indentures, they answer in every part; their harmony is wonderful and is of itself a conviction. No human contrivance could have reached it; there is a divine majesty and foresight in the answer of every ceremony and type to its completion; and there is one yet to be completed. Oh the glorious day when that shall come, that is, the grafting the Jews in again to their own olive tree, the fatness, the sweet, the marrow of their own law fulfilled in the Messiah.

Some visible causes harden the Jews in obstinacy; as, for instance, they have quite altered their doctrine since Christ came, on purpose to avoid plain proofs of His being the Messiah. The Septuagint thus which used to be read in the synagogues since the Hebrew had ceased to be the vulgar tongue or well understood, and which was a translation deemed of divine inspiration, has been rejected for a spurious translation of a person called Aguila. For the same reason they have altered in prejudice to our Messiah, the principles and notions which they received by tradition from their fathers concerning the *Logos*, or Word of God, being God, yet a distinct Person from the Father. They now also will allow no type in the Law, or the office of the Messiah to extend beyond temporal conquests, whereas Jews formerly, Philo and those before him, did make the mystical the principal end of the law. They have invented new and strange conceits, as of two Messiahs to answer to the two states of suffering and triumphing foretold and fulfilled in our Saviour.

They say we disbelieve the Gospel, because our fathers tell us that those things related in it were not so done. The fathers have not told them so, but confessed to the matters of fact related there. The question is not between the tradition of the Jewish fathers and Gentiles, but of those fathers who did believe and those who did not. We have surer evidence even than the affirmative testimony in attestation of the Resurrection, namely, the many miracles performed by apostles as flagrant and notorious as those which Christ Himself had wrought, and which have all the four marks.

They now contend that men were never under the curse of God by the Fall, and therefore needed no deliverance from it; that Israel was a holy nation because they are so called in Scripture. If they can reconcile their being the holy people with being such sinners that the Messiah's coming is delayed as they say, then by the fall of Adam men were put under the curse of God, from which there were no sacrifices in their Law sufficient to purge the soul, therefore another and more efficacious sacrifice was necessary. . . . Plain reason does evince that the qualifications of a Messiah for the conversion of the Gentiles could be no other than what were found in our Jesus. His miracles vouched Him sent of God, and malice itself could find in Him no sinister or selfish end. His conquest of the Gentiles by their conversion did not begin till after His ascension, to obviate an objection of seeking temporal rule. Christ would not permit kings to become His servants till He had first endured three hundred years of their persecution; to teach them that His Church was not built upon their shoulders nor depended upon their authority. Moses was not designed for the ultimate and universal Lawgiver; he never pretended to it, but pointed to One who was to come after him, and had few of those qualifications which the Gentiles required in the supreme and universal Lawgiver. On the other hand, there is not any one circumstance or qualification, which they could desire in a Messiah, which is not filled up, nay, far exceeded in their own way in the person, life, and death of our Messiah, and in all His conduct: showing that He was a Legislator sent from heaven.

CHAPTER V.

NATIONAL DEBTS, ETC.—BISHOP OF ELY AND NONJURING FRIENDS—ARCHBISHOP SANCROFT — CONSECRATIONS — CHARACTERS OF PRELATES AND CLERGY IN THE TWO COMMUNIONS—"REGALE AND PONTIFICATE"—DR. WAKE—KENNET—ATTERBURY — MASSACRE AT GLENCOE — TILLOTSON — BURNET — PRINCE OF ORANGE—SUPPLEMENTS—"GALLIENUS REDIVIS"—"REGALE AND PONTIFICATE" ABRIDGED.

LESLIE upon return to London found it in a general state of gloom, panic, and peevishness. William had gone to the Hague for the purpose of organizing a new coalition against France, by which alone he kept his hold upon the throne of England. His policy was to make himself necessary to this country in the conduct of a war upon the Continent, and thus divert attention from affairs at home. The burden was sorely felt in taxation and debt to an enormous and unprecedented extent. Yet English people did not venture more than feeble remonstrance and secret grumbling against their chosen tyrant. When in Holland he assured his own countrymen, in reply to complimentary speeches, that their interest had been the paramount object of all his undertakings. Then came the story of a plot against his life, attributed of course to the French and the Nonjurors. Even a bad harvest and the increase of crime was laid at the same doors, and Macaulay is not ashamed to say appearances gave colour to the assertion; though it is apparent, from his own reluctant admissions, that the Revolution introduced into England more misery, wickedness, and profligacy than had at any period disgraced it before.

In the autumn of 1692 the Usurper came back to London, supporters making great efforts to lend a false glow of enthusiasm to his reception. Russel, the admiral who had betrayed the king, being discontented with the reward from William's Government, was pronounced by his comrades in treason "insolent and a villain;" and Parliament spent a session in wrangles about the ill conduct of the war and scandals of naval administration. Not much comfort was afforded by William's speech, assuring them that the sacrifices were necessary to the English nation and Protestant religion. A new claim for gratitude was devised in the National Debt, an idea never entertained by the house of Stuart, being no less unwise and immoral on the part of a nation than an individual. Burnet has been credited with this invention, though Whig historians dispute his title. It is only certain that William's wars entailed the burden of debt; that Burnet quite approved the plan of borrowing instead of paying, and that once such a system began it naturally and speedily increased. Together with it, a suitable concomitant, came in the practice of stock-jobbing and swindling on a large scale under various pretences, which also has continued to increase under the indefinite name of speculation. Companies and lotteries were started, the very names of which might have been supposed to warn people to beware, if there were any known limits to either folly or avarice. Now the English nation apparently prefer to be robbed by Americans and Germans, but then their own countrymen and chosen ruler emptied their pockets. No plan suggested itself for imputing to Nonjurors the misery resulting from the bursting of those various bubble-companies. Yet it is surprising that Leslie found repose from his vigilant adversaries at this time, because the society he kept exposed him to suspicion and false accusation. Since the prohibition of divine service at Ely House, Bishop Turner had lived at Putney, where he frequently visited with several Nonjuring Prelates, Lord Clarendon, Dr. Hickes, Mr. Wagstaffe, and others. Therefore he might have quite as reasonably been fixed upon for a false charge of conspiracy as the Bishop of Ely; who found it necessary to retreat therewith to France from his persecutors, though their efforts to involve him in what was termed the Preston plot proved a failure. Thus Leslie was deprived of one whom he highly esteemed on many accounts, and who always accorded to him a cordial welcome. Still were left many friends and a wide circle of genial acquaintances, including the accomplished Mr. Evelyn and Mr. Samuel Pepys, among whom he was favourably known for his humour and conversational powers.

In 1693 an event occurred which concerned him very seriously, namely, the consecration of Nonjuring Bishops. Archbishop Sancroft, after his violent ejectment from Lambeth Palace, retired at first to Palgrave Court in the Temple, where intimate friends were graciously received, and from thence to Fressingfield, in Suffolk, his native place, but at both he sought, as far as possible, seclusion from the world. His eminent piety and learning were only equalled by his gentleness and bountiful liberality. It is therefore surprising that Whig historians should have industriously laboured to decry his merits, because the only failing he exhibited, a want of resolution and perseverance, was a chief cause in the success of the revolution so dear to them. Having suffered so much, and nearly spent with age and infirmity, he may well be excused for shrinking from leadership in a tremendous struggle which he foresaw might involve an ocean of blood; while King James showed him, for his determined attitude previously, scarcely less animosity than William and Mary. One reproach has been needlessly cast upon his memory, of having written to the Princess of Orange, inviting her and her husband over to England; for nothing can be more satisfactorily proved than his own assertion that he, though urgently pressed to do so, firmly refused to write any letter at all, to avoid possibility of misconception afterwards concerning its contents.

When Lord Aylesbury burst into tears at the sight of his reduced estate, his reply, "Oh, my good lord, rather rejoice with me, for now I live again," was characteristic of the beautiful humility which adorned him through life. He went to his rest November 24, 1692. Before that event he made provision for the continuance of the apostolic succession among the Nonjurors. A list of persons deemed suitable for the episcopal office was submitted during his lifetime to King James at S. Germains for his sanction, from whom two were selected for consecration, which took place on the Feast of S. Matthias in the following year. These were Dr. George Hickes, already mentioned, and Mr. Wagstaffe, by the titles of Suffragans of Thetford and Ipswich. The latter's name is now scarcely remembered; but he was justly esteemed in his day. After being deprived of the Chancellorship of Lichfield, he practised as a physician with great success, so that he was better able than several of the Nonjurors to support himself in the Office. Macaulay's hereditary antipathy to the clergy, and utter ignorance of ecclesiastical customs, frequently apparent, have combined to betray him into a ludicrous blunder concerning this excellent divine. He says that "Wagstaffe used to visit his patients in full canonicals."

This is indeed now a customary formula with reporters of the sectarian press for describing vestments of which they do not understand the distinctive differences. Wagstaffe simply wore an academical gown and wig, such as barristers wear still, no "canonicals at all," the ordinary habit of a clergyman in public at that period and for a century afterwards—as much so as a black cloth coat is now; and he might have known this had he ever considered the origin of his own father's straight collar. Any other dress for a clergyman was deemed a disguise, like the "blue waistcoat." Both at the time and ever since, this step of consecration by Nonjurors has been severely condemned by opponents. Yet it is very difficult to understand what alternative lay open to them, or how otherwise they could have justified their position, when even Dr. Tillotson confessed that presence at Prayers which their conscience disapproved would be "a cheat in religion, of all cheats the worst." Many persons expressed surprise that Leslie was not selected for appointment. Whether he would have accepted it, there is nothing to show. He was certainly consulted on the general subject by King James, and warmly concurred in the selections made at the instance particularly of the good archbishop and Bishop Lloyd of Norwich, another of the deprived, the very antipodes of his namesake. The whole matter was very carefully considered by the persons best qualified to decide what ought to be done under present circumstances, so no doubt they acted for the best; nor can regrets be entertained on Leslie's account, still less that of the work to which he devoted himself. Indeed, good reasons are apparent for the omission. His Irish birth and connection might have possibly occasioned prejudice among English people, very undesirable to evoke. His disposition to engage actively in politics, if curbed by the restraint of the episcopal office, was too well known not to have risked greater unpopularity to the whole body. Nor were his pecuniary circumstances such as to have enabled him conveniently to have undertaken it. Whereas his advice contributed greatly to settle the matter to the satisfaction of all parties, and left him free to support their cause further by the powerful use of his pen. This assistance was immediately rendered by "The Case of the Regale and Pontificate," of which the first edition was published while the new consecrations were yet in view.[1] These of course stood upon somewhat different grounds from those afterwards performed, when the deprived prelates had all been removed by death, and the same objection to connection with the Establishment could no longer be urged as imperative on conscientious persons, when also political questions had undergone material alteration by events occurring in the course of divine Providence. If in the first instance names had been of any account—if characters thrown into the scale had possessed any weight in determining which body should be esteemed the Church of England, then Sancroft, Ken, Lloyd, Turner, Kettlewell, Frampton, Dodsworth, Hickes, Wagstaffe, and Leslie formed an army of learning, piety, and integrity, against whom a Tillotson, Sherlock, Stillingfleet, Burnet, Lloyd, and Tenison presented a very feeble staff for comparison. It was quite otherwise. Revolutionists were master of the situation, with tremendous interests at stake, for every one of them was steeped above the lips in treason, and they could not afford to allow weight to such considerations. When the head of any body has become corrupt, it cannot be but the rest is in an unwholesome condition. And such was the state of society in England at that time, both ecclesiastical and civil, by

[1] Greatly enlarged when republished.

admission of their own party writers. None could point a finger of reproach at moral delinquency among Nonjurors, though Argus eyes were on the watch for detection of the slightest flaw. Even so late as the eighteenth century Colley Cibber's satire upon "painted piety," an impoverished translation of stolen ideas, was equally false in its pretended application to any among them. Whereas the jests and jibes, the sneers and scorn elicited by personal failings of the Establishment clergy among their own adherents, were unhappily as just as they were numerous and notorious. It was a consciousness of this disparity and inferiority which infused such venom into the attacks of Christian prelates upon nonjurors; though they abstained from retorting generally, and exposing these scandals in the terms they richly merited. Human flesh and blood could not have helped sometimes to be stirred with indignation at cruel calumnies, or refrain from repelling injurious accusations in scathing language. So if Leslie stood somewhat conspicuous for this, it was because he was conspicuously made a target for the other. In general he and other Nonjurors abstained from personalities, addressing themselves to the arguments or exposing errors of their opponents in a manner which should render their works permanently and widely useful when those controversies had passed away. This character the "Regale and Pontificate" clearly bears. Its immediate object of vindicating the new consecrations produced a masterly discourse upon a subject of vast consequence to the whole Church at all times, and the principles laid down are enforced by historical facts and precedents which do not admit of dispute. Subsequently to its publication a controversy rose among some leading divines concerning the points treated of here, to which, therefore, he alluded in a preface to the second edition, but without altering his own book, or entering himself into the dispute further than by way of supplement in reply to some objections which had been made. Nor did he fully accord with the disputants, who were Dr. Wake, afterwards Archbishop of Canterbury; Dr. Kennet, who then held the living formerly occupied by Bishop Leslie, and became Bishop of Lincoln; Dr. Hody, already noticed sufficiently as the manuscript discoverer; and Dr. Atterbury. Dr. Wake was a man of fair abilities and attainments, kindly and graceful in manner, who, fond of controversy and a good preacher, soon recommended himself for preferment, being entirely on the revolutionary side, without stooping to unworthy arts to obtain it. Unhappily he lost the use of his mental faculties during the later years of his life; but before that discharged the duties of his high office with great credit to himself and general satisfaction. He wrote on one occasion to Dr. Charlett at Oxford, a mutual friend, but entirely agreeing with him rather than the other: "I hear that Mr. Leslie is about to fall upon me," referring to this question, but probably anticipating from rumours a more direct attack than any intended, and they were on friendly terms. It is remarkable also that he proposed a scheme for uniting the Anglican and Gallican Churches, the very idea of which, when first suggested by Leslie, brought down a vial of personal abuse in the House of Lords upon him from Burnet, as a papist and "most furiocest of all Jacobites." Dr. Kennet entertained the same sentiments, and even more strongly expressed them. His history and some other works bear the same stamp; and he incurred much odium among nonjurors, so much so that he was commonly denominated "the dean, the traitor." A horrible portrait of Judas, in a picture of the Last Supper over the altar in

S. Luke's Church, Whitechapel, was said to be intended for him.[1] Really Burnet had been designed to be represented, but fear of him led to this substitution with some miserable verses. In either case it was a discreditable exhibition, properly ordered by the Bishop of London to be altered so as no longer to convey any such idea; the disgrace of which, however, did not lie at the door of Nonjurors. Dr. Kennet deserved no such treatment, however erroneous his opinion may have appeared, for not only was he a man of extraordinary ability, immense learning, but great kindness, in which Dr. Hickes largely shared for a long time.

Almost his equal in learning, his superior in the arts of controversy and debate, on the opposite side was Dr. Atterbury, a very great friend of Leslie, and more deserving of superlative censure in the elegant grammar of their adversary. From the deanery of Carlisle he passed on to that of Westminster, and the bishopric of Rochester under Queen Anne, but no man was looked upon with more suspicion in William's time. Mr. Walpole is reported to have held this conversation with him: "Why don't you restrain yourself in the House of Lords?" "I cannot." "Then why not stay away?" "I have no excuse." "Yes, my lord; say you have the gout." "I cannot." "You may, and I often do. Be quiet, and I undertake to give you privately £5000 a year till Winchester falls." His devotion to the exiled king first brought him to the Tower, when prayers were offered up for him in churches, and his portrait in shop-windows, with these words—

"A second Laud,
Whose Christian courage nothing fears but God,"

collected thousands of admiring spectators. Banished at

[1] By Dr. Weldon.

length by a vindictive ministry, he died in exile at Paris, 1731.

All four showed in Leslie's opinion more heat in discussion than occasion required or than became the subject, so he did not hesitate to say, "I wish with all my heart they had put on more decency and moderation on both sides in the management, and forbore those personal remarks which are a deformity to such learned tracts, wherein the latest is still most to blame, especially where he takes upon him to represent the same fault in others." He pointed out in what respects each had made this mistake and some loose admissions by Dr. Atterbury, "perhaps to smooth the way," then laid down a valuable maxim often overlooked by disputants and critics. "Undervaluing is not the heroical way; the more I give my enemy when he deserves it, it shows I am the less afraid of him, and renders my victory more manly wherein I overcame him."

The importance of this subject at the present day cannot be overrated, when the divine character and original rights of the Church are denied by persons within her own fold, and insidiously encroached upon by successive, often stealthy, steps of State officials, while the excuse for silent submission is the old one, "Better bear this and the other than hazard a breach with the State," so that by this the Church must bear on without end. "If rights are divine, how can they be given up? No human authority can either supersede or limit them; it is a sacrilege to invade them. Suppose the Church were independent of the State as to her purely spiritual power and authority, this would make no separation of communion, nor exempt members of the Church from being likewise members of the State and answerable to it in all civil matters. If the clergy must not so much as speak for their inherited rights to execute the office which Christ has committed to them, how will they give up their lives for it? Let not the fault be laid altogether upon the State till these have been instructed by those whose office it is to instruct them ... and so despoil the Church of the proper army of her ministry. Many content themselves to wish every Ash Wednesday that discipline were restored, send one poor longing wish after it once a year, but move neither hand nor foot towards it." How few people warmly interested in what they deem Protestantism are aware that such State control over the Church as they desire mistakenly in her interest is the very thing for which the house of Stuart lost the throne, and which Parliament then forbade ever to be restored. The Star Chamber ordinance, then so obnoxious, has been revived to conceal the means by which policy judgments are procured. One more quotation, out of many reluctantly omitted for the sake of brevity, must close these introductory remarks, and form a double apology for urging the necessity of "resisting invasions of secular authority," standing upon primitive principles, of exorcising that "poor fear of temporal powers" which Erastianism has begotten, and to venture something upon divine protection.

"I have not the least apprehension that I hereby give offence, either to the civil government or to the clergy and true sons of the Church of England; but I would warm some frozen souls if I could, who say 'there is a lion in the way,' and 'are afraid where no fear is.' Let us do what we are commanded and leave the issue to God. If bishops will submit themselves to the yoke of Erastus, who can speak in their defence? They find the keys of their discipline hung at his belt, and would persuade us it is best so, lest Pharaohs increase our burdens." So "circuitous methods" have been openly recommended for interpretation of the Prayer-book, and a "not" interpolated into a rubric to explain its meaning in the middle of the nineteenth century. One of the most recent steps of Erastian encroachment has been to alter the form in which preferments to the Episcopate are announced in the public prints. Formerly the authorized statement was that the sovereign recommended a certain person to the Dean and Chapter for election. Since 1880 this has been altered into an announcement that the bishopric has been conferred by the Sovereign. An insidious innovation, which if permitted to pass unchallenged may after a few repetitions be quoted as a precedent, and so the wedge driven further in.

The ceremony of consecration for Nonjuring prelates was performed with all essential rites, and care to obviate any such spurious objection as had been raised concerning the case of Archbishop Parker. Of course it had to take place in a private house lest Government should interfere, a circumstance which could no more affect its validity than that of an Apostle for the same reason. A stronger objection apparently consisted in the instrument empowering the Bishop of Norwich to act as the archbishop's delegate being said to have lost its power by his death; but this did not invalidate the ceremony canonically and ecclesiastically, whatever its effect in a political point of view. Want of territorial jurisdiction or misapplication of titles was of no consequence at all. The fact that such a step was taken served to put some check on the Government's evident design of completely muzzling the Church of England at the time; and it remains both for a warning and consolation should any similar attempt be repeated at a future period.

A reply appeared which called for a supplement from our author, but it is of no consequence, as the writer evidently misapprehended the whole subject. Yet in the nineteenth century a prelate could adopt such a statement of his as this: "Whatever courts are in this country must have their origin in the sovereign." He has been answered by Charles Leslie, therefore, already.[1] "This is the most magnificently scandalous part of the Regale which submits even Christ to the king, for he cannot by this ratify the censures of His Church in heaven without his Majesty's licence." Such objectors do not understand the distinction between jurisdiction *in foro exteriori* and jurisdiction *in foro interiori*. There can be no end to contradiction, if exploded and disproved errors are to be reproduced as if they had not been so. And when men are told that this or that "will not be tolerated in this country," it is some comfort to remember the same sort of prediction was ventured about other things now taken for granted. Whatever happen to establishments and "those who warm themselves at palace fires," the Church and the people will find a *modus vivendi* together. Regale may in a general way be taken to denote the sovereignty or royal power; the Pontificate spiritual power in the episcopate, or Sacerdotal authority, by readers of this Treatise.

Whilst these matters engaged attention in the ecclesiastical world, a terrible crime had been committed in the political, to which Leslie's thoughts were much diverted. The massacre of Glencoe had been mentioned in his answer to King, but little heed or credit was attached to the story, though freely commented upon at Paris. News travelled there from Scotland almost quicker than to London, where also the English Government exerted great pains for concealment. Every allusion was diligently suppressed in public papers; pamphlets like the "Answer," being unlicensed,

[1] Bishop of Carlisle's Visitation Charge (Dr. Goodwin).

had only a limited circulation, and in that the matter appeared to be overweighted in interest by the rest of its contents. Scotch authorities even more anxiously than English endeavoured to hush the matter up, or dismiss it as a mere piece of "Jacobite mendacity" unworthy of denial. Gradually, however, whispers grew louder; this very laboured silence provoked inquiry; and at length our author by republication of the tragic circumstances in detail rendered longer secrecy impossible. Even then, when the subject was mooted in Parliament, inquiry was promised and pretended only with a view of stifling it; only by degrees the truth came out that the scenes described had been really enacted in all their horrible enormity under express direction from William. If the transaction did not wear so ghastly and guilty a complexion even at this distance of time one might smile at the feeble artifices employed by Whig historians to conceal his deep complicity. None of them, however, can do more than repeat the poor shameless plea first suggested by Burnet, who also held his tongue as long as possible, affecting ignorance or incredulity that William signed the order for massacre without reading it.[1] Macaulay improves on this, by saying that all who know anything of business can testify it to be a common practice! One who was the minister of an English Sovereign in these better days ought to have refrained from an excuse which most people rejoice to think is not the case. Were it even so, William's conduct remains as black as ever; for what Macaulay has omitted to mention, though he borrowed his account from Leslie's pamphlet almost entirely, is a most condemning fact, that the order was signed by William in two different places —at the beginning and the end; a most unprecedented

---

[1] "History of England," vol. vi. p. 211.

circumstance, the reason of which is obvious, that criminal agents responsible for its execution wished to provide for their own security when discovered, as they foresaw must be the case sooner or later, and to shelter themselves behind the throne. In result, the scheme of evasion and delay proved only too successful; inquiry dragged its length along so slowly that interest in the subject became superseded by other events. Action was deferred again and again in Parliament by ministerial manœuvres; a few inferior agents ultimately were sentenced to punishments never completely executed, though of no severity commensurate with their crimes. The prime movers escaped, and the guiltiest of all remained shrouded in the pretence of ignorance. Leslie's account narrated a similar enormity perpetrated in Ireland, and appeared in 1695, on its republication under a new title, "Gallienus Redivus, or Murder will out; being a true account of the Dewitting of Glencoe, Gaffney," etc., which he explained himself to have been adopted from a parallel in ancient history, fitting the present case so exactly that one might suppose the one to be copied from the other. This atrocious massacre of seven hundred and fifty persons, intended to include six thousand, is hardly paralleled even by his story of Gallienus. William wrapped himself in impenetrable silence, as usual, leaving Sir J. Dalrymple, commonly called the Master of Stair, a secretary of Scotland, his chief assistant in the plot, to invent the best excuse he could for himself, pledging to secure if he could not screen him. What did the prelates and priests of the Establishment say? Did the pulpits ring with declamation when they heard it, which had sounded so loudly against James for a Declaration of Indulgence? No; they were silent as the grave. Did seven prelates go with a protest to the king, ready for the Tower? Not they. All knew it, archbishops and bishops, but not a word escaped their lips in Parliament or Church. Burnet confided his guilty knowledge of this with "secret vices" to his manuscripts, and smoked on serenely. Did Sharp say nothing, who had been foremost to sound a trumpet of alarm in London in the former reign? No; he aired the imperious insolence of an upstart Archbishop of York, and stamped out any embers of pious zeal among the clergy, but on this matter had no suggestion to offer. And Sherlock, if he sent circulars to the clergy, Xantippe must have adroitly detained them from the post. Surely, dissenting ministers proclaimed their abhorrence? No; they too now remained passive and silent as the priests of Baal when Naboth was murdered. Only one man acted the part of Elijah in the little remnant of Israel, and openly, with unfaltering voice, denounced the shedding of innocent blood; but, as a Nonjuror, his impeachment was ignored as a piece of Jacobite mendacity. Here are proofs of guilt: "It will be proper for the vindication of public justice to extirpate that set of thieves.—W.R." Dalrymple says in the letter enclosing these bloody instructions, "Argyle tells me that Glencoe hath not taken the oaths, at which I rejoice. It is a great work of charity to be exact in rooting out that damnable sect. This is the proper season to maul them in the cold nights."

When an order was desired for the execution of that butcher, his own intimate associate and secretary, William refused to sign it; yet we are to believe that he signed and countersigned this order for extirpation of the Macdonald tribe without knowing what it was! Leslie thus seems almost prophetically to have remarked, "The Dewitting in Holland was almost forgotten; he wants but a good historian that he may not lose his character to after ages."[1]

[1] See Macaulay, vol. vi. p. 206.

Another person most deeply involved in the whole transaction was William's private counsellor, chaplain, and secretary, Carstairs, a Presbyterian minister commonly nicknamed the "Cardinal," on account of his influence in ecclesiastical affairs in Scotland. It is said he could do kind acts when they did not interfere with his designs, as for instance providing poor episcopal clergy in Scotland whom his party had reduced to destitution with clothes and money, who never knew their benefactor. He ought to have this acknowledgment whatever it be worth as a set-off against his many crimes, for he was a man with whom conscience was an unknown quality and blood a familiar thing.

Leslie performed a painful public duty in dragging into light this horrible business at no slight risk to himself. The seizure of his "Answer to King," no doubt, had been partly in consequence of this exposure of Glencoe and Gaffney's affair; but the second publication could not be so easily suppressed, or else the Government had been spared the necessity of even a mock investigation.

A narrative from the venal pen of De Foe was issued for the purpose of exculpating William, which only made the matter worse; for, avowing its inspiration from "his Majesty's lips," it proceeded to justify the slaughter on grounds of nature and necessity in war, such as "giving no quarter to a garrison which resists," "desperate mischiefs require desperate remedies," etc., which were at once obviously inapplicable and shocking.

The affair in Ireland of Gaffney was equally atrocious, though fortunately less extensive. No one cared to defend it or answer Leslie's complaint; and of what consequence could be the death of a single Irishman, however unjustifiable to that party which has always wished to "rest and be thankful" in office?

Dr. Tillotson died on November 21, 1694, stricken with apoplexy four days previously during evening Service at Lambeth Chapel. Shortly before he had published Sermons preached on several occasions, with additions and corrections, to clear himself from a charge of Socinianism widely prevalent. To that volume Leslie undertook to reply, because if let go by default the imputation might be presumed sufficiently refuted. Here it might be supposed was occasion for remembrance of the old maxim, "*De mortuis nil nisi bonum;*" and that was his own view, so that, though his treatise had been already written and a licence obtained for its being printed, he resolved to withdraw it. But vindicators came forward, professedly in honour of Tillotson's memory, to assail Nonjurors in unmeasured terms; the most eminent being Burnet, a Dr. Williams, and Sir Robert Howard in the Establishment, with a number of Socinians, Deists, and Dissenters outside. This altered his intention, and any apparent harshness must justly be attributed to their officious zeal. Moreover, Dr. Tillotson had been well aware that heretics quoted his sermons in their own justification without repudiating this inference till the very last, and had read Leslie's "Reflections" if he liked before licensing them. He had also allowed Burnet and Williams to attempt his defence, while alive, in terms as objectionable as the productions of his own pen. Nay, still he is held up as a pattern by Latitudinarians in assemblies where a majority can have no intelligent appreciation of his real conduct or opinions—a proceeding not reflecting much credit upon the honesty of such eulogists.

Therefore a brief sketch of his history will fittingly precede consideration of the charges against him. He was the son of an Anabaptist minister in a Yorkshire village.

A question respecting his baptism has been satisfactorily settled since, therefore he was justified in not condescending to answer it in his lifetime, like a successor against whom the same objection was current. At Cambridge University he acquired popularity and the credit of considerable talent among contemporaries. After Ordination his easy and lucid style of preaching in various posts won general admiration, and though now his sermons are accounted dull reading, it is sufficient that such judges as Dryden and Addison have pronounced in their favour. A charm of voice and manner lent additional attractiveness in large audiences, so that preferments quickly fell to his share. His loyalty at the time of King Charles II. admitted of no question, passive obedience being a favourite theme. Yet there were, including the king, some who entertained suspicions how deeply it was seated. On the eventful Sunday for reading the Declaration, the Doctor like some other divines had occasion to go into the country, returning when William had secured the throne of King James, and swimming henceforth on the full tide of revolution. The slight reluctance felt or feigned to be installed in the archbishop's place was easily overcome, nor did he offer him any portion of the revenues when in straitened circumstances; but he cannot be charged with avarice, for he left but a poor pittance for his widow, a niece of Cromwell, which had to be supplemented by a generous donation from William for her comfortable maintenance. That his private life was exemplary need hardly be added. William and Mary were naturally much grieved at his death, and his loss by the revolutionary party deeply felt. Those who could not mourn had been well content if permitted to observe a respectful silence. What Leslie was concerned alone to arraign were his public conduct and opinions, and these because so ostentatiously and defiantly extolled. That he was to some extent unconscious of heresy is very probable, and certain that he was sincere and honest; but these considerations do not meet the necessity of defence for a Metropolitan of the English Church. The gulf between its doctrine and his cannot be bridged over by any vindication yet offered, while his practice on different occasions pointed decidedly in the same direction. He said himself that his "merits forced some who had no kindness for him to advance him;" yet King Charles whom he meant pretty well gauged his character as an anecdote shows. In divine service at the Royal Chapel, instead of bowing at the Saviour's name, Tillotson used to step a little backwards, glancing upward with an air of superior devotion, upon which Charles observed that he "bowed like Quakers to their friends, the wrong way." His inclination, in fact, anticipated that substituted for the honest curtsy of old ladies in modern circles of fashion. Another well-authenticated story illustrates the same inconsistency. In a funeral sermon upon Dr. Whichcote, Tillotson spoke highly of his liberality in allowing his predecessor when deprived of a College Provostship, half of the income, and bequeathing to his son £100; the very thing himself did not, nor even offer a farthing to Dr. Gunning, a poor man wrongfully deprived of a College office to which he succeeded. Then his practice of administering the Sacred Elements in the Blessed Sacrament of the Altar to persons up and down the church in various postures, was in direct disobedience to the rule of the Church, which he above all others was bound to observe. Blount, Toland, and other infidels were on terms of familiarity at Lambeth Palace, when it was equally notorious devout Christians found no admission there. He professed to "leave men to their own discretion in small matters," but what were small he reserved to himself determination of. By the same rule of liberality a modern prelate can countenance omission of the Athanasian Creed, while prohibiting a vestment which he dislikes. Lathbury has undertaken to throw a shield over the Doctor which can only damage his cause, for in it he betrays too clearly that he possessed a very limited acquaintance with the works on both sides which he presumed to criticize. Had Dr. Tillotson remained in the communion to which he originally belonged, it had been better for the Church over which he was unfortunately called to preside, and for his own reputation. The above particulars, among several others that might be related, will indicate sufficiently whether he did not furnish grounds for the suspicions entertained of his heretical tendency, which an impartial examination of his writings abundantly confirms. The proofs furnished in Leslie's examination and charge are overwhelming, therefore it was his duty to make them public, for an archbishop is a public man.

Another prelate involved in the same charge, or rather who volunteered to share it, was Dr. Burnet, Bishop of Salisbury, of whom the less is necessary to be said, because his lifelong antagonism to Leslie renders mention of him frequent in other parts of this volume. His father was an attorney at Edinburgh, who, nominally an Episcopalian, had decidedly Puritan tendencies, and his mother a Presbyterian, which accounts for the sectarian leaven so strongly developed by young Gilbert in mature years. Relinquishing study of the law, and ordained in 1665, he became Professor of Divinity at Glasgow; but intimacy with the Hamilton family opening better prospects in England, he obtained the preachership of the Rolls and a Court chaplaincy. From this latter post he incurred dismissal by a most improper sermon, insinuating a charge of Popery against King James, which he had not courage to stand by, and retired to Holland, where he was noticed as the chief plotter of the Revolution. His writings are voluminous, and like his sermons, which, though carefully committed to memory, were delivered with an easy fluency much admired, distinguished by marks of great ability in composition, but so tainted with bitterness and a want of veracity towards opponents as to have lost all claim to credit. No man ever hungered more for popularity yet was less popular all his life, for he embittered adversaries, made friends afraid of him by bustling and gossiping habits, insulted the clergy, and had so little sympathy with the people that even at the grave his remains were shockingly insulted by a mob.

In the same year, shortly after Dr. Tillotson, died Mary, Princess of Orange. A woman who, with many amiable qualities and good intentions, spoilt all in devotion to a husband, who tempted her to rob her father's crown, and quarrel with her sister, yet gave her not the love to purchase which these things were done. So when she turned her back upon the Countess of Dorchester, no wonder the affronted woman, though richly meriting her own rebuke, exclaimed, "I beg your Majesty to remember that, if I broke one of the commandments with your father, you broke another against him." Her death was occasioned by the small-pox, and perhaps hastened in some measure by injudicious treatment of physicians, who did not recognize the symptoms till the disease had made rapid inroads upon her constitution. When assured of her danger she made what preparation she could, and calmly met her end;

though she never acknowledged her offences, nor was moved to repentance by the attending prelates in her last hour.

ABRIDGMENT OF "GALLIENUS REDIVIVUS, OR MURDER WILL OUT. BEING A TRUE ACCOUNT OF THE DEWITTING OF GLENCOE, GAFFNEY," ETC.[1]

Gallienus (emperor A.D. 253–265), as he was dissolute and abandoned, so was he passionate, severe, and cruel against both soldiers and citizens. There is extant a letter he wrote to an officer about such another massacre as Glencoe, showing how a luxurious person can be most cruel if necessity furnish occasion. "You will not satisfy me if you only destroy those in arms, who would perish by the fortune of war. The whole male sex, even old men, must be extirpated without fear of censure. . . . Slay, kill, destroy; you can understand my disposition." Here was a great deal to do, and many words about it. Our milder order bade only to extirpate, not making distinctions, only the whole tribe. Short work best, and few words.

MacJan, Macdonald, Laird of Glencoe, a branch of the Macdonalds, one of the greatest clans or tribes in the north of Scotland, came to Colonel Hill, Governor of Fortwilliam, at Inverlochy, some few days before expiration of the time for receiving the indemnity appointed by proclamation for January 1. He entreated him to administer the new oaths so that he might have the government protection.[1] The Colonel received him with all expressions of kindness, yet shifted administration of the oaths as not belonging to him but to the Sheriff. MacJan, complaining that he might be wronged by time and weather and roads, got protection under Colonel Hill's hands, and was assured no

[1] Reproduced by Macaulay, vol. vi. pp. 196, 216.

order should be put in execution against him till he had time to appeal to king or council for his safety. With all imaginable haste he posted to Inverary, and craved of the sheriff, Sir Colin Campbell, the indemnity, who scrupled about the time, but on his representing weather, etc., administered the oath to him and his attendants. MacJan went home and lived peaceably and quietly. A party of the Earl of Argyle's regiment came to his country, Glencoe being convenient for quartering, on pretence of collecting hearth tax (never known in Scotland till 1690, after the English Parliament had eased themselves of it). The Laird and his sons asked them if they came as friends or as enemies; the officers answered as friends, and gave their parol of honour to do no harm to him or his concerns; upon which they were welcomed, and promised the best entertainment their place could afford. They lived in mutual kindness for fifteen days, and the last day of his life he spent in company with Captain Campbell, playing cards till six or seven in the evening, and parting with mutual protestations of friendship. That day Campbell had orders from Major Duncannon to fall upon the Macdonalds and put all to the sword under seventy, with a special care that the old fox and his sons did not escape, by five o'clock in the morning at the king's special command.

Duncannon's orders from Colonel Hamilton were of the same date, February 12, 1692. The soldiers being dispersed three or four in a house, according to the numbers they were to assassinate, the poor people little suspected their guests were to be their murderers. At five o'clock in the morning they began their bloody work, surprising and butchering thirty-eight persons. MacJan himself was a stately, well-favoured man, and of good courage and sense, as also the Laird of Auchentruchen, a gentleman of more than ordinary judgment, who had Colonel Hill's protection in his pocket. I cannot without horror relate how a boy about eight years of age was murdered. He, seeing what was done to others, ran out in a terrible fright and grasped Campbell by the leg, begging for mercy, and offered to be his servant for life. Campbell inclined to spare him, but one Drummond barbarously ran his dagger through him. MacJan was killed while dressing and giving orders for the entertainment of his murderers; shot through the head, he fell dead in his lady's arms, who through grief and bad usage died the next day. Most were killed when asleep. The night being boisterous, many had an opportunity of escaping. They set all the houses on fire, drove the cattle and sheep to Inverary, which were divided among the officers.

It pleased God that two of MacJan's sons escaped, for the younger, having a strong impression that some mischievous design lurked under specious pretences, prevailed at length upon his brother to go with him to their father, who allowed them to try what they could discover. Hearing some remarks of a soldier, that he "liked not this business," they retired as quickly as they could to inform their father, but hearing guns and shrieks preserved their lives.

The instance which I have to give exceeds that of Glencoe. The murder of Gaffney in Ireland by command of Lord Coningsby. The very words of the article against him and Sir Charles Porter were—that the lords justices did in council, by word of mouth, order one Gaffney to be hanged without trial, being a witness against one Sweetman for murder. Sweetman, giving all his real estate, beside £500 for bail, was never prosecuted, and the said Gaffney was immediately executed. Every tittle of the charge was proved, all Coningsby saying in his vindication being that "unless he had hanged him so, he could not have hanged him at all." Now comes the astounding wonder; the House of Commons could not frame any excuse for the execution without trial, yet, considering the state of affairs, they did not think fit to ground on it an impeachment. What was the state of affairs? It was in the winter of 1690, when all Ireland except Limerick was in the obedience of William, the courts of justice open and lords justices sitting in peace and grandeur. If any rebel parliament could have found a Gaffney or Glencoe against King Charles I. or his sons, what a noise would they have made!

An Abridgment of "The Case of the Regale and of the Pontificate." Stated in a Conference concerning the Independency of the Church.

It has been agreed on all hands that the State cannot deprive bishops of their episcopal character, and their episcopal acts are valid except acts of jurisdiction in that particular diocese out of which they are ejected by the State; but because bishop is a relative word, and implies a flock since the days of the apostles, therefore the question is whether the State can dissolve the relation between a bishop and his particular flock, and deprive him of the exercise of his jurisdiction within his own proper district, and substitute another bishop in his place. To stop the execution of a commission is to render it ineffectual. No authority less than that which gives any commission can stop its execution. There is a spiritual relation instituted by Christ between a bishop and his flock, and those who keep outward communion with their bishop partake of inward communion with Christ. This relation or marriage cannot be dissolved, nor we divorced and married to another bishop by any other means than those which Christ has appointed, and a second bishop is an adulterer while the first lives not divorced by competent authority. The Church has suffered more under heretical kings than heathen; and an heretical king can corrupt the doctrine of the Church more than a heathen. A good and orthodox king may turn apostate. How can he then be head of a Church who denies the faith of it? Or be the head of different communions? Who shall judge of a King's apostasy? It is not to be supposed he will condemn himself. A king may return from apostasy or heresy, and if he lost his Regale for that, recover it. So that it is not fixed, but fleeting and casual. And then who shall be judge of the sincerity of his conversion or pretences to religion? The professions of princes when a crown is the bait are a slender security. We can have no security to our religion, at least none equal in human appearance to the primitive foundation whereon Christ placed the Church; independent as to her whole spiritual authority of any earthly power, though with sufficient guard for obedience in civil matters. Then we need be in less pain for the religion of our prince except for the good of his soul. In revolutions and rebellions the Church must either change sides and principles or undergo persecution, and her spiritual authority, like secular commissions, take out a new charter under every new head. It is said that upon the conversion of kings and states to Christianity there was a compromise made between them and the Church; that it being incorporated into the State, made concessions to it in lieu of protection and other advantages.

No such compromise appears, nor is there any record of it. Kings disown it, and claim the Regale to have been given by God, attested in holy Scriptures, and to have been always so. Such grant if made would be void, because no trust can be transferred, especially that in which the souls of men are concerned. Bishops may assist one another, but cannot delegate their power to those who are no pastors, to presbyters without episcopal consecration, much less to laymen. The Church in England and other places has been reduced. If she gave up her power to the State for advantages, the bargain is broken. ... Whereas no society can subsist without meeting and consulting concerning affairs, and giving orders as occasion shall require: if one cannot meet without leave of another, then is that society dissolved, being dependent upon the mere will and pleasure of the other. The common objection of an *imperium in imperio* breeding nothing but confusion is answered thus, that sacred and civil powers are like two parallel lines which never meet, so that each act independently upon the other withot confusion or interfering. Confusion arises when the one will put a sickle into the other's harvest; when the civil power will take upon it to control the Church in the exercise of her spiritual authority, or the Church do the like to the State in temporal authority. Our blessed Saviour, in His all-wise providence, set up His Church independent of all powers upon earth, so He gave her no authority that could possibly interfere with civil powers. He gave to Cæsar all that was Cæsar's, but the things of God and the administration of the spiritual kingdom of heaven upon earth He left in the hands of His Church, accountable to none but Himself. Bishops being made lords of Parliament, the king should have the choice of them, but this ought not to extend the Regale to the choice of persons, because that is an encroachment upon the divine commission to the Church, and carries with it all the consequences of Erastianism. As she has no title from heaven to make choice of kings, as little has a king for the nomination of bishops.

In all ages and religions those who served at the altar were reckoned distinct, and the Chief of the Estates of the nation. We find by experience that the State, particularly in England, have been out in politics in reducing the Church to a low ebb of credit and authority with the people, for laws and constitutions have proved too weak to restrain the unruly passions and ambition of designing men. The State has no such security as when the people are taught to obey for conscience' sake. But when they see bishops made by the Court, they are apt to imagine that they speak to them the Court language, by which means the State has lost the greatest security of government; and it insensibly draws men into a disesteem and suspicion of religion in general, whose foundation they cannot think to be divine while they see the Church disposable by the State. The Erastian principle has had two visible effects in England; it has turned the gentry Deists, and the common people Dissenters—for the Dissenters one and all pretend to divine commission independent of all the powers upon earth; therefore the people run to them and look upon the Church of England as a Parliamentary religion and establishment of the State; and Deists can never think there is anything divine in that which they see to stand or fall by their vote.

The Regale is a perpetual seed of jealousy and discontent; for a king may look upon those who are zealous for religion and the Church of Christ as seeking to impair his prerogative; and friends of the Church may be tempted to think his Regale an encroachment upon her original and inherent rights.

In Sweden the king is absolute in civil affairs, yet leaves the Church entirely free in all ecclesiastical; nor is he offended that in the Liturgy they pray for the Church and clergy before him and ministers of State.

It is thus in all Liturgies except ours.

The king in our Litany is thrust in between the Church and the bishops, and the whole royal family are drawn in with him.

The effects in Sweden are remarkable, for they have no Dissenters there; and between the Church and State are no disagreements, for the ground and foundation of them, the Regale, is out of the way. Can the king be a nursing father and yet have no authority of her? This objection vanishes when the whole of that verse, Isa. xlix. 23, is read out—" They shall bow down to thee with their face towards the earth, and lick up the dust of thy feet." David ordered the courses of the priests and Solomon thrust out Abiathar; what they did by extraordinary commissions from God is not to be brought in precedent for the ordinary power of kings. What David did was given to him by the Spirit in writing; and not needed if he had done it by his own power as king. If kings had such power, then had not the great and victorious Uzziah been smitten with leprosy, nor Saul dethroned, nor Jeroboam cut off.

The sentence upon Abiathar was a civil, not ecclesiastical one; banishment and a reprieve as to his life, but not a full pardon. If the text be understood to imply a deprivation, it will also prove a degradation which our kings do not pretend in regard to bishops; and so the text would imply an extraordinary commission to Solomon. But from apostles' times to this there have been no bishops in the Catholic Church but of particular districts. And if the secular magistrate can put another bishop in the place of one deprived, then may the State alter and model the whole episcopal college, and consequently the whole authority of the Church of Christ. Putting Zadok in place of Abiathar was not advancing Zadok above Abiathar, for he always was so, as if the Archbishop of Canterbury had the rule given him over the province of York during an incapacity. In the time of our Saviour the succession of the high priest was reckoned from Zadok. And in all things the temple economy was wholly divine, and not established by an ordinary Regale or any human authority.... If Eli was high priest not from God, it is most probable he usurped the office when he was judge, and then he will stand the first example of the civil magistrate's encroachment upon the Church; which was attended with remarkable judgments. But it is to be considered how dangerous and uncertain an argument is mere example in Holy Scripture where many things are told very shortly, and the reasons not always set down. There being but this one example of Solomon, it is a very dangerous method to build upon it.

The commission that Cranmer took out for his bishopric from Edward VI., and the like done by other bishops, is to be understood only of civil power and authority derived from the king, nothing of which was granted by Christ. In Cranmer's commission there was an exception made "over and above those powers and authorities given by God." These the king did not pretend to grant. And it was asserted by the bishops that they were the messengers of Christ to teach the truth of the gospel, and to loose and bind sinners, etc.

The convocation who made the submission of the

clergy under Henry VIII. were all Roman Catholics, though we ever since have been upbraided with it. As our laws stand at present, the Church is left wholly independent of the State as to her purely spiritual power and authority. Article 37th excludes precedents drawn from extraordinary acts of Moses, David, or Solomon, giving to godly princes such prerogative as had always been given, to restrain with the civil sword. The bishops opposed the oath of supremacy, therefore Queen Elizabeth laid aside the title of "head of the Church," instead of which the word "governor" was put in, as it stands to this day. See also the Homily, second part, on the "Right Use of the Church."

Encroachments are made by degrees, and the best time to stop is at the beginning, before we have given precedents against ourselves, have yielded the cause and are entirely subdued; then it will be too late, the power will be more irresistible, and men's courage grow less. To comply with the wickedness of another is to make myself guilty of it. Therefore to admit lay deprivations to be unjust and invalid, yet to argue for our compliance with them, is to do evil that good may come.

Dr. Wake sets up the Regale to the very height merely upon precedents, which is the same as saying it has no other right. Some of these precedents are modern and of no authority; others are not truly related with the necessary circumstances; and others truly related make nothing to the purpose, while some are directly against it. But none are of authority sufficient to establish or justify the Regale; beside contrary precedents, and that Dr. Wake, when he comes to reasoning, overthrows all the power of the Regale which he had built upon the authority of precedents. Donatists were the first who appealed to the secular power in any ecclesiastical cause. But Constantine refused their appeal as not belonging to him but to bishops only, which he called "the heavenly judgment." After heretics carried on the same cause. In France, when Pope Lucius II., to court the favour of Louis VII., A.D. 1148, sent him a bull to dispose of the first vacancy in every cathedral and enjoy the mean profits, he burnt it with indignation. Count Alphonsus not only renounced the Regale, but condemned it.

Bishop Burnet's "History of the Regale" shows its dismal effects in the Greek Church. There can be no supposed consent of the Church, for none dare oppose absolute emperors; and there are several canons of councils called general against the Regale. There are precedents against it in Britain of the most primitive times, which are the more considerable because they were before Austin the monk came into England, and consequently before there could be the least umbrage that this was any part of Popery.

After this the Regale began to obtain in England, and is an effect of Popery; though at first sight it seems contrary to it. Popes found they could not maintain their usurpations over other bishops without the assistance of kings, with whom, therefore, they were content to divide the prey; both enlarging their powers upon the ruin of episcopacy. The *congé d'élire* in England, though to no purpose but to show the ancient right of the Church to elect her own bishops, may one day prove a handle to recover it. Its form originally was not by way of command to the clergy, but of request and desire only. The king called it his petition to the clergy, which shows plainly where the right of election lay. We must date the original of the Regale in England from the times of Popery, and not pass it as a novelty of the Reformation. Its principle has carried with it consequences totally inconsistent with the notion of a Christian Church.

He who has no right but possession has no right by his possession; it may continue so long that those who have a better title are all extinguished; then a right grow up, since there are none who claim a better. There are those who, to make way for the Regale, deny all priesthood; but Church and priesthood seem to be convertible terms. We must either part with our priesthood or the Regale. Dr. Wake, speaking of the power of the prince, says "it reaches not only in matters of discipline but in matters of faith too." This he proves by the example of Henry VIII. in modelling the Articles; and he makes the law the standard of heresy. But he comes round and overturns every stone that he had laid; for he says that "princes may abuse this power to the detriment of the Church. And whenever the civil magistrate shall so far abuse his authority as to render it necessary for the clergy by some extraordinary methods to provide for the Church's welfare, that necessity will warrant their taking of it." This makes the clergy judge of the necessity, and then they may take these methods when they see cause. No necessity can create any authority, though it may sometimes excuse the exercise of it in an extraordinary manner, therefore the clergy have authority independent of the State. If Christ left no more authority with His Church than He thought necessary for the ends for which He instituted it, then a less authority will not be sufficient. The Church is a society spread over the earth, and therefore cannot be dissolved in any one kingdom; nor can the concession of any national Church oblige the Church Catholic, nor that national Church herself, otherwise than according to the rules of the Catholic

Church. It is not one of the least evil consequences of this principle of the Regale that it begets a secular spirit in the clergy, which soon eats out the evangelical spirit of Christian simplicity, the (*parrhesia*, or) open and fearless but modest courage in asserting the truths of the gospel against all opposition. The pope's claim to universal supremacy was the great cause of schism in the Western Church; and the doctrine was not known in the days of Gregory the Great, who wrote against it when set up by John of Constantinople. We may lay good claims to other popes also before they arrived at their full height. When they had got free themselves the popes were content that other bishops should be kept still under the yoke, and made a new diversion of the spoil, allowing to kings by concordats the presentation to some preferments that they might securely enjoy the rest. A remedy has been thought of for all these things; and it may be said the Western Church has (like her Divine Master) been crucified between the usurpations of the Pontificate and the Regale.

If the king's supremacy and power of the State were reduced to a civil power only, though in ecclesiastical causes and over ecclesiastical persons, and if the pope's supremacy were brought back to the limits of his first patriarchate, then the primitive episcopacy would revive, and their correspondence by communicatory letters. Then, and not till then, religion will be restored to its ancient lustre, will be venerable and glorious.

The notion of priesthood has been dwindled in late times to make way for those who have no commission to show for usurping the sacred office. Therefore they have reduced it all to preaching, and loved the name of preachers better than that of priests. Whoever has thought himself a gifted man has applied himself to the liking of the people; and poor people have been very fond of having authority put into their hands to give a call for their teacher. It is blasphemy against God to act in His Name or give commission to others without His express warrant. Such commission must be outwardly given, and God never made a priest but by an outward commission. Christ did not take this honour to Himself till outwardly called; nor leave it to the inward call of any of His disciples to make themselves apostles. The same commission has descended by outward ordination, given by those to whom He left that authority. Some who call themselves "clergymen" deny there is any priesthood at all. If the people's dishonouring the priests of God be a profanation of Him, what must their condition be who prostitute and profane their own character?

The root and bottom of all this was the bringing of the priesthood at first under the Regale, whence it became subject to everybody else, even to the beasts of the people. The true notion of a Church and priesthood has been utterly lost where Erastianism has prevailed, consequently the reverence due to religion and to God has sunk with it, also the benefits annexed to the holy offices of the Church, as means of grace appointed by Christ our Lord, on which are founded our hopes of glory. Political government is called earthly, secular, or temporal, because it operates only in this world. The Church lasts for ever; and it is the same which is in heaven and upon earth; they are not two Churches, only two parts of the same, one militant the other triumphant, having the same Head and King. The communion of saints extends to heaven; we bless God for them, and pray that with them we may be partakers of the heavenly kingdom. They pray for us, for our consummation and bliss, and rejoice with us at our conversion.

Hence the Church on earth is called the kingdom of God; and her government is dignified with the same name as that of the heavenly host, a hierarchy or sacred government, as being all of the same family or society. The power of the Church extends to the other world, and will be exercised there over angels as well as the world.

The successors of the apostles must be content to pass, as they did, through evil report and good report; as deceivers and yet true. They must not, to save themselves from reproach, let religion go to wreck, expose the commission of Christ to be trampled upon, divest themselves of the proper arms of their ministry, and suffer the devil without opposition to ravish out of their hands those souls for which they must answer. Christ left no more power with His Church than He knew was necessary; to make it less will be to defraud themselves and render it ineffectual to the people, as S. Cyprian said: "It is a most dangerous thing in divine matters for any one to recede from his full power and authority." The Regale among us has much varied and lessened from the height in which it was set up by Henry VIII. The writ of *congé d'élire* was taken away by Act of Parliament (Edward VI. ch. 2) as too great an encroachment upon the Regale, but our kings, ashamed of that, still continue the method.

The terrible schism in the Western Church might be healed if every bishop would make himself free from encroachments both of the Pontificate and Regale, and act according to his own conscience. If such should remove images, forbear elevation of the host, and invocation of saints, give the cup to the laity, and have the service in the vulgar tongue, what should hinder our communion with such a bishop? No man is bound to ask or tell his private opinion on other matters. On the other hand, there is nothing in our Liturgy but what Roman Catholics approve; they may think it deficient, but not in any necessary point. While we stand out against the plenitude of papal supremacy it is not the interest of the Church of Rome to heal the breach of communion, because that only keeps up the breach of parties amongst us. The schism between Rome and our Reformed Church is of much greater consequence to the Christian Church (as a whole) than that of Dissenters, and takes in even them; therefore if healed would cure the whole: but whatever lawfully may be done ought to be done for the healing of any schism. Our rites and ceremonies are not the cause of their schisms, only a pretence. Episcopacy was the heir of which they said, "Come, let us kill him, that the inheritance may be ours." Their case, therefore, can be no parallel to that reconciliation proposed with bishops in communion with Rome. The same method and the same principles would open communion between the Eastern and Western Churches, whose liturgies and public worship might soon be adjusted so as to give no cause for a breach. It is the papal supremacy which alone stands in the way to oppose such a glorious reunion of all Churches.

In the great work there is a most glorious step to be taken by that king whom God should inspire to take his Regale out of the way. He would truly deserve the titles of "most Christian," "most Catholic," and would be in good earnest "the defender of the faith," following the examples of Constantine and Louis VII. of France, rather than of Jeroboam, Saul, Uzziah, Constantius.

ABRIDGMENT OF THE "CHARGE AGAINST DR. TILLOTSON CONSIDERED."

This author in his four sermons, though he seems to speak home sometimes, yet has taken special care to avoid the only shibboleth which the Christian Church could find out to discover the several sorts of Arian and other heretics who denied the Divinity of Christ, which was consubstantiality—that God the Son was of the same substance with His Father. Several of them would allow Christ to be of like but not of the same substance. It is very strange that he should forget this only material word, the very heart of the whole cause and expressly asserted in the Creed, especially considering that in the third sermon he quotes the words which follow them. To say that Christ is truly and really God "by office and by divine appointment and constitution" is a vain distinction; for God by office must be by nature, other He could not be so really and truly. Being necessitated to use the word Persons, he does it very grudgingly and slightly. "Here then I fix my foot: that there are three differences in the Deity which the Scripture speaks of by the names of Father, Son, and Holy Ghost; and everywhere speaks of them as we used to do of three distinct Persons; and therefore I see no reason why in this argument we should nicely abstain from using the word Person; though I remember that S. Jerome does somewhere desire to be excused from it." This "somewhere" of S. Jerome's was a strange quotation for so grave a doctor. A much more learned person than himself has shown that S. Jerome did not scruple to use the word Person and in the same sense with us at the present day, but his scruple was concerning the Greek word hypostasis, which he thought needed some explanation or caution. For example, in Phil. ii. 6, the doctor would have the sense to be, "He did not arrogate to Himself to be equal with God" —quite contrary to the words literally translated—He thought it not robbery to be equal. To bring himself off from seeming to favour Socinians, he pretends to prove the divinity of Christ from it thus—"He made no ostentation of it." That means more easily—He had none to make ostentation of. Let the text lie in its plain grammatical interpretation and its words are not to be answered by Socinians; for if it was no robbery in Christ to be equal with God, it follows unavoidably that He was true and real God by nature.

Let us come now to the doctrine of satisfaction. The doctor mumbles it like thistles. He says there is no certainty, because there was no need of any satisfaction to God's justice at all; and that God's justice is to be considered no otherwise than as a "politique" to secure His government, and therefore does not infer any punishment of sinners, but that His threats may be only *in terrorem*, or so far to be inflicted as may secure His government from the rebellion and usurpation of wicked men; as if God were afraid of being deposed by them—a strange notion of the justice of God! But this new doctrine of making hell precarious totally overthrows the doctrine of the satisfaction of Christ, and plucks it up root and branch; for if there be no certainty of a hell there can be no necessity of satisfaction for sins, which by this means are remitted without it. He says that "remitting sins by the death of Christ was a way very honourable to the justice of God and the authority of His laws;" and this is every word he says on the subject. The nature of justice requires that a full and adequate satisfaction be made, otherwise God is no more justice. Besides, if there was no necessity of satisfying justice, it was not only not very honourable in God, but even not reconcilable to any notion we can have of justice to take the life of an innocent person. He makes the foundation of it to be some foolish and wicked fancies which got into people's heads, in compliance with which God sent Christ, and took His life. Those revelations which God gave at the beginning to Adam and afterwards to the patriarchs and prophets, more expressly of the promised seed—and those types and institutions which God from the beginning did appoint as shadows and sensible representations of the expiatory death of Christ upon the cross, such as sacrifices which were commanded to Adam, and descended by uninterrupted tradition even to his heathen posterity,—all these the doctor thinks to be only fancies and imaginations, and that to comply with these was the end of Christ's incarnation, death, etc. Whereas the institutions of false and idolatrous religions were but imitations of the true religion instituted by God; that the devil was but an ape of God Almighty; whence arose the saying, that where God has a church the devil has a chapel. Hence the devil has his sacrifices, his priests, his feasts, etc. He did not invent, but only imitate, as 1 Kings xii. 32. But this author turns the tables, and would have the devil, or wicked men by his inspiration, to have first invented these religious rites, and then God to have framed His religion after the pattern of theirs. The notion of a Mediator he calls "superstition." If it were superstition, is it not so still? And yet to comply with this the doctor makes the end of Christ's coming to be our Mediator. This man makes no more of the mysteries of our religion than to satisfy men's foolish curiosities. As if Christ was incarnate for no other end but to make people wonder and gaze, that He was crucified only to outdo the inhumanity of heathen sacrifices; that is, to cure the wickedness and folly of men by overacting them in both!

They were wont to sacrifice not only beasts, but one man for another; an innocent person for the guilty. Was this not a very wicked and inhuman custom? Yet the doctor would have compliance with it to be the reason why God sacrificed Christ. On the contrary, Christ Himself assures us that He came to destroy the works of the devil, not to compound with him; much less to gratify him in following his wicked suggestions. The doctor gives two answers to this objection, first that God did not command His Son to be sacrificed, but His providence permitted the wickedness and violence of men to put Him to death. If there was no more than bare permission, how was Christ's death a sacrifice more than the death of any other man? Was not God's covenant with Him before it more than a bare permission? How did God then make Him both a priest and a sacrifice by His death? This cannot be called bare permission. "God did determine it before to be done." Though He permit evil, you will not say that He does determine or order it to be done; and God sent His Son for this very end or purpose. It was His express will and pleasure that He should suffer, therefore Christ said, "Not My will, but Thine, be done;" and did voluntarily and resignedly submit to it.

He says that "the sacrifice of Christ was to comply with an unreasonable expectation men had of being saved by the vicarious suffering of some other in their stead." If it was unreasonable for them to expect it, it was unreasonable in Christ to suffer it. God could not have pardoned sin without satisfaction made to His justice, either by the offering of the sinner himself or of a sacrifice in his stead.

"God did not want goodness to have forgiven sin freely and without any satisfaction." Now, justice cannot be satisfied without full payment made. God is not crippled or stinted in His justice more than in His mercy, for He is justice itself; what is necessary to the nature of justice must be so to His nature, for they are the same. In his sense the attributes of God fight against one another; but in ours they rejoice and exult together, and one extols and glorifies the other. Then God's justice is magnified in requiring full satisfaction, His wisdom in finding it and His mercy or goodness in giving that satisfaction for us. I say that from the very nature of justice, which is God, there was a necessity for a full and adequate satisfaction to be made. The person must be infinite who could pay an infinite debt (for such is sin, being an offence against infinite goodness), and likewise must be man, that the same nature which offended should make the satisfaction. Hence He took all our natural but none of our personal infirmities; our Redeemer must be God-man, none other but Christ. He prayed that "if it were possible, the cup might pass from Him," which shows that it was not possible for Him to accomplish the redemption of man without suffering death; otherwise, no doubt God would not have refused the petition of His well-beloved Son. It is no impeachment of the wisdom of God to say there was no other way possible; on the contrary, it is carrying wisdom to the utmost height to find it out. Socinians say Christ suffered for us or for our sakes; whereas others would have it, in our stead, which the doctor thinks "a mere controversy of words." He would make us believe there is no more between Socinians and us, than whether Christ died for our sake or in our stead.

He not only speaks the very Socinian language of the

Trinity, but he really undermines the unity of God by setting it upon a foundation which himself overthrows. His great proof is the "general consent of mankind concerning the unity of God." And yet, speaking of the heathen idolatry, he says that "the generality were grossly guilty both of believing more gods and of worshipping false gods." All the salvo for this most palpable contradiction is what he offers—"that the unity of the divine nature was the primitive and general belief of mankind, and that polytheism and idolatry were a corruption and degeneracy from the original notion."

I do not doubt but Adam worshipped the true God. It is as true that idolatry came in very soon; some say Cain introduced it. The Scripture tells of a general corruption before the Flood; after it we know the whole world was swallowed up in a universal idolatry, except only the family of Abraham, and after him of the Jews, who were continually lapsing into it. What then becomes of this author's "greatest part of mankind" and his "always"?

Next, as to the Trinity he speaks the very Socinian language. "Neither the word Trinity, nor perhaps Person, in the sense of divines are anywhere to be met with in Scripture." But he brings himself off thus: "Yet it cannot be denied that there are three spoken of by the names of Father, Son, and Holy Ghost, in whose name every Christian is baptized, and to each of whom the highest titles and properties of God are in Scripture attributed." And in conclusion he is willing to compound for the word "Person," so long as we mean by it neither more nor less than what the Scripture says in other words. Yet he said before there is no such thing to be found in Scripture in the sense of divines; and what other sense he means is easy to tell, for the present controversy is only between the sense of divines and of Socinians.... When his sermon on Hell was first published, it was handed about among the great debauchees and small atheistical wits more than any new play. Dr. T. has opened the way to heaven so broad and wide as to let in the latitudinarians; and he has determined that God is not obliged to execute His threats, though He is to perform His promises. Again, he makes the chief and only business of religion to respect the peace and quietness of the world.... He makes a woman giving out her child to nurse to be a more heinous matter than to renounce Christ and all revealed religion, because it is a natural duty. Yet he justified the present revolution from the visible finger of God in it ; and from miraculous interpositions (such as the uncertainty of the weather) he justifies those whom he calls " the worthies of our nation," who deserted, betrayed, and took arms against King James. I compare our natural light or knowledge to the creation of the first day. And it is the light of the first day which we enjoy still, but not as it was that day created. It was regulated and modelled on the fourth day into the sun, moon, and stars ; and now we have no participation at all of the light of the first day, but what we have from its regulation on the fourth day, and conveyed to us from the sun ; which I compare to revealed, that is the Christian, religion.... Now that Christ is revealed, the true knowledge of God is to be had only in the face of Jesus Christ ; for none know God truly "but the Son, and he to whomsoever the Son will reveal Him."

SOME REFLECTIONS UPON THE SECOND OF DR. BURNET'S "FOUR DISCOURSES CONCERNING THE DIVINITY AND DEATH OF CHRIST," 1694.

Here is set down such a notion as should make a Christian's ear tingle. He gives the same account as Unitarians of S. John i. 14—"the Word dwelt in or did inhabit the person of Jesus Christ." This is far from the full import of the words "was made flesh," which means much beyond bare inhabitation. Our soul may be said to dwell in our body, but there is something more; the properties of each are attributed to the person who partakes of both. Man is called mortal because his body is such, and immortal because his soul is such. So Christ is called God in respect to His divine nature, and man in respect to His human. All the attributes of the divine, and properties of human nature, are predicated of Christ. Nothing short of impersonation could make Him to become flesh, or make that flesh adorable without the highest idolatry. Dr. B. thinks to solve all this by comparing God's indwelling in Jesus to that in "the cloud of glory" in the temple, and says that "the Jews worshipped the cloud of glory because of God's resting in it." They did not; that were idolatry; and upon such reasoning it were idolatry to have worshipped Christ. . . . God spoke out of the fire on Mount Horeb with an audible voice; yet He strictly forbade the worshipping of anything they saw there, or making any similitude of anything there, lest it should corrupt them to idolatry. If God has not assumed our nature into His own person, only dwelt in Christ as in the temple cloud, though in a higher degree, Christ cannot be our God, and we are idolators in worshipping Him, as much as the heathen in worshipping their idols from the supposed inhabitation of God in them. "Christ is our Lord, as the Eternal dwelt bodily in Him," says the doctor. How then is He adorable? How is He God by nature? Worshipping of Christ must by this rule be the most direct idolatry, if we suppose no more than an indwelling of divinity in Him, and not that His human nature was impersonated with the divine.

He adds that "this indwelling is a vital one, not an assisting one like inspiration." But this will not meet the consequence above told, for there may be a vital indwelling, short of impersonation (Acts xvii. 28). He says that "the union of the divine and human nature in Christ is represented in Scripture as the compounding one person, as much as in other men the union of soul and body makes one man." This, indeed, is fairly said if it be as sincerely intended; but thus he could never have explained it by the indwelling of God in the cloud, nor scrupled against use of the word "Person," nor have made a distinction between Christ's assumption with a high dignity, and the dwelling of the eternal Word in Him. It is very plain that he does not think the man Christ to be God, or that Christ is God and man, but only God in man.

Dr. B. passes on to the other great point, the satisfaction of Christ. He first endeavours to remove the groundwork of any satisfaction being due to God's justice for sin, by advancing that notion of justice which Dr. T. did in his sermon of hell. He calls it only "a right of punishing vested in Himself which He may either use or not use at His pleasure." God is not accountable to any other, in respect of outward compulsion. But on the other hand He is, as I may so say, tied up to His own inherent rectitude and all the perfections of His nature. This is no stinting of His prerogative, but the height of it. Now, justice is as much an attribute of God as His mercy. . . . To forgive is no part of justice; it will exact to the uttermost farthing, otherwise it were not justice; and whatever is essential to it must be so to God. But mercy and justice do not thwart or overcome one another in God as in man, because in Him each is infinite.

Upon their ground of the no necessity to satisfy God's justice for sin, they cannot find out any reason why Christ should have died. Sometimes they say to confirm the truth of His doctrine. But that does not confirm it, for men have died for errors. And Christ vouched His miracles, not His death, to confirm the truth of His doctrine. At other times they say it was only to show God's abhorrence of sin. How? To excuse the guilty and punish the innocent? This upon their way of reasoning would show rather God's acceptance of sin and abhorring of innocence. It cannot stand with justice any other way than upon the doctrine of satisfaction, nor can the death of Christ be otherwise rationally accounted for. What need was there for Christ being sacrificed? No need at all, say the doctors; but we find in Scripture often mention of God's covenant in Christ, and we suppose this to be it. But the Scripture gives quite a different account, namely, that in order to remission there was a necessity for Christ's suffering. Sometimes they fall foul upon God's justice for suffering an innocent person to die. But if they could understand Christ as our Surety, satisfying the utmost demand, they would find the reason of the inexpressible agony of Christ our Redeemer, who had an adequate notion of the infinite demerit of sin.

The doctrine of satisfaction as I have set it down is strictly pursuant to the doctrine of the Church of England, which they once stated in the prayer of consecration in the service of Holy Communion, in the Homily for Good Friday, and in the Homily of Salvation. Yet these adversaries roar in the midst of our congregations, and set up their banners for tokens.

"A Supplement upon Occasion of a History of Religion supposed to be written by Sir R. H——d," calls only for a very brief notice, because the book itself was for the most part a compilation from such writers as the infidel Blount; and the best points of this review are expressed elsewhere in reply to other writers. Sir Robert Howard was a man of some genius, with a taste for poetry, but too indolent to have ever accomplished any great work in prose or verse. His politics were adapted to the times in which he lived, like those of so many more under King Charles II., James II., and the Usurper. In religion he professed to be an admirer and disciple of Dr. Tillotson, but his practice was as negative as his creed.

CHAPTER VI.

ORDER OF PUBLICATIONS—QUAKERS—"SNAKE IN THE GRASS"—PENN—OLIVER'S PORTER—CRISP—CALUMNIES—CONSPIRACY—TITHES—SOCINIANISM—ANECDOTES—SUPPLEMENTS—QUAKER AND SOCINIAN CONTROVERSIES—QUALIFICATION FOR ADMINISTRATION OF SACRAMENTS.

DURING several years from 1694, our author continued his original design of providing a complete armoury of defence for the Church of England against her various antagonists, within and without. Circumstances neither suggested nor materially affected this design, though they influenced both the time and manner of its prosecution. Some subjects were so interwoven and related to each other, that his treatises upon them proceeded simultaneously or alternately in parts. But the design itself was not altered by those circumstances which arose from time to time to vary slightly the manner of its execution. Deists, Jews, Quakers, Socinians, ranged themselves outside the Catholic Church in a natural order for consideration. Then followed other communities professing connection with her—Nonjurors, the Establishment and Erastians in the Church of England, the Gallican and the Roman branches. Intercourse with individuals or passing events only modified his plan so far as to affect the order of publication in some respects. Biographers, therefore, have been mistaken in ascribing the origin of several treatises to casual circumstances, as in the case of the next production of Leslie's pen which calls for notice, the " Snake in the Grass," with its sequels and supplements directed against Quakers. They formed a numerous and prominent sect at that time, compared with their present condition. And one main reason among others of their gradual loss of influence and consideration, was the completeness and effectiveness of his confutation of their tenets and pretences. They never recovered from the blow he dealt, and after a few angry recriminations the leading professors of Quakerism subsided into that silence which the community has generally maintained ever since. Hostility to the Church has not been abandoned; but its current is directed into safer, more secret channels of political antagonism, merged in the common flood of sectarian opposition to the Establishment. Adders' poison is under their lips still, but they do not bite so venomously and frequently in the nineteenth century as in the seventeenth. Nor with one exception have any parliamentary scorpions risen above the meanest level of mediocrity. Quakers now for the most part, if insignificant in numbers, yet really are more esteemed and respected than formerly, because they have receded from their aggressive attitude, and sloughed off earlier eccentricities and extravagances. Some other sects might advantageously take a lesson from their decorous and peaceable character. Why they should discard the name Quakers, and almost resent its application, is not very intelligible, for certainly it originated with their own founders, and was justified and gloried in by Fox, Penn, Ellwood, and others, as involving some moral or spiritual resemblance to Moses and Habakkuk. Leslie had no personal antipathy to any amongst them; on the contrary, a very kindly feeling to several. He wrote entirely in the interests of truth against error, as he earnestly assured them in his first treatise, wishing them to consider not who said it, but what was said. Before its publication he presented in a formal and respectful manner several productions, to which he invited a reply from their chief assembly in London; but this was evaded by lame and paltry excuses from one meeting to another. Nor could they reasonably object to inquiry or interference from outside, because Quakers themselves actively interfered in public affairs affecting the Church's interest, denied her doctrines, and denounced her discipline in most violent terms. No members of any sect, even Anabaptists, committed greater outrages against decency as well as the law of the land, or indulged in more scurrilous and abusive language against the clergy. Therefore they would have had no just ground of complaint had severer retorts been provoked by their offensive demeanour than he had any inclination to offer. But his object was not to quarrel with Quakers but refute Quakerism; and providential circumstances brought within his reach means and opportunities of performing what he deemed "a holy duty" towards them and society at large just at the most needful season, and in conformity with the original plan sketched out for himself.

London has undergone such immense and frequent alterations that little idea can be formed of a locality and its condition, or clue afforded for its identification by furnishing its name or situation two centuries ago. It may be mentioned, however, that our author, shortly before his treatise on Quakerism, had taken lodgings in the house of a member of this community, the Society of Friends, facing the new Exchange, into which his sitting-room looked, and where he remained for about twelve months or more. From this it may readily be inferred that his pecuniary circumstances were not in a very flourishing condition, for he had a wife and now two children to provide for. The neighbourhood was on some accounts favourable to him from its contiguity to churches the most numerously attended, and to clubs or coffee-houses which his own friends frequented, religious, literary, and political. There was the real London of that day, the centre of its life and activity; where people brought the latest news and inquired for it; where plots were hatched or pretended; where men and books were discussed by friends and foes unceasingly. Society was not so exclusive as at the present day, nor religion and politics so palpably subjugated to material considerations of rank and wealth. A name meant something, whether that something were good or bad. Then also literature and literary men stood in higher estimation, though not so many persons pretended to education among the higher and middle classes. To have written a learned treatise, or a really able and vigorous pamphlet upon any side of a question, was a sure passport to admiration, with of course some envy or detraction, much more than to possess a fine house, hold a lucrative post, or slaughter numberless birds. Nonjurors and Jacobites naturally resorted to London, not only because of a similarity of plumage and congeniality of tastes, but, their resources being greatly crippled, they thus could more readily enjoy that relaxation and social intercourse which the majority, being men of cultivated intellect, desired, but could not find elsewhere. Oxford was also a favourite resort for the same reason, and the still greater advantages it afforded for study of books, so as to give rise to the saying that "its streets were paved with the skulls of Jacobites," though the real author of that saying was not Dr. Johnson, as commonly supposed, but Sir Simon Harcourt.[1] The great lexicographer consciously or unconsciously adopted it, to stereotype an important fact of history.

[1] In De Foe's trial.

Whether Leslie selected his lodging with an eye to the object he had in view of confuting Quakerism or not is a point of little consequence; but nothing could have proved more opportune, for thus facilities were afforded of acquiring full and accurate information concerning their peculiar tenets. Conversation with his landlord produced so strong an impression as to lead to discussion with many more of the Society invited to be present on various occasions, who brought with them their own books for reference, and stated in the freest manner their opinions and objections. The happy result of these conversations and debates was at length the conversion not only of the landlord and his family but also of several other persons.

Another special reason served to concentrate attention on this subject about the same time. Leslie's known adhesion to the cause of the Royal family in exile necessarily brought him into contact with a great number of persons, some of whom proved occasionally a source of embarrassment; for acquaintance with them furnished a handle of suspicion among Government spies and tale-bearers, though the Government themselves showed no desire to meddle with him. Appeals for pecuniary assistance were not unfrequent, which it was difficult to refuse even by one whose own resources were slender, and in some cases, as that of the family of the late Bishop of Oxford, friendship strengthened the claim of most undeserved suffering. Many who complained most loudly of that poor bishop's subserviency to James, might have formed a more lenient judgment had they known how much he needed some office *in commendam* to eke out a very scanty income, and in what absolute destitution at last his family were left, so that the burden was even beyond the power of a few friends like Leslie to sustain alone. Dr. Kennet, the intruded bishop at Peterborough, was one who, with his characteristic kindness even to opponents, assisted in this case when made known to him. But there were many more claimants upon Jacobites and Nonjurors, of whom none knew but themselves; some good, and some bad perhaps, none the less possessing a strong title to commiseration when fellow-sufferers for conscience' sake. Now conspicuous as a Royalist among his acquaintances stood the famous William Penn, whom Macaulay the historian has so ungenerously laboured to depreciate, owing to a family pique against the Quakers. He was really a man of superior powers and education as well as of good birth, united with winning manners and address. Had he not possessed more than ordinary talents he could never have attained the position which he had gained, in spite of his peculiar opinions, under two Sovereigns. Nor is there any reasonable ground for imputation upon his integrity in the various matters of business which he was called upon to undertake at different times. On all occasions he seems to have acted uprightly as a Christian gentleman of more than ordinary sagacity; and the only inexplicable thing is how such a person could have apostatized from the Church of England, in which he had been brought up, to embrace the delusions of this fanatical body. Most of them were notoriously illiterate, especially the founder, George Fox, a journeyman shoemaker or cobbler, who could not write or speak English grammatically, and who, in presuming to interpret Holy Scripture, made the most extraordinary blunders about simple texts and matters of fact which children are supposed to understand. Probably Penn was the only person then of the slightest pretence to learning in the whole community, though they had since their origin in 1650, and introduction into London in 1654, increased in wealth and importance beyond most other sects. Several undertook to write books and pamphlets, which only showed them to be without the most elementary rudiments of education, so that they had done better to adhere exclusively to profession of inspiration and infallibility. Whereas a majority of Quakers were republicans and radicals; though Leslie shows how they could shift their ground before and after the Restoration in addresses to the king; Penn steadfastly and sincerely devoted himself to the house of Stuart both in prosperity and adversity. His loyalty to the Throne remained beyond dispute, even when he had unhappily apostatized from the Altar on which it most properly rested. His position, accordingly, was an anomalous and influential one, which he knew well how best to turn to advantage without detriment to his high character. Such a man could not fail to enlist the sympathy and esteem of many who otherwise might have held aloof or even shunned his acquaintance. Leslie treated him with a particular respect upon every occasion. More than that, deeply deploring to see one of such breadth of understanding carried away by a spirit of fanaticism, he addressed to him several personal remonstrances. Sceptics, who cannot understand a Christian's feeling in converting even a Gildon from the error of his way, would deem it no doubt a great triumph to have recovered Mr. Penn. Leslie, who fully estimated the influence of his example, appealed the more earnestly to his sober judgment, but failed; not because his arguments were unconvincing, but because prejudice was more powerful than argument. It should be remembered, moreover, that what first warped and alienated the mind of Penn from the Church of England was the flagrant treasons and inconsistencies of a multitude of her own professing teachers and disciples in the revolutionary ranks. The effort to win him back, though it failed, was a noble one. Equally creditable was Penn's conduct in one respect. He displayed no feeling of indignation at the remonstrances or censures addressed to him upon his religious system. All was taken in good part as intended, and, whereas he could make use of very severe and decided language when he thought proper towards co-religionists as well as others, none of those abusive epithets and angry taunts in which they lavishly indulged ever escaped his lips against Leslie. The friendly footing established between them continued unimpared by the determined adherence of each to his own system.

A larger amount of space was devoted to the Quaker controversy than relatively to others it might seem to merit. None, except the Socinian, has been treated at such length. This arose in the first place from the number and variety of points disputed; for Quakerism was but "one branch of enthusiasm," and a form embracing errors held by other fanatics. To confute one, therefore, was to confute them all, whatever name they might pass under. In the next place, from the necessity of supporting charges made against the community by evidence capable of test at the time when they were made. Now such particulars are not worth repetition or remembrance; perhaps they never were deserving the pains bestowed upon verification of dates, times, and persons. And as they greatly serve to encumber the subject, may be advantageously omitted with the remark that not a single assertion could be disproved, only the plaintiff's attorney abused, and that the heresies imputed to the Quakers were derived from the published writings of their own acknowledged leaders. The controversy can thus be reduced to narrow limits; but the main features here reproduced deserve serious consideration by Christian people who deem themselves in no danger of becoming Quakers. For heresies have their roots in human nature, and may spring up almost imperceptibly in assimilation to the truth they design to strangle, like weeds in different soils, which are often difficult to distinguish from the plants they fasten upon for destruction. The value of these treatises eminently consists in the masterly method of stripping off disguises and exposing the danger and falsehood of doctrines speciously clothed in evangelical terms, to pass current among communities which have no idea of their real origin and tendencies. Fortunately for himself, the subject of this biography possessed a sufficiently cheerful disposition for acrimonious attacks to produce little impression. Had he, however, been more sensitive, the kindly demeanour of a considerable party among the "Friends," and the result of his labours, would have afforded ample compensation. The "Snake in the Grass" obtained celebrity far beyond their circles; no publication of its kind enjoyed a wider circulation, three editions being called for in as many years, though greatly assisted by some of them.

The "Friends" by no means formed a single, undivided, happy family. They had their separations and divisions and strivings for superiority like other sects. And bickerings sometimes rose to a white heat among them, when they could assume quite a papal tone of authority, denouncing and excommunicating each other. Even the sober, sedate Penn confessed that upon one occasion, when his own interpretation of a text was contradicted by one who had no idea that he was doing so, and whose opinion no Christian could doubt to be correct, was so transported with indignation as "not to know whether he was standing on his head or his heels." As may be supposed from this admission, the unfortunate offender incurred a malediction of no very gentle or soothing description. It was also rather in defence of another poor victim, George Keith, than from the need of any reply, that one was made in "Satan Disrobed" to "An Antidote for the Snake's Venom," by George Whitehead—a very feeble performance. One objection, however, of his deserves notice. He asked, Why should failings of individuals be chargeable against their society more than those of individuals against the Church, or any other community to which they belonged? This in itself was fairly and forcibly urged; but Leslie's answer was equally pointed, that Quakers make pretensions to inspiration and infallibility as individuals, which members of no other communion do. When, therefore, they disagree, who can presume to apportion the amount of inspiration or infallibility qualifying one to condemn another?

Leslie was the first in England who opposed the fallacies and fanaticism of Madame Bourignon, of whom he has given a brief account as the real author of Quakerism, which he had hoped to be done at greater length by his learned friend, Bishop Hickes. No originality was pretended in the title "Snake in the Grass," which had been frequently employed, and very recently in a caustic and able pamphlet on political matters, supposed to be from the pen of Somers or Rochester, but its application is explained thus: "There is no enthusiasm where there is no pride, which, being dressed in the garb and guise of humility, is literally the devil transformed into an angel of light; and then he is most a devil because he can most deceive."

Muggletonianism has nearly died out. Its very name only lingers in the purlieus of old-fashioned towns among traces of bygone credulity and ignorance. Yet it sprang into existence from the same source and in the same year with the other heresy, and under auspices quite as distinguished; for its founder, Ludovic Muggleton, was a tailor, whose thoughts revolved on an axis of equal power to that of the man's with the awl and wax. Personally the two agreed together, but their disciples soon became rivals for popularity, and Penn termed Muggleton "the sorcerer of these days;" while both appealed to light within as their ground for leaving the Church of England. At length the Quaker light eclipsed or extinguished the Muggleton; but they were, in fact, " twin enthusiasts, which, though like Samson's foxes drawing two ways, their tails were joined with firebrands to set the Church in a flame." In order to do no injustice to his system, Leslie took pains to become personally acquainted with this man, and learned it from his own lips.

Divine authority declares that "of writing many books there is no end, and much study is a weariness of the flesh." Our champion of orthodoxy was not so closely pinioned to his desk as to have no relaxation from his self-imposed tasks, nor compelled to find it only in discussion classes. These proved less irksome to him than they would have done to most persons even of a literary turn, not only because there he learned practically the fallacies and delusions which most readily found favour with different minds, and the best mode of treating them, but also because they afforded experience and an agreeable sphere of usefulness. Other means of recreation filled up intervals of leisure. Jacobite and Nonjuring principles did not restrict his society to any particular set, nor residence in lodgings prevent cards and invitations coming there from more fashionable quarters. He and his wife had many visitors, and spent a considerable portion of time from home. Among members of Parliament in both Houses were a great number to whom his politics, instead of being an objection, proved rather a recommendation. In Oxford, Berkshire, and Surrey they had several friends, and especially at Bagshot a warm welcome could always be counted upon. If he never concealed his opinions nor forgot his ecclesiastical character, yet he knew there is a time for everything, and with his gaiety of manner and conversational powers could unbend whenever a proper occasion offered to lay aside controversy of every description. Country sports and amusements had a great charm for him, so that he was not one of those guests whom a host can only leave in the library for the best part of the day, but was equally ready to shoot, or ride, or drive with the rest of the company; while he seemed as well acquainted with lighter literature and the current topics of the day, as the more favourite subjects of his study. These accomplishments not only served to dissipate unfavourable prejudices and prepossessions and secure him a general popularity, but contributed to invigorate his own health of mind and body. His constitution was by no means so strong as his father's, for he suffered frequently and severely from the gout, which could neither be attributed, at least immediately, to inheritance from him nor to luxurious habits, for he was equally temperate and moderate. But each recurrence of a more painful attack synchronized palpably with some excessive mental strain or excitement, so that there can be no doubt, that without the pleasure and relief afforded by such innocent indulgence, he never could have accomplished the amount of intellectual work he did, or performed it so satisfactorily. Another reason of success in writing was his habit, instead of bottling up his wit and learning for sudden surprises, of discussing freely the subject he had in hand with qualified friends, that he might benefit by their criticisms, whilst few authors have been less indebted to other persons for their ideas than he was.

An amusing adventure is mentioned in the "Snake," which the author met with in 1696. He went to visit another prophet generally called Oliver's Porter in Bedlam, where he was confined on the ground of insanity. His Christian name was Daniel, and his proper surname nobody seemed to know or cared to inquire, but accepted the designation conferred upon him in memory of his former employment in the hall of the great usurper. Perhaps there was some "method in his madness," for the probability is, that by being supposed to have gone off his head, he escaped the penalty of losing it altogether in the first excitement of the Restoration, for having occupied so prominent a position during the Rebellion. Whether his mental aberration was genuine or affected, his education and accomplishments were equal to those of other prophets. He had studied some books of a mystical kind, and was so fond of reading that his library was allowed to him in the asylum, among which was a large Bible given by Nell Gwynn, because perhaps she found little time for its perusal at Court. Though constant war raged between him, Fox, and Muggleton, they calling him mad, and he them wicked and profane for despising his gifts and mission, he was popularly credited with having foretold the great fire of London and other remarkable events. Preaching occupied a considerable portion of his time, when crowds collected to hear, and sat many hours under his window at the end of the building overlooking a grass plot. Observing among some women on this occasion, busy turning over the leaves of their Bibles for the texts

Oliver's Porter quoted, one grave, sober-like matron, Leslie had the curiosity to ask her what profit she could expect from listening to such a mad man; when she, with a composed countenance and as pitying his ignorance, replied that "Festus thought Paul was mad." This made him, he says, reflect that there were several sorts of madness; and what ill luck some mad folks had to be closed up, whilst others went about the streets. Undoubtedly also the line of demarcation between preacher and audience was slighter than stone walls indicated; and acquaintance with inmates of such establishments has led some people to doubt whether more reason is generally displayed inside or outside them on religious subjects.

Among Leslie's converts was a youth called Crisp, who relapsed into his former heresy. This was a triumph vaunted with high exultation among the Quakers, yet the poor creature could not be properly accounted a gain or loss to any community, being subject to fits of insanity, which appeared very evident on his admission to Holy Orders. He would stop in the middle of public service for private ejaculations; and when this was made a cause of complaint by congregations who were discomforted, he resigned his office, saying, "He could not stay where he had not time for his devotions." He had promised that if any fresh scruples should arise in his mind, he would take no step without first apprising his converter. Under the influence of certain members of the sect this promise was broken, and only a scurrilous letter sent upon remonstrance with him. Such an apostasy formed a small set-off against the many converts who never could be seduced back to their former heresy. But the circumstances have an interest in a very different light as showing the wisdom and fairness of Leslie's own conduct in regard to such persons. It was not to Nonjurors as such in opposition to the Establishment, but to the Church of England, he reconciled his converts; not attempting to impose upon them or even recommend the political obligations which he felt binding on his own conscience. The same attitude he consistently maintained in other respects; one entirely devoid of the faintest character of schism any more than heresy. So much so that when Quakers taunted him with "expulsion from the ministry for refusing oaths," the reproach easily recoiled on themselves and damaged their community, whose only boast was "non-swearing" in the eyes of the public. Another charge pained him, because he knew that a calumny of the kind can be circulated amongst numbers who never hear its contradiction. They called him a "mercenary priest who wrote for bread, and for hire against them;" "necessitous and malicious; who employed his skulking leisure for base ends, and found means supplied by the contents" (of his books). With many more such choice epithets and flowers of rhetoric, in favour with a peace-professing community fond of making quarrels, but which does not fight. Their victim need not have experienced even a moment's discomposure, had he but known what contempt and indignation they brought upon themselves, and how universally their insinuations were scouted by all classes. Now that the circumstances are all forgotten, it is due to Leslie's reputation to repeat simple facts. His treatises were composed and published, without concert with any single being, at his own cost and risk. If he did not suffer pecuniary loss, that was entirely owing to their popularity; but on the whole he did not "make a single guinea," nor ever received a retaining fee for writing in his life. Had he done so, however, he would have been in company with the ablest and most honourable of literary characters then or ever since.

The crime of being necessitous is unfortunately too prevalent at all times to need any apology; but his accusers really only aimed random blows in the dark, knowing nothing beyond what was apparent to the world of his real circumstances, of which there never was any reason or attempt at concealment, but under a false impression that he had lost enormous emoluments with his ecclesiastical preferment.

His real offence was exposure of the inconsistencies between practice and profession on the part of the sect. Such as these. George Fox objects to "the painting of a likeness upon any sign," yet when a simple Friend called upon them at a meeting to throw away their money as having images of heads, lions, etc., it was of no avail, though Fox professed that he dictated his "doctrine from the mouth of the Lord." They say "thee and thou" to the world's people, but do not like it back from them; and therefore prefer Christian servants who "speak in the language they approve of." Scoffing at observance of Church festivals, yet keeping their own yearly meetings in London at Whitsuntide—which, if it mean anything, must mean what the Church commemorates, and suits their worldly taste of a visit to the metropolis in the height of the season. Costly furniture, fine houses, luxurious living, carriages and liveries—at first denounced as signs of pride, whilst to the Fox and his children grapes were sour; but with increase of wealth became not only allowable, but characteristic; for they have a method of eliminating poorer members from their society. To such an extent did the indignation of the more furious zealots rise, that a conspiracy was formed for the murder of Leslie. It was most deliberately organized by the Quaker leaders; and so eager and exultant were they in the prospect of its accomplishment, that nothing but a want of reticence on their own part, under the merciful care of Divine Providence, prevented its accomplishment. Leslie had an intimation sufficient to assure him of the reality of the design against his life; also to take the necessary precautions for his safety; and he was no more wanting in physical than moral courage. When, however, urgently pressed to proceed against the guilty persons involved in this cowardly attempt, he nobly and most properly refused to produce the evidence in his hand; and this not on account of his informants, who made no such conditions, but because he preferred to overcome evil with good; though very great stress was put upon him for a complete disclosure of the facts. For once, at any rate, the priest must have felt thankful that he no longer was a magistrate, between two stools on the Justices' bench.

Several replies appeared at intervals beside the "Antidote" of Whitehead, the more noticeable one being Ellwood's reply to "Satan Disrobed." All of them were answered, but they contained so little of argument and so much of repetition, with mere angry recrimination, that now few readers would have patience enough for their perusal. What is material will be found in the supplement to this chapter, which deserves attention as containing expositions of Scripture, and statements of sound doctrine of great value, independently of the particular circumstances which called them forth.

Controversy has its pitfalls and disadvantages for champions of orthodoxy as well as disseminators of heresy. And Leslie was betrayed into some statements of doctrine which do not bear the stamp of theological accuracy, upon a subject which required most cautious handling. One Eccles had said that "the blood of Christ is no more than the blood of another saint." When this properly called out reprobation, Ellwood came to the rescue by explaining Eccles to have meant only that "blood forced out of the Saviour after He was dead," but admitting it to be an "unjustifiable expression." It was a great deal more—very wicked, false, and wantonly shocking language; and the apology did not mend its false doctrine. Yet it would have been better to leave the matter there, than invite speculation about a mystery further by these words: "S. John lays much stress upon, and tells this with more particular observation than of the shedding of any other part of His blood. Then it was the blood and water issued forth out of His side, the two sacraments." What the Quakers intended was to deny the union of the divine and human nature in the one Person of the Redeemer. But both the error and its irreverent statement might have been reproved without suggesting, as Leslie unintentionally did, a question of the relative value of the blood, shed and unshed. Upon that nothing can be rightly hazarded, either in word or thought. And his own reference to the Sacraments in the latter part of his sentence shows the unguarded character of the former, affording an opening to materialistic considerations which himself was the furthest from entertaining.

Again, his statements on Justification and Sanctification were defective, or not so satisfactory and explicit as to prevent misconception. What he wrote is true enough so far as it goes, and applicable to the points under discussion, but falling short of the full doctrine, and drawing distinctions which, though finding favour among Protestant writers of note, seem to countenance a part of the Calvinistic system of modern invention, unwarranted by Holy Scripture, the teaching of the early Fathers, or the formularies of the Church of England. Justification is a state as well as an act of absolving, and a man cannot be made or become righteous solely and simply by imputation of the Redeemer's merits. To be accounted righteous before God, he must really become so; for there can be no pretences or false assumptions with Him, therefore righteousness must be imparted. Even Isaac Barrow is not quite consistent with himself upon this subject in his sermons,[1] for much the same reason as Leslie—a desire of pressing a single view of truth against error, or the suspicion of holding it among Protestants, to the exclusion of another equally necessary view. Points of difference between the Church of England and Rome are numerous and serious, nor will a faithful and wise member of either try to conceal or obscure them. The interests of truth are best secured by unreserved candid admissions. But neither truth nor the interest of either Church is served by inventing differences, or exaggerating them to widen the breach. Bull and Bellarmine were no more at variance than S. Paul and S. James concerning justification, though earlier controversialists have contrived to represent these in antagonism. Now that the heat and blindness which disfigured all religious discussion in former times have in some degree abated, writers and teachers, who remember that theology is a science, should use technical terms with accuracy, and forbear the use of distinctions and cloudy verbiage which insinuate opinions incapable of support by acknowledged standards of orthodoxy.

Tithes are touched upon in this portion of the Quaker controversy, and more fully in another special treatise, which will be considered in its place. It therefore suffices here to

[1] Vol. ii. pp. 123–131.

press one point arising from his remarks upon the consideration of those who approve of receiving them. Tithes are inseparably connected in the Law and the Gospel with priesthood; those clergy, therefore, who represent their own titles to Orders as a mere solemn sham, and repudiate the name and notion of priesthood for themselves, ought consistently to refuse them. Their claim at the very best is a parliamentary title to an income which the same power bestowing it can as properly take away. They deprive themselves of any religious obligation or authority for demanding tithes, so would do well to weigh our author's forcible words, or reconsider their position.

Quakers professed themselves particularly aggrieved at being charged, among other gross corruptions, of doctrine and worship with Socinianism, because they knew how abhorrent that was to the many who only smiled at their other excesses as foolish eccentricities. Socinians, on the other hand, were indignant at being classed with people who indulged in language and conduct of the most shocking description, of which superabundant evidence had been produced. That Leslie should have condescended to particularize these so amply remains a matter of deep regret, for they have greatly disfigured his pages, and unfitted some for general perusal. Though the facts could not be gainsaid—nay, there were things worse than he related notoriously practised by members of the community, and heaps of profanity and nonsense written by their recognized authors—yet it would have been more consistent with the dignity and solemnity of sacred subjects to have omitted them altogether, or at least relegated not only a portion but the whole to the obscurity of an appendix. He apologized himself for "cleansing the Augean stable" from a sense of duty, and for indulging occasionally in coarse wit and banter suited to the minds of his opponents. No doubt serious subjects may be treated with advantage sometimes in a light and pleasant vein of raillery; and one may even play the fool to answer one according to his folly. But both Solomon and S. Paul have suggested cautions in doing so, which seem to have been insufficiently kept in view. Accordingly Socinians expressed no small indignation at any identification of their sect with the other. Their special plea for attention lay in the reasonableness and sobriety of their system; and it must be admitted, if they could write angrily, seldom violated decency. Nevertheless Leslie was fully justified in connecting the two systems of error together. Nor was it possible for him, in collecting materials for confutation of the one, not to be struck with its family resemblance and fundamental relationship to the other. True indeed that Quakerism was the offspring of Romish corruption. Its mother, Bourignon, lived and died in that communion. The wonder is she has not yet been canonized, but Romish dignitaries testified to her odours of sanctity; whereas Arius and Macedonius at least had the merit of antiquity. But then the heresy of Bourignon and all her offspring was in reality a revival and reproduction of heresies condemned as long ago. Leslie, therefore, only followed the natural and proper order of things when *pari passu* and simultaneously he carried on controversy with these two sets of opponents for several years; since what else in either required confutation had already received it in the " Short and Easy Method with the Deists." This plan helped to lighten his labours, and afford a prospect of their earlier termination. How he dealt with the more sober, rationalistic, no less heretical body, comes now under consideration.

Certain circumstances had occurred to render most necessary execution of our author's design of directing his artillery against Socinianism. When the Emperor of Morocco's ambassador visited the court of Charles II., its adherents had taken the remarkable step of presenting him with an elaborate address, in which they described themselves as the proper representatives of Christianity in England, denouncing Church-people as mere "idolizing Christians," while Mahomet was declared to be "the scourge whom God had raised up for their punishment," and his disciples their "own votaries and fellow-worshippers of the sole supreme Deity, with other wholesome doctrines." Since the indulgence to Dissenters granted by William, they had set up a meeting-house in the metropolis for the first time, to which visitors were being earnestly invited. And still more recently a series of pamphlets against the doctrine of the Church had been gratuitously circulated. It was time, therefore, that something should be done before this fresh crop of deadly heresy should seed itself in the hearts of an ignorant multitude, and Leslie girded himself for its extermination. The name Socinian has been commonly and indiscriminately applied to all who deny the Christian doctrine of the Trinity and our blessed Saviour's divine nature, derived from Lælius and Faustus Socinus. Of these the elder was born at Sienna, in Tuscany, of a distinguished family, who travelled through several countries in search of a religion to suit him, and settling at Zurich, died at an early age, in 1562, nominally in communion with the Protestant body there. His real opinions were expounded and developed by his nephew Faustus, with additions probably of his own. Other persons soon associated with him, and helped to mould his heretical opinions into a formal system, whose head-quarters were fixed in

Poland, where it was disseminated widely in surrounding countries, and passed into England. Here it met with little success for a considerable time, and had to conduct its operations secretly for fear of the Government. The real founders and fathers of the sect were, however, as themselves admitted in their letter to the ambassador, none other than the heretics Paul of Samosata, Arius, Marcellus, Macedonius (though they did not mention him), and such like, long ago condemned and excommunicated by the Christian Church.

Leslie opened his battery by a published "Letter to a Friend," in 1694, briefly explaining the irreconcilable difference between the Christian doctrine and their notions, with the inconsistency and self-contradiction involved in these, as stated in "Biddle's Confession of Faith," lately published. Instead of repudiating the name Trinity, Socinians then, as now, studiously retained it for the purpose of veiling their real teaching under a false pretence. "Some made the Second and Third Persons to be creatures; others denied them to be persons at all, but only manifestations of divine power and wisdom. Both are equally false, while contradicting each other. First, if the Word and the Spirit are only creatures, to worship them were idolatry of the plainest description. If they are only manifestations, then all the attributes are equally divine, so there would be more than a Trinity, some twenty or more. How could the Word be made flesh, as Holy Scripture says, for a manifestation is nothing in itself? If there be only one Person in the Godhead, it would follow that He became incarnate and died, so there could be now no God. Why should men have been commanded to be baptized in the Name of the Three Persons if there be only One? Or again, if there be not Three Persons, how could it have been said by the Saviour that blasphemy against One might be forgiven, but not against Another? How could One be made flesh and the Others not? Then observe their differences between themselves, the one part making God their object of worship, the other part only a creature; the one to say there are Persons, the other there are not. . . . There is as great and sublime mystery in the Holy Trinity of God as in His nature, and even in human nature, which yet is no reason for disbelief, nor any contradiction, because the Persons are not Three and One in the same respect."

An interval of three years elapsed without this letter eliciting any reply, though plainly issued as a challenge. A second then followed, coming to closer quarters. First, Leslie protested against assumption of the title Unitarians, as if Socinians believed in the unity of the Godhead more than Christians, and the designating these Trinitarians when themselves professed, not only one, but different sorts of Trinitarianism. Then English Socinians are shown to be with more propriety termed Mahometans, as greater enemies to Christ than disciples of the false prophet, for they refuse Him divine honour. It is not enough to believe there was such a man as Christ, or that He was the Messiah which Mahometans confess, and His mission and miracles. Again, English ones were not reckoned Christians by the main body of Socinians in Poland, because they denied divine worship to Christ, though themselves affirming Him to be only a Creator. Herein lay the germ of the controversy, which was fully unfolded in six dialogues supposed to be held between a Socinian and Christian upon the subject, as treated in a book entitled "A brief History of the Unitarians compared with the Words of Scripture and the Current Sense of the Church from the First."

The profession of Arianism and Socinianism has dwindled down to a vanishing point during the last century in this country, till in the year of grace 1884 the very name has disappeared from enumeration among a hundred and eighty sects in public Returns! Such is the stigma affixed to memory both of ancient and modern founders of the heresy that their children disown, and are ashamed of their proper parentage. But the deadly thing itself still exists with its former vitality, and remains lurking and hiding under various disguises of piety, purity, philosophy, or Protestantism. As the snake in the grass has been scotched but not killed, only is more silent and sleek, so the old serpent's other brood are being hatched in various coverts, and the slimy track may be traced here and everywhere abroad. They bask in the warmth of princely smiles, and fold themselves in ermine and lawn. They glide through gilded saloons, Council chambers, and circles of fashion. They are dressed in the garb of superior enlightenment and rough common sense. They sit in Decanal Stalls, and even claim to be the peculiar guardians of sound theology. Their poison is diffused through the press, still gratuitously offered and decked out with rhetorical artifice and flourishes of over-punctuated, glittering platitudes from the pulpit in Cathedrals and churches. Anabaptist, Congregational, and Independent sects are saturated and drenched with Socinianism; and even Methodists are drenched with it to the heart's core, though their churchless, creedless community are too deficient in learning or intelligence to know what they worship. If there were not Arians and Socinians in Parliament, and among prelates and priests of the Establishment, such frantic anxiety would not be exhibited to mutilate the Book of Common Prayer and eliminate that bulwark of orthodoxy, the Athanasian Creed. These constitute the real danger to the Church of England—her treacherous dealers, who would play with the serpent and enemies within the camp. Leslie pointed out the deadly character of their heresy and their wiles in his day. These are more perilous two centuries later, in proportion as their devices are more concealed. They want to sting true religion to the death, and therefore it is infatuation to let their system steal insidiously closer and closer, till it has coiled itself round and sucked the very heart's blood out of the Church of England. The old names and the old profession will be resumed if ever disciples of Arius and Socinus feel strong enough openly to confront and defy the Catholic faith. Meanwhile that faith is a precious heritage and a trust which her children have received to preserve at all hazard, and transmit uncontaminated to their children's children. It is not theirs to pollute or dilute, to barter or surrender. Let people and things also be called by their right names, at least among true Christians. What Leslie stated negatively and positively is true, and should be acted upon now. Arians and Socinians have no title to the name Unitarians. That, and Trinitarians if they will, not in opposition but as correlative terms, belong exclusively to professors of the Catholic faith—the faith once delivered to the saints— that "we worship one God in Trinity, and Trinity in Unity." To apply it to deniers of this fundamental verity is to make the word a meaningless misnomer, and break down the barrier between truth and falsehood under a spurious, suicidal pretence of charity. Arianism and Socinianism are not Christianity, but a form of Antichrist, as the Evangelist S. John declared;[1] nor is there any such genuine charity as that which "speaks the truth in love." It may be sincerely hoped that some outside the Church

---

[1] S. John ii. 22-24.

hold unconsciously more sound and exalted views concerning the doctrine of the Trinity than their particular sect confesses, as it is to be feared that inside the Church there are some who do not fully believe her confession of faith. An able minister of the Arian body in the north of Ireland, now dead, used freely to speak of letters from a late distinguished Conservative statesman, containing acknowledgment of agreement in his particular religious opinions, while publicly in communion with the Church of England. Is it any wonder that he dealt some terrible blows to her establishment in the sister kingdom? Within the last twenty years there resided in a large English town a Jewish gentleman deservedly respected on several accounts, with whom a clergyman had long been on a friendly footing. Meeting accidentally one Sunday morning, the priest inquired whither he was going, when he replied, "To my place of worship." "I did not know," said the other, "that you had a Synagogue here." "No," said he, "but when I am well served there, and hear nothing to the contrary, why should I not be well content?" indicating at the same time the Arian meeting-house. His testimony was confirmed by another Jewish gentleman of as high character. The facts illustrate most forcibly the position established by Leslie with uncontrovertible evidence that Socinianism or Arianism has an essential connection with Deism, Judaism, and Quakerism, but no affinity with genuine Christianity. Here again is the trail of the serpent. A tract widely distributed within the last few years bears this title, "What Unitarians believe," the contents of which are only their old rank heresy disguised in Christian terms and popular phraseology, to divert incautious or uneducated readers from asking, What Arians do *not* believe? which is the main question requiring an answer. The last *brochure* of their printing company is a so-called "Prize Essay," just as disingenuously entitled "History of the Doctrine of the Trinity in the Christian Church," which history it misrepresents, and which doctrine it labours by garbled quotations to destroy. If no more skilful performance could win a bribe of fifty guineas, then some people and their money are easily parted; and it stands out clearly that, so far from advocates of this system having advanced beyond their fathers or gained by apostates, they have seriously retrograded in intelligence. They do not possess at least the wisdom of the serpent now, or would leave its defence in the old hands. Another sceptic, apparently unattached to any particular sect, has impugned some of Leslie's arguments; but as he only repeats the purport of objections by his contemporary opponents Biddle and Clendon, without adding anything to their weight, readers had better consult their own writings for a statement of their case. Leslie termed Biddle "a mere pragmatical schoolmaster," and complained of his "rude" language personally to himself. Certainly his feathers appear to have been considerably ruffled by the rigid scrutiny his History underwent. Nor was Mr. Clendon so courteous in his language as became a "calm judgment" and "philosophic plainness." But on the whole the controversy can be read with much interest and profit, on account of the thorough investigation of scriptural texts which it affords. Mr. Clendon unfortunately suffered a prosecution for some statements of doctrine which offended the Government; but the fault of this lay, in the first instance, with his own imprudence in trying to force his publication upon the attention of distinguished persons, with not a little grotesque kind of flattery. Nobody regretted his misfortune more sincerely than Leslie, because he disapproved of persecutions and prosecutions on account of religion, as weapons of carnal warfare, though those who urged their use against High Churchmen, Jacobites, and Nonjurors could not with much reason complain of retaliation upon themselves. Nor could he feel much indignation at some hard speeches into which the names of Dr. Tillotson, Burnet, Sherlock, and Stillingfleet were needlessly dragged. Defence of the two former by an avowed Socinian could not help to clear them of the suspicion of heresy, and comparison with the two latter was rather a compliment than anything else to Leslie's ability. The controversy continued for a long period in the shape of supplements, replies, examinations, and answers, which only served to darken counsel by words and involve the necessity of re-slaying the slain. All its main features and elucidation of important texts are, it is hoped, fairly indicated in a brief sketch or outline at the close of this chapter.

Rejoinders by Biddle and Clendon led to restatements and enforcement of the previous argument from Scripture. The text Isa. liii. 11 had been explained by him to mean that God the Father had seen the travail of His Son's soul, and was satisfied with it as an offering for sin—which they termed "not so happy as ridiculous." Nevertheless the context is wholly in favour of this interpretation, nor is there anything in the original to prevent it. The ordinary one which they preferred—that Christ saw of the travail of His own soul and was satisfied—has nothing else to recommend it but its popularity, which is chiefly owing to want of consideration. The same remark applies to Gal. iii. 13.

Dr. Stillingfleet's name came up again, but inasmuch as he subsequently acknowledged many errors and mistakes in the writings of his youth, it is fair to suppose his apology was intended to include those upon more important subjects as well as less—a point of great importance, which has been overlooked frequently by writers appealing to his authority in support of their views. The question about the eternity of punishment has been revived in the present day by a few latitudinarians as ambitious of success, but of less ability, and they have thrown no light on the subject nor answered Leslie's arguments, because most probably they have never read them.

Two other treatises, in 1698–99, were published during the same period, and in reply more immediately to Quaker objections, but equally applicable to other schismatic bodies and their pretensions. (1) The qualifications necessary for administration of the Sacraments lie at the root of the whole matter; and the want of these is one main reason why Sacraments themselves are so glaringly made light of. If it were not for decoying ignorant people from their mother Church, the pretence of retaining Sacraments would be totally discontinued among the pretended followers of John Wesley. (2) Tithes are objected to now simply on the score of covetousness. Tenants delude themselves with the notion that if the legal obligation were removed they should pocket the difference. This is a practical error, which experience alone perhaps may remove; and when the day shall come, surrender must be still larger on the part of lay impropriators than of clergy. But for those who wish to know the sacredness and justice of the claim to tithes on the part of priests apart from political questions, nothing can be more clear and convincing than the account Leslie has furnished. It is, of course, a great difficulty to undo a pernicious system long established, or revert to the original practice in any institution. Where the receipt of money is concerned this difficulty is increased, because people readily suspect there is some crafty purpose at the bottom of any proposed alteration. Nevertheless the collection of tithes in a thoroughly secular way at lawyers' offices, or worse, at public-houses, is so alien from the idea of a religious duty, that some united movement among the clergy ought to be devised for removal of the evil. Until a sacred association be restored instead of these degrading and desecrating customs, tithes will continue to be reluctantly paid and awkwardly received, or be swept away altogether. The spirit of Hophni and Phinehas makes the offering of the Lord abhorred.

> "In sooth, the sorrow of such days
> Is not to be express'd,
> When he that takes, and he that pays
> Are both alike distress'd."[1]

More unjustifiable are lay impropriations. A fact will illustrate Leslie's observation. Five thousand workmen were a few years ago charged a shilling each for admission to the grounds of a Peer in Yorkshire, every acre of which was originally taken from the Church with the obligation of maintaining the ancient hospitality to the poor.

ABRIDGMENT OF THE "SNAKE IN THE GRASS," "SATAN DISROBED," AND "AN ANSWER TO THE SWITCH."

Quakers inherit the hypocrisy as well as heresy of Arians and Socinians, and defend themselves with the same distinctions. Their notion of the one light within is of that which lighteth every man that cometh into the world, therefore every man has it; not natural reason or conscience, but a divine light. We doubt not there is an influence from above, as of the sun upon all the earth, so of the Holy

---
[1] Cowper's "Yearly Distress."

Spirit shining upon the consciences of the most profligate, till by repeated provocations He is banished. But George Fox makes the light within not only an illumination from God, but itself to be the essential God and Christ. Hence Quakers call their souls a part of God, of His being and essence. This monstrous notion is the foundation of all their other errors and blasphemies; they assume to themselves the name of Christ, and make themselves equal with God, infallible and perfectly sinless. Damning all the Christian world from the days of the apostles, while worshipping and adoring one another because of the light, or Christ, or God, which they suppose to be in them; though, if every man has it, it is no peculiarity of the Quakers. Their meaning must be that none but Quakers follow this light. If a man may leave it without knowing he does so, then all Quakers have left it, for ought they know. If he cannot, then there can be no sin of ignorance, which is to contradict both the Law and the Gospel. . . . A man may think himself in the right and be mistaken, which will destroy all the Quakers' certainty. George Fox replies to this objection in the case of S. Paul, that "Christ said it was hard for him to kick against what pricked him, and the light within was that." The apostle himself tells us there were no such pricks of conscience within, for he was fully persuaded and zealous in persecution of the Christians.

Fox says the soul is "infinite, not a creature," which is making it God. Mr. Penn makes excuse for him on account of his ignorance; for by equality with God he meant only unity; and by infinite, something that is not finite. It is a strange excuse for infallibility. Fox affirmed himself to be equal with God, and to be the Christ—the Way, the Truth, and the Life. To have outward visions and revelations. He said, "they (Quakers) are come to what the apostles were in: the Spirit of Christ, the Spirit of God; they witness immediate revelation." "They can discern who are saints and who are devils, and who apostles, without speaking ever a word." "They have the Word of God, Christ which is eternal and infallible, in their heart to judge persons and things."

At other times, when pressed, they bring down this infallibility to mean nothing that distinguishes them from other men. Quakers preaching up the light within, is not only derogatory to the satisfaction paid by Christ for our sins, but it is blasphemous in ascribing to ourselves a power sufficient to work out our own salvation, whereas no wisdom less than infinite could have found out the means, nor power less than infinite could have effected our salvation. Is Quaker infallibility limited to speaking only? They can judge hearts, and tell who are saints and who are devils by winks and glances.

Extraordinary inspirations are not to be credited unless vouched by miracles, and if pretended to come from Him but are not, then they are demonstrated to be from the devil. Here is a mark. Those from the devil generally tend to rebellion, as in the case of Jeroboam and the Ten Tribes. On the other hand, though God sent many prophets to reprove kings and priests, yet they neither rebelled nor set up opposite Altars. When our Saviour came He did not separate from the public worship and communion of the Jewish Church. The apostles frequented the Jewish temple and liturgy, though they had separate meetings for institutions of the Christian religion till the destruction of Jerusalem.

The Quakers' notion of the light within must necessarily cut off dependence upon Holy Scriptures as a Rule either of Faith or manners. Because these are often brought in contradiction to it. Some of their authors called the Holy Scriptures by the wicked and contemptible names of dust, death, serpents, meat, etc.; which one Whitehead says was only in opposition "to some ignorant priests in the north, who would have the very paper and ink and characters to be the Word of God and the gospel." That had not been reason for these barbarous expressions, but there never were in the north or anywhere else priests so ignorant as to say it.

Besides, these were not the words of the languages in which the Scriptures were written, though it is likely enough Fox and others thought so; and they made conscience of sticking to the letter, and saying "thee" and "thou" instead of "you." As the scorpion is said to carry oil which cures its own venom, so the wise providence of God has disposed of most errors, that they carry contradictions to themselves in their own bowels. If the Holy Scriptures must not be called the Word of God because written in letters, why must the Quakers' blasphemous and profane scribbles be styled the Word of the Lord? Have they not broken off from the Church government established in England and all the Christian world? Yet they call any opposition to their "Church" no less than rebellion against God Himself.

In short, enthusiasts have no principles, no rule, but their own fancy, which they take for Inspiration; and there never was any enthusiasm in the world that exceeded the Quakers'. None have ever so condemned and vilified the Holy Scriptures as they have done. Nor was there ever, from their first appearing in the world, one Chapter read at any of their meetings, though many of their own epistles have been frequently, and enjoined to be read there; pursuant to which principle, in their disputes among themselves, they appeal to their own writings instead of the Scriptures.

So have they committed the wildest idolatry to one another, putting themselves in the place of God. Fox said, "The Quakers are in the power of God and in the authority of the Lamb, and are upon the throne." In a letter to Oliver Cromwell he called himself "the Son of God," "the Branch," "the Star," "the Door that ever was, the same yesterday, to-day, and for ever." Though they will not give their hat or a nod to men of the world, it is their custom to bow to one another as to the light within, which is Christ. A woman threw herself on her knees at Fox's feet, saying, "Thou art the Son of the living God." Another preacher in a public meeting accosted him, "Thou art the King of saints." At which another woman being offended, her excuse was that it was not to Fox she spoke those words, but to Christ who was within him. This was the very ground and foundation of all idolatry, namely, the supposed presence or inhabitation of the divinity in creatures or images. In a book called "The Guilty Clergyman Unveiled," they make the Quakers' blood to be the blood of Christ by which we are saved. It cannot be surprising if we find them altogether heterodox in the fundamental principles of the Christian religion. They acknowledge a Three, but deny a Trinity, which is to confess the same thing in English and to deny it in Latin; but their meaning is, they would not have the Three in heaven to be Persons before Christ was born, and so these must be creatures.

They say Christ took flesh, but, as they explain, no otherwise than as angels assumed bodies; or as He inspired or dwelt in the prophets of old. They deny any proper incarnation, or that Jesus and Christ were one Person, or that Christ did carry up with Him a body into heaven, nor know what Christ did with the body of Jesus after He had raised it from the grave. There is no other

Scriptures misrepresented.

Christ but what is within them, and they call themselves His body and Church. Mr. Penn will not have the true Christ to be a Person, but only a moral principle. And that the "body which suffered at Jerusalem was the body of Christ, not assumed into His person, but as a cloak or veil like that in which angels appear for a time; but that the outward person which suffered was properly the Son of God we utterly deny."

They construe the imputation of Christ's righteousness to be only within them, but have a notion of inward blood-shedding, expressly denying Christ's outward blood to be the blood of the new covenant, or more than that of any good man. Mr. Penn says the serpent is a spirit, and nothing can bruise its head but something spiritual; consequently the seed of the promise is an holy principle of light and life, which, received into the heart, bruiseth the serpent's head, and this is Christ, the light within. A supposition of so pernicious a nature that it unchristianizes any one who holds it; for the faith of Christians is built upon Jesus Christ as the Seed promised to bruise the serpent's head, and that this was performed by the shedding of His blood outwardly upon the cross, as a propitiation and satisfaction for the sins of the whole world. By the help of this distinction of an outward and inward Christ's blood, etc., the Quakers can subscribe to the whole Creed yet not mean one word of it. Quakers are direct Socinians, for they deny positively the satisfaction of Christ, and copy their arguments, though it would seem without knowing it. Mr. Penn understands that long and elegant description of the resurrection of our bodies in 1 Cor. xv., "only of the spiritual state of the soul in this life." Now, among other names of reproach Mr. Penn bestows upon one of the Separate Quakers, are Hymenæus and Philetus, not minding how near home this brought the accusation (2 Tim. ii. 18); for those were direct Quakers who spiritualized the resurrection from the letter, and meant it only of the rising up of Christ in our hearts, which S. Paul calls "overthrowing the faith."

As they deny any outward resurrection, so they deny any outward heaven. The text, 1 Cor. xi. 6, of "showing forth the Lord's death till He come," they explain to mean coming spiritually in our hearts, and so suppose there is an end of that ordinance; though they cannot deny that Christ was come in the hearts of the apostles and primitive Christians, none of whom dreamed of the time being expired—the same time appointed for the other sacrament—"always, even unto the end of the world." Christ has promised His gift to go along with His institution by the hands of His ministers, and therefore the outward ordinance is necessary, even where the inward gift has been already attained (Acts x. 47). Their neglect of these ordinances has lost to the Quakers the reality and the thing signified. The devil having stolen the body or outward part of religion, the soul soon disappeared; for religion can no more live without outward and corporal means, than the soul while here without the body; and hence this corporal service, Rom. xi. 1, is called "reasonable." Whoever goes about to separate bodily from spiritual service does as much murder religion as he that should separate a man's soul from his body. Quakers never give us any creed or summary of their faith. They find fault with others, but tell not plainly what they hold themselves. G. Whitehead has at last done it, and comprises it in just twelve articles, but in such dubious and general terms as to deceive an unwary reader, yet keep from contradicting the heart of the heresy.

There is no point wherein the Quakers are more fierce

and positive than in opposition to tithes, because if they were taken away they suppose the clergy would sink of course, and be deprived of their subsistence, and so the total ruin of the Church follow. What if the light within should allow some to pay, as being legally established? Would their rulers give them leave to follow their light? When some did so they were proceeded against as rebels to God. It is an ingenious excuse that Fox only wrote against payment to the Popish clergy, not the right of the Church of England as settled by the civil government. Yet there were no tithes paid to any Popish priest in England ever since Quakerism appeared. And why do they boast of sufferings and imprisonments for not paying tithes as a sort of martyrdom for the truth? Now, the evangelical priesthood is after the order of Melchizedek, and tithes are claimed as being due to that; so that all their arguments as to the Law and Levitical priesthood being superseded operate nothing against a superior and more excellent Order. I have no manner of doubt but they are as ancient as priesthood itself; that is, as Adam, from whom descended the knowledge of tithes, as of sacrifice and priesthood, which are relative; the one being the maintenance, the other the office of the priesthood, therefore the one must be as ancient as the other. God reserved the tenth part of our substance and the seventh of our time as a tribute and acknowledgment to Him from whom we receive all. They are called "His inheritance," not as then instituted, but then given to the Levites. Nor is Melchizedek's tithing mentioned as the beginning or first rising, but as a thing well known and received even in those early ages. The word enthusiasm signifies inspiration, and may mean a good as well as evil one; though from frequent false pretences it is generally used in the worst sense. The sort owned in the Church of England is full as much as any sober Quaker can mean by the light within. It is the Alpha and Omega of our religion, as shown in our Offices of Baptism, Confirmation, and Holy Orders; in our Catechism and Common Prayers. Then why do they break off and separate from our communion? Miraculous gifts are of much less value than saving graces, so are not to be greatly coveted or prayed for; and to pretend falsely to any such gifts is downright blasphemy.

Quakers say in the "Switch" that it is "impossible for man to withstand and leave the light without knowing that he does so." This is to answer a suggestion in the "Snake," and they suppose that such men as Paul, while a persecutor, had before resisted the light, for punishment of which it was hid from their eyes. This will not help Quakerism; for by their own argument this strong delusion may be sent for former resisting of the light. Besides, this casts a foul reflection upon S. Paul, as if he had been a wilful sinner against his own convictions, contrary to his testimony (Acts xxvi. 4; Phil. iii. 6); whereas his great sincerity was the cause of his obtaining mercy. They will needs have his miraculous conversion to have come, not from the glorious apparition and outward voice from heaven, but from the pricks of his light within, against which he could not kick. Where was the inward command before the outward voice? See how unwilling Quakers are to allow anything to the outward revelations of God. It is mere fancy, and nothing else, which they mistake for divine light within them, and the power that accompanies it is the delusion of Satan.

Here is the mystery of their perfection, their saintship, and their being equal to God; for this seed in them they suppose to have been first conceived in their virgin hearts by the Holy Ghost, then to grow up in them to be a Son born in them, and at last to become the everlasting Father. At the same time they own they have the evil one in them too; and what evil they do is only his, and not theirs. If so, then the good in them is no more theirs than the evil. And why should the evil deeds of other men be accounted theirs any more than those of the Quakers? They think their faith in the light within as God and Christ makes them acceptable, and atones for their sins, which will not be imputed to them, but to others who have not this faith. So the Quakers and we are at the utmost distance possible. We differ about the object of faith—they or we are blasphemers and idolaters; there is no compounding; their doctrine is totally exclusive of any Christ without. And they mean that it was the same in them which suffered at Jerusalem, and that He was then not outward more than now. The Quakers having rejected our Lord and Christ, it cannot be expected that they should place the satisfaction for sin in anything He did or suffered. Now, this satisfaction made for our sins by the perfect obedience, sufferings, and death of our Lord and only Saviour, Jesus of Nazareth, performed in His own person for us, is the only meritorious and procuring cause of our salvation. And all this is wholly without us; we have no share in the propitiation, atonement, or satisfaction made for sin; that is wholly attributed to Christ. The satisfaction is applied to us by a true lively faith, and this is our justification. A true and sincere repentance succeeding this faith, with amendment of life, and a due thankfulness for our redemption, is our sanctification, which cannot be wrought in us but by the inward operation of the Holy Ghost. But the Gift is not the Giver. That is the great mistake into which Quakers have run. The light within is the gift of God, but not God; it is not the sufferings and spiritual blood of this which makes the atonement; our faith must not be in this, but the meritorious passion of the Son of God wholly without us, though inwardly applied to the heart by faith. Justification and sanctification are distinguished; one wholly the work of Christ without us, the other of His Holy Spirit within our hearts; the one but once performed, the other daily to be renewed.

AN ABRIDGMENT OF THE SOCINIAN CONTROVERSY.

The "Switch" quotes from William Penn that very positively he determines the resurrection is a change, not of accidents, but of bodies; and that the body which dies shall never rise any more. We mean by the resurrection of the body rising of the same body. It can be meant of no other; for if it be a perfectly new body which is given to the soul, it may be called a creation, or anything but a resurrection.

The whole question concerning the doctrines of the Trinity and Incarnation is, whether they are revealed in Holy Scripture or not. And the way to know this is twofold. 1. From the very words of Scripture itself. 2. From the current sense of the Church in those ages when the Scriptures were written and downwards; they who learned the faith from the mouths of the inspired writers, and conveyed their writings down to us, being the most capable of any to give us their true sense and meaning.

We not only ought not, but it is not in our power, to believe anything but what we think we have reason to believe. We are forced from plain reason to acknowledge a First Cause, which gave being to all other things, and from whom all other things proceeded. Then from the same reason we must believe that the First Cause did not produce itself; likewise that this First Cause had no beginning. We believe, though we cannot solve these difficulties and seeming contradictions; yet because you cannot solve difficulties, as in the Trinity and Incarnation, you reject the revelation in the Holy Scriptures, and the current sense of the Catholic Church. . . . A contradiction is only of the same thing, and in the same respect. That three persons may be in one nature is no contradiction. Nor must that be a contradiction in one nature which is so in another. What is a contradiction to body is not to soul; what is to time is none to eternity; what is with men is not so with God.

If there were words which could express the nature of God properly, or as He is known to the angels of heaven, they would be as unintelligible to us as the word seeing is to one born blind. Thus we understand the word Person quite differently from the person of a man upon earth. Is it not a contradiction that the Son should be as old as the Father? Because it is among men it will not follow that it is so in God. . . . Light and heat are necessary effects of the sun; it is before them in nature, because they proceed from it; but not before them in time, because they are necessary effects, and the sun cannot be without them. Though it cannot be in human nature that the son should be as old as the father, yet it may be in the divine, for the production no doubt is necessary. These are only illustrations, nor can there be an exact parallel betwixt God and any creature. I go on to show what is no contradiction in the faculties of the soul—understanding, memory, will. These are of the constitution of the soul, and it could not be a soul without them, therefore each must be as old as the other, and all as old as the soul; though these faculties act distinctly yet not separately, and the soul is not divided or multiplied, but acts in each or all of them.

There are Persons and not faculties in the Godhead. Scripture calls Christ the express image of His (Father's) Person, the image of His subsistence or personality Again, a person being the most complete and perfect subsistence, as subsisting by itself and not in another (like faculties or qualities), must be given to God. Passions come and go, but faculties in the soul are of perpetual necessity, as dimensions in a body. And our blessed Saviour, in the parable of the Sower, describing the several ways by which the seed becomes unfruitful, arranges them after the three faculties of the soul, but not after the passions, which are many. We may rise up higher as on a ladder to view more of the perfection of God.

To be beneficial to others is an image of God: this is expressed in the heavens and their influence upon earth, but they are not sensible of it. It is then a nearer image to know when we do good and take pleasure or satisfaction in it, as God did in His works, and saw that they were very good. But there is a higher degree of happiness, a yet nearer image to God, when we ourselves are made the object of our own benefactions, when we can do good to ourselves and taste our own happiness. This is performed by what we call self-reflection, whereby we become the object of our own knowledge and love. In this consists the essential happiness of God, in the knowledge and love of Himself; and this, reflected perfectly from one Person to another, is infinitely more complete than the shadow of it in the reciprocal reflection of the faculties in our soul.

This leads me to another step on the ladder. To the happiness there is in thought, there is a further added, which is to communicate that thought to another; without which the soul would be a very solitary thing. Without conversation life would be a burden; the Son is called the Word of God. He is also called the Word, as He was the instrument by which God made all things, and commuciated Himself to creatures; and the creation is described as being all spoken. For there is another communication beyond that of thoughts by words—to communicate one's self fully and entire in full perfection. Since the communication of one's nature is a perfection, it is of necessity that God must have it.

S. Athanasius did not invent the terms and distinctions of his Creed; he but followed the same used in Holy Scripture and by the Catholic Church before him. God is not compounded or made up of anything; His unity is the most perfect of all unities. But in every unity there is a union of diverse things, for there is no union of one. Unity in bodies is by way of composition. Spirits are not compounded, and cannot be divided. And the Persons are not parts of God, nor is He compounded of them or divided among them; but the whole Deity, flowing in its full infinity perpetually from one Person to another, is in the eternal enjoyment of its own beatitude blessed for ever in itself: in so perfect a unity as can be but faintly represented in the unity of any creature even of a soul.

Enjoyment and satisfaction in the union of bodies is from the union of their souls; this is what we call love. Friendship is the strongest tie among men, and the chief cement of conjugal affection. S. Paul speaks how intimately we are united to Christ, and in Him with the whole blessed Trinity, which the apostle calls "a great mystery."

... By the word God in Holy Scripture always given to the Father only, the whole Trinity is meant; but is sometimes used even in distinction from the Father, and sometimes the term Father is given to the Son. Even heathen philosophers held three supreme and almighty principles which they called likewise persons from the Jews, but fell into sundry errors.

There is another point—the Incarnation; that the divine and human natures should be both joined in one Person: in the words of S. Athanasius, "as the reasonable soul and flesh is one man, so God and man is one Christ." Now, there are no two things in the world so different as the natures of body and soul; hardly anything except that of being agrees to both. Yet how are they united so as both to make but one person? The parting of them is the destruction of the person, and even while they remain united their natures and properties are no ways confounded and blended together. By what links and chains God and man can be joined together so as to make one Person, the same to be finite and infinite, I cannot tell, nor how God communicates of Himself to creatures; no more than how the same creatures can be mortal and immortal, nor the links and chains by which spirit and flesh are joined together. But what is impossible with men is easy to God. In order to our right understanding of Holy Scripture, the ground and foundation we have to go upon in disputed passages is the sense in which they to whom they were delivered, who learnt them from apostles, taught them again, and so on through the several ages of the Church. What was the common and received doctrine in far-distant Churches must be what was delivered to them, and could not by any concert or contrivance be the same. And this was the method taken with Arius in the Council of Alexandria.

They did not go with him upon his logic, nor criticism and etymology of words, but, "Who ever heard such things before?" And the new notions started by Arius were rejected as novelties and breaches upon the Christian faith.

One Cerinthus, an arch-heretic and disciple of Simon Magus, affirmed that Jesus was the son of Joseph and Mary; that Christ came upon Him in the form of a dove at His baptism, inspired Him with the knowledge of God the Father, and with the power of working miracles; that when Jesus suffered Christ left Him and flew up into heaven without partaking any of His sufferings. Against this Cerinthus and his followers S. John wrote his Gospel. Two answers which the "History of Unitarianism" gives to this text contradict one another, that by the Word is only meant God's power and wisdom; and that the appellation of God is given to angels and men, as Moses was called a God to Pharaoh. The first makes the Word not to be anything different from God, the second says that it is man and not God. We do not say that any of the Persons are distinct from God, but in God. And there is an example of this among men; we do not say that John is a distinct person from human nature, but in it, from other persons who possess the same. The Word is a distinct Person from the Father, because personal actions are attributed to Him, and because He is set up as the Object of our adoration. In Psalm cx. 1, the second Lord spoken of was Christ is plain from S. Matt. xxii. 44, and the Jews so understood it; nor can there be a greater distinction of persons than for one to speak to the other—one to sit on the other's right hand, one to subdue the other's enemies. Therefore by the Word a Person must be meant, and not only a property or attribute of God. S. John xvi. 13, 14 proves the diversity of Persons in the Godhead. How could one Person be more distinguished from another or from a naked quality than to say, as here, "He shall not speak of Himself," and "He shall receive of Mine, and show it unto you"? Again, in Acts viii. 29, and Acts xiii. 2, it is clearly a Person who spoke, the Holy Ghost.

S. Matt. xii. 31. It is said of Moses "they provoked his spirit," meaning him; then this is the meaning put upon the text, that sins against God are to be forgiven, but sins against His Spirit are not to be forgiven. But the spirit of Moses was not a person, that is, not subsisting by itself, therefore we cannot affirm anything of it otherwise than of Moses. And it would be the same absurdity to say anything of the Spirit of God otherwise than of God, if He were not a Person, that is, subsisting by Himself.

S. Matthew xviii. 19. Mr. Biddle's exposition of the text is, baptizing unto such a one is sometimes meant of baptizing in his name. As our fathers are said to have been baptized unto Moses, and some persons unto John's baptism. So it is not a proof that such a one is God. Being baptized in the name of such a one includes being baptized unto him; but being baptized unto such a one does not include being baptized in his name. Unto such a one may mean no more than his ministry, but in one's name is owning him the author of my religion, a dedicating and devoting myself to him, which is not lawful to do to any creature (1 Cor. i. 13–15). And there is not an instance in all the Scripture of any that were baptized in the name of any creature. To be baptized into Christ's baptism is all one with being baptized in the name of Christ, because the form of His baptism was in His own name, together with that of the Father and of the Holy Ghost; but to be baptized unto John's baptism was not to be baptized in the name of John, for his baptism referred to Christ, who should come after him. The question is not of being baptized into the profession of a doctrine, for all are obliged by their baptism to profess the doctrine of that person in whose name they are baptized; as no man is enlisted in the name of a cause, but of some person for whose cause he fights. S. John iii. 13. Socinians understand literally, and say that before our Lord entered upon His office of Messiah he was taken up to heaven to be instructed in the mind and will of God, as Moses was into the mount; and from thence descended to execute this office and to declare this will; and that the same is hinted in S. John vi. 38, 46, 51, and viii. 40. None of these passages say so. Before His incarnation He was there, and came down; nor any need was there for Christ being taken up to heaven to be instructed in the will of God, since upon this author's own principles the Word of God, His whole wisdom and power, abode in Him. S. John viii. 58. Socinians explain this, before Abraham was it was decreed that Christ should come. The words will not bear it, and the Scripture is to be understood, like other writings, by the common use of words. If he meant in decree only, it was no answer to their question. Our Lord did not speak sophistically. Irenæus understands this text of Christ's existing before Abraham. But why should the Jews go to stone Him for this answer? There was no sort of difficulty in it as Socinians explain it. The Jews say these misunderstood it. Then they must suppose that He spoke with a mental reservation, on purpose that they might mistake. Yes, say they, He spake "in parables, that seeing they might not see," etc., but not to hinder men from believing.

Christ says, "I and the Father are One," by which Tertullian proves that we pray to the Son when we pray to the Father. And S. Cyprian quotes this text as proving the natural union of the Father and the Son. "Thou being a man makest Thyself God." A natural son partakes of the true nature of his father; in which sense to call any one the Son of God is to call Him true and real God, as the Jews here understood it; in which sense Christ is God's only begotten. They explain their own meaning past dispute. They could not say, "Thou makest Thyself God," if they had meant only a man. On the other hand, if He had not been such as they meant, without doubt He would have renounced the blasphemy, nor suffered the Jews to go away in so mortal an error, nor lose His life for it. "Ye believe in God, believe also in Me." No prophet, nor apostle, nor angel durst thus compare himself with God. "He that hath seen Me hath seen the Father." He who will not hearken to a herald despiseth the king that sent him, but one cannot say that he who sees a herald sees his king. "If ye ask anything in My name I will do it." No man or angel ever spoke after this manner.

"The Holy Ghost shall receive of Christ's." Why? Because, says He, "all things that the Father hath are Mine, therefore said I that He shall receive of Mine." And "I will send Him unto you." Will one give to a creature the power of sending the Holy Spirit? It is objected again, that the Holy Spirit appeared in the form of a dove on Christ, and of cloven tongues on the apostles. The first was to signify the meek and peaceable spirit of Christ, and the second to express the gift then bestowed, not the form or shape of the giver. It is a vulgar error that there was any shape of a dove at our Saviour's baptism. There was a bodily shape, else people could not have seen it, which descended leisurely, hovering as a dove, that people might take more notice, and to express the overshadowing of the

Holy Spirit, and it abode and remained upon our Saviour. Rom. ix. 5. The Person spoken of here is over all and blessed for ever, and is God. The apostle is only speaking of Christ from the beginning of the chapter. Tertullian quotes the text as proving Christ to be God. S. Cyprian does the same. And that other expression, "as concerning the flesh," shows plainly that He had another nature derived to Him from His birth of the blessed Virgin (Acts xi. 30).

S. John ii. 24, 25. There is a difference between this and Elisha's knowing what the King of Syria spoke in his bed-chamber, and it can be no parallel.

Phil. ii. 6. The form of a thing is its essence, not its shadow or likeness, and therefore whatever is in the form of God is of His essence, and consequently must be God. The inference of the apostle is, that because Christ was in the form of God, therefore He was equal to God. If Christ was originally a creature, as the Socinians would have Him, and advanced to the divine honour, or a made God, then indeed it could not be excused from a great robbery, presumption, and blasphemy for Him to pretend to be equal with God. The apostle in this text seems to have foreseen and obviated the Socinian heresy. Again, if Christ was nothing but a servant and a man, how can it be said that "He took upon Him the form of a servant"? It is not said that He took upon Him the form of God, because He always was in that form, and so could not take it. As to the objection that the apostle urges Christ's example of love and humility, this must suppose a choice in Him; for who calls it humility to be born poor? Does a man choose to be born? Therefore it must have been before coming into the world that He made His choice.

Heb. vii. 3. Melchizedek is compared to the Son of

God, but the Son of God really was what Melchizedek was said to be. Then how came Melchizedek to be like the Son of God if there were none when he was made? The pattern after which anything is made must be before the copy. How can these things be reconciled upon the Socinian principle? But in the Christian scheme it is most easy; namely, the eternal Son of God was before Melchizedek, but in time incarnate after him. And yet it was the same Jesus, yesterday, to-day, and for ever, as expressly said of Him, Heb. xiii. 8, and other places of Scripture. It is objected that Christ should have assistance of the Holy Ghost, Himself being God? Christ submitted Himself to the infirmities of our nature, for He came to be an example to us, which He had not been if His divinity had exerted itself to the utmost. Therefore He was perfected as we are by the unction of the Holy Spirit. All the Three Persons are joint—as in their nature so in all their operations; though yet some operations are more peculiarly but not exclusively attributed to one than to another.

In the Creed God is named at first as a nature or species to individuals; then the several Persons follow in their order. If this be sufficient with us to express our meaning, it was much more so before the Arians had disturbed the doctrine of the Trinity, which occasioned a further explication in the Nicene and Athanasian Creeds.

"They whom we now call Socinians were by the Fathers and first ages of Christianity called Nazarenes, Ebionites," etc. They were so called and condemned as heretics, and they stand condemned as such to this day by the whole Christian Church. The spirit of antichrist is the same with the Socinian opinion, that Christ had no being before He was born of the Virgin. S. John does not only say that Christ was flesh, but came in a body of flesh. Must

He not then have existed before He came, as was so clothed? He says also that "He was" in the beginning with God, was sent by God to take upon Him our flesh, that He came to do this—to deny it is an antichrist. Mahomet should be accepted as one of the fathers of Socinianism, only he is much more Christian than these heretics; but they are not so well known in the world now as he, therefore Socinians do not own him to be of their party.

The doctrine of satisfaction is a main foundation of the Christian religion. God gave his Son to be a propitiation for sin, and received from Him satisfaction for our sins; and this proves Him to be both God and Man. God because none else could pay infinite satisfaction for infinite goodness offended; and man, because that which offended must make the satisfaction. But human nature could not do this, "in that it was weak through the flesh;" therefore, says S. Paul, God sending "His own Son in the likeness of sinful flesh, and for sin," or by a sacrifice for sin (as our margent reads it) "condemned sin in the flesh." The Socinians argue against the satisfaction, that it would hinder piety because sin is called a debt. But the sophistry consists in not distinguishing aright betwixt a debt of sin and money. God does not lose by sin as a man loses his money; that is a gross conception. It is an offence against love and goodness, and "God is love." Sufferings in hell are not intended for the amendment of offenders, but as a satisfaction to justice, the time for forgiveness being over. There is not in Scripture any intimation of the abatement or non-execution of its eternal punishment, which would not be so if the worm should die or the fire be quenched. I will not say that everybody must be damned that does not believe the satisfaction of Christ, but that none can be saved except by it; infants, fools, and madmen, and those who never heard of it are excused from believing it, yet are saved by virtue of it.

ABRIDGMENT OF "QUALIFICATIONS FOR ADMINISTRATION OF SACRAMENTS."

These qualifications are of two sorts—personal and sacerdotal. Personal, the holiness of the administrator. Though this be a great qualification to fit a man for such a holy administration, yet it does not alone qualify any man to take this upon him. But there is moreover required a sacerdotal qualification, that is, an outward commission (Heb. v. 4.; S. Matt. iv.). What other man can pretend to it upon the account of personal excellencies in himself? So Christ did not leave it to His disciples, to every one's opinion of his own sufficiency, to thrust himself into the vineyard; but chose twelve apostles by name, and after them seventy others of an inferior order, whom He sent to preach. His apostles did proceed in the same manner after His Ascension (Acts xiv. 23). And those thus ordained had power to ordain others (1 Tim. v. 22; Titus i. 5). S. Clement says the apostles had known through the Lord Jesus Christ that there would be a contention concerning the name of bishop; on this account they did themselves appoint the persons, and established an order how, when they should die, fit and approved men should succeed them in their ministry.[1]

This succession is preserved and derived only in bishops, as the continuance of any society is deduced in the succession of the chief governors, not its inferior officers. And wherever Christianity was planted, episco-

---
[1] 1 Ep. Corinth., pp. 43, 44.

pacy was established without exception. The words bishop and presbyter are sometimes used in the same sense; they may as well prove that Christ was only a deacon, because He is so called in Rom. xv. 8; or that apostles were aldermen, or emperors no more than generals of armies, or kings only dukes. It was charged to Timothy how he should sit in judgment, etc., upon his presbyters (1 Tim. v. 19), which destroys the Presbyterian claim of parity. If they will take S. Jerome's word, whom they boast to favour them so much, then what Aaron, his sons, and the Levites were in the temple, that same are bishops, presbyters, and deacons in the Church.

Presbyterians alone of all Dissenters have any pretence to succession; so what has been said must operate still more strongly against others who set up merely their own pretended gifts. It is objected that idolatry and other great errors unchurch a people, and consequently break the episcopal succession. But Scripture supposes a Christian may be an idolater, therefore it does not unchurch (1 Cor. v. 11). There were frequent lapses to idolatry in the Church of the Jews; yet this did not unchurch them, nor deprive them of a competent measure of the Holy Spirit. Apply this to the evangelical priesthood which is as surely fixed in the bishops of the Church, and its succession continued, as the Levitical priesthood was confirmed and continued in Aaron's line. Abuses in the sacerdotal commission do not take it away, till God do so.

The whole Christian world, as it has always been, is episcopal except a few Dissenters, who in less than two hundred years last past have arisen like a wart upon the face of the Western Church. And among them every class does condemn the rest; and each denies the other's ordination. What allowance God may make for those who think their ordination to be good, I will not determine. But they have no right to expect this allowance who have been warned beforehand, and notwithstanding venture. To state the case most impartially, to receive baptism from Dissenters is at least a hazard of many thousands to one; but to receive it from episcopal clergy has no hazard of validity at all, even disowned by themselves. The only objection of Quakers is the necessity of great personal holiness in the administrators, without which they cannot see how the spiritual effects can be conveyed.

His greatness is often most magnified in the meanness of the instruments by which He works.

The argument will hold more strongly as to the Sacraments than in the office of preaching; because in preaching much depends upon the qualification of the person as to invention, memory, judgment, etc.; but in the administration of an outward Sacrament, nothing is required as of necessity but the lawfulness of the commission. It is contrary to all God's former institutions; the wickedness of priests under the law did not excuse any of the people from bringing their sacrifices, nor were their offerings less accepted. We should be in a much worse condition under the Gospel demonstration if the effect of Christ's institution depended either wholly or in part upon the personal holiness of His priests (1 Cor. iii. 21). This was the error of the ancient Donatists, for which reason they rejected all baptism except performed by themselves, arguing, "How shall a man give that to another which he has not himself?" But Optatus answers that "God was the Giver, and not man." They were nothing but ministers or workmen, and that as when a cloth was dyed, the change of the cloth came from the colours infused, not from the virtue of the dyer; so that in baptism the change of the baptized came from the virtue of the sacrament, not from the administrator. Therefore let us work that God, who has promised, may bestow the effect. Consider the grievous sin of schism no less than the rending of Christ's body; and therefore great things ought to be borne rather than run into it—even all things, except what is sinful. There is an objection not worth an answer, but that I would condescend to the meanest and leave no stumbling-block; viz. that no visible effect is seen from our baptisms, and therefore it is concluded there is no virtue. To make this argument of any force, it must be proved that none do receive any benefit; for if some do and others do not, this must be charged upon the disposition of the recipient. Simon Magus received no benefit; the devil entered into Judas; yet the other apostles did receive benefit. Therefore we are commanded to examine and prepare our hearts.

Modern Presbyterians have departed as much from Calvin and Luther as from all the Christian world; while at the same time they would seem to pay the greatest reverence to these reformers, and much more than to the first and purest ages of Christianity. In this they imitate the hardness of the Jews, who built the sepulchres of those prophets whom their fathers slew, while at the same time they adhered to and outdid the wickedness of their fathers in persecuting the successors of those prophets.

Abridgment of "Divine Right of Tithes."

The subject of tithes is the great Diana of the Quakers. Milton has more wit, but little more argument than them. His fancy was too predominant for his judgment; his talent lay so much in satire that he hated reasoning; or rather he had not leave to make use of it while he wrote for hire against his own opinions, which appears by what he wrote unbribed, contrary to what he afterwards had a pension to set up. He sacrificed a noble genius to the vices of the age. Nothing else could have made him set down the cry of the ignorant Quakers, that we "made use of the Popish arguments for tithes," whereas all that have any skill in these matters know that Popish writers were the first corrupters of the doctrine of tithes. If the name "hireling" be meant of those who take anything for their preaching, it flies directly in the face of our Saviour (S. Luke x. 7). But if it be meant that they are the culpable hirelings who value the hire more than their work, that can be only known by Him who knows the heart, and can be guessed at only by us from the consequences. And for S. Paul's preaching gratis, it tells against Milton, for the apostle asserts his right to have been burdensome. He, abating of that for prudential considerations at that time, is far from a precedent for all times and places; for the same apostle tells us that the other apostles did not, and himself did otherwise at other times and places.

Selden, on what he calls the "History of Tithes," carries on his more underground, and gives such an account of them as would effectually overthrow them. Covetousness is so the root of sacrilege, that as no man would rob God for nought, so can none return from his sacrilege till he is cured of the covetousness which caused it. And covetousness cannot be cured while we are possessed with that distrust of God which is the cause of it. When God created man He instituted a worship for the happiness of man, not that He wanted anything from him. God required our absolute dependence upon Him as to necessaries of life. He reserved great portions of time to be employed in His worship. He required a tenth part of substance as a yearly tribute. To this end were tithes and sabbaths instituted, to use us to daily acts of faith; and till we are used to these we can never rise to higher. The command is often repeated that none should appear before the Lord empty. This part of worship cannot be paid after our fancies, but as God has appointed. Therefore what part of our substance God has reserved as a part of His worship is not to be reckoned among bare acts of charity, but must be offered in such manner and method as He has prescribed.

It is evident that a tenth part of all increase under the law was reserved to be offered to the priests, not only for a maintenance, but as to the Lord. And the tithes were reckoned in the same rank with the sacrifices and other offerings (Lev. xxvii. 30; Numb. xviii. 24; Deut. xii. 6). And the substraction of tithes was called "robbing God" (Mal. iii. 8). That this institution was before the law is evident from the example of Abraham and Jacob. The apostle argues the greatness of Melchizedek over Abraham from the paying of tithes to him; if a gratuity it would have argued the other way, for a giver is greater than a receiver. And the preference given to Melchizedek was because of his priesthood. The word is observable—"tithed" Abraham, that is, exacted tithe as his due. And because it was part of the priests' office to receive the Lord's tithe, a receiver of tithe and a priest are synonymous (Heb. x. 8, 23).

Selden infers that only a tithe of the spoils were given. It would prove nothing but that spoils taken in war are tithable, as well as profits of labour in peace.

The word signifies literally "tops of heaps," being the choicest and best parts. Suidas says that Abraham gave to Melchizedek a tenth part of "all" before mention of the tithe of the spoils, which cannot limit the other. Jacob's vow was not only a vow but a further declaration that the

Lord only was his God, because he would offer his tithe only unto Him. However Gentiles paid their tithes, the notion was received time out of mind, and tenths generally mean the same thing; and though not always, yet often in sacred writings. If tithes were thought so sacred that they made conscience of paying them without compulsion of any temporal law, this shows the notion they had of a higher original, *jure divino*. The notion which all the world had was as of a tribute to God for what He had bestowed, and to procure His further blessing which holds as well for one year as another. If the end of offering tithes can be no other than a due acknowledgment of what we have received from Him, the reason must reach to all things. And this was the notion of the Gentiles. There is no account how the practice of tithes began among the Gentiles; it was time out of mind. Melchizedek is the first of whom express mention is made that he received them, and the first called priest. Yet no one doubts that there were priests before him; as little can we doubt that tithes were paid before, for his tithing of Abraham is not mentioned as the introduction of a new custom, else who had known what it meant? and we should have been told. On the contrary, the apostle argues that it was paid as a tribute due to Melchizedek, and thence infers his superiority. Selden supposes him to have been Shem, the eldest son of Noah; so that we must pass the Flood to search for a higher original of tithes. Sacrifices were appointed as types of Christ our true Passover; and Adam could have no knowledge of Him but by revelation. It is allowed that sacrifice and priesthood and marriage were instituted at first by God, and descended by immemorial tradition from Adam. Now tithe, as well as any of these, was universally received among the Gentiles, and must have been from the beginning. How else should all the world have hit upon a tenth more than any other number, in nations far distant and without any correspondence? The gospel was not meant to overturn anything in the law, but to confirm by fulfilling it. Tithes were no part either of the typical or ceremonial laws; therefore were not fulfilled in Christ. He has given express approbation to them as an act of worship to God. He would never have commanded that to disciples; which He would not have His disciples to fulfil more abundantly. The apostle says that Christ received tithes (for his words, Heb. vii. 8, can be meant of no other), and then He has confirmed them not only negatively but positively, Himself now in heaven ever living to receive them.

Again S. Paul, 1 Cor. ix. 13, 14, makes a comparison of the tithes and offerings of the altar. "Even so" Evangelical priests should live of the gospel—to have a revenue like that of the temple—else it were not "even so." The only dispute which could then be, was to whom they should be paid, whether to the priests of the Temple or the Gospel. The priests of the temple were then in possession of them, and would have raised a much more severe persecution against the Gospel, if its priests had pretended to them. When the Papacy had grown great upon the ruins of Episcopacy, the Pope took upon him to alienate the tithes of the Church, forgetting the first and chief end of them as a worship and tribute due to God, and insisting only upon the secondary consideration of being a maintenance for the clergy. Schoolmen made a new scheme about the year 1230 A.D., that the particular quantity of a tenth was only of ecclesiastical institution. There is no stop in the art of encroachment, so the Begging Friars after this got up and made tithes to be perfectly arbitrary at the will and pleasure of the giver, mere alms which might be given to any religious beggar; a shameless preaching of greed to rob the Secular clergy. Popes have in several ages taken upon them to sell the tithes of the Church to laymen. In England we have the sacred sanction of vows to that general obligation. Tithes have been dedicated to God by kings and parliaments, with the most solemn imprecations upon themselves and their posterities who should take back or retract any part, from before the Conquest down to Henry VIII. Selden yields that they are unalienable and irrevocable. And Spelman, in his "History of Sacrilege," has given many remarkable instances of the ruin and destruction of those families who shared most of the Church lands and tithes in the beginning of the Reformation, and before Henry VIII. had lived to see that incredible mass of wealth which he had robbed from the Churches all melt away like ice before the sun, and his own vast treasure with it, insomuch that he was at last reduced to coin base money.

There can be no pretence for the lawfulness of impropriations, when those very Acts of Parliament which took them from the Church and gave them to laymen, acknowledge they are God's dues and His rights; and they were obliged to frame a particular Act to enable laymen to sue for tithe, which before they could not do, though in it tithe is named as being due to Almighty God. Tithes are to be paid out of all our gifts and goods. Some part of our substance, a tenth at least, is due to God as an act of worship, which is different from an act of charity; therefore we must give to the poor out of our own nine parts. Though we give the full proportion, yet if we do not give it of the very best, we fail as to the quality of our gift, and forfeit the blessing.

All who worship God ought to pay tithes. All that

expect His blessing upon the remaining nine parts. This is no harder to the poor than to the rich, because they pay proportionably; and it is accepted by God as much, if given with a good heart, as the offerings of the rich. He did not give the Levites temporal possessions among their brethren, but settled upon them "His own inheritance," which, as the priesthood had its original and institution, so it should have its revenue and maintenance and dependence from God alone. "Even so hath the Lord ordained that they who preach the gospel should live of the gospel," that is, of those things which are due to God under the gospel. The offering of our tithe ought to be performed with prayer and adoration of God. What benefit has the farmer for tithes being taken from the clergy? They are still paid, only with this difference, that the impropriators generally throughout England set their tithes a shilling or eighteenpence an acre dearer than the incumbent. Impropriators have taken these lands in reason and law, as well of God as man, with that charge that was put upon them by the donors of the lands, and by God upon the tithes of maintaining the poor. Therefore the impropriators stand chargeable to keep the poor at least from being a tax to the nation. And at the beginning of the Reformation, when the laity were first put in possession of these lands and tithes, they did make a show of keeping up the former hospitality. But when the fish was caught they soon laid aside the net.

There was another and a greater burden upon these lands, etc., the cure of souls; and that also they undertook.

CHAPTER VII.

Convocation — Innocent XI. — King of Spain — Duke of Gloucester — King James — At S. Germain — Death — Appearance — Character — Death of William — Offer to Leslie of Preferment — Robert Leslie — Bishop Huntingdon — Queen Anne — Occasional Conformity.

Leslie's attention was diverted now for a while to public affairs in Church and State by events of more than usual concern to all parties in the kingdom, and especially interesting to him. There was first the Convocation question, which, having slept for several years, suddenly revived. That body is the sacred Synod of the nation, and presumed to represent the Church for settlement of all ecclesiastical affairs, except her constitutional principles of doctrine and discipline; much in the same way that Parliament is supposed to represent the nation in political matters. And the uniform custom had been for Convocation to be consulted, and deliberate in those which affected her interest. At the same time, it must be admitted that a practice had existed or grown up gradually in many former reigns of regulating some things without regard to this authority, partly for convenience and partly from neglect, both by the king and the bishops. So these had undertaken to speak and act in the Church's name till a *quasi* sanction seemed to be established for their acceptance generally as her own proper voice. But this had no real authority nor a validity independent of, much less in opposition to, the priesthood. Very naturally, however, they preferred a system which contributed to magnify their own power and importance as a superior order, and the expression came into use under their auspices of "the inferior clergy," to denote some necessary and inherent difference of the priesthood from themselves. When assemblage in London and York also involved a tedious and expensive journey, it was equally natural that persons of slender income should have easily fallen in with this practice of leaving the bishops supreme control, without stopping to consider what consequences might ultimately ensue from such default. Dr. Tillotson, at the commencement of the usurpation, summoned a meeting of Convocation in the hope of passing a comprehension-scheme for admission of Dissenters into the Church, by levelling down her barriers and alteration of the Prayer-book in conformity with their prejudices, which was a pet project of William. He had no other object in view, for Convocation was really more distasteful to him and the latitudinarian party than to his predecessors on the episcopal bench. Only they hoped thus to gain a great lever of advantage for their project, by committing to it the representative assembly of the whole clergy. The device signally failed, and had to be dropped after a considerable amount of heat and angry discussion, to which reference has already been made by anticipation in connection with the case of the Regale and Pontificate. After that, till his death, Tillotson adopted a different plan. Since he could not make the clergy speak with his voice, they should not speak at all. Since they would not accept his *ipse dixit*, they should be condemned to an ignominious silence. At the opening of Parliament he went through a form of summoning Convocation, but always immediately proceeded to prorogue it. And his successor, Tenison, a man scarcely more orthodox and still less able than he, selected by William for the post on account of this inferiority of character, as likely to prove a supple instrument for his purpose of keeping the Church in shackles, intended to continue the same artifice. Murmurs at length began to grow louder and louder among the clergy, and a demand for restoration of their ancient and undoubted right of meeting for the dispatch of business. A great impulse was given to the movement by a tract published under the title of a "Letter to a Member of Parliament," authorship of which has been differently ascribed to Sir Bartholomew Shower and Dr. Binks. Wake replied in a pamphlet which surrendered all the rights of the Church altogether to the king happening to be in possession, who was effectively answered by Samuel Hill, and not so forcibly by Atterbury, though with more eloquence and rhetorical power. The only argument of any weight put forward by the obstructionist party, that the meeting of Convocation formerly being only for the purpose of voting subsidies, and therefore unnecessary when this right had been surrendered, had no foundation in fact. That right had never been formally surrendered by the Church or Convocation, and therefore could not be lost to successors, because the archbishop of the day had taken upon himself to yield. Silence might have been a mistake on the part of the clergy and imply acquiescence for themselves, but could not be justly pleaded to involve any consent in the future.

Nor was it true that this had been the great business of Convocation, or that discussion had been ever limited to such a subject. All ecclesiastical matters properly belonged to Convocation, the only limit lying in the need of royal licence from the very nature of the case for giving practical effect to any conclusions which might touch upon the temporal rights of the crown or people.

In this contest Leslie was deeply interested, and though his position as a Nonjuror precluded him from direct interference, he threw all the weight of his influence into the scale with the so-called "High Church" party, for preserving their right unimpaired. Many of those who had succumbed to the Revolution had long felt gallingly the weight of the chain they had hung round their own necks, and sighed for relief which could not be obtained without fresh swearing and another revolution. They had, therefore, to rest content with efforts to rescue what little of ancient liberty remained from destruction. To some extent in this they succeeded, for Convocation met again February, 1700, with the well-dissembled reluctance but affectedly cheerful consent of William, upon writs issued by the Bishops of London and Rochester, who thus established their independent rights as Suffragans, and Tenison had to yield a grim acquiescence. Such a temper as both Houses displayed, and such a diversity of sentiment as they professed, boded ill for their harmonious working. So no sooner had the usual formalities of assemblage been performed, than the war of words commenced. The chief subjects of contention were respecting the condemnation of heretical books, and a claim of the Lower House to continue sitting after adjournment of the Upper, both of which the latter resolutely opposed.

Now that Convocation has regained its long withheld powers of deliberation upon ecclesiastical affairs, it is easier to consider these matters calmly than it was then. And it can scarcely be denied that while prelates by no means exhibited that spirit which became them, they had the best of the argument on their side. It could only lead to anarchy and dissension perilous to the Church's welfare, if the Lower House of Convocation were permitted to assume a position of irresponsibility and insubordination to the Upper in the face of the nation. The whole purpose of their joint constitution would be inevitably destroyed; but for this very reason prelates should have been more careful than Tenison and his brethren for the most part were, to adopt a conciliatory attitude, and carefully consider the matter of every grievance submitted to their notice by the representative body of the clergy. Again, though the Lower House was within its province in discussing the character and tendency of books widely circulated, it became evident their intention was rather to censure individuals than their books, and individually strike at prelates with whom these were justly enough presumed to be in too high favour, including Burnet, the author of an "Exposition of the Thirty-nine Articles." If, therefore, the bishops, instead of obstinately refusing concurrence, had suggested to the Lower House the propriety of endeavouring to answer these pernicious volumes before condemning them, it would have been a more dignified and speedy method of composing differences. What might be the issue of their continuance none could predict, when happily that was interrupted by the calling of a new Parliament. One or two pamphlets which appeared during the heat of the controversy were ascribed to Leslie's pen, for which a different authorship has since been claimed; nor do they bear the characteristic marks of his style, therefore may be dismissed from consideration. If he did write anything upon the subject, at least it cannot be said that he confined his disapproval of heretical writers to mere declamation, or the fulminating of censures against persons. His method of combat was both a fairer and more successful one—to dispute and disprove their tenets from Reason, Scripture, and the Authority of the primitive Church. Opponents who may deride and deny the powers of Convocation cannot so easily decline to accept the arbitrament of public opinion when their arguments are clearly proved erroneous in this way. A few prominent partisans of the bishops endeavoured to start a fresh cry against Nonjurors and Jacobites, representing the whole thing as a conspiracy of theirs, and protesting against their title to interfere at all. Such an idea was amusing, coming from those who readily accepted support for their own opinions from every quarter, and only wanted a convocation so far as it might be an instrument for opening the Church's gates to a creedless heterogeneous mass. Such an objection was altogether untenable. Nonjurors and Jacobites had never formerly separated themselves from the Church of England; they only claimed to represent her more truly and consistently than others who had been intruded into their offices. They had never been excommunicated, nor had any one ventured to propose such a thing. Therefore they had both a moral and legal right to interfere in any matter which concerned her welfare; nor were Leslie, Hickes, and Wagstaffe in the least deterred from doing so, but rather the contrary, for the complaint showed palpably what an influence opponents felt them to possess in spite of all which had been done to depreciate and disparage them. Least of all did this objection apply to Leslie, because, so far from fanning the flames of dissension, he endeavoured as much as possible, by kindly remonstrance with both parties, to moderate their warmth; and even made a point of attendance at public services in Parish churches with his family, wherever Nonjurors had no chapel of their own, rather than seem to sanction schism, or widen the breach unnecessarily. Though this course did not commend itself to any of the party then, there are clear proofs that he did so on several occasions and at different places.

The eighteenth century, which thus opened with stormy prospects for the Church, ushered in events of a still more portentous character to the world at large. Innocent XI. was dead—the Protestant pope who had signally aided William in robbing his own infatuated devotee of his crown —and no one could expect the newly elected pontiff to walk in his steps. Then followed the death of the King of Spain, indicating a new European war for certain, in which England sooner or later must be involved, with fresh expenditure of blood and treasure without any adequate result to the nation. But the hand of death was to be busier still among royal houses and crowned heads. Its next victim was the only child of the Princess Anne and George of Denmark. He was the last of seventeen children, the rest of whom had scarcely survived their birth. This one had reached his eleventh year, and was taken ill just after celebration of his birthday by great festivities at Windsor. Commonly called the Duke of Gloucester, it is said that, owing to an old and natural prejudice against that title, the patent of creation had never been drawn out, and now the formality was rendered needless. Dr. Burnet says nothing about his moral disposition, of which, indeed, at such a tender age little idea could be hazarded, though generally "the boy is father to the man," and some later historians have taken upon themselves to form sanguine guesses on the point. He, however, formed a high opinion of the young prince's intellectual powers and thirst for knowledge, neither of which he could be presumed to have inherited from his parents. From the doctor's own account of the method of instruction he adopted as his tutor, though no doubt in a conscientious desire to do his duty to the utmost, it is surprising the poor boy lived so long; for his brain was overloaded with lectures for several hours every day on subjects of every possible description, beside elaborate explanations of the bishop's own views about political and ecclesiastical affairs, of which the less he heard then the better and happier he might have been. What made his death so serious was not only sympathy with parents for a loss not likely to be repaired, but the view it presented of fresh complications to the State. The Prince of Wales had been discarded, and this child substituted as heir to the throne after his mother. He had been, therefore, the very hope of the Revolution, and now that hope suddenly was extinguished. Its contrivers began to tremble for the future, some to cast about with Marlborough for ways of providing against all emergencies, and making their peace with the exiled family. Jacobites and Nonjurors looked up and thought they saw the sky clearing for a restoration. Anne bore her loss with patience and resignation, in some measure owing to constitutional impassiveness, but it may be hoped also under the influence of better motives. She herself despatched a secret messenger with tidings of this bereavement to her father. It was not her first communication since that unfilial desertion which cut him to the heart so deeply, but no response had been made to her professions of submission and penitence, because obviously these could not be sincere so long as she continued to wait upon opportunity in England; though her sister, and "Old Caliban," as she termed William, had given her some bitter pills to swallow. No more notice was taken on this occasion than before of her letters, for their little value appeared only too conspicuously. Even William, in 1697, made an overture of reconciliation through the King of France, on condition that James should formally resign to him the crown for his lifetime, and that then it should revert to the rightful heir, which the king very properly disdained to consider. The fact of such a proposal being made demonstrates beyond question how untrue had been the usurper's pretences for invasion, and how little he had at heart anything but gratification of his own ambition. He and Anne were engaged in similar work, and prompted by similar motives, trying to out-manœuvre one another, their consciences ill at ease, but overpowered by a terrible temptation. The time had arrived for James himself to turn away his sad and wearied eye from this world altogether, and leave its hopes and disappointments behind him. Indeed, after 1697 he had discontinued any efforts, if not abandoned all hopes, for recovery of his throne. Nearly all correspondence too with loyal subjects in England had dropped, and he spent a perfectly uneventful existence at S. Germain, only varied by occasional visits for deeper seclusion and devotion in the monastery of Latrappe. Some show of state was maintained, and several English persons formed part of the royal establishment, but those who had not been brought up in the Roman faith, or apostatized, had a very hard time of it indeed. One after another, chaplains who wished to minister to their spiritual wants had to retire; for while one or two had sacrificed their all for the king's sake, they were not only forbidden to exercise their functions openly, but treated with a contumely and cruelty beyond human nature to endure.

Leslie went over upon two or three occasions for a short period to confer with his Majesty upon the state of affairs, and enjoyed his full confidence as well as that of the Nonjurors and Jacobites in general. Personally, on all such occasions James manifested towards him the utmost favour and condescension, both on his own account, and for the still greater sacrifices which he could not but remember Leslie's father, the bishop, endured for his. He knew very well his staunch attachment to the Church of England, as steadfast as his own to Rome, and listened very patiently to his urgent entreaties for assurances which might be repeated to English people of protection to her rights in future, as an indispensable condition of restoration. Nevertheless, little tangible security of this kind could be extracted suitable to the extremity; for whatever modifications James himself might be convinced his former headlong policy required, the queen and her priests were as inveterately bent as ever upon insisting that Rome should not only have ascendancy, but supremacy, whether at S. Germain or S. James's. A knowledge of this convinced Leslie of the inexpediency of more decided efforts, and his visits were only such as duty required, when he encountered none of that ungracious and ungrateful treatment of which Dr. Grenville and other clergymen had so much reason to complain.

King James had been seized with convulsions, from which he appeared to have recovered, when another attack prostrated him; and it is remarkable that each of these occasions was while engaged in Divine Service, just when the plaintive words of Jeremiah were being sung— "Remember, O Lord," etc. When the last hour was at hand he forgave all his enemies, mentioning more particularly the Prince of Orange, the Prince of Denmark, and the Emperor of Austria. To the generous and chivalrous King of France he tendered his hearty and deserved thanks for all his kindnesses, who, deeply moved with emotion, burst into tears, and pledged himself to recognize the young prince, his son, as rightful heir to the throne of England. There ensued a slight rally after that for some hours, but on the next day, September 16, 1701, King James II. breathed his last. His conduct and character have been estimated differently, but the subject need not be pursued further here. His personal appearance and demeanour may interest some readers, as drawn by one who saw him frequently: "Something above the middle height in stature, well shaped, very nervous and strong. His face rather long, and complexion fair, with an engaging expression. His carriage a little stiff and constrained. Not so gracious as courteous and obliging. He offered no formality, and was easy of access, though none knew better what ceremony was becoming, or, when necessary, could be more exact in observance of it. His conversation was rather adapted to the conviction of his hearers by reasoning, than by the use of fine language. He abhorred every sort of duplicity, and proved a sure friend where he professed to be one; nor when he could not serve a man did he hesitate to let him know it. Naturally his temper was hot and fiery, of which in later days he got the better; and even when younger seldom was overpowered so far as to act unbecomingly. A great lover of walking and manly exercises, no diversion made him neglect business; and he had an inveterate aversion to intemperance or gambling."[1] Form and features are to some extent emblematic of the mind within, so in the Stuart portraits of the National Gallery any one can easily trace in that of James II. the characteristics which distinguished him from other members of the royal family.

Louis XIV. lost no time in fulfilling his promise to the deceased monarch, of openly proclaiming his son by the title of King of Great Britain, against the advice of his

---

[1] Nairnin Macpherson, "Original Papers."

ministers. William's wrath was excited to the highest pitch, and though the French ambassador endeavoured to explain away the proceeding as a mere formal courtesy required by long friendship, not intended to signify any interruption of peaceful relations with him, he was not to be so appeased; but ordered the English ambassador to leave Paris without the customary ceremony of leave-taking, and prepared for an active resumption of hostilities. He also instructed his Government to set about a new Act of Settlement for exclusion of all the Stuart family attached to the Roman faith from succession to the throne. This measure diverted it over the heads of fifty-seven persons in the natural order to a remote branch, the Electress Sophia of Hanover and her son, who up to this period had always professed sympathy with the unfortunate Prince of Wales, but of course saw immediate reasons for changing their opinions. The old lady, being asked a question on one occasion concerning the education of her daughters, frankly replied that they were not taught any religion till it should be seen whom they were to have for husbands—a policy which explains a good deal of royal indifference ever since. Curiously enough, the favoured individual selected for introduction of this Act of Settlement into the House of Commons was a Sir John Bowles, whose sole distinction up to that moment had been a disordered intellect. Nevertheless it was carried with little opposition, for the revolutionary and Hanoverian party were strong and resolute, adherents of the Stuarts were weak and irresolute, and funds were abundantly supplied for direction of doubtful votes. The Princess Anne's secret message to her father had not escaped the vigilance of William. A bird had carried the matter from S. Germain; and though he dissembled his displeasure so far as to pay her a ceremonial visit of condolence, and permit some regal honours which had been withdrawn when they were notoriously at variance, she was meant to feel in due time the weight of his vengeance. A paper lay in his cabinet, which showed that he had studied in the old school of the Tudors how to dispose of women who venture to make themselves distasteful in any respect. When this secret in its turn, as all State secrets do, became a matter of public rumour, it was vainly attempted to be discredited by saying that search had been made and "no such document as described" could be found, which artifice has been repeated since by William's eulogists. True in a certain sense to the letter of these particular words, the denial was in spirit utterly false, and no fact was ever more fully established by evidence of sight and hearsay, than that Anne's head was intended for the block on Tower Hill.[1] But man proposes in vain against the will of Providence. William's own course was run out, and his account to be rendered where neither arbitrary power, partisanship, nor society can avail to hinder a sentence of inexorable justice. He had but very lately returned from his native country in shattered health, with a racking cough and a ghastly countenance, in which courtiers could see depicted unmistakably the premonitory symptoms of a speedy death, even if no event occurred to hasten its approach. Himself had strong suspicions of the truth, and since physicians could give no relief, he had, like Saul, recourse to a famous quack affecting occult arts of healing, with the usual result of such applications. The end came in an unexpected manner. A fall when out riding near Hampton Court on a favourite horse, which stumbled in a rabbit-hole, broke his collar-bone; and though this was rightly reset, his system was too far injured to bear the shock.

[1] See "Advice of Church of England to her Children."

It soon appeared, after arrival at Kensington, that he was rapidly sinking. His last hours were disturbed by French and English doctors disputing about their favourite theories for delaying the inevitable; statesmen and courtiers bustling in and out with proposals and suggestions, which betokened more concern for themselves than their master; and Drs. Tenison and Burnet to offer such religious consolation as their wisdom and piety deemed suitable. The dying man spoke no words of forgiveness, expressed no contrition for his sins, refused admission to Prince George, who certainly could have afforded little help or comfort on such an occasion, nor did he desire to see the Princess Anne. He behaved devoutly while prayers were offered in his behalf, and acquiesced in the proposal to administer to him the last sacrament, though he had scarcely strength remaining for its reception. The two prelates present were severely blamed by Leslie and many more among contemporaries for not moving William's conscience to make some confession. It was, indeed, much needed on his part, with the memories of De Witt, Glencoe, and many other crimes beside the Revolution, and "secret vices" which Burnet knew; but those prelates were consciously disqualified for performance of such a duty. The noblest, tenderest act of his life must not be omitted. After entrusting his papers to the care of Lord Albermarle, a favourite whom he had raised from the meanest condition by sudden leaps to the highest rank, he inquired for the Duke of Portland. This other favourite, elevated in the same rapid manner to even greater wealth and distinction, but possessing at least some more title to respect in himself, had almost entirely withdrawn from court, out of jealousy to his rival. His affection for his master had been most faithful and sincere, too deep to bear with any semblance of composure the strain put upon it in seeing the upstart Keppel supersede him. When he responded to the summons and came close to the sick man's ear, it was too late for any intelligible or articulate utterances. But what was intended could be all too fully understood by Bentinck, the oft-repeated assurance of unchanging attachment, which had failed to soothe his wounded spirit, once more. A faint feeble whisper, a tear-dimmed glance of that once eagle eye, then William took his hand and placed it upon his own heart just ere the lamp of life went out. So touching a proof of fond affection sheds a softness on the death-bed scene, and relieves with a solitary gleam of light a dark and terrible career. Another trait of tenderness for the memory of his wife, inferred from her ring found suspended by a ribbon round his neck, is unfortunately shadowed too deeply by some other circumstances to be of much account.

William's funeral was conducted with a scantiness of expense and ceremony which reflected much discredit upon his ministers and Parliament. The need of economy was pleaded, or supposed to be the reason of this neglect, yet no profusion or extravagance had been grudged on far less important occasions, or for purposes far less exceptionable. Beside the burden of an enormous national debt created under their auspices, thirteen millions had been spent during his reign, of which no explanation was furnished in State accounts; and it was a fact too well understood that it went in bribery and corruption among those very officials and members of Parliament who now declined to pay honour to their patron's remains. Although a soldier of surpassing bravery—never so bright or happy as in the midst of a campaign or on the field of battle—he never earned the reputation of a skilful general or great commander, a success of which he was almost more ambitious than the crown of England. Among Dutch friends and favourites he could throw off his constitutional reserve, and show himself a genial, even gay, companion. But his unconquerable aversion to English tastes and habits made him shun their society as much as possible, and adopt a cold dry manner, which gave great offence. Any professions of strong religious feeling would have suited ill with such a career as his, and his creed consisted of little more than a belief in a Supreme Being and the Calvinistic theory of predestination, with a morbid aversion for the Church of Rome. He attended, however, when occasion required, upon the services of the Church of England in a sufficiently reverent and decorous manner; though never confirmed, or pretending to approve of her doctrines or worship, from time to time receiving the Sacrament of the Altar from the hands of his latitudinarian prelates. Dr. Burnet complained that he did not like opposition or reproof; but perhaps William did not deem him the person best fitted to administer it. If also this man had not been allowed to meddle in other concerns they might sometimes have issued more prosperously. For instance, no one could have been more unfortunately selected than he to win over Leslie from the Jacobite and Nonjuring cause by the offer of ecclesiastical preferment, which he essayed to do with characteristic self-confidence and maladroitness. Whether he acted under authority or solely on his own behoof cannot be stated with certainty, but he made the attempt in a manner which only gave pain and offence. Such a proposal as his might have been foreseen to meet a disdainful rejection from a man of the highest conscientiousness, who had already counted the cost of loyalty to his rightful sovereign, and whose honour and reputation were now manifestly bound up with adherence to it. If he had not forsworn himself while yet unknown and under strong inducements from his own kindred, how was it possible he could abandon the cause without burning first every line he had written? The next act had properly been a second retractation, and, like Cranmer, to hold out his guilty hand to the flames. Burnet's failure at negotiation served to whet his hatred; but this reason was one of those things on which he could maintain reticence when necessary— alluding only to "one Leslie" as a mere stranger. Towards Leslie, either before or afterwards, William himself never betrayed any personal animosity, though he could not but have read and felt sorely the exposure of his own part in the massacre of Glencoe. For some reason or other he estimated, beyond its real worth for any impression it could produce in Ireland, the Dean of Dromore's accession to his side, and very liberally rewarded it by grants of land and money on two occasions.[1] This brother, a learned man, and no doubt conscientious in his way, possessed none of Charles's talents or mental powers to make his support of great consequence to either side. Shortly before the occurrence of that fatal accident which left the throne vacant, some circumstances occurred showing how honourably men could act together for the interests of their common country, however widely separated by religion and politics. The English Government received an intimation in December, 1699, that French wines were imported from San Sebastian and neighbouring ports in Spain, under pretence of being manufactured in that country. A difficulty was experienced by custom-house officials in detecting the fraud, though tests were several times applied to seizures of consignments. At length a prosecution was ventured against a wine-merchant named Creagh, when Robert

[1] February and April, 1696-97, State Papers.

Leslie, son of Charles, came forward and gave evidence of what he had witnessed at San Sebastian. He proved that several vessels then under seizure had taken in their loadings there, which had first been shipped from French ports, and this evidence was confirmed by another witness named Bishop. The jury, however, gave the verdict against the king, as was strongly suspected under sinister influences. But when a fresh trial was demanded, another person called Gamell, who had been engaged in these transactions, came forward and made a clean breast. So the merchants were glad, in dread of further exposure, to offer an accommodation and pay a fine of £22,000 to the Crown. For Robert Leslie's conduct on the occasion, he was awarded by the Lords Justices £500, and the same was given to Gamell by the lords of the Treasury under William's orders. Robert, in acknowledging its receipt, styled himself "the most wretched being upon earth," but in what his excessive misery consisted he left no conjecture.[1]

Youthful and buoyant natures are liable to occasional fits of depression, but soon recover their wonted elasticity. And this disturbance was only temporary. He was but a very young man then, who afterwards was known for his gay and lively disposition, and whose sparkling powers of conversation attracted admiration from Dean Swift and other eminent persons in society, both at home and abroad. His present good fortune, no doubt, contributed to restore his normal cheerfulness, and the award must be acknowledged a very gracious and generous act on the part of William. What is yet more strange, among the last persons who engaged the latter's favourable intentions again was Robert's father, and the circumstances altogether furnish a curious and interesting episode for relation. Readers may

[1] State Papers, 1701.

remember that after Bishop Leslie's translation to Clogher at the Restoration the see of Raphoe was conferred on his young friend and kinsman, another Robert Leslie, who succeeded him again in the other. There followed three at Raphoe, the last of whom deserves particular mention—Robert Huntingdon, a distinguished fellow of the University of Oxford. He travelled for eleven years in the East, visiting Jerusalem and the sites of the Seven Churches, during which he acquired great proficiency in languages, and made a valuable collection of manuscripts preserved in the Bodleian Library. Upon returning home he reluctantly accepted the Provostship of Trinity College in the University of Dublin, the duties of which he discharged with eminent success, but retired during disturbances in King James's time to the parish of Hallingbury, in Essex. In 1701 he accepted, at urgent entreaties from the Archbishop of Dublin and other prelates, the See of Raphoe, eight years before having refused Kilmore, owing most apparently to scruples about deprivation of Bishop Sheridan for refusing to take the oaths. Though he may have taken them himself in England, it does not follow that he considered a vacancy properly made on the Episcopal Bench by refusal. However, at the death of Dr. Cairncross, making no further demur, he was consecrated Bishop of Raphoe on August 21, 1701, but within a fortnight was no more in this world.

Then it occurred to many leading personages in Church and State what an admirable success would be achieved if Charles Leslie could be persuaded to accept the vacant mitre, and among these the Duke of Ormond made a strong representation to William. He promised to give it his full consideration, and evidently cast about for the best way of making the offer, when at this very juncture occurred the catastrophe which ended his life. The See remained unoccupied for some months, and eventually was filled by Dr. Pooley, under Queen Anne. She was not likely to have objected to Charles Leslie, for the political importance of such a recruit appeared too obvious for question, and personally she must have been favourably disposed towards him on account of his intimacy with her own family, whom she was anxious to conciliate. It therefore remains for presumption that, on being sounded, he intimated his disinclination, to prevent a formal proffer of the appointment causing embarrassment. His natural delicacy of sentiment would have suggested this consideration for the queen and her advisers in return for their kindly intentions towards himself, while it left him free to act under the very novel and peculiar circumstances of her accession to the throne as his conscience should direct. What his duty should be, or what course he should pursue, it was impossible at once to determine, for it depended materially upon proceedings beyond his ken or control in a newly opened page of history. "Circumstances alter cases" forms the general and ready plea for persons anxious to justify a desertion of principles not coincident with worldly interests. This had been abundantly experienced at the Revolution; but Leslie had shown too clearly his abhorrence of all subterfuges and salves of conscience for any one to suspect that less than the clearest conviction of duty would alter the attitude he had long assumed, or that he could be induced to "sacrifice to his own net."

The Princess Anne of Denmark ascended the throne without opposition, and the apprehension which she and her governess secretly entertained that this apparent tranquillity was only like the calm which precedes and betokens a storm, soon became exchanged for a sense of confidence and security. An amazing opportunity bolder spirits among the Jacobites thought to be lost by not at once making a dash at the crown in the name of James III. And if this had been attempted with energy and determination, supported by an invasion from abroad, the probabilities are it would have been successful, with what ultimate results it is unnecessary to speculate. During the last few years an intense and increasing unpopularity of William had seriously threatened another revolution to terminate his usurpation. But circumstances on the whole conspired in favour of Anne's peaceful accession. Her ministers in the critical emergency acted speedily and determinedly. Before her brother-in-law's death had been reported in three parts of the realm, she had been proclaimed, made a seasonable and felicitous little speech, and active measures had been taken to crush the first symptoms of resistance to her authority in any quarter whatever.

Friends of the Royal Family in exile had been astonished at the suddenness of William's death, and before they had recovered from their first surprise found the ground pre-occupied, and a new Sovereign formally if not firmly established in his stead. English people in general stood again waiting to see which way the stream would flow, as they had waited in dubious inaction when the Dutch fleet arrived at Torbay, till the tide carried them forward in the direction wanted by those superior and clever enough to have the management. Anne had in her surreptitious communication to her father requested permission to take the crown, holding it as it were for her brother in reversion, which pretty plainly indicated an intention of taking it whether that permission were accorded or not. Nor did she hesitate when the moment arrived for action.

Another cause operated greatly in her favour. Nonjurors and Jacobites were highly gratified at her early assurance of warm attachment to the Church of England, and thought reasonably enough that nothing would more incline her to restoration of her brother's right than refraining on their part from disturbance of her reign in the mean time. Every one knew that she differed as widely as possible from her predecessor, not only in sentiments, but in character, though she might possess, under a dull placid exterior, some similar dogged determination to push on to an object in spite of all obstacles. Such things could never be said of her as of him by a pope, that "he was master of the world, and commanded Catholic princes like slaves." Her very dulness, domestic nature, and sex combined to make the chances on her side, when the nation needed time at least for consideration before embarking on a perilous experiment of recalling the discarded family with no security for good behaviour but promises, and reported to be as thoroughly ingrained with Romanism as ever—a scare of most portentous efficacy manufactured first by their own infatuated conduct.

Now, it plainly appeared that the next sovereign must be a foreigner, come from what country he might, and whether professing himself a Romanist enamoured of liberty of conscience for his subjects, or a German with only Protestant negations. Nor could Anne expect to be more than a nurse of the throne till then, though actually only thirty-eight years of age at this time, after the loss of all her numerous offspring. Many deemed this a Nemesis for her unfilial conduct, like the melancholy ends of her sister and William. Doggerel of the day unmistakably expressed prevailing popular impressions as to their deserts; but it is presumptuous for fellow-creatures to interpret confidently the meaning of divine dealings. "Some men's sins go before to judgment, some they follow after." Her own ambition or talents never ranged beyond the idea of present possession of royal power, and nothing but experience could convince her how "uneasy may lie the head which wears a crown." Perhaps so commonplace a character was best suited for the crisis, disarming opposition, and leaving scope for contrary expectations concerning the future. Quite as erroneously is she credited with the exclusive merit of restoring to the Church the firstfruits sacrilegiously seized by Henry VIII.;[1] for Mary, his daughter, had most nobly and piously renounced all pretension to them. But Elizabeth, inspired by no such scruples, deliberately setting aside her sister's act, reclaimed them for the crown, in which grasp they remained till this time. Nevertheless Anne ought to receive her proper meed of approbation for a righteous intention: Dr. Burnet also for the special efforts he made to persuade her to it, after the disappointment he experienced in pressing the same point upon the attention of William and Mary in vain. That fund, still denominated "Queen Anne's Bounty," has been for a long period alienated again from its original intention of benefiting poorer clergy, to the very great discredit of Episcopal and State rulers, and is now at the present day simply one of several buttresses nominally for the Church's support, but really employed to find salaries for lay officials who desire easy berths. Anne must be further acknowledged to have throughout her whole reign continued steadfast in her attachment to the Church of England, and what she conceived the promotion of the best interests of religion. How well this was understood by the great mass of the people appeared from their conduct on exciting occasions. A recent historian has attributed

[1] Stanhope.

inaccurately to her the title of "Good Queen Anne."[1] Most certainly she never was so called during her lifetime by any considerable section of the populace, nor did the title ever properly belong to any occupant of the throne in England but the wife of Richard II., daughter of the Emperor Charles IV., who died at Shene Palace in 1394—the virtuous and affectionate woman to whose sorrows Shakespeare makes the gardener at Langley so touchingly allude.[2] In no previous reign did Church questions obtain a larger proportion, if not a monopoly, of public attention, by no means to the ultimate benefit of the Church herself. She never has prospered so truly as when let alone, and left to pursue her proper work unfettered or unfostered by injudicious attempts at State legislation on her behalf.

With assemblage of a new Parliament there was also a meeting of Convocation, which commenced with renewal of the old dispute. The bishops made a concession about the mode of conducting business more conveniently for the Lower House, which was not deemed sufficient, but they were masters of the situation; and though some of the queen's new ministers evidently sympathized with the clergy, their resistance practically proved of no avail, and she herself looked coldly upon their proceedings as calculated only to do mischief. But a far more generally interesting and exciting contest was that which sprang up in Parliament simultaneously, concerning a Bill against Occasional Conformity arraying the Lords and Commons in violent opposition to each other. By the Test Act in 1673 it had been provided, professedly in defence of the Church of England, that no persons should be entitled to hold certain public offices who did not receive the Blessed Sacrament at her Altar at least once. This measure, which

[1] Stanhope, vol. i. 43.   [2] Act iii. sc. 4.

was intended to exclude Dissenters from admission, soon became a door of entrance; for many candidates qualified themselves by a single reception, immediately relapsing into regular attendance at their own conventicles. Thus the intention of the Act was palpably defeated, and a gross profanation involved of the most solemn act of Worship. Accordingly, the new bill was introduced to forbid Occasional Conformity, rendering the Test applicable to a larger number of offices, and requiring reception of the Sacrament three times a year, with severe penalties upon office-holders who should attend places of worship not in connection with the Church. To this the House of Lords, including a majority of the bishops, offered uncompromising resistance, when pressed by the House of Commons, as a violation of the principle of toleration sanctioned at the Revolution. At first the court were in its favour so far that Prince George voted for it, while he privately whispered to Lord Wharton, "Me heart is wid ye," for he customarily attended the Lutheran chapel. But afterwards the Court changed sides and discountenanced the bill. It was a most objectionable proposal, because it provided virtually for a frequent repetition of the very profanation by unscrupulous persons which it condemned, whilst framed in the worst spirit of that religious persecution which its preamble disavowed. Nor had those who volunteered so eagerly to champion the interests of the Church for the most part any higher conception of her character than the low Erastian notion of a political institution. If Spiritual and Temporal peers did right in warmly opposing the new intolerant and persecuting measure, unfortunately the grounds on which that opposition was based deserved as little approval, and was as inconsistent with any high spiritual views of the Church as those of opponents. Ultimately the bill was lost, but meanwhile other questions and other issues became involved, in which the original question was obscured and almost forgotten, although the old war-notes continued to be repeated. Pious and earnest Dissenters gravely disapproved of such base tampering with conscience and dishonest compliances for the sake of worldly advantages; but their voice was drowned in the agitation which political parties maintained for their own purposes on both sides under the cover of religion. Even some Dissenters, who were not pious nor recognized by those who were, felt the inconsistency of this occasional conformity too strongly to conceal their dislike. On the other hand, Leslie, with his friends, severely and loudly protested against it, not from entire concurrence in the political aims of the party in Parliament—for Nonjurors would have been exposed to its sweeping persecution—but because they felt shocked at a corrupt and impious abuse, the tendency of which was to degrade the blessed Sacrament to the most secular of all uses, and destroy in people's own minds all sense of reverence and honesty. A shower of hostile comments followed upon some of his utterances, and he was held up to odium as the very incarnation of bigotry; but this was no more than a natural consequence of associating and identifying himself with a political party, which really sympathized with Nonjurors and Jacobites less than with Dissenters, but accepted their assistance for the time. Whilst this agitation proceeded, the party for hereditary right in England refrained from direct efforts in behalf of their exiled sovereign, though an active correspondence was being carried on between S. Germain and some of their supporters in Scotland. Government had forestalled them upon William's death, and they had neither plans ready nor means of putting them in execution if prepared. A rising proposed up there soon proved abortive; and one of the chief agents incautiously trusted to some degree a man of infamous character. Simon Fraser, or Beaufort, also styling himself Lord Lovet, was discovered to be only a spy and traitor in the hands of the Duke of Queensberry, whose principal design was the ruin of noblemen whom he hated, the Dukes of Hamilton and Athol, and Lord Tarbot, by entangling them in a charge of treasonable conspiracy. Although Leslie did not participate in any of Fraser's proceedings, nor was even suspected of any concert in them, no one doubted he would have approved any open and fair attempt to restore the throne to its rightful owner if a suitable opportunity should offer. Therefore King James III. sent him a paper of instructions authorizing him to assure his English subjects, if they should recall him, that former errors should not be repeated, but the Church and University be maintained in all their ancient privileges, and even the nomination of bishops surrendered to a properly constituted commission, with other pledges for their complete security.[1] Meanwhile Leslie threw himself into the arena of political conflict with a fresh vigour, dealing out some severe thrusts, and receiving a full average in return.

[1] Macpherson's Papers, vol. i.

CHAPTER VIII.

Renewal of War — Comprehension Scheme — Theatrical Amusements, etc. — Ecclesiastical History — Mr. Parker — Mixed Marriages — Origin of De Foe — Occasional Conformity — Sacheverell — New Association — "The Shortest Way with Dissenters" discovered — Supplements — Private Judgment — Ecclesiastical History — Mixed Marriages.

Almost the first act of Queen Anne upon her accession was to proclaim war against France. It was in full accordance with the interrupted policy of her predecessor, with which in other respects she materially disagreed. Her Ministers by no means were unanimous on the subject, but the more powerful section, led by Marlborough and his relative Godolphin, had their way. That distinguished man combined in his own person the two very different offices of a Cabinet Minister and Commander of the forces abroad belonging to England and her Allies. His avarice and ambition are as notorious as his shining military talents, and conspicuously influenced his urgent counsels for renewal of this unhappy war, which had already cost oceans of blood and treasure to every nation in Europe, though a fairer opportunity could not have been wished for leaving peace undisturbed.

Another motive was at work of an equally sinister description. Marlborough had long engaged in a double game of politics between the revolutionary party at home and the exiled family at S. Germain. Both knew fully his disingenuous character and distrusted him, for they held proofs in their hands of his simultaneous negotiations with them both; but neither could afford to reject his support on any terms, so long as a prospect remained of securing it to their own side. He was determined to avoid as long as possible committing himself irrevocably to either, and continued to express fervent devotion by secret communications to "that young man in whom he had the deepest interest," while commanding the forces of England against his powerful patron and protector the King of France. Nor was he sorry to have a valid excuse for absence from his Sarah, while profuse in assurances to her of unfailing devotion; like those of the sparkling Irish melodist to his "darling Bessy" left in the seclusion of a Devonshire cottage, while he enchanted and enjoyed fashionable circles of the metropolis. The Tory party Jacobites and Nonjurors strongly objected to war and wished for peace; both on account of the enormous military expenses, and that they might bestow more undivided attention upon party interests at home. Revolutionists favoured the war just because it necessarily distracted such attention, and afforded time for strengthening their own position against eventualities of the future. On their side also were a majority of Dissenters, especially Presbyterians, who in London comprised the more wealthy commercial classes. The expensiveness of war was no great consideration with them, since the burden fell upon the landed interest, which consisted of their opponents; whilst the bugbears, if peace were established, of a French invasion and a "Popish Pretender," perpetually repeated, would have lost half their weight for fostering disaffection against the Church of England.[1] An

[1] See Swift's *Examiner*, xxiv.; Works, vol. vii. 115.

unsuccessful expedition to Cadiz was attributed by them to design on the part of the Admiral Sir George Rooke, till a lucky capture of Spanish galleons laden with booty turned the rising clamour into congratulation, and the splendid successes of Marlborough gratified the national pride of all parties if it did not heal their animosities.

Poor religion had to suffer as usual among contending factions, dragged into every question as the stalking-horse and victim upon which most of the blows fell, while all alike pretended to disinterested zeal in its service. To overthrow the Church of England was the grand aim of Dissenters by one means or another, and as a step towards that first to get rid of the Establishment. A party inside the Church who sympathized with them in dislike to her doctrine and discipline had another plan in view. Their object was to preserve the Establishment with all its worldly advantages intact, by reducing the condition of holding them to an empty negation. A common platform was to be erected, upon which sects of every kind might stand, only bound to objure Popery and the Pretender. So far had this proceeded that these latitudinarians had persuaded Mary before her death, to lend the weight of her influence towards a scheme of comprehension, which at one stroke would have swept away apostolical succession, to establish in its place Presbyterianism, cloaked under the false and specious pretence of a moderate Episcopacy. Leslie, therefore, performed an inestimable service in exposing this most disloyal and dangerous conspiracy, though it embittered and infuriated its contrivers more than ever against himself. The most eminent of the party Archbishop Tillotson, like many, had died before any attempt could be made to put it into execution; but that such a scheme had been deliberately framed by men sworn to defend above all others the Church's polity affords the most irresistible testimony to the justice of those suspicions of unfaithfulness for hinting which Leslie had incurred unsparing censure. Now that he brought this to light, people understood the meaning of mysterious intimations about the excellent intentions which her late Majesty had conceived for the benefit of the Church of England, frequently repeated in sermons and other publications. The scheme itself was preposterous, without either the merit of originality on the one hand, or any successful experiment on the other to recommend it; being no more than a revival of the miserable Tulchan Episcopacy, which in Scotland had perished after scarce a generation's existence amid the scorn and derision of all classes.[1] Even so short a duration as that could not reasonably be expected in this more sober country, and it must have melted away like a rope of sand within a year or two. Henceforth Dr. Burnet, who had been deeply implicated in the plot, exchanged his tearful elegies over Mary's loss for complaints against the "insubordination of the Lower House of Convocation in an essentially episcopal Church." And this comprehension scheme was consigned to the limbo of abortive expedients, its very memory only revived some years ago by a projected Pan-heretical Synod, which fortunately also was nipped in the bud by a timely protest in the public press.

Leslie had other subjects to occupy his attention. Arrears of controversy had to be cleared off, occasioned partly by restrictions under which the press then laboured, of which writers at the present day have fortunately no experience. To publish any work without a Licence involved considerable danger, and to obtain one certain delay, even

[1] Life of Bishop Leslie.

if the contents of a manuscript included nothing which could wound the susceptibilities of the Government. The delay also was due in a measure to his own desire to answer whatever his Socinian and Quaker opponents might have to say concerning his previous publications. This accounts for several bearing the same date in appearance which were written at different times, as for instance, a "Treatise on Water Baptism," and the "History of Sin and Heresy," with some additions to the "Snake in the Grass." On the Quaker side fresh champions came forward, but they were only persons of very inferior ability, who could do nothing to alter or improve upon the position of their predecessors in the field, Fox, Penn, Elwood, and Eccles. They called, therefore, only for some restatements of the case established against them, which need not be repeated. But the tract on the "Sin of Heresy" is interesting because it dealt with a subject as the author observed, "seemingly abstruse and out of the common road," under the title of "Meditations upon the Feast of S. Michael and All Angels." His object was to discredit and discountenance the "adventurous flights of poets who have dressed angels in armour, and put swords and guns into their hands to form romantic battles on the plains of heaven—a scene of licentious fancy." To such an extent had this proceeded that the subject had been introduced upon the stage, and so religion greatly injured by being made an entertainment of "profane raillery." Many good people were grieved and pained by such exhibitions, so that William had been induced to put severe restriction on the licence of theatrical representations. Jeremy Collier, the eminent ecclesiastical historian, made a powerful and sweeping attack upon the stage, with whose views Leslie pretty nearly coincided. Those who take the same now may feel a cold shade of disappointment at learning that Nonjurors were the first who set their faces against theatres as places of sinful and immoral amusement. They need not be so of necessity, and properly conducted afford scope for the exercise and exhibition of peculiar talents which certainly were never intended to lie dormant; nor has any other sphere of employment for them been as yet suggested. Besides, many entertainments at which pious persons attend without scruple under the specious guise of charity involve a greater waste of time and frivolity. But how far theatres are rendered conducive to rational and innocent recreation among the people will of course depend upon the manner in which they are conducted, which no general statement can determine.

That with which Leslie more immediately concerned himself was the abuse of Scripture to furnish subjects. He designed also to give a more serious and authentic view of the War in heaven, mentioned in the Revelation, than Milton's groundless supposition, which makes the angels ignorant of the blessed Trinity, and to have revolted because the Second Person was declared to be their King upon a certain day before creation of this world. Leslie suggests as more probable and practical than this idea, while consistent with sound doctrine, the cause of dissatisfaction to have been the Incarnation of our blessed Saviour when revealed to them. This speculation, however, has no more authority than Milton's, though untainted by his heresy; nor does he sufficiently meet a serious objection to it, in the fact that the Revelation is a volume of prophecy concerning future events, not a relation of the past, though he does say S. John may have applied the history to illustrate these. Readers must be left to form their own opinion of his argument; but at least they will find in a brief epitome of the discourse sufficient to repay an attentive consideration.

Two other publications of this date fittingly claim notice here. The first was a "Dissertation concerning the Use and Authority of Ecclesiastical History." It appeared as a letter addressed to Mr. Samuel Parker in his "Abridgment of Eusebius," intended to serve the double purpose of warmly recommending that work to public favour, and expressing his own views concerning the need of such studies being more sedulously cultivated among the clergy. Mr. Parker was the son of the bishop who had incurred odium in King James II.'s time, in the disastrous dispute at Oxford already mentioned. He inherited his father's misfortunes as well as his learning and ability, which were increased by his attachment to the Nonjuring cause, therefore no more appropriate or seasonable service could be rendered to him than this testimonial. That it was well deserved is evidenced by examination of the histories themselves, and some other books which he subsequently published, though his talent lay rather in the way of condensing and epitomizing the works of others than any original or inventive faculty of his own. His "Commentary on the Books of Moses" deserved more commendation than it has ever received for the research it showed into writings of the early Fathers, and it laid the foundation of a modern work which is more justly esteemed.[1] But the remarks of his reviewer upon the general subject are still scarcely less applicable than to the time in which they lived; because crude suggestions and new-fangled experiments for improving the Church frequently bear witness how unconscious their well-meaning authors are of an utter want of novelty, and the fundamental objections which lie against their adoption. Observations about the

[1] "The Library of the Fathers," Parker.

necessity of adapting machinery to changing circumstances have, of course, a modicum of truth; but their practical application involves a very serious risk, unless accompanied with careful remembrance of the fact that the Church is a divine institution of great antiquity, the constitution of which was never designed to undergo incessant modifications or readjustment according to the ever-varying tastes and caprices of mankind. New wine may be good, but the old is better than it or water.

The second dissertation was on the subject of mixed marriages, the substance of a sermon also previously noticed in connection with the name of Leslie's esteemed friend Henry Dodwell, with several additions. Its subject is as little out of date as that of the other, for one of the most baneful and prolific sources of separation from the Church in the present day, is the facility afforded to marriage at her altars without inquiry or attempt at compliance with the plainest rules of the Prayer-book. "The hands of princes and rulers are chief in this trespass, and at the least it is a tentation." If, therefore, priests or prelates connive at its continuance, they need not be surprised to see the offspring of such unions and the parents themselves alienated instead of attracted to their communion. Almost insurmountable difficulties stand no doubt in the way of a rigid discipline, nor is it desirable to create a ferment by insistance upon it in every instance. But half the difficulty has arisen from sheer neglect of conditions which the laity understand as well as the clergy, and impute that neglect to a hankering after fees, or a poor fear of newspaper reviling. Let the examples cited in this sermon be fairly considered with the inferences drawn from them, and the conclusion cannot be escaped which it endeavours to enforce, that the safety of the Establishment would be best secured by maintaining as far as possible in their integrity the Church's own provisions for solemnizing matrimony among her people.

"An oath for confirmation is an end of all strife," said S. Paul; but, as if to give a double contradiction to the inspired precept (and perhaps because ingenious commentators had disputed his authorship of the Epistle), the sacrament of Holy Eucharist suffered a double profanation in the matter of Occasional Conformity. First it was desecrated by one party into an instrument for restriction of civil rights, and then still more profanely perverted into a qualification for their possession by unscrupulous persons who winked with their eyes, kneeling before the Altar. Nobody dreamed of terminating the scandal and cutting the Gordian knot by the simple process of abolishing the Test Act, or at any rate had the temerity to propose such a thing in the commencement of the seventeenth century. Prelates and peers who valued themselves upon their liberality of sentiment only rose to the idea of compounding for offences by a money payment. Ultimately enforcement of these penalties ended, as other infringements of liberty have done, in overthrow of the very system of protection which they were intended to secure, because its foundations were laid in folly and injustice. The nearest to a right conception of the Church's proper position as the representative of true religion in the nation was Leslie's statement in his "Regale;" but so far from this meeting the approval of Dissenters or Church-people in general, they shrank from it with equal alarm as a perilous and impracticable proposal for establishing an *imperium in imperio*, a free and unfettered organization in the midst of the State. So it was, but upon Christian principles of mutual independence and co-operation for the good of the nation at large. Church-people were too deeply leavened with Erastianism and accustomed to Egyptian bondage to appreciate liberty. Dissenters of all sorts thought it the shadow of papal tyranny returning in disguise. Politicians eyed askance any plan which would deprive their own party in its turn of the advantage of ecclesiastical patronage and control. In other treatises Leslie insisted upon this primitive constitution very frequently, nor has any one ever yet ventured to confute his arguments; but meanwhile he had fain to content himself with support of those persons whose views upon the whole most nearly approximated to his own, both on ecclesiastical and political affairs. While the battle for and against Occasional Conformity raged with unabated fury in and out of Parliament, the country was flooded with pamphlets; which were sought with greater avidity than they would be now, because intellectual appetites were not sated and jaded with a superabundant supply of speeches and articles in the daily press. The quality was often better if the quantity was less, though of course among a heap of productions many were miserable enough. Quite as many others displayed superior powers of reasoning, wit, and learning, but consideration of them must be omitted in this biography, and attention confined to those and their authors with whom Leslie came more immediately into conflict. It will be well to premise further a few circumstances connected with the origin of the dispute which illustrates forcibly "how great a matter a little fire kindleth"—no more than a spark of vulgar ostentation. A weak-headed Lord Mayor of London in 1697 availed himself of his election to attend a Presbyterian conventicle with the insignia of his office in a foolish procession. Hitherto little or no notice had been taken of the practice of occasional conformity in a private manner. But this, being intended as a demonstration to some extent of the effects of toleration, created a flutter of excitement in orthodox circles. No doubt there was a touch of bravado in the proceeding, but much more of petty vain-glory which might have been overlooked with a smile of contempt. And the imprudence was not repeated when it was seen what an amount of irritation it had produced; till a Sir Thomas Abney, in 1701, conceived the idea of gaining notoriety by a similar extravagance. He like the other was a Presbyterian, whose community were the wealthiest and most important among Dissenters in London, and eager for a recovery of their former domination in place of the Church. The note of defiance being renewed at once summoned opponents into the field, when the first prominently to reply was not a churchman but a Dissenter calling himself De Foe, his real name being Foe. One of his three biographers has made a silly attempt to trace his connection with a family of Norman descent; and the man has suffered much at the hands of these biographers, for they have imitated his worst faults without a scintillation of his genius. This Foe, son of a butcher in S. Giles in a small way of business, showed his ambition and romantic tendency first by change of his patronymic, making the initial letter of his Christian name, Daniel, into a syllabic prefix "De;" and subsequently improved this idea by merry allusion to his "grandfather's pack of hounds," which had about the same foundation in historical truth. His education was no more than a private dissenting academy could afford, and its limited extent never more clearly appeared than when he ventured upon scraps of Latin quotation and other shows of learning. He failed completely in business transactions, though the blame of this he laid upon political prosecutions. That he did not behave honourably to his creditors, and lived in an extravagant manner, keeping a coach and liveried servants with a fine house when he had not the means is beyond dispute. Otherwise his failures would leave little reproach on his memory; for he was not naturally fitted for any other pursuit than that of an author, in which he succeeded so far as was possible under drawbacks he could not help. The surprising thing is that, despite of these, he accomplished so much, and earned so extensive a popularity by his writings. Low scurrility, malice, and unscrupulousness disfigured them continually; nevertheless, they discovered unmistakably a genius of no common order, which if cultivated would have qualified him for the foremost rank among writers of his day. Perhaps no one ever wrote so much or upon such a variety of topics, and if he betrayed necessarily often a very superficial acquaintance with the subjects he presumed to handle, yet it was accompanied by much wit, smartness, and force of expression, which was very attractive. Even his versification, which was much coarser and more illiterate than his prose—though his great ambition was to be a poet—contained some happier bits of fancy well deserving remembrance, as for instance the simple lines so often repeated, without an idea of their origin—

> "Stone walls do not a prison make,
> Nor iron bars a cage;
> Minds innocent and quiet take
> That for a hermitage."

And—

> "Wherever God erects a House of Prayer,
> The devil always builds a chapel there;
> And 'twill be found, upon examination,
> The latter has the larger congregation."

Again, a wholesome truth, much forgotten by descendants of the mushroom nobility which sprang up after the Restoration and Revolution, was well expressed in the following, though his immediate object was defence of "new-made noblemen" of William's creation against those who boasted of a much earlier existence—

> "'Tis well that virtue gives nobility,
> Else God knows where we had our gentry,
> Since scarce one family is left alive
> Which does not from some foreigner derive."

Divorce and police courts seem to show an increasing deficiency of that patent which is the only basis of security for permanence of the peerage or any other privileged institution. De Foe's prolific pen never rested for many years, and its utmost fury was directed against Jacobites, Nonjurors, Tories, and High Churchmen, at the head of whom he always placed Leslie for a special share of virulent invective, as will be seen further on. Now he came forward in a different character, and it was almost his earliest appearance in print, as the writer of a letter not in favour of the bill for prohibiting Occasional Conformity, but against the practice itself. It was a very sharp remonstrance indeed, yet couched in decent and respectful terms to Mr. Howe, minister of the Presbyterian congregation to which the Lord Mayor belonged, for countenancing his conduct and that of all other offenders in the same body, whom he did not hesitate to denounce as immoral, dishonest, and inconsistent with the genuine principles of Dissenters. Mr. Howe replied by an indignant rebuke for introducing his name into the question, but declining to discuss it with an anonymous writer; and though some further correspondence followed, it provoked little more from Mr. Howe than a repetition of his rebuke, in which he showed his discretion rather than valour or ability.

A complainant of an opposite description was Mr.

Sacheverell, destined to become famous shortly with the new title of Doctor, and occasion a disturbance vastly out of proportion to the importance of anything he said or did, owing to the ferment then prevailing in the nation. He was a man of fair ability and moderate learning, who could write an effective sermon and deliver it still more effectively. Leslie afterwards espoused his cause most warmly, and defended him through thick and thin, at the cost of much obloquy to himself; for which he met with an ungenerous and ungracious return that gave great offence to his friends. But it made little impression upon himself; nor when Sacheverell signified his intention of attacking him in a pamphlet, though he wisely reconsidered this determination, did Leslie betray the slightest sense of animosity.[1] His first public appearance of any importance, though admired as a preacher in London among Tories and High Churchmen, was in June, 1702, at Oxford, where he preached a sermon entitled "Political Union," which caused a great deal of excitement, owing mainly to the general state of feeling, and to the manner of the preacher himself. It is absurd to say, as many have done since, apparently upon a very superficial acquaintance, that the sermon was a most wretched, flimsy production, though equally undeserving of the extravagant eulogy bestowed by admirers at the time. Apart from consideration of the opinions expressed in it, which were those entertained and proclaimed by many more clergy every Sunday quite as strongly, it was a well-reasoned and carefully written discourse, above the average. But a sermon for its effects depends upon delivery in some measure, with a striking phrase or two, and very much more on the occasion, audience, and the amount of sympathy between them and the preacher at the time. A

[1] Hearn's correspondence.

few extracts will furnish a specimen of the doctor's style so that readers can form their own opinion.

"This great and wise prince Solomon knew that the royal palace and the divine altar were protected by the same Power and Providence, and that the Throne and the Church stood upon the same bottom. That the welfare and destruction of both were bound up together; that they were subsisted by the same common principles; that what struck the one in like manner affected the other; and that when the pinnacles of the temple tottered, the crown was found very seldom to sit unshaken on the prince's head. . . . We may talk for ever about the danger of religion, and the obligations every man lies under to defend it, and yet perhaps never make a single proselyte to our party. Men are under such a cold neglect and indifference towards that which relates to the naked soul and conscience, they have so little feeling of these spiritual matters, and so much jealousy of trick and design, that they are very backward and cautious to be betrayed into the belief of it. The other world lies at such a distance from our sight, and is so far removed from our prospect, that very few can raise an idea of its glories, or be touched with its concerns. But when the affairs of this life come to be called in question, or the least of its enjoyments exposed to any danger, flesh and blood rise at the summons, and how ready are we to defend, how resolute and obstinate in the vindication of them! When liberty and property lie at stake, they command our spirits and courage; few men are cowards in this case, whatever they are in others; it sets the whole man in alarms, and calls up the strongest powers of nature in their assertion. What, therefore, the interest of religion cannot engage men to do, perhaps the advantages of their temporal welfare may prevail upon them to perform. For when our duty comes enforced with a double obligation and reward, when it proposes the joint satisfactions of both lives, and lays before our choice all the blessings of two worlds at once, what motive can it want to encourage mankind to its practice? Now, to set this matter in a clear and convincing light, I shall examine it under the double consideration of experience and reason. . . . A ruined Church and prosperous Government are irreconcilable contradictions in experience, confronted and confuted by the united, universal, and concurrent testimony of all ages, and histories, sacred and profane. . . . Atheism and anarchy have always gone hand in hand; they are the mutual spawn and genuine production of each other, and, like vermin, are bred out of the same filth and corruption. Where the principles of religion come once to be shaken, or ever happen to be subverted, the State never fails to follow it, and to take share in its misfortunes and ruins. . . . The four grand pillars upon which all Government is raised and supported, are justice, counsel, treasure, and religion. But doubtless the main column that keeps up this fabrick, and preserves it both from shaking and falling, is religion. The others are only under-props. Heresy and schism have such a natural communication with rebellion and usurpation, that where the ecclesiastical body is infested with the one, the body politick is seldom free from the other plague. As long as men's opinions govern their actions, errors in judgment can produce nothing else but errors in practice. Innovations in the Church are but the forerunners of those in the State; and where doctrines and discipline of the first are shaken or corrupted, the powers and privileges of the second very seldom remain entire. What alters the fundamental constitution of the one, will infallibly destroy both. Presbytery and Republicanism go hand in hand; they are but the same disorderly, levelling principle in the two different branches of our State.... It is as unaccountable and amazing a contradiction to our reason, as the greatest reproach and scandal upon our Church, that any pretending to that sacred and inviolable character of being her true sons, pillars, and defenders, should turn such apostates and renegadoes to their oaths and professions; such false traitors to their trusts and offices, as to strike sail with a party, that is such an open and avowed enemy to our communion; and against whom every one that wishes its welfare ought to hang out the bloody flag and banner of defiance. But in this, as well as in most other circumstances, both our Church and State share the same common fate, that they can be ruined by none but themselves, and that if ever they receive a mortal stab or wound, it must be in the house of their friends."

Now, this sermon's political tone throughout clearly distinguishes it from pulpit addresses in the Church of England at the present day. Politics are still a staple commodity in town and country conventicles, but allusion to them is exceptional in churches. It must, therefore, be remembered that in Sacheverell's time such was not the case. A solecism often gives more offence than a more serious fault; but there was no breach of custom or good taste as then understood on his part. That which caught the ear, and lingered impressively on the minds of his audience, from an indefinable something in the way it was uttered by the preacher's melodious voice, was the single phrase—"hang out the bloody flag and banner of defiance." This repeated from mouth to mouth more than all the rest of the discourse, in which were many other things equally belligerent and eloquent, gave the key-note to commotion, and in a week Sacheverell had become famous, throughout the kingdom—the idol of one party and the abhorrence of another.

The change of feeling in favour of Toryism perceptible in the nation greatly disturbed De Foe's restless spirit, the more because accompanied by a sensible loss of personal influence and resources to himself, having been a secret-service pensioner for several years under William; Othello's occupation was gone, and he could not fail to be angry. Accordingly, his displeasure found vent in a publication entitled "A New Test of the Church of England's Loyalty." This was directed against a sermon of Dr. Binkes' before Convocation, but proceeded most impartially to level censure at the whole body of the Church, and accuse her members of "wholesale persecution for more than thirty years, while themselves apostates from the very fundamental doctrines of their Church, perjured in the sight of God and man, notorious hypocrites and deceivers," with a long disquisition about the Origin of Government in the consent and for the benefit of the people governed. Many other attacks issued from the press simultaneously, but De Foe's was conspicuously the ablest, though Dissenters declined to acknowledge him as their proper champion and representative. Its sting lay in the fact that such numbers of professing members of the Church of England, especially clergy, had shifted their ground at the Revolution. The old theory of absolute passive obedience was an absurdity for them to revive, who had after proclaiming it for a generation cut it down by the roots. Dr. Drake and others replied, but failed effectively to meet this count in the indictment. Nor could Leslie do so successfully in his "New Associations," because it was true and indefensible with regard to the Tory party—all, in fact, but Nonjurors and Jacobites, who for acting up to their old principles of loyalty had been left in the lurch. Therefore, while severely rebuking De Foe's acrimonious tone, he employed himself mainly in defending the doctrine of non-resistance, and confronting his theory of the Origin of Government with the Scriptural scheme.

As this subject was pursued in other subsequent publications, the contents of " New Associations" require no more minute description at present; though it attained much popularity, and included a forcible reply to Denis's "Danger of Priestcraft in Religion," an attack upon Sacheverell. A more cunningly devised and formidable weapon was next employed against the Church. A pamphlet issued from the press, entitled "The Shortest Way with the Dissenters," complaining in bitter terms of their demeanour towards the Church for many years past, and holding them up as a fitting object for resentment and revenge, now that her time of triumph had come. It professedly was written by a clergyman, and as such passed current for some time, infuriating Dissenters or frightening them by the horrid vengeance it seemed to invoke, and covering Church-people with confusion, that any one clothed in the garb of her ministry should have propounded anything at once so wicked and foolish. When excitement had cooled down a little to permit of more dispassionate consideration, a suspicion of its genuineness crossed the minds of a few persons, because after most careful inquiry it could not be traced to a single known author or publisher connected with the Church. Among these was Leslie, who communicated his suspicious impression to Lord Nottingham, with remarks upon the style of the pamphlet compared with other compositions. His lordship held in his hands as one of the Government the means of following up the scent, so that after a while detection was complete, nor did

De Foe attempt denial that he had fabricated the atrocious hoax. He very naturally tried to ride off upon the lame excuse of only having done it by way of jest; but the malicious intention of bringing odium and disgrace by his infamous imposture upon the clergy in particular and the whole Church in general, was too apparent. So sorry a pretence, and the cowardly attempts he made to escape punishment, only aggravated his first offence, and he was condemned to the pillory, to be then imprisoned, with a heavy fine, which it must have been impossible for him ever to pay. That he richly merited punishment none could reasonably doubt, but that inflicted far exceeded the necessity of the case, betrayed a spirit like that which prompted his offence, evoked a good deal of natural compassion for him among the populace, and embittered De Foe more than ever against his opponents. A mild and moderate penalty might not have altered his malignant disposition, but it would have disproved most effectually his taunts about persecution, and deprived him of all claim to sympathy in any class. De Foe had particularly intended suspicion and odium to fall upon Leslie, therefore he would have been justified in demanding punishment; but so far from this, he deprecated anything being done beyond a public exposure of the cruel forgery.

Abridgment of "Private Judgment and Authority in Matters of Faith."

All religions and sects are built upon dispute whether men ought to govern themselves by their own private judgment, or be determined by authority of others in their faith. The effects of private judgment are multiplicity of sects and opinions, and it is the chief pretence of war. To remedy which evils, some would have a settled judge of controversy for appeals and determination of all disputes in religion. Supposing the Scriptures to be an infallible complete rule of faith, how shall we agree about the true meaning and interpretation of them? We see every sect quote Scripture and have its own interpretation. On the other hand, there are difficulties in submitting our private judgment to authority. First, because it is left to private judgment to choose that authority. If I should believe in God upon the authority of any Church, it would follow that my faith was more in that Church than in God; and I have no more for the authority of that Church than my private judgment still. Secondly, private judgment can never be so fatally mistaken as in submitting to authority if it should judge wrong. The question will remain whether greater mischiefs and inconveniences have befallen mankind in the one way or the other. If it be found that greater have attended private judgment, that would be no greater argument against it than against free-will or any other composition of our nature. Perhaps men make use of their hands to more destruction than any good they do with them, yet this would be an ill argument for cutting off the hands of our children. Christians allow heathens to be misled by authority, who go on in the track of their fathers without examination; yet heathens have no notion of an infallible judge. Jews stood out and continue in infidelity upon the single point of authority, because Christ was rejected by their Church, a principle common to them and the Church of Rome, upon which I see not how a Jew can be converted. Christ Himself owned, they say, their Church all His lifetime, and so did His apostles. Yet it said His miracles were wrought by Beelzebub, and that He was a deceiver in His doctrine. It was the only judge of God then in the world, whereas other Churches now dispute this point with that of Rome. Both Jews and Romanists are here upon one basis, the authority of the Church, and both cannot be right.

The Jew has this advantage, that whereas the Romanist must allow his Church to have been once the only true one, the other does not allow the Church of Rome at all; which retorts the argument it uses against the Church of England, but against which the Dissenter again asserts his private judgment. There is not one word in the Scriptures either of the Pope or the Church of Rome, so that this must be determined purely by private judgment. If private judgment is to be determined by vote, there are ten to one against the Church of Rome. But she is said to be the mother Church? How can she be the mother of Churches which never descended from her? It is certain the Jewish was the mother of all. The promises mentioned were first made to her, and if these can be transferred, then they may be from Rome as from Jerusalem, and so without end. There is no promise to secure any particular Church, that her candlestick may not be removed as others have been. It was to every particular Church Christ spoke when He said, "Tell it unto the Church;" for the case there put is of private difference. There was nothing at all of faith concerned in it. Neither God nor Christ does send us to a judge of faith, nor can there be any but God alone. The Creed will test this, because where anything is determined by authority, such authority must be superior to what it determines. We receive not the creed upon the authority of the Church. I receive the Scriptures upon the testimony, not authority, of the Church, and I examine that testimony as I do other facts, till I have satisfied my private judgment there is no other way. God has taken more care of our souls, and not put our faith under the dominion of any. The apostles disclaimed it (2 Cor. i. 24; Gal. i. 8). Should the sun borrow light from the moon? Yet this pretence of the Jews is again taken up by the Church of Rome, and we have seen strange effects of it in both. ... We know the canonical books of Scripture not by authority of the Church but by her evidence. The heretics could not produce their originals, nor did their copies agree one with another, which was deciding not by authority but by evidence. The twentieth Article says "she has authority in matters of faith." But far from infallible authority; "as a keeper and a witness," to determine controversies of faith only ministerially, not absolutely and authoritatively. Has He, therefore, given no power at all to His Church? It was a great power when He said, "Go and teach all nations, baptizing them." And He left power to invest others with the same authority, without which none can preach the faith; for "how shall they preach except they be sent?" Likewise there is the power of the Keys, which implies all authority of government, as being the ground and pillar of the faith; and He has promised to ratify in heaven the censures of the Church when justly inflicted upon earth. A condition is here implied as of contrition in the penitent, so of *clave non errante*, that is justly. While Christ exposed the fallibility of the Church (in His day), He yet supported her authority by owning that the scribes and Pharisees sat in Moses' seat.

Dissenters will do nothing they are bidden, for the very reason of being bidden. This is the spirit of contradiction; it is crossness for crossness' sake, of which they would soon be sensible if exhibited in their own children. I allow the Church to be judge of faith upon earth, yet there is an appeal to God. The Church is the interpreter of Scripture, as the judges of the law. But the ultimate decision is in God, and we must make use of our private judgment in the great matters of Faith and Worship. The Church of Rome requires every man to trust blindly to her guidance. The Church of England shows her commission to be a guide on the road to heaven, derived by Succession from the apostles, with a competent though not infallible authority. Dissenters have no commission nor authority to show; they have thrust themselves as guides upon the road. If any will answer me, I desire him first to join in this prayer, that it would please God to strengthen those that are in truth, and convince those that are in error; towards which I have cast in my mite.

ABRIDGMENT OF A "DISSERTATION CONCERNING THE USE AND AUTHORITY OF ECCLESIASTICAL HISTORY."

The study of history, especially the ecclesiastical, will serve best to the ends of promoting the interests of God's Church where she is so far lost as to be almost forgotten; unknown to most what she truly is, or what it is that belongs to her. The best method will be to show her in her primitive face. A picture allures more than description, and matter of fact beyond many arguments; discourses tell us of things, but history shows them to us. Of all history ecclesiastical is the most beneficial, as much more as the concerns of the Church are beyond that of the State, our souls above our bodies, and our eternal state more than the moment we have to stay in the world. Thus we see the rise and growth of heresies and schisms; and how these tares were sown while the husbandman slept. There we see the beginnings of Erastianism, more fatal to the Church than persecution; when court bishops gave up the sacred deposit committed to their charge, into the hands of kings for worldly considerations. Controverted points must be determined by matter of fact—what that faith was which was at first delivered to the saints. Those doctrines and that government which has this evidence must be the truth. Those who have not read ecclesiastical history and the primitive fathers must take their knowledge at second hand upon trust from others. The best method is to examine upwards and read downwards from the beginning; there we shall find many of these seemingly exalted and new notions set up by various sects, to have been old exploded heresies condemned by the Catholic Church, and only new vamped by subtle enemies crept in among us to divide and distract the ignorant and unstable. Even the fanatics would fain have antiquity on their side if they could get it, and when it will not do they rail at it. By consulting the original records and histories of the Church, it will appear how groundless and contemptible are the pretensions of both Pope and Presbyter, who are joined like Samson's foxes with firebrands, though they look several ways, to ruin and depress the primitive Episcopacy. As God in His infinite wisdom has not thought it best for the world to set one universal monarch over it all, but many independent kings who may balance one another, so, S. Cyprian has observed, Christ did make the College of bishops numerous, that if one should prove heretical or seek to devour the flock, the rest might mercifully interpose for the saving of it. But, as S. Gregory the Great argued, if a universal bishop should fall, a universal Church may fall with him. On the other hand, the Presbyterian party would unhinge all particular governments, and render the government of the world a mere chaos and a mob. A stronger argument is that of fact—what was the government of the Church as established and left by apostles? for that must continue till a greater, at least as great an authority shall alter it. Some make no matter of the government so as the doctrine be preserved, not considering that the government was given to preserve the doctrine; and no instance can be given, from Jeroboam downward, where the change of government did not bring with it a change of doctrine, as the apostle argues (Heb. vii. 12). For the priesthood being changed, there is made of necessity a change also of the law. If the Church goes, the truth which she supports goes with her, is impaired or improved with her; for Christ has built the faith upon the foundation of the apostles and prophets, Himself the chief Corner-stone. While the Church retained her primitive discipline and preserved the bounds of the Sanctuary free from popular and all lay usurpations, how was the faith made glorious, and Christian zeal shone far and wide to the disarming and conversion of her adversaries! . . . I have now but one word more concerning the abridgment of histories; they are of use to those who have read the histories at large and to those who have not. To the former they serve as indexes and revive them in their minds with little pains; and to those who have not leisure or application to go through great works, they afford that knowledge which they would otherwise totally want.

ABRIDGMENT OF A SERMON ON EZRA X. 4: "AGAINST MARRIAGES IN DIFFERENT COMMUNIONS."

What this matter was appears from the context. Ezra reproved the people of Israel for their having married with idolatrous nations contrary to the command of God. The

Jews were then the peculium or holy seed; which is the reason why their genealogies are set down with so much exactness even before the Flood. The prohihition was not on account of their nation, but religion. "For they will turn away thy son from following Me, to serve other gods" (Deut. vii. 4). They turned away the heart of Solomon; and if the wisdom of Solomon was not proof against the witchcraft of this sin, what other man's presumption can be guiltless. We find the same reproof against the Jews for marrying with idolaters of their own nation. Thus Jehoram and Jehoshaphat. But it was lawful to marry with heathens who changed their religion, as Ruth and Rachab. And the case in Ezra was of marrying with Babylonians during the captivity. It is a maxim in law, that where there is the same reason, the law shall be the same. And none can deny there is at least as much reason for Christians to avoid idolatry as the Jews. It is strange to hear some deny there can be any idolatry among Christians; proceeding upon the supposition that it is a total and absolute forsaking of God. Many Christian idolaters may have the instruction of God's good Spirit, and may be men of devotion and great zeal as Jehu was, and their labours may be profitable to the Church; yet this Christian idolatry is more inexcusable than the heathen or Jewish. You may say, if idolatry be not inconsistent with the protection of God, and even the instruction of God's good Spirit, why should it be so unlawful to marry with idolaters? I answer, the sin is not the less for the goodness of God; it is rather a greater aggravation of it. It is a bewitching sin, and the nature of fallen man is bent to this spiritual fornication. And this is the reason why marriages with idolaters were forbidden more than with other sinners. Idolatry, that serpent-sin, insinuates itself under the notion of the worship of God, and is transformed even into zeal for His glory. There is no sort of reason for thinking that idolatry is not the same under the Gospel as it was under the Law, more than that there is another sort of adultery or murder. S. Jerome, S. Cyprian, and S. Augustine speak against these marriages, and there are several Councils to the same effect.

It is objected 1 Cor. vii. 12. But this is of divorcing, and not of marrying. In the first conversions to Christianity it must happen that many might be converted, and not their wives or husbands. S. Paul says, "not to put away;" but he does not say, "marry such a one." There is more in it than this; for if it were supposed lawful to marry such, there could be no dispute about the lawfulness of living together after marriage; and if Christians had a doubt whether they ought not to divorce their wives for idolatry, it is past a doubt they thought it unlawful to marry with such. The apostle, though he would not absolutely dissolve marriages made before conversion, yet in case of a second marriage ties them up that it shall be "only in the Lord"—words meant of marrying only the faithful, the interpretation of S. Ignatius and our early reformers.

Nor will this decision of S. Paul conflict with that of Ezra, who commanded to put away such wives as were idolaters. For the cases are totally different. That in Ezra was Jews (believers) marrying with idolaters, which voided the marriage from the beginning. That in S. Paul was infidels or idolaters marrying with one another (which was undoubtedly lawful), and afterwards one being converted. This is the particular sin for which it is said God sent the flood. After the flood Ishmael was born of Hagar, and the influence of the mother appeared in his persecution of Isaac, and his marriage of a wife out of Egypt, which warned Abraham as to the marriage of Isaac. Lot suffered his daughters to marry in Sodom, and they perished. We find the same ingredient in the ruin of Esau ; and the miseries of Judah, son of Jacob, proceeded from his marrying a Canaanitess. In the New Testament we find no examples, for the case was so positively ruled by the apostles. To come to an end, this will be granted me on all hands, that marrying into another communion is at least a tentation, and then how can any one without mocking of God repeat the Lord's Prayer, " Lead us not into temptation," when at the same time, even while the words are in his mouth, in the office of holy matrimony, he deliberately, wilfully, and avowedly throws himself or exposes his child to this great tentation ? How can any priest with a good conscience deliver over with his own hands one of his flock to another of a different communion? If they should fall thereby, would not their blood be required at his hand? God says of such marriages they will be a snare to you. With whom does the power of reforming lie ? " Arise," said the people to Ezra ; " for this matter belongeth unto thee." Matters of religion are to be reformed by the Church.

CHAPTER IX.

Party Nomenclature—Intimacies—Whigs and Tories—"Rehearsal"—The Church in Scotland—"Cassandra"—The Three Estates—Calves'-Head Feasts—Club—Occasional Letter Writer—Burnet's Calumnies on the Clergy—High and Low Church—Nonconformity—Dr. Davenant—"Wolf Stript"—Owen—S. Wesley—Supplement—"Cassandra"—"New Associations"—"Wolf Stript."

Party nomenclature ought to undergo alteration when, owing to any causes, former principles are abandoned. Thus properly Sir Robert Peel relinquished profession of Toryism from a conviction that he no longer was prepared to stand upon the old lines. Since then more than one new departure has taken place; even what he intended by Conservatism ceased to form the policy of the party professing it. A fresh style is required to indicate with any propriety of meaning their aims and object. Conservative as much as Tory is a misnomer out of date in application to those who are concerned to defend the Throne without the Altar, the Crown but not the Mitre, the Temporalty in the State without the Spiritualty, and what are sometimes termed "sacred rights of property" apart from the rights of sacred property. How this great party in the State ought in future to be designated, or what service it can usefully perform for the remnant of a much-altered constitution, its leaders may be left to define, but its interests cannot be forwarded by retention of this palpable contradiction. A similar observation does not apply with equal force to the other large political party. For although Liberality is absurdly employed to designate free handling of other people's property and ancient institutions, nevertheless these have a reasonable claim to the old appellation of Whigs who still favour Democracy, Republicanism and Dissent even if their ultimate intentions be occasionally kept in the background. Originally Whig and Tory were designed to be terms of reproach and opprobrium, nicknames bestowed by their respective adversaries, but speedily adopted and gloried in by the parties themselves upon whom they had been affixed. It is worth while to note what changes occurred in their significance during the period in which their use continued most common, with some reference to their first intention. They began almost simultaneously, the one derived from Ireland, the other from Scotland, though Tory had somewhat the start of Whig; in 1697 being taken to describe those previously called Royalists, Loyalists, or Yorkists, who resisted the proposal for depriving the Duke of York of his right of succession to the throne. Tories in Ireland meant Romanists and plunderers, who committed depredations upon owners of property, especially of estates which had been confiscated to Protestants. There long continued on the statute-book, perhaps is still unrepealed, an act authorizing arrest and imprisonment of "all rogues, vagabonds, Tories, and Irishmen calling themselves gentlemen." Such a nickname suggested itself as very suitable and happy to imply the predatory and lawless character of a party who objected to a new and enormous stride in legal confiscation on behalf of Protestants. Its sting was extracted immediately that they accepted and boasted of it.

Within a year those called Exclusionists and True Blues, to signify Protestantism of deeper colour than the Church's, or "Birmingham Protestantism," a name for spurious courage, after casting about in various directions for a short, pithy, and contumelious epithet like the other, got the title of Whigs—meaning sour milk or whey, as illustrating their acrid, distempered character in general.[1] But no sooner did they also in turn adopt their new designation than it lost all its odour of contempt. Historians have failed to discover and record who were the authors of these appellations, or else, in an age so conspicuous for its love of memorials, testimonials, and centenary celebrations as the present, those departed worthies could hardly fail to have a church, a conventicle, a monument, or a new university erected to their honour. At the Revolution the terms went somewhat out of fashion, because it was felt to be a manifest incongruity either for the partisans of a Usurper to style themselves as defenders of Hereditary right on one hand, or on the other for Democrats and Republicans to have become the powerful supporters of a stolen crown. Under Anne their use revived with a partial return to former meanings, but involving an inconsistency still on the part of Tories who were Exclusionists in fact, while professing to support old constitutional principles. With extinction of the Stuart race hereditary right has ceased; and the settlement of the Hanoverian dynasty upon a parliamentary basis opened quite a new question for debate between the rival partisans of monarchy and republicanism in this country.[2] The Church has now no necessary con-

---

[1] Burnet ("History of his Own Times," vol. i. p. 58), not liking this, suggested Whigomers or drivers.

[2] Stanhope makes Macaulay virtually to agree with him. Both, for obvious reasons, omit the real point.

nection with either party; members of both are equally capable of honourably engaging in her defence, and the promotion of her material interests for the sake of the nation at large. From which alternately she has suffered more in the past it might be difficult to determine; but the fault lay mainly in the short-sighted Erastian policy of prelates and priests trying to wed and confuse her with the State.

Charles Leslie regarded Whigs in his time with an utter abhorrence. He had no friends among them. It never occurred to him to separate men from their principles and professions, as is done in the present day, and in private life be on terms of intimacy and cordial alliance with those who in public are denounced as holding dangerous opinions, and prejudicial to the welfare of the nation. He did good unto all men, especially those of the household of faith, so far as lay in his power. He was affable and courteous in demeanour towards schismatics with whom he was brought into personal contact, but his charity was based upon truth, therefore he abstained from all spurious or hollow intimacies which involved a departure from principle. For this reason he laboured the more to win converts to his own opinions through the public press or discussions, which were the only means left open to him; nor these without some severe and inconvenient restrictions. It speaks well for the general good temper and fairness of English people that a man thus rigid in adherence to a particular standard, making no attempts to win popularity, and subject to continual misrepresentations, should, notwithstanding, have secured so large an amount of favour among all classes as he did. He never met, in the most excited times of political turmoil, with any rudeness or interruptions in the streets of London, though his appearance was pretty well known. With exception of Burnet no unkind words or allusions concerning him occurred in Parliament from speakers of very opposite sentiments. And if a few Quakers had formed a plot against his life, a far more numerous portion of the Sect upon another occasion invited him to a public entertainment in testimony of their esteem and good will, which afforded him great gratification, because so spontaneous on their part and unexpected on his own. Little option or choice was afforded to him if he engaged in politics at all as to the course he must adopt. He disapproved of all plots and conspiracies of a secret or private character, nor desired any question to be raised concerning Queen Anne's title on several accounts. What affected him most was the condition of the Church of England, both spiritually and temporally. Already he had exerted himself to great advantage for her in the former way. Defence seemed requisite in the latter, and only the Tory party could be said to have this at heart. Therefore he allied himself with them—when, too, they most needed writers of credit and ability. What he thought of the Whig party at that date one or two passages of his writings will most clearly demonstrate. "I now say that a true Whig is not so good as a pagan, for the pagans did and do acknowledge a God, and never had so foolish and blasphemous a notion as that His power over them was derived from themselves. . . . Are not these men literally heathens? For what is a heathen but he that denies the Holy Scriptures of God? They are worse than Mahometans. For the Alcoran acknowledges the Scriptures of both the Old and New Testament. . . . Behold! O Englishmen, and consider a set of men among you combined to depreciate and overthrow your whole religion! To run down revelation by which only we know that Christ came into the world and died for our sins. In short, they would turn us all heathen, would wrest your Bible out of your hands, and bid you believe it no more, but follow the green boughs of corruption against which you have declared war at your baptism. Therefore your giving heed to these men, or bidding them God-speed, is directly lifting yourselves under the banner of the devil. Who else could or durst call the Holy Scriptures of God a withered branch? . . . I have long made it my observation of the Whigs that they pay the least regard of any to men of quality or place. They take a particular pleasure to despise men in power, and treat them with the greatest malignity and contempt; they think none above themselves, and themselves above all others; they have a perfect aversion to the word superior, to keep their distance or pay respect. And this comes upon them as a natural consequence of their principle deriving all power from the people. For while they look upon themselves as the original of kings and parliaments, and that all these are accountable to them as their substitutes and servants, how can they think anything of lesser honours derived from the crown? What is a lord or a duke to me? I am an Englishman! is their common saying. This makes them insolent even in conversation with any that are above their own level, and they love to expose them. The less respect they pay to others they think themselves the greater men. But none value power more when they get it into their hands. Then they think Government is upon its right basis, for they look upon themselves as the original and foundation of it; and that therefore they have a right to exercise it without control. For you may take this as a sure rule that, whenever you hear men cry up the power of the people, they mean only themselves; not other people. No, but they seek to depress them; and whoever opposes themselves, they say are against the power of the people, and ought not to be suffered in a commonwealth. This is their language, and ever has been in all popular commotions. They will suffer none to judge but themselves; if any differ in opinion from them, they reckon such not to be of the people. . . . Hence, when one of this stamp comes into any little magistracy his crest rises above the moon, and he thinks himself equal to the greatest man in the nation. He is busy and restless and pragmatical, and keeps the neighbourhood perpetually in hot water; none can be quiet for him. But if he can affront any man of quality or in high post, then he is in his element, and cries about justice and putting the laws in execution without respect of person. . . . A true Whig is for religion a Deist; he will own a God, but banters revelation; he believes no Church, but complies with any which is in fashion, and will overturn one Church and set up another as he thinks it serves his interest and ambition to be the head of a party. . . . He is as dangerous in the State as in the Church; he loves revolution and hates hereditary government because it is a settlement, and the worse title the better king with him, because it keeps the king more at the mercy of the people, and makes way for new changes. And yet he may think these changes for the better, and really may design what he thinks most for the public good; and many of them endeavour after it in earnest, and do many generous and popular things; are men of probity and honour, and sincere in what they profess, and have many noble and lovely qualities as the patriots among the Greeks and Romans, who durst even sacrifice themselves for their country. But their misfortune is, not rightly understanding the nature of government, its original, and the obligation of conscience to it, as to God, and not to man. . . . Our Whigs, not consulting the Scriptures in this case, or little regarding them, have fallen into the error of the heathen, of placing government upon the foot of the people, and in that frame can find no end or last resort; but every man makes himself judge, and nothing can follow but eternal confusion."

No person still enamoured of the title Whig will be expected to recognize his own portrait in these selections from many passages in the *Rehearsal* to the same effect— a new publication, at that time only in embryo, which will follow for consideration almost directly in these pages. It may be presumed that if Toryism has become extinct, Whiggery has improved from the same causes. Even then the picture was not intended to apply personally to individuals, but to be taken as one typical of the Whig character in those who put themselves forward prominently to represent and speak for the whole party. A great mistake or omission on their part was the leaving of principles and objects in the hands of low scribblers, when certainly there were many noble and generous men amongst them who must have shared to the full Leslie's disgust and indignation at the profane and abominable writings issued in their name to inoculate the masses; when also men of ability were not wanting in their ranks to rescue their cause from such degradation. Entertaining the view our author did of the principles of Whigs in their natural and necessary tendency to set popular authority above revelation itself, it is no wonder that he lent the whole weight of his influence to resist them.

Before embarking in the project which he had conceived of doing this by publication of a weekly paper, he committed to the press some other pamphlets, which formed a sort of transitional stage between theological treatises and mere political ones. Not that he intended such a graduation of proceedings, but in actual fact it occurred. What he wrote in the interval was all of a semi-theological and political character, which could not be correctly referred to the same class as that of preceding or subsequent publications, yet partaking largely of both. "New Associations" may be placed at one end of this line of demarcation, and the "Wolf Stript" at the other. To the first was added a second part, which also acquired an extensive popularity, running through three editions in a few months. It continued discussion of the same subject, occasioned by remarks of several belligerents, the chief of which was in a tract on the "Danger of Priestcraft to Religion," the purpose of which is sufficiently indicated by its title, but written with a good deal of vigour. In all these great abhorrence was expressed of Leslie's proposals for union with the Gallican Church, as a step towards Rome; and the "Regale" with its supplement[1] which had contained that, came up for fresh animadversion, but none of them attempted any argument concerning the proposal itself.

Another subject introduced by him was the illiberal treatment of Episcopalians in Scotland. They had been deprived of their establishment, and now were refused even the barest toleration by Presbyterians. When they applied for permission to have their own bishops and use the Liturgy in their churches, the most violent outcry was raised against them. At the very time when not only toleration but equal civil rights were being demanded on behalf of Dissenters in England, in Scotland any toleration at all was refused to Episcopalians. To justify so flagrant an inconsistency, the only reply deemed necessary was a comparison between the numbers of Dissenters in the two countries, and the fact of a legal establishment of Presbyterianism across the border; although that only had been of

[1] This was written much later than the "Regale" in its first state.

recent institution, and as if the converse were not exactly the case on this side! Deficiency in argument had to be supplied by invectives against Jacobites and Nonjurors, with insinuations against the character of priests in Scotland who had to be ordained in England, for which not a vestige of foundation in fact existed. Nothing, indeed, testified more clearly their disinterestedness, sincerity, and integrity than the simple fact of seeking Orders for ministering in a country where they were certain of exposure to ill-treatment from enemies, at a scanty pittance scarcely sufficient to provide them with necessaries of life, when they could if disreputable have found a safer, more congenial, and remunerative sphere of employment in the ranks of their opponents in either country. A Mrs. Astell volunteered to interpose in this controversy with amusing impartiality, recommending to Dissenters their extinction as a party because "it would make for their interest and real good," while she carefully assured the public that her publication was "not writ by Mr. L——y, or any furious Jacobite." Her compliment and proposal were accepted with a similar impartiality of silence on both sides, nor did her reputation ever incur the suspicion which she had sought to obviate by this anticipatory disavowal.

"Cassandra (but I hope not) telling what will come of it" was in reply to an occasional letter criticizing his "New Associations," the anonymous author of which he "supposed to be of a higher figure than the senseless scribblers." No attempt to identify him can be deemed satisfactory, therefore he must be left in the disguise which he preferred to assume. He termed "New Associations" "the most malicious and virulent book of the age," and consigned Leslie to the pillory as a writer who had the best way of turning everything to his own humour of any man he ever met with. The pamphlet showed thought and education, but hardly deserved so complete an examination as it received, because what its author opposed to the Scriptural[1] scheme was only that which De Foe and other Whig champions had already sufficiently explained concerning the origin of government from the people by election. He was willing to admit its institution by God in this sense, that if He set a ruler over every nation, the people had as much a divine right to his protection as he to their obedience. The question, however, remained, if the right of protection were invalid, did this justify the people in taking arms, deposing the ruler, and appointing another in his room ? For this the Occasionalist contended upon ground of necessity, which Leslie deemed a usurpation of divine authority. He repeated that mistake so frequently objected to by our author in Whig writers, and so common still, of making the Sovereign one of the three Estates of the realm, and the Balance of power to consist in their good agreement ; a false assumption which of course involved the main point in dispute. King, Lords, and Commons are not these Estates, but the three are the Spiritualty, the Temporalty, and the Commons under the sovereign, and deriving their powers and privileges from him. Whether this constitution be a good one or not, whether also it be derived from divine authority, will remain open to question with all who are not convinced by Leslie in "Cassandra," and Sir Edmund Filmer's work on Patriarchal government; but that it is an established thing in England from Henry VIII. to the present day, and for centuries preceding, no one conversant with Acts of Parliament can reasonably doubt ; even though in practice for a century the authority of the crown has been limited by

---

[1] Leslie's was not identical with Filmer's.

consent of the three Estates, and though either Temporalty or Spiritualty should suffer further restriction in the future.

Calves'-head feasts were an institution among Republicans and Dissenters in mockery of the annual Church fast to commemorate King Charles's martyrdom on January 30. When Leslie censured them severely in "Cassandra," and other publications, a majority protested entire ignorance on the subject, and even questioned their existence at all. But the fact was abundantly proved, that in London, Oxford, and other places these revels were practised and attended by considerable numbers. It is not necessary to suppose they received any countenance from the more religious or respectable persons of Whig sentiments, or that they had extended beyond a few principal towns.[1] Yet, as was pointed out, the matter for consideration was not how many deemed it prudent openly to participate in such proceedings, but who held calves'-head notions regarding the dismal tragedy of that day in secret triumph, or treated the Church's Fast with profane contempt. "It was not the meat, but the principles, which rendered them detestable;" nor was Leslie far wrong in surmising there were not only a few profligate men, but many more of the party on behalf of whom the Occasional letter writer undertook to answer. At one of these impious meetings a sort of symbolical ceremony was performed of sticking knives into the largest calf's head all at once, in token of their union for the restoration of a commonwealth and extirpation of monarchy, with music and verses to travesty and burlesque Church services on this anniversary. Had, therefore, "New Associations" and "Cassandra" possessed no other merit, their author deserved thanks for bringing public opinion to bear so decidedly against these parodies of a solemn observance,

[1] Milton was accused of being the founder.

that men became alarmed to be even suspected of attendance at them, and they had to be completely abandoned. If the "higher figure" were not Dr. Burnet himself, yet he had admission to some of his most intimate counsels, and undertook to defend it in his "History of his Own Times," then in course of preparation, with more than ordinary partiality for a stranger. Leslie had been made acquainted with a portion of that book's contents, while yet unpublished, through a deceased friend, to whom they had been shown without any condition of secrecy expressed or implied. Accordingly, he ventured to protest against reflections upon men of honour and reputation still alive, and against sweeping accusations upon the whole body of the clergy, not only of the Restoration period, but of that date, being reserved for publication when none should be able to defend themselves. Burnet's apologist or amanuensis took him severely to task for this exposure, complaining of the manner in which his information had been acquired, but not able to deny the fact of such calumnies being in the manuscript. They remain to this day unaltered, and have furnished the sole authority upon which many gross attacks on the clergy have been repeated. Had Burnet's charges been true, his mode of dealing with them was most unbecoming and ungenerous for a prelate; but they were not true. What made the matter worse was that when thus challenged as an "accuser of the brethren," who vilified his own contemporaries and predecessors in the ministry, "not as an admonition to amend, but to asperse them to after ages," neither had the honesty to verify his accusations by any evidence or retract them; while admitting that he could "not speak from personal observation, for he so abhorred the clergy in general as to avoid their conversation, but kept better company among statesmen and politicians." His book had been pretty well discounted already from this disclosure before its appearance in print, and because that was confirmed by his notorious practice of discrediting and reviling the clergy upon every possible occasion. In the pulpit of S. James's Church, Piccadilly, Leslie heard him denounce "the corruption of them all over Christendom," and stentorically declare "priestcraft, a modish term borrowed from Dryden," to be its spring and source—he the one Elijah left stainless and immaculate in evil days.

"High" and "Low Church" had been terms already frequently employed to distinguish men holding different opinions on several ecclesiastical and theological subjects; but more happily designated as "schools of thought" by a late Dean of Ripon (McNeile). Now they began to be more generally and invidiously applied, dividing clergy and laity of the Church into separate and hostile camps, according as these were presumed to uphold or derogate from her ancient doctrine and discipline in their integrity. It has never been discovered who was the ingenious inventor of these unfortunate epithets any more than of Whig and Tory, or perhaps even he, too, might have some memorial from posterity! But Burnet never more boldly displayed his customary recklessness than when he publicly attributed the first adoption and recognition of them within the Church to Leslie, for at that very time he had before him in "Cassandra" and other publications of his a statement directly the reverse. Leslie correctly ascribed their origin and first application to Whigs and Dissenters, saying here, "They have invented this name of distinction on purpose to give themselves full liberty to vent all their spleen, unseen as they think, against the whole Church." Again, elsewhere, "The distinction of High and Low Church was invented of late on purpose as a handle to blacken the whole Church of England more securely and run down her whole constitution." Therefore it was obviously a very wanton piece of spite to cast the odium of their introduction upon him; but of course Leslie had, like Burnet himself and many others, while objecting to the terms upon principle, occasionally to adopt them when in general use so far as to signify his own unmistakable adhesion to one party rather than the other. Here lay an essential difference, of course, which has continued ever since; for the terms unfortunately have not fallen into desuetude. Burnet explained Low Church to mean those that "treated Dissenters with temper and moderation, and were for residing constantly on their benefices and for labouring diligently in them, that expressed a zeal against the Prince of Wales" (a slip with him for the person otherwise denominated pretended, and Pretender) "and for the Revolution"—in which excellent class of course he included himself. High Church were "those who loaded the other with false and invidious characters, were not for those moderate counsels, and took all pains to enforce their tragical apprehensions concerning the Church being in danger into the nation."[1]

Dean Swift, who now began to appear above the political horizon, concurs with Leslie as to the origin of the names, and in his characteristic method of sarcasm defines and describes both parties rather in regard to their political than ecclesiastical aspect. "Some time after the Revolution the distinction of High and Low Church came in, which was raised by the Dissenters in order to break the Church party, by dividing the members into high and low; and the opinion raised that the high joined with the Papists inclined the low to fall in with the Dissenters. . . .

[1] "History of his Own Times," vol. iii. 484; iv. 120.

To be against a standing army in time of peace was all High Church, tory and tantivy; to differ from a majority of bishops was the same. To raise the prerogative above law for serving a turn was Low Church and Whig. The opinion of the majority in the House of Commons, especially of the country party or landed interest, was high-flying and rank Tory. To exalt the king's supremacy beyond all precedent was Low Church, Whiggish, and moderate.[1] . . . The Church thermometer is supposed to have been invented in the reign of Henry VIII., about the time when that religious prince put some to death for owning the pope's supremacy, and others for denying transubstantiation. . . . It is adapted to the present constitution of our Church as divided into high and low. . . . The Church is placed in the middle point of the glass between zeal and moderation, the situation in which she always flourishes, and in which every good Englishman wishes her who is a friend to the constitution of his country. However, when it mounts to zeal, it is not amiss; and when it sinks to moderation, it is still in admirable temper. . . . Whether zeal or moderation be the point we aim at, let us keep fire out of the one and frost out of the other. But alas! the world is too wise to want such a precaution. The terms High Church and Low Church, as commonly used, do not so much denote a principle as they distinguish a party."[2]

Leslie objected to the terms *in limine* on account of their invidious origin, and further because of their constant misapplication, as of another word, "Nonconformist," which is a misnomer still as absurdly and injuriously employed by Church-people to designate Dissenters. What he said upon both subjects is well worth notice. "The Church of England

---

[1] Swift's Works, vol. vii. 258.
[2] Ibid., vol. viii. 222, 224, 226.

is but one, though there may be in her men of different complexions. She has for all one and the same charter, canons, articles, homilies, liturgies, rites, and ceremonies. Whoever keep not up to these are transgressors against the rules of her society. Those whom they call High Church are for supporting these, and those Low Church who would give them up. . . . Whoever lives in a society and do not conform to the rules, are thereby nonconformists to that society. These are they who are called Low Church; that is, who have but a low regard to the preservation of that society of which they are members, and therefore take upon themselves to dispense with its rules and orders. Not to mind the rubric, to mangle and curtail the Liturgy, and to speak very indifferently of episcopacy and our whole constitution. . . . A Dissenter ought not to be called a Nonconformist, for he who quite forsakes any church or society, and is no longer a member of it, cannot properly be said not to conform to its rules. If a man quits any club or company he may be said to dissent from them, but cannot be said not to conform after he has left them. Or if I turn off a servant, or he leaves me, he cannot after that be said to be an irregular servant. . . . From henceforth let the word Nonconformist be applied only to the Low Church, and that of Dissenter to those of separate communions; then we shall understand who is who."

In more recent times the appellation "Broad Church" has been adopted and appropriated by the members of another party, not imposed upon them by outsiders or opponents. So far from being affronted or taking umbrage, they ostentatiously profess it, as an indication of intellectual superiority and comprehensive charity, which disdains to study theology or recognize its distinctions. In this indifference they resemble the latitudinarianism of the seventeenth century and its general political character. But they are deficient in the simple, unselfish piety which often accompanied the excessive Protestantism of their predecessors. What is worse, the new school or system chiefly finds favour among professors and schoolmasters. If priesthood be not regarded as conveying an indefectible character, but only a title to some ministerial profession of indefinite signification, then its solemn duties and obligations are best left to those who believe in its reality. Low Church prelates and priests do sometimes perform functions in a strange manner, as if they had little conception of their proper meaning; but such exhibitions do not occasion the painful sensation produced by Services and Sermons which betray a radical and instinctive scepticism concerning essential doctrines of the Church. Papal usurpations and mediæval accretions upon the Primitive Faith have been distinctly discarded by the Church of England, with the cumbrous ceremonial required for their expression; nor will any high party ever succeed, if it wish, in restoring them. Puritanism and Calvinism, on the other hand, have struggled ineffectually to graft themselves upon our Prayer-book, for their exotic origin and character are manifestly incongruous to its whole system. Still more alien is the Saducean and semi-heathen philosophy which would evacuate the whole doctrine and discipline of the Church of their real meaning and continuity. Theology is a history and a science with which reformers ought at least to make themselves fully acquainted, and the more extensive this acquaintance the less disposed they will probably be towards crude suggestions for improvement and new-fangled experiments. Height in faith, depth in humility, and breadth in charity have ample scope for exercise among the varied wants and distinctions of a teeming population without tension in any direction of the terms of communion definitely prescribed for clergy and laity.

The soul of wit did not lie in Leslie's title to his pamphlet, "Cassandra," etc., nor obscurity arise from brevity, for to understand its meaning requires more than ordinary consideration. A strange thing is, that he did not in the first instance volunteer that explanation which was afterwards elicited. Some anthologists of the press, in presenting him with a nosegay of their appreciation—"son of a Jesuit, high-flying, tyrannical, nonjurant, renegade, tantivy, hare-brained priest, as mad as a Bethlemite, inspired by the devil"—therefore ridiculed his view of Priam's daughter, asserting that she was "a mad prophetess;" whereas, of course, the Trojans rather were infatuated who disbelieved her prediction of their city's destruction. His application of the classical story stands thus: "There are a parcel of Greeks within the walls of London, called New Troy, covered with a wooden wall of pretence to religion, liberty, and property, who will come out armed men and set her on fire, as they did once before, if she believe not Cassandra in time. That these men would have us pull down the walls of our laws, the Corporate and Test Acts, which exclude Dissenters from places of power and trust, to let in this horse, which we must not look into as being sacred, though we hear the clashing of armour within." The story made her prophecies to be true, and the moral of it is to express the fatality attendant upon those whom God has determined to destroy—"that no advice or ever so plain demonstration will convince them." This application stands on all fours with the story; but had it not, their criticism would have lost nothing of its value by being couched in decent language. If Cassandra misconceived the best mode of preserving the citadel by penal laws and restrictions, none the less was the wooden horse intended for its ruin, and the principles she denounced of a most fatal tendency. "The Jesuit Unmasked," by De Foe, in reply, requires no other notice than that it endeavoured to turn against him an idea of his own with an impertinent address and accusations.

Difficult to keep pace in perusal with the swarm of pamphlets which appeared, any answer to more than a very small portion would have been impossible. It was said that a society existed among Whigs and Dissenters for the support and encouragement of writers on their side —a much more justifiable course than has frequently been adopted for keeping alive an agitation. What remains for regret is that such a topic as "Occasional Conformity" should have occupied the time and talents of some other men, to the exclusion of much more important subjects. Such a one was Dr. Charles Davenant. He had distinguished himself as the author of Essays upon "Public Grants and Pensions," "The Treaty of Paris," and other subjects, which not only contained valuable information in a compact and convenient form, but were lucidly and forcibly written. That, however, which had gained him most reputation was not the more solid and useful productions of his pen, but an inimitable satire in a dialogue between Mr. Whiglove and Tom Double. Even the party against whom his shafts of ridicule had been directed did not fail to appreciate its humour, and they soon had a much deeper satisfaction. For a man cannot live upon fame, so Davenant turned round and realized his own ideal by devoting his talents to the Whigs, if not for, yet simultaneously with, an appointment to a Scotch secretaryship worth £1200 per annum. Leslie could hardly be expected to regard such a recusant with much respect, and he dismissed his remarks in a few words of severe contempt. He selected as a foeman more worthy of his steel with whom to cross swords the top and chief among the faction, and wielding the most masterly pen. Yet it does not say much for his estimate even of him, that he proceeds to accuse him of being a notorious "plagiarist," who had borrowed from and abused the speech of a noble lord in Parliament. This person was Mr. James Owen, a Dissenting minister at Shrewsbury, who had some reputation for learning, and had previously engaged in public controversy. His present pamphlet, "Moderation a Virtue," in favour of Occasional Conformity, and undertaking to defend it by Scriptural and Ancient precedents, had an extensive popularity, and was deemed by his own party to be unanswerable. Therefore Leslie found a congenial occupation in replying to it, in the "Wolf Stript of his Shepherd's Clothing," to which Mr. Owen again replied, though he had pretty well exhausted his stock of arguments, in a second essay, "Moderation Pursued." The "Wolf Stript," etc., was dedicated to "the Queen and three Estates of Parliament," following the example of opponents, which they affected to deem a piece of presumption on his part. It was an indirect testimony of allegiance, and showed that he entertained no desire to question Anne's title to sovereignty under existing circumstances. Much of the contents were occupied with the same subjects treated of in "New Associations" and "Cassandra," and defence of High Churchmen as the truest friends of moderation, and reconciliation with Dissenters, because they are the most sensible of the evils of separation which the soothing practice could contribute nothing to effect. For why should men change their principles if they were sound and safe? It concluded with a challenge to the leaders of Dissent that they should furnish to Convocation a list of "indifferent things," the removal of which would satisfy them, and test whether the high or low party in the Church would go further for reconciliation, especially prelates who had already been concerned in schemes of comprehension. De Foe undertook to scout such a proposal as useless, considering the character of the majority in the Lower House of Convocation. That, of course, was only an evasion, and Dissenters disclaimed his authority to speak on their behalf. The rest maintained a prudent and very intelligible silence, for they knew full well that any acceptance of the challenge could only serve to confirm Leslie's statements about the unreality of their pretences and incurable differences among themselves. If separation be only on account of things admittedly indifferent, its sin must be very great. If any things necessitate or justify it, they cannot be deemed indifferent. Dissenters have not a single point of union or cohesion but political antagonism to the Church, and some are far more widely separated from others in principle than from her. The Hampton Court conference remains on record a proof of the futility of all attempts at union based on removal of indifferent things. To remove only some would leave the door of schism as widely open as before; to remove all would be simply a clean sweep of the whole formularies of the Church, together with her episcopate and priesthood. What a medley of confusion and discordant elements would ensue, no Cassandra true or mad can predict.

"A letter from a country divine to his friend in London" concerning the education of Dissenters in their private academies was printed in 1703, which declared that destruction of Episcopacy root and branch was a maxim commonly inculcated, with several other statements of a similar kind. What gave these importance was the fact of their coming from one who professed to have been trained in one of these Seminaries, and therefore spoke from experience of the poison-instilled into young minds evidently incapable of judging. His testimony, therefore, most legitimately was cited in the " Wolf," and startled a great many people into reflection—upon the dangers of what was silently in their very midst, under a pretence of Christian education. Dissenters naturally felt much disturbed by the exposure; and the facts, though questioned, were not disproved by De Foe or any of those who volunteered for the task. The author of this letter was Samuel Wesley, father of a more famous man, John, who had renounced his schismatic connection to be admitted into the Church, and been ordained. Stories are told, similarly authenticated, of this sort of teaching being still pursued in some of these Seminaries which need not be detailed. But the reflection is immediately suggested by Wesley's letter, how moral as well as physical qualities often reappear and reproduce themselves in a second or third generation. It had become an adage then that men conspicuously engaged in undermining and subverting her principles were "Fathers of the Church who never had been her sons." It is true now as then, and the mischief wrought by them is incalculable. Converts are proverbially zealous, but the value of their zeal depends materially upon the disinterestedness of their convictions. A fatal love of proselytizing often renders their admission and welcome far too easy; or they pass muster in the crowd of a University simply to gain thus a passport to temporal advantages. But even in cases of unquestionable sincerity, conversion affords no security that the neophytes have fully grasped the extent of renunciation properly required before embracing a new system. So, when the first fervour of emotion has subsided, old tastes and tendencies deeply ingrained resume their suspended power, and, it may be quite unconsciously to the persons themselves, but all the more fatally, are at work. The seeds of schism and insubordination must have been deeply sown in John Wesley's constitution to blossom so freely as they did, and so speedily. Again, the Nemesis he inflicted upon his father's memory has been terribly repeated upon his own by the schism which so falsely bears his name.

ABRIDGMENT OF "NEW ASSOCIATIONS" AND "CASSANDRA."

When God has determined destruction to a nation, He takes away their senses, that they have eyes and see not, ears and hear not; they will not understand.

The Ten Tribes who never returned after their second defection were finally cut off, and their name lost. And it is observable that in the succession of nineteen kings there was not one good, though all of their own choosing. The root and foundation of republican schemes and pretences for rebellion is this supposed radical power in the People, as of erecting government at the beginning so as to overturn and change it at their pleasure. To obviate this the author of the "New Associations" carries us to matter of fact, how political government did begin in the world, and how the world was divided into several nations; and shows that this was not done by the election of the People, but by that stupendous miracle of the division of tongues, whereby, all of one language sorting together and God placing a governor over them, they became a distinct nation.

That hypothesis of the election of the People would render all government precarious, and eternally liable to change and confusion. It was never known, nor can be, what is meant by the People in this scheme. The whole never chose, and a part is not the whole. The question remains as to the Origin of government, whether by election or the institution of God. I grant that people have a right of protection of their governors by the divine law, and that right cannot be invaded. The king is called the one Supreme Head and King. The body Spiritual were not taxable by king and Parliament, but only by themselves, till the Revolution of 1641, which overturned all foundations. A precedent once being made it has been carried on to this day. The division of nations was one act, done at one time, when the name of Peleg was given to the son of Eber (Gen. x. 25), which was one of the most memorable eras of the world, and ought not to be forgotten by us. This was about a hundred years after the Flood, when mankind were so increased as to be thus divided. Before which time we may well suppose that Noah had the chief government. Several families might have a distinct government of their own, with a due subordination to their common parent. But before this time of the division of the earth we read nowhere of nations. It will follow, from the original of political government being immediately from Divine institution, that no ruler can be limited by the people or any of them, and consequently all governments must be absolute and arbitrary, which makes a dreadful sound to English ears.

There are limitations of concession and limitations of coercion. Thus God is pleased to limit Himself, when He makes covenants and grants conditions to mankind. Thus fathers may limit themselves to their children. And thus kings may limit themselves to their subjects by granting them such and such laws, and giving them the assurance of their solemn oaths to observe them. Laws are made by kings, therefore kings must be before laws; and these are wholly concessions from them, as our Magna Charta proves.

Lord Bacon sets this down as a maxim of our law, as well as of reason, that "the supreme power may dissolve itself, but cannot limit itself." The best security we can have against tyranny in our governors is by a dutiful submission to encourage them to be good to us. And by loyal principles to render them safe and secure in whatever concessions they shall please to give us. Moses was the meekest man upon earth, yet never was any so tormented with continual insurrections. The Israelites were for popular elections, and to choose for themselves a captain.

They rebelled twice against David, a man after God's own heart. Solomon, of his own choosing also, gave the people perfect peace and plenty unparalleled; yet they complained of taxes, and rebelled against his house. God did once vouchsafe to be King Himself. But they grew weary of this Theocracy, and in the days of Samuel rejected Him and chose for themselves.

No kingdom was ever yet destroyed by the tyranny of a king, but by rebellion many have been. Let the "*jure divino* doctrines" be true or false, it cannot surely be called "slavish" to submit myself to one royally born, sprung from many kings, whom I believe to be invested with a divine commission? There can never be any government fixed without a certain foundation, centre, and ultimate arbitrator, which can never be the people. They are the party to be governed, and therefore cannot be the governors.

In the contests of York and Lancaster, both parties pretended to be next in blood to the crown. That was the whole dispute, which shows that hereditary right was the rule. Many Acts of Parliament in England acknowledge the crown to be hereditary, and that *jure divino* too. . . . Our laws know of no treason but against the king.

Murder of Archbishop Sharp, of S. Andrew's, in Scotland, by the Presbyterians, May 3, 1679.—It is related[1] that one of them "fired a pistol at him, which burnt his coat and gown, but the shot did not go into his body." For what end this is told you shall see presently. But first, for the falsehood of it, I refer to the certificate of the Doctor of Physic and three Surgeons, who by order of the Privy Council in Scotland viewed and embalmed the body of the Lord Archbishop, which is upon record in the Council-books. It was propagated to countenance another invention of theirs, that the archbishop was a wizard, and had purchased a magical spell from the devil to keep him shot-proof. A true account of the murder was published by authority the same year, 1697, and from the depositions of many witnesses examined upon oath, which has since silenced their clamours, being undeniable matter of fact. This author pursues him with a stroke more barbarous than any the assassinators ever gave, and says "he begged his life in a very abject manner of them, and was in great disorder." The contrary of which appears in the narrative last mentioned. No man could show a more Christian courage and resolution. He gave them caution of shedding innocent blood, and when he saw they were resolved to murder him, he prayed them to spare his daughter, who was with him in the coach, and to give him a small space of time to recommend his soul to God; which they refused, saying God would not hear the prayers of such a dog, and cut and mangled his hands while he held them up in prayer even

[1] Burnet.

for them, that God would forgive them; which were the last words he uttered while they were hacking and hewing him. No history since S. Stephen can show a greater example of composure of mind and true Christian magnanimity under so sudden and cruel a martyrdom.

If King Charles I. would have turned Presbyterian, have destroyed the Church and revenged the Presbyterians upon the Independents, then the Presbyterians, having no other game to play, would have let him live a little longer till they could have done their business without him, and set up their commonwealth in the State as well as the Church. And I doubt not but the Independents would have done the same if they had been hewed down by the Presbyterians, and that they could have made the king a tool to have set them in the saddle again. The like would the Anabaptists, or any other of the then sectaries have done, if it had been their case; and have had as much cause to boast of their loyalty as the Presbyterians! But the destruction of the Church was the *causa sine qua non* with them all. None of them would have the king preserved upon any other terms. They all agreed in that point, though they quarrelled with one another about dividing of the spoil and setting up their own different models. But Episcopacy was their common enemy. Let the Dissenters of several sorts divide the murder of the king among them; they were all guilty of it. The Presbyterians began the rebellion against him, and brought him to the block; and just as they were ready to strike the stroke, the Independents snatched the axe out of their hands, and did it themselves. There is no difference betwixt rebellion and regicide; the one is in order to the other. In vain, therefore, do these rebels lay the murder of the king upon one another! One disarms him, another binds him, and a third cuts his throat! Which are most guilty? Even all alike! However, it is among the Dissenters and Whigs.

ABRIDGMENT OF "THE WOLF STRIPT OF HIS SHEPHERD'S CLOTHING."

Socrates wished Æsop had written one fable more on this moral of the new resemblance of virtue and vice, insomuch that one is often taken for the other; and yet there is so vast a distance in their nature as that no things upon the earth are more opposite. Thus, Laodicean latitude and indifferency in religion which God abhors recommends itself to us at this day under the specious name of moderation. Therefore it is necessary to inquire what sort of moderation is a virtue, and what sort is a vice, seeing the name of moderation may be applied to both. This word is found but once in all our Bible, and there it is mistranslated. It is in Phil. iv. 5, "Let your moderation be known unto all men." The word means, plainly by the context, a patient and cheerful suffering of afflictions, with full reliance and trust in God in all distresses. In the vulgar Latin the word is translated "modestia," cheerful and modest suffering. The same Greek word is rendered by our translations "patience," in 1 Tim. iii. 3; "gentleness," in 2 Cor. x. 1; and "clemency," Acts xxiv. 4. And as to the word moderation, I have no quarrel to it, it is a good word; but in Phil. iv. 5 there is nothing meant or intended of the sense that is screwed from it—of moderation that is indifference as to religion, which speaks wholly upon another subject.

Moderation is generally understood as the opposite to zeal, but in this sense it must be understood to be a vice, and a great one, as zeal is a most necessary and heroical

Christian virtue. Therefore, to make moderation a virtue, we must take it in such a sense as not to be inconsistent first with zeal for the faith; for we are commanded "to contend earnestly for the faith which was once delivered to the saints." Secondly, not with zeal for the Church and her unity, without which all faith and all knowledge profit nothing. The sin of Schism is called by no less dreadful a name than the tearing of Christ's body in pieces. But this heinous sin makes no impression at all upon the Church of Laodicea, where moderation is a virtue; which is very angry with those who mention it, or hinder their flocks from straying into schismatical congregations. We should have little quarrel with Dissenters if it were not for that fulsome word Schism. If they did not gather separate congregations in opposition to the Church, they would be no Dissenters. I will go as far as any man in extending moderation to other matters and persons. But I must give heed to that earnest exhortation of the apostle (Rom. xvi. 17), "Mark them who cause divisions and offences, and avoid them." And he tells us how they make these divisions: "By good words and fair speeches they deceive the hearts of the simple." Again, he pronounces that "they serve not our Lord Jesus Christ." None can do so who would divide His body. The apostle says, "charity beareth all things," but they would bear nothing from the Church, their mother. Yet quarrel with her for the colour of her clothes, for her gestures, habit, and everything; for her very looks.

They make the difference small to justify Occasional Conformity for obtaining profitable places or employments. They plead their right as children to have their share in the management of her family, though they own themselves not of it, and to have adopted a new mother, whom they love better, and who has more than once got her house from her, turned her out of doors, and dashed her children against the stones. Let us see the utmost that can be said in defence of this Occasional Conformity.

The title is, "Moderation a Virtue, or Occasional Conformity justified from the Imputation of Hypocrisy." He does not justify it merely for a place, which is "scandalous, a reproach to religion, and offensive to all good Christians." Who can prove it was merely for a place? But men must judge by actions; no hypocrite can be otherwise discovered. If a man never came to church before he was called to it by a good place, can any one judge otherwise than that he was brought to it for that reason? And if he return afterwards to the Dissenters and rail at the Church as before, can any judge him not guilty of hypocrisy? Error and false principles are never true to themselves, for to serve another turn they are forced to declare the practice "scandalous," etc., till they have another occasion of taking it up again. It is a sure mark of some mischief when these saints cry out about persecution. But let us examine their precedents. They bring in our blessed Saviour, because He taught in private houses, on mountains, and in the wilderness. Had He not authority to do so, superior to that of the Jewish establishment? But can Dissenters plead such authority over that Church which He established? They observe not that moderation towards His Church which He did to that of Moses. He never dissented from public worship, but was a constant, not occasional conformist; and confirmed the authority of those who sat in Moses' seat, though very wicked men. He observed not only feasts ordained by the law, but the feast of dedication, which was purely of Church authority.

S. John Baptist never separated from the communion

of the temple, nor taught men to do so. So the apostles and Jewish converts. Certain things (Acts xv. 28) were made necessary than by the decree of the Church, which are indifferent in their own nature. Let Dissenters look to this, who quarrel at things enjoined by the Church.

Our author shows that sacrifices and supplications were offered in the temple for heathen kings. It would have been more to his purpose to prove that the Jews held occasional conformity with the heathen. But is desiring the prayers of another conforming to the worship and religion? The Thirty-nine Articles are not made articles of communion, far less of faith, and required only from the clergy for an uniformity in doctrine publicly preached. It is well known what a slight esteem Dissenters had of the Sacraments while they had the government. At Oxford the Sacrament was not once administered from the time Episcopacy was thrown out, 1648 to 1660; the like was in Ireland and Scotland.

I would have no Dissenter come to the Holy Sacrament with us till he were fully satisfied in his own mind, and then he ought not to leave us. But to be at one time of different and opposite communions is dissolving the very notion and being of a Church. There is but One, and one Episcopate (as S. Cyprian speaks) throughout the whole world, and there ought to be but one Communion; whoever break this are guilty of schism.

Now, the Dissenters have set up communions not only different, but opposite to the communion of the whole Catholic Church; for they have thrown off the episcopate itself, which is, and was ever thought in the primitive Church to be, the principle of unity. The Church will not admit any presbyters without reordination. If Dissenters would agree among themselves and set down a list of such indifferent things as, if granted, they would comply and come into the Church, herein would be a proper subject for the exercise of moderation; but to deform our worship and scandalize the best part of those in our own communion who find themselves greatly edified, and their devotion much raised and enlivened in the excellent composure of our Liturgy and the decency of our ceremonies, perhaps dispose them to be Dissenters, or run over to the Church of Rome, and all this to gain nobody—this is what would happen. But as we are not to give just offence to those that are without, so neither to the Churches of Christ; we are not to disgust the members of our own church merely to gratify the petulant humour of Dissenters and yet not reconcile them. The beauty of a face is in the symmetry which gives a pleasant air, and the way to bring over Dissenters is to keep our Liturgy entire. Episcopacy is the thing they strike at, though their advocates would cast a mist before our eyes. There is no curing without settling the true notion of the Church and the priesthood, as instituted by Christ and practised in all ages of Christianity since. All must be thrown loose, even to the heart's desire of the Socinians and the very Deists; while they continue to despise and trample upon Church authority, which God has made "the pillar and ground of the truth." They are but wolves in whatever sheep's or shepherd's clothing; for without the belief of a Divine authority lodged in the character of bishops and of kings, it is impossible for any one to be a sound Churchman or a loyal subject.

I end as I began, with the near resemblance of virtues and vices, though there is the greatest opposition in their nature. An enthusiasm which is the excess of pride recommends itself to many well-inclined and religiously disposed people, under the notion of abstraction from the world, of humility and self-denial. What greater delusion than to think that we can contrive a shorter and a surer way to heaven than that which God has commanded? All this is the effect of enthusiasm. Most heresies and schisms have come from this fountain, and generally have begun with setting a low esteem upon the outward Ordinances.

CHAPTER X.

HISTORIANS OF QUEEN ANNE'S REIGN—SCOTLAND—IRELAND—CONTINENTAL POWERS—"REHEARSAL"—LOCKE, ETC.—MINISTERS AT CLACKMANNON—PROCESSION AT EDINBURGH—PLAYHOUSE—SUPPLEMENTS—EXTRACTS FROM "REHEARSAL."

A GREAT desideratum is a good history of Queen Anne's reign, an exciting and most important period of English history, and none less so than its second quarter. It gave a strong bias to the course of events during succeeding ages, and the effects are still in operation. Volumes, professedly undertaken to serve this purpose, are obviously defective or objectionable in various respects, but more especially because written with such undisguised partiality. Boyer, Tindal, Hallam, Burnet, Mahon, Burton, have all pursued the same track of indiscriminate animosity towards Tories and High Churchmen as one odious class, though these were by no means all united in sympathies or objects. Tindal the copious plagiarist, and Hallam the affected philosopher, are simply Whig Deists of the old school, betraying, in their scorn of religion, a latent fear it might after all be true. Burnet's incurable prejudices and personal antipathies against all who did not stand upon the latitudinarian platform are quite as conspicuous, or else his unpolished narrative is more pleasant reading, and contains more information. Boyer is very dull as well as partial, and

Burton over-fond of many-syllabled words to clothe ordinary ideas wanders into byways of remote connection with the subject or title of his work, apparently out of his depth from an incapacity to understand English ways of thought upon religious subjects or their controversies, any more than Scotch Calvinism is intelligible to the ordinary English mind. Mahon's history of Queen Anne is the weakest performance of all, and might more accurately be termed a life of Alexander Stanhope[1] from the prominence afforded him in its pages. Whig conceptions are rended down without clearing them of their grosser particles, and his notion of the Church in England resembles that of old-fashioned upholsterers concerning a piece of furniture to serve the double purpose of a family chest or bed for a stranger. The Whig cause against Tories and High Churchmen had something in it originally strong and effective; here it is represented in a modern Conservative and Erastian style of far less attractive description. Till a comprehensive and impartial work can be produced, or a qualified advocate shall undertake to defend the unpresented side of the question, one who wishes to ascertain the exact truth must be content to pick his steps cautiously, and leave much that he reads under a Scotch verdict, "not proven." For the purpose of this biography it is not necessary to have more than a general authentic sketch of the state of the nation from time to time, and of those questions in which our subject particularly interested himself. Both at home and abroad events had occurred to strain attention to the highest pitch, but unfortunately the country was divided into parties and factions which could not agree upon any one. They distrusted and opposed each other with a virulence which they did not feel or

---

[1] "Queen Anne," vol. ii., *passim*.

pretend towards foreigners. The Pretender and France in reality were but names and pretexts under cover of which Whigs and Dissenters sought excuse for inveighing with untiring pertinacity against Tories or High Churchmen, Jacobites or Nonjurors. These, on the other hand, at heart as little inclined to the French, and bitterly regretting the enforced exile of the rightful sovereign from among them, yet were tempted to conceal their pain and affect indifference upon the subject, in consequence of the taunts and grievances daily experienced from their own countrymen.

They were content to leave the question of right in abeyance till the queen's occupation of the throne should terminate in the course of nature. No doubt many sanguinely trusted her feelings would more and more gradually incline to her own family as that time drew nearer, and a chapter of accidents facilitate her brother's succession. Her ambiguous silence helped to encourage such hopes, for which no blame can be justly attributed, as hers was a very novel and peculiar position, and the faintest syllable uttered on the subject liable to exaggeration or misconstruction which might have done irreparable mischief. "Blood is thicker than water," and she had betrayed qualms of conscience, though she could not have felt any very warm affection for a brother she had almost never even seen, whose birth she had regarded as a misfortune, and contributed to render it suspected more than anybody else. To suppose she would secretly desire to repair that wrong, is to give her credit for remorse rather than repentance, without a vestige of proof. On the other hand, she could have no affection for the Hanover family; they were alien to her kindred and personally unacquainted with her. Yet, again, she had an invincible repugnance to Popery, in which her brother had been educated; and they were Protestants of some sort, ready, moreover, to embrace the Church of England for the sake of a crown. The probability is that, though swayed at times by varying emotions like other people, and provoked or flattered into a seeming tacit acquiescence to hints and insinuations dropped on behalf of her brother in conversation, she never once seriously entertained any idea of trying to set aside the Act of Settlement. It would have been dishonourable, because only on the faith of that engagement had the Whig party in power secured her easy accession, without whose support it would have been impossible. Whatever her impenetrable silence really meant, it was the only safe policy to maintain from first to last, and was the highest stretch of wisdom so narrow an intellect was capable of developing without assistance. If Jacobites and Nonjurors misunderstood it, as most of them did, all the better for her purpose of remaining in undisturbed possession, and that was their own affair. Some in Scotland could not be so easily satisfied as those in England to wait upon Providence.

During the years 1703 and 1704 communications passed between them and S. Germain, the general intention of which could not reasonably be doubted, and Sir John Maclean, a man named Kirk, and a few other persons were arrested upon charges of treasonable correspondence which very nearly cost them their lives. Fortunately the business of examination became a bone of contention between the two Houses of Parliament; and the Duke of Queensberry, in over eagerness to exhibit his astuteness, foiled his own game of a grand conspiracy being detected, for proofs were wanting, and the prisoners had at last to be released. He studied the Presbyterian interest in that country as the stronger, so that the Episcopalians were exposed to fresh acts of persecution, and more galling measures against the bare profession of their faith than ever. By a strange irony of fate, under a queen professing the same, it was more severely inhibited than had been the practice under William, who, if anything at all in religion, was a Calvinist like the Presbyterians themselves. Queensberry, with all his servile submission to them, was caught in his own snare, and became as unpopular in the Scotch Parliament as he had feared a just and honourable policy might make him. To what height their intolerance could reach appeared on a proposal to carry the Succession Act there. It was demanded that the Royal prerogative should be limited, all public appointments vested in the Privy Council, and, as if this reduction of sovereignty to a bare shadow were not sufficient, upon pretence of an apprehended invasion, persons suspected of any Jacobite tendency were to be disarmed. Whereas forty thousand standard of arms from the Tower of London were to be dispatched for distribution among her Majesty's loyal subjects professing the Covenant, yet of these a large part had repudiated her title to the crown at a public meeting.

In Ireland the Duke of Ormond had superseded in the vice-royalty Lord Rochester, the queen's uncle, who preferred to live nearer the throne, and desired to have more control over public affairs. However, as he continued much the same line of action, his government gave little more satisfaction to Presbyterians or Romanists. The Test Act had been introduced there with a view of more rigorous exclusion of the latter from any civil office or post of honour, with the strong support of the former. But it was much more cruelly and intolerantly framed than in England, because it also enacted that estates of Papists should be equally divided among their children, except any one of the family should join the communion of the English Church; a very unfair method of reducing the wealth and influence of Romanists, and a very base bribe to apostasy. But the artifice recoiled upon its Presbyterian promoters, for a clause was slyly introduced analogous to the bill against Occasional Conformity, which, of course, served as effectively to cripple themselves by exclusion from the power and influence in public affairs they so much craved for, in order to become predominant in the country after a while. But such are the double-edged weapons which religious and political factions so often inconsiderately manufacture to wound themselves, while aiming to deprive opponents of all liberty of conscience. High and Low Church could find no acceptance as terms descriptive of parties there at that date, because Protestantism among members of the Church of England inclined so invariably downwards. But Whigs and Tories found at once a cordial welcome, and speedily echoed and re-echoed it with a warmth which showed they had been transplanted to a congenial soil.

Europe continued to be drenched with blood, while crowned heads moved their pieces on its chess-board, and generals sought for fresh laurels. Louis, King of France, lost nothing of his chivalrous bearing because fortune seemed to have turned against him. His generals began to lose heart under defeats, but he maintained an imperturbable show of confidence. The Dutch dare not think of peace, lest they should be submerged behind their own dykes. So long also as they could lay the chief burden of the war upon England, and insist that their troops should not be carried far from their own territory. The emperor was in a very awkward plight. Hungary in a state of half revolt, and Vienna threatened with a siege. The King of Poland was deposed, his own sons being concerned in the conspiracy, to make room for a mere adventurer, Stanislaus, whose usurpation, however, did not last long. The King of Portugal and the Duke of Savoy both joined the Alliance; but their support meant simply that their pecuniary resources were exhausted, and that they desired retaining fees from England for loyalty in future.

Flushed with conquest on several fields of battle, the Duke of Marlborough sought for fresh opportunities of displaying his marvellous military capacity. He had suddenly lost his only son by small-pox; but, after a brief retirement, set out again to drown his grief amid the stirring scenes of the camp and the roar of artillery. Schillenburg, Ingoldstadst, Hockstœdt, or Blenheim (as it came to be called, more euphoniously if less accurately, by Englishmen), Triers, and Landau, one after another, were inscribed upon the brilliant roll of his successes; and the gallant Prince Eugene scarcely acted a less distinguished part, with a generous cordiality rendered more conspicuous by contrast with the pitiful jealousy and incompetence of the Prince of Baden. The one blot upon Marlborough's escutcheon was his utter disregard of the enormous cost to his country at which his victories were purchased, while insatiably eager for self-aggrandizement. His avarice and cupidity were amazing, and his beautiful and tempestuous duchess was as grasping as himself. Ten days after the great battle of Blenheim Sir George Rook bombarded Gibraltar, which the efforts of Spaniards failed to recover, and defeated the French fleet; so that both by sea and land the arms of England were triumphant almost beyond any former experience. But the practical results were nothing.

Neither the gravity of these affairs drew off attention from the old subjects of dispute at home, nor put

English parties in good humour with each other; nay, rather served to inflame their resentments. The war was as eagerly recommended by Whigs as peace was demanded by Tories; and while the former sedulously depreciated the naval achievements of Sir George Rook because he had the credit of being a High Churchman, the latter put him for much the same reason on a par with Marlborough.

Such, then, in brief, was the state of affairs generally, when Leslie assumed a new character, not without misgivings or reluctance, as the editor of a weekly paper entitled the *Rehearsal*, in opposition to the many which were published in the Whig interest, such as the *Observator*, the *Review*, the *Flying Post*, and the *Mercury*. None of them were newspapers in the modern acceptation of the term, for only a small portion of their columns was devoted to the supply of general information about occurrences or affairs taking place either at home or abroad. They mainly consisted of discussions upon the favourite subjects of contention, highly flavoured to suit the popular palate; and when anything in the shape of news was detailed, it was generally some scandal or story upon which to hang a leading article to the praise or prejudice of a party. Tories and Churchmen had been unrepresented up to 1704 by any regular organ, and accordingly were placed at considerable disadvantage with their opponents, when he volunteered to fill up the gap in some measure. Many of his friends and acquaintances had deplored the want of an antidote to the poisonous literature industriously circulated among the masses, but shrank from the task of providing it, either from a consciousness of their incapacity, or disinclination to brave the odium sure to be incurred. The writer's name could hardly be expected to remain a secret, and his attempt was very like disturbing a wasps' nest. However,

Leslie's spirit was stirred within him continually by what he saw and heard of the mischief done by these papers being read in coffee-houses, and recited by hired readers to crowds of eager listeners in the streets, generally poor ignorant people who believed what they heard, when coarse and calumnious attacks were directed against the Church or persons in high office; and the coarser and more calumnious they were, the more adapted to the taste of a mob audience. He did not conceal from himself nor underrate either the difficulty or disagreeableness of his undertaking. No pleasure or profit could possibly accrue to himself from condescending to meet scurrilous opponents on their own ground, and fight them with their own blunt, unpolished weapons of plain language and broad humour, such as the commonalty would appreciate. But this he designed to do, so far as he could, without falling into and imitating the viciousness of their style. De Foe and a man named Tutchin, who had been engaged in Monmouth's rebellion like him and had escaped the heavier penalty of treason with the loss of his ears and a barbarous whipping, were the most notorious of these scribblers. The one conducting almost single-handed several of the above-named papers at the same time, or in succession; the other manager or proprietor of the *Observator*, a journal formerly edited upon exactly opposite principles by the brilliant Roger Lestrange. It could not be wondered at, if an implacable resentment burned in the breasts of these two men against the party naturally associated in their minds with the cruel punishment inflicted upon them. But their wrongs afforded little palliation or excuse for the indecencies of abuse and slander in which their revenge frequently indulged against clergy and gentry, who personally had never in the most indirect manner been concerned in any offence towards either.

Leslie's hope was, by adopting a plain and humorous style, to gain the ear of the public at first; then, when he had disabused it of common fallacies and misrepresentations, to elevate the tone of thought and win attention to convincing argument on higher and more serious topics; in which endeavour he soon succeeded beyond his expectation. Though some, who approved of the enterprise, regarded it as hopeless; and others as beneath the dignity of any one of ability and character to pit himself against such adversaries as he had to encounter. Some had even ventured to designate themselves accurately enough as the Scandalous Club, but with defiant imprudence; for English people, even when supporting a bad cause or bad advisers, have seldom been so lost to self-respect or a sense of the fitness of things as to relish the appearance of approving scandal only because it is scandalous. His own conscience afforded the answer to these objections, though he fully appreciated their weight under other circumstances; and, as he said himself, he "was content to be a servant of Christ and abase himself to the lowest degree if thereby he might do good," and contribute in any measure to popularize the cause of truth and righteousness, taking for his motto the admirable old maxim, "Magna est veritas et prævalebit,"[1] which, however, cannot be said to be confirmed by universal experience. The title "Rehearsal" was adopted to indicate in a general way his purpose of innocent ridicule and banter, from a very famous and successful play, acted in 1671, and published the next year. It was a joint composition of several wits—namely, Butler, author of "Hudibras;" Villiers, Duke of Buckingham; Dr. Sprat, afterwards Bishop of Rochester; and Martin Clifford, highly eulogized by Sprat as a critic, but leaving nothing to justify this

[1] Apoc., Esdras iv. 35, 41.

reputation among posterity, unless it has been his share in the "Rehearsal" which has never been defined. Originally this farce was intended against Davenant, but afterwards understood to be directed against Dryden, in parody of his "Conquest of Granada," and other plays. Johnson has pointed out an objection to this view, that these were not published till after the "Rehearsal;" and several personal allusions, which suited Sir William Davenant, who had been a soldier and friend of Milton, have no application whatever to Dryden. But it is enough to say, in reply to this, that he took it to himself in his dedication of the translation of Juvenal. Much of the satire, which is now unintelligible for loss of reliable references, was supposed to be well understood at that time, and Leslie had derived great amusement from its perusal, as appears from many allusions besides the use of the title. Dryden declared "the author sate to himself, and was the very Bayes of his own farce, and therefore scorned to reply." But he felt its sting severely, while he met with scant sympathy, because most people deemed his conversion to Rome an act of hypocrisy of a piece with some other unpleasant passages of his history.

The first number of the *Rehearsal* appeared in print upon Saturday, August 5, 1704; commencing by way of introduction with some remarks upon a fictitious number of the *Observator* assailing "Cassandra," and in the form of a dialogue, which was retained during the continuance of its publication. Then its earlier pages were chiefly occupied with a discussion about Sir George Rook's merits as a naval commander. Writers since have been as much divided upon the question as his contemporaries. It appears plainly enough that at that time his political and religious character gave most of its warmth to the dispute, and that had this borne a different complexion he would have been spared the greater part of the censures, taunts, and complaints heaped upon him. Two great generals, Schomberg and Wellington, have asserted the inaccuracy of most descriptions of battles ventured by historians; and the probability is that none but professional men are competent to criticize either naval or military achievements. It is well known they are not exempt from jealousies and partialities, but at least they possess that technical acquaintance with their subject, the want of which must deprive the comments of mere outsiders of any great value; just as they are ill qualified for pronouncing peremptory decrees upon ecclesiastical subjects to which some nevertheless are very prone. His admirers showed a lack of discretion in exalting his services in a manner which seemed rather to disparage the magnitude of Marlborough's victories; for, though it failed to excite any unpleasant rivalry between the two heroes themselves, it manifestly provoked Sir George's adversaries to more violent reproaches. Leslie defended him warmly, but in a more prudent manner, by reciting his previous exploits and the praise bestowed upon them by high authorities. At the same time, he fully admitted the justice of all which was said in praise of the duke, and of Sir Cloudesley Shovel, another commander who was being extolled for the same ungenerous purpose of depreciating his superior officer in these engagements at sea. He objected to any comparisons being drawn between the merits of such men, and exposed the real source of Sir George's unpopularity among Whigs and Dissenters; while, to prevent any imputation on his own motives, he carefully announced that, so far from being his friend, he had no personal acquaintance with him, nor even knew him by sight. Such a dispassionate and impartial testimony proved more effective in discountenancing clamour than many extravagant eulogies. After these heats had somewhat subsided, or other victims were found for attack by partisan writers, one thing remained which all persons in England could regard without any semblance of satisfaction; that was—Gibraltar itself. It has remained a source of satisfaction ever since; but whether, like Calais or Dunkirk, some government of the future will not surrender it for a consideration, or the carrying out of a grand policy to legitimate issues, appears within the range of speculation already, and England hold no more the key of the Mediterranean.

Our Rehearser by no means espoused Tory schemes and proposals of Tories with undiscriminating zeal, but considered each one simply on its own merits. When, therefore, the Earl of Rochester proposed that the Electress of Hanover or her son should be invited over to this country, it met from him uncompromising resistance. Such an idea had originated with the Whigs, who intended to have at hand a counter-irritation and camp of intrigue, whilst the queen sided with their opponents. When her influence began to be thrown into the opposite scale, and her ministry to change its character, then Rochester thought to trump the Whig card by this strange alteration of front. It was a disingenuous manœuvre, the object of which was obvious beyond all concealment, and therefore Whigs were justified in their immediate change and withdrawal from their former position. Leslie opposed it from first to last as a most injudicious proceeding, whether supported by one party or another, naturally calculated to cause uneasiness to the queen, to intensify political dissensions and strengthen the revolutionary principle of making regal dignity elective, and the throne dependent upon the will of the people. He pointed out distinctly and emphatically the dangerous issues involved in the proposal, and how badly it had worked when such an experiment had been tried before in English history.

Few can doubt the force of his reasoning, that a prince placed in such a position necessarily becomes the leader of a party, and a rival of the sovereign in possession; while the people become inured to that fatal, injurious doctrine, "the worse title the better king," because he must be more subservient to their wishes in proportion, as he is dependent upon their favour. That doctrine, as insisted upon with unceasing vehemence and pertinacity in the *Observator* and other papers, need have claimed no more than a cursory notice had it not been borrowed from and supported by champions of far higher calibre, such as Algernon Sidney and John Locke, both men of great intellectual power. It was, therefore, to these and their arguments upon several topics, especially the latter's, that an elaborate reply was addressed in many numbers of the *Rehearsal*. Locke attained high eminence among men of letters entirely by his own talents and untiring assiduity, but never received from his party that reward to which his services entitled him, though he had shared exile and misfortune with some of its leaders. If his religious opinions were widely apart from true Christianity, yet that could have been no offence or excuse for neglect in their eyes, while his private character was unblemished, and his disposition kind and liberal. But the theory he propounded in his two "Treatises on Government" will not stand the test of Scripture, to which himself appealed. One is not bound to adopt the rival scheme of Filmer in its integrity, or any other, in order to arrive at this conclusion, for his premises are inconsistent with plain facts, and texts are strained to convey a meaning which they cannot reasonably bear. Still he laboured carefully to substantiate his idea of the origin of government by evidences convincing to his own mind, instead of adopting the much easier plan of "summarily brushing aside" the arguments of opponents with the lofty disdain of professedly merciful critics of a modern date.[1] It should be remembered that the refutation contained in the *Rehearsal* had to be written in simple and homely language according to the author's original plan; yet substantially it was complete and convincing. Tutchin and De Foe were glad to drop the subject, while numbers of persons among the uneducated classes who had imbibed their notions openly avowed a change of opinion. Those who care to form a just conception of the whole controversy ought to read both Locke's treatises and the *Rehearsal* together; a labour which will well repay the time and attention it requires by the clearness of thought produced, whichever view they may adopt, upon a subject of permanent interest. But a majority of readers will be content with a slight specimen of our author's arguments in his own words, which have not lost their native force because a revolution succeeded in overthrowing an hereditary monarchy two centuries ago, only to establish a new one in its place upon a different basis.

The really important question remains for consideration—what system of government, if any, has the better claim to divine authority? Comparisons between particular sovereigns and royal houses do not touch the one point in debate; nor that other question introduced to escape a plain issue—what remedy subjects may justly have recourse to, when a tyrannical or vicious monarch persists in disregarding the teaching of reason and religion to the detriment of a whole kingdom.

[1] Stephen, "English Thought," ii. 135.

Many topics fully treated in the *Rehearsal* have frequently recurred to be discussed in newspapers and public circles with an amusing air of novelty, as if they had only just sprung up and nothing ever been said about them before. Errors and blunders and misstatements are repeated by speakers and writers, quite unconscious that they have been completely exposed and refuted long ago; whilst on the other hand, with an equally charming simplicity, weapons from time to time are produced in defence of truth as of the most recent manufacture in clever heads, which, after doing good service, had been laid by and gone to rest in the libraries of our forefathers. Terms of communion or separation; the argument for an Established Church; the relative position and use of the Thirty-nine Articles; popular preaching, its use and abuse;—few persons would readily admit that there is not a great deal to be said upon any one of these. Nevertheless they would find by turning over the pages of the first volume of this journal they might save trouble, and could hardly more effectually strengthen their position at least on the orthodox side, than by simply reproducing what has there been stated. There is nothing new under the sun except men and women themselves. Their imaginations, devices, ways of thought, philosophy, and discoveries are all old, for the most part poor imitations and repetitions of what went before.

Leslie managed to procure early and authentic information, which often took his opponents by surprise and greatly disconcerted them; sometimes also effectually unravelling the falsehood of reports which their papers disseminated. Yet he had no regular staff of assistants or correspondents, but simply relied upon friends and voluntary communications for the trustworthiness of his statements or corrections;

and never in a single instance was he convicted of any material error concerning a matter of fact, the reverse of which was notorious with the other side. And the plain reason of this difference lay in his honesty of purpose and design. He had no desire to supply news, detail scandal, false or true, against individuals, or wound private feelings; but to discuss public questions so far as they involved the Church's welfare, and carry on a crusade against principles which he deemed pernicious and dangerous to society. In prosecution of this purpose he did not hesitate to condemn proceedings whether of persons or parties in any public place. Such, for instance, was a sermon preached by a Presbyterian minister at Clackmannon, in 1705, who told his poor ignorant hearers that Christmas Day, which in Scotland is called "Yule," was observed only in memory of a dog which had been hung upon a tree for six hours, but when taken down as dead ran away yelping and "yuiling" in a strange manner. The name and place were distinctly specified to give room for inquiry or disproof, if possible; but the story was fully confirmed. That such an incident should not have elicited a single expression of regret, reproof, or apology from Presbyterians, illustrates unmistakably the prevalent spirit amongst them. Indeed, it was no such exceptional sort of occurrence as to demand much attention; and when exposed, the only surprise expressed in Scotland being that English people should disturb themselves about the matter, while some deemed it a good joke. Nor was that the worst instance of profane jesting. A procession passed through the streets of Edinburgh, wherein were the public hangman and prison officials dressed up to represent priests, with crosses on their caps, a Bible, a chalice, and the Holy Sacrament, taken from an altar, in their hands, together with a picture of the blessed Saviour upon the point of an halberd, which then were burnt in a bonfire! Now, this profane exhibition was no sudden freak or excess of a mob under circumstances of some extraordinary excitement, but deliberately ordered and executed under the authority of the Privy Council as a protest against Popery and prelacy. All that was uttered in defence of the proceeding was by De Foe in the *Flying Post*, who did not venture to deny the accuracy of the narrative as a whole; but quibbled about the certainty of a Bible being included in the conflagration, because it was a copy of the Latin Vulgate, and the terming of the sacred Host our Lord's body. That Presbyterians might not feel themselves outdone by their brethren in Scotland, since the anniversary of King Charles's martyrdom happened to fall upon a Tuesday, which was the weekly lecture day at two of their meetinghouses in London, they sang by way of thanksgiving this rendering of Psalm cxviii. 23, 24—

> "This was the mighty work of God,
> This was the Lord's own act,
> And it is wondrous to behold
> With eyes that noble fact."

The same party who sanctioned and united in these things were they who pleaded the virtue of moderation, and complained of being suspected of sympathy with those regicides of 1641! Then there was the Playhouse, built and opened with great ceremony under the auspices of the Kitcat Club, an institution precisely similar to the Calves'-head, and to which the queen was unhappily induced to give her name, at the time when S. Paul's Cathedral languished in a condition of most unseemly neglect for want of funds to repair it. These are only a few out of many proceedings of the same party condemned in the *Rehearsal*. And surely it was a noble enterprise to undertake, before the nation should be hopelessly saturated again by principles, the terrible result of which was burnt into Leslie's mind by his own remembrance and his father's sufferings for nearly twenty years? No amount of obloquy turned him from his path, so that by the close of 1705 his paper had a circulation equal to any of its contemporaries, with a far higher reputation. This success suggested an insinuation by the *Observator* that he was—though his identity could only be shrewdly guessed at as yet—hired by a party to write for them. It came with cool assumption from Tutchin, who himself occupied that very position, as well as De Foe; but he could with the greatest sincerity assure his readers that he had not pocketed a single penny by his performance; and if inquiry had been pushed further, the publisher could have testified, with equal or greater satisfaction, that he was losing nothing by his venture. Beyond, however, his reasonable remuneration, all the profits accruing from publication went towards the increase of its circulation; and De Foe's accusation, repeated by one of his venomous biographers, of "being busy about raising contributions," had not a shadow of foundation, though a very innocent charge if it had been true. That Nonjurors and Tories distributed copies gratis is very probable, but without any concert or even acquaintance with its author. They did so simply in self-defence, and to promote their own principles, therefore the fact serves only as an additional testimony to the paper's value in public estimation. Nor was support long required, for so soon as it became sufficiently known it paid its way. If subscriptions had been required, they could have been easily procured, or even secret-service money such as De Foe received at the hands of Harley, who had succeeded in ousting Lord Nottingham and installing himself in the ministry. But Leslie could not have accepted either one or other, because he had no intention of crippling the freedom of his pen, or adapting his principles to the exigencies of any party by becoming their tool or hireling. Indeed, a little attention to the selection of his subjects of discussion ought to have obviated the necessity of any denial; for nothing would have been more easy and acceptable to the popular taste than discussions about elections and various matters of gossip, or a column for a rival scandal club, which were rigorously excluded, because inconsistent with the author's single aim. Neither was any pen engaged in the composition but his own—except, perhaps, his son Robert's occasionally. As he said, "politics were not his talent, nor his taste, but to write and converse upon argument and reason, fact and Holy Scripture, except so far as the best politics had a foundation, and were involved in these." An illustration of this lay in a matter already noticed—the proposal to bring over to reside in this country a member of the house of Hanover during Queen Anne's lifetime. If he had wished to cultivate the goodwill of the Tory party in Parliament, no finer opportunity could have been sought. For the changing of both sides from their former professions on the question rendered the charge of inconsistency no heavier against the one than the other; and this artifice of Lord Rochester met too ready an approval as a fine piece of policy against the court and the Whigs. But his disclaimer, with that of other honourable men, was so decided as to give great offence to some in high position, whose friendship could have been of service, and even to win an expression of admiration from the lips of his adversary, Dr. Burnet. He alluded now in terms of the utmost respect to the queen, even of regard; though she never noticed him, nor was he prepared to accept a favour. This proceeded not only from a chivalrous disinclination to disturb her reign, but also—for he knew she saw the *Rehearsal*—that he might remind her of her own solemn professions of affection and assurances of support to the Church of England. Dr. Drake, an able writer, was employed to defend the Tory change of front, on the ground that now was a seasonable time for that which was improper before. Leslie did not know for certain who the author was or his design, while he expressed a high opinion of him if being the person reputed as such. At the same time, he begged to disclaim this poor pretext on behalf of High Churchmen as advanced upon mere Whig principles, nor, if otherwise, allowable when distasteful to her Majesty. Further, he declared himself no enemy to the succession of the house of Hanover "in God's own time, and if His providence should make way for it according to truth and right," in the Act of Succession lately passed, though he could wish the queen had issue of her own. Not, indeed, that he meant to imply that any change of feeling and opinion had come over him since the death of James II. But for the present he stood released from any necessity of actual service in behalf of the Heir of the Stuart family, until he might be reconciled to the nation, and give a satisfactory pledge to govern according to law. His admissions, however, so far from smoothing the irritation of either party, were only distorted into reflections upon the House of Hanover, and presuming to limit Providence, with a view of course of prejudicing him with that family, for it kept a keen eye upon the various currents of opinion in England. This he dismissed with a curt denial, but replied more warmly to another charge against him as a Nonjuror of "belonging to some other Church than that which the rubrics and canons appoint and establish." His answer is worthy of attention, because it defines the attitude which he assumed, and wished to be understood to assume at that date. "When did I distinguish myself from that Church which the rubrics and canons appoint? I'm sure I never had any other Church, and I hope I never shall, unless she be taken from us. I'm resolved, with the grace of God, to keep close to her while one rag of hers is left together. And now I'll tell you freely, sir, if I have any scruples concerning the Church of England, it is that she may leave me and not I her; that is, that she may die before me, which God of His infinite mercy prevent." Once more, also, he repelled the accusation borrowed from Dr. Burnet of inventing the distinction of High and Low Church in these vigorous terms. "You cannot but know that in all I have wrote I have constantly declared my abhorrence of it, and said that it was set up by the Whigs and Dissenters on purpose to have a handle, under the name of High Church, to blacken the whole Church. . . . If by adopting you mean using it, you do so too on speaking against it. It is now become the language of the nation, and a man would not be understood if he did not use it."

Abridgment of "Rehearsal."

1. *Set Forms of Prayer.*—Are we not to sing with the Spirit as well as pray with the Spirit? Are they not both in the same text, 1 Cor xiv. 15? Then, if by the spirit be meant extempore, we must sing extempore psalms, and to extempore tunes. It is the spirit of devotion which is here meant, not the spirit of extempore effusions, or ready invention and turning of words, which is gained by art and

custom, as we see even in schoolboys. Forms of prayer are no more an hindrance to devotion than a form of psalms and set tunes; rather a great furtherance and help in easing the speaker from the labour of invention, and the hearers from expectance and curiosity of what comes next: which is a set form to them, without the security of proper matter and words. So that all the choice left to hearers of any sort is only this—whether they would have a form of sound words, which they know beforehand to be such, as the Lord's Prayer, etc., or a form as to them, whatever it be with the speaker, wherein there is great hazard, and frequent experience of both words and matter being very undigested, unseemly, and even unsound. The alternative is whether they would have a good form or a bad one, since form it must be; and whether they should sing well or ill, if singing they will have.

2. *A Church Establishment, and Terms of Communion.*— It seems as impossible for any country to profess a religion without having some Church established, as for a State to exist without a government established. The Church (so now let me call it, for I speak not of true or false) which was established among the heathen as well as among Jews and Christians, was always a part of the State, and the principal part of it; all contravention to it was reckoned an infraction upon the State. Even in Holland, that place of toleration, they have an Established Church, and so guarded that none of any other communion have access to magistracy or share in the government.

When Christ our Lord founded His religion, He established a Church, not upon secular power, but to show its independency and prerogative above all others, with authority in the governors the apostles, and their successors the bishops, to the end of the world, to admit into and govern this society, and to exclude out of it and from al the privileges of it, both in this world and that to come. Without a Church no religion can be preserved, therefore the Christian Church is called the pillar and ground of the truth. No man can be excommunicated or turned out of an opinion, or the privileges of it; but he may out of a society. Therefore the Church is a society, with governors, rules, and privileges; not a company of professors only, far less of mere thinkers without restraint or limitation.

When any man has a mind to come into a Church, and inquires what are the terms of communion, the meaning is, what are particular to that Church, and not used elsewhere. And of this sort I know none in the Church of England but the Apostles' Creed, which is required at baptism. To be reconciled to the Church of Rome, one must subscribe to the Creed of Pope Pius IV., which includes the twelve new articles of Trent, which that council added to the twelve of the Apostles' Creed. Therefore they make these properly terms of communion. For the Church of England the Thirty-nine Articles, Canons, and Homilies, are required only from the clergy as a test of their doctrine, that they all may teach the same thing, and to prevent various and erroneous opinions being preached among the people to their distraction. No such subscriptions are asked of any layman. And in all Churches and societies there are other tests required from the officers who are entrusted with the affairs of the society, than from the common members.

Indifferent things, about which Dissenters make such a stir, were not imposed upon them as terms of communion, for they were fixed and established before they broke off from the Church, and were complied with by them as well as by others. Therefore, when they broke off, they made those indifferent things terms of separation; but they were never made by the Church any terms of communion, nor are at this day. Dissenters quarrel with them because they can find no other cause of quarrel; that is, indeed, no cause at all, for none yet ever held that an indifferent thing was a sufficient ground to embroil a Church or State. Let such a principle into an army, what fine work it would make! It would be like the fellow at Bothwell Bridge, a Covenanter, who at exercising never budged a foot at the word of command to the right, left, or about, but stood musing like a stake; and when his captain bade him mind, he said, "No, he didn't approve of his way of exercise." "Why?" said the captain. "Because," said he, "we are fighting against set forms, and it is a set form."

3. *Canonization.*—The Church of England canonizes none, nor keeps the memorials of any but who are recorded for saints in Holy Scripture. Putting a man in heaven is something like it, if we cannot take him out again, as Dissenters have done. Baxter, who bragged that he had "spent gallons of blood fighting against the king (Charles I.)," in his "Saints' Everlasting Rest," edition 1649, translated those of the regicides then dead straight into heaven, and named several of them—as Brook and Pim, Hampden and White, and Twiss, who was "Moderator" of the "Assembly of Divines." And he described heaven in the form of a Parliament, and called it the "blessed Parliament"—he meant it in that form which which was then, that is without a king. Having canonized these, he again riveted and confirmed his grant to them in the next edition, 1652. Yet, after all, he took them out of heaven, or dropt them; for they were left out in the new editions of his book after the Restoration, 1660. He was then ashamed of his saints, or afraid to own them, and left them to shift for themselves, lest he might have been sent

to bear them company, which for all his assurance he had no mind to do.

A word about one of these saints, respecting the manner of his translation. Lord Brook favoured the Parliament against the king; we must suppose trusting for his reward to Baxter's Parliament of heaven. On March 2 (day of S. Chad, the bishop who built Lichfield Cathedral) this man was seated in his chamber in the town, out of all danger, and exercising his "talent of praying" publicly, though his chaplains were present; for the pale of the Church was then broken down. All men and women acted the priest, and took heaven literally by violence. He prayed that " if the cause he was in were not right and just, he might be presently cut off." Presently he was shot in the eye with a bullet from the close, by a common soldier, and instantly died. Whence Mr. Baxter sent him to that heaven governed by a Parliament. It had been better to have followed the ingenious Milton, who, in his " Paradise Lost," makes Lucifer to have called a Parliament in hell, himself the first speaker, to assert their " rights and liberties " against the " arbitrary " government of the king.

4. *Mr. Locke's Treatise on Government.*—" Concerning the infirmities of health and avocations of business, which in a number, though much less than that of a commonwealth, will necessarily keep many away from the public assembly: and the variety of opinions and contrariety of interests, which unavoidably happen in all collections. 'Tis next to impossible (that the consent of every individual should ever be had)."—Locke, vol. ii. 318. Yet, in the very page before, he makes the consent of every individual to be necessary, and the foundation of all political society. If it "never" could be had, then not upon one occasion more than another. Nor can any

occasion be mentioned more likely to create variety of opinions and contrariety of interests than the contrivance of government and the choice of governors. So that Locke himself is plainly shown to confuse himself, owning that the foundation of popular government is nonsense and an impossibility.

Legislative power, wherever it is placed, in any sort of government is, and must be, arbitrary and absolute; it is impossible to be otherwise, and every man sees this in all governments upon the face of the earth. The legislature is not bound to its own laws, but may repeal them at leisure; or before repeal may dispense with them, or leap over them and act contrary to them. In short, may do what they will, and make what they will to be law, for their will is the law. Therefore if, as Mr. Locke say, she has proved "no man can subject himself to the arbitrary power of another," no man can subject himself to any government, of what sort or size so ever. Nor can there be such a thing as government kept up in the world. And if, as he says, "no man has power over the life or property of another," then the whole community cannot force upon any single individual who shall gainsay their constitution, nor compel him to leave them or his native country and birthright. If, as he says again, "no man can transfer to another more power than he has in himself, and that no body has power to destroy his own life," then how came any government to have power of life and death? Mr. Locke confesses the individuals could not give it. Who else was there to give it? I doubt a little divine right must come in here. What else can give to another that power over my life which I have not myself? Again, "He is in a much worse condition that is exposed to the arbitrary power of one man who has the command of 100,000, than he that is exposed to the arbitrary power of 100,000 single men." This is so very senseless (with all respect to Mr. Locke's judgment) that it is even a shame to answer it. A general or a king may command hard things, as to march upon the mouth of a cannon and hang a man for a very small matter, stepping out of his rank or taking an egg, though he were starving and had not a penny to pay for it, or for asking his pay though it be due to him;[1] yet, with all this arbitrariness, is not this a better state of things for these 100,000 men than anarchy, and letting them all loose, upon one another, to rob, plunder, and kill at discretion? If the number be greater, as of millions in a kingdom, the confusion and destruction would be proportionably greater; and if the whole world were in this supposed "state of nature," it would be one Aceldama, and nothing but hell could equal the wild uproar. Yet Mr. Locke thinks this much preferable to living under the absolute government either of a king or a commonwealth.

In ch. xix. p. 422, he says, that "if a government be arbitrary it is dissolved, and the people are restored to their original state of nature;" but he does not "suppose the people will continue in that state, but may choose a new legislature for themselves, in what form or manner they think fit." Suppose, according to him, the government dissolved, and all the individuals of England and Scotland rendered wholly independent of each other, in his supposed state of nature, all and every one of them upon a level. I dare say it would be doomsday in the afternoon before they could frame any sort of government whatever, upon the free vote and consent of every individual. Besides

[1] These iniquities here instanced were actually perpetrated under William the usurper.

what is said above of investing the government with the power of life and death, which Locke confesses they could not give as not having it in themselves, and which would be much worse than the state of nature or pure anarchy.

I have quoted Locke thus particularly on purpose to show that the most acute and celebrated of the Whig writers can speak no more sense upon this subject than John Tutchin, etc.

5. *Vox Populi vox Dei.*—Whatever founds government must be superior to it. Government must derive its original and whole authority from it, be accountable to it, and dissolvable whenever it thinks fit. Government among men cannot be derived from mere human authority. This is so very obvious, that all governments whatever, of whatever sort, and among all nations and religions, do pretend to a divine right. Whigs and commonwealth men do. Their maxim is, "Vox populi vox Dei," that the voice of the people is the voice of God; so that whomsoever the people set up is set up by God, is God's anointed vice-regent, etc. The heathens pleaded a divine right, but, not knowing the Holy Scriptures, groped in the dark after it. On all hands it is confessed that no government can stand without a divine original right and authority; for what else can give one man power over another, over his life, liberty, and property? Besides, it is utterly impossible for any government to have been set up by the free vote of every individual, which is the foundation of Mr. Locke's and all republican schemes. So that if I should allow their maxim, and by the voice of the people mean the voice of every individual, fairly and truly collected, without force, fear, or any other collision, I need not be afraid of the divine right of any such act of the people, since they never did any act what-

ever, from the beginning of the world, much less so material an act as the contriving and erecting of government, by any such free and unanimous consent. In histories, and even in Holy Scripture, it is said the people did so and so, by which phrase is not meant every individual, but the greater part. Belial put that notion, of the generality of the people being the voice of God, into the heads of his sons, whom he stirred up to vindicate their "liberty" against David, and to set up his son, a vain young man, in his stead. This is the first instance we have of "Vox populi vox Dei." After this, ten tribes rebelled against the house of David, and became a distinct kingdom, and their kings were elected by the people. This case is determined by the mouth of God Himself (Hosea viii. 4): "They have set up kings, but not by Me; they have made princes, and I knew it not." To conclude this point, was the voice of the people the voice of God when they preferred Barabbas to our blessed Saviour, and their voice prevailed with Pilate to condemn Him? Go through all the histories and instances, you will find it oftener the voice of the devil, especially in matters of government; for God ordained the people to be governed, and when they usurp the office, they invert the institution of God and are actual rebels against Him, and enlist themselves under the banner of Belial, whose service, instead of God's, they take to be perfect freedom. In the kingdom of Judah, the hereditary right of succession being preserved, the people were in quiet, and the kingdom prospered until the Babylonish captivity. In the other of Israel, where little regard was had to succession, what else is to be met with but seditions, murders, and destruction? As their kings mounted the throne by blood of their predecessors, and were not removed without blood, so the people that chose them were continually butchering and destroying one another.

6. *The Original State of Nature one of Government, not Independency.*—Government is dependency when one depends upon another. It is superiority when one is superior and another inferior. Therefore they who would have the original of government in the people are obliged to suppose a state of independency among all mankind, when no man in the world had any dependence upon any other, and when no man was superior to another. This they call the state of nature; and if such a state cannot be shown, their whole scheme falls to the ground. They happened ill to call this the state of nature among a race of mankind who all came into the world by generation. Nature has imprinted nothing more strongly upon all mankind than the duty and dependence of children towards their parents, and the superiority of parents over their children. Where either parents or children offend against this law of nature, the parents in not taking care of and providing for their children, or the children in not returning duty and obedience to their parents, such are called unnatural. This is the common sentiment of all mankind; therefore this supposed independent statement must be looked for among the pre-Adamites. Or we must suppose a shower of men dropping out of the clouds without fathers or mothers, all upon the level. Or that men were created in multitudes like the beasts, etc. Then, indeed, two men created at the same time, and not deduced the one from the other, would be independent as to nature. Without that, the independent cannot be the state of nature, but contrary to it. Now let us observe how God, designing man for government, expressed it in the economy of His creation, and founded it in very nature. He created but

one man, and did not create the woman at the same time, lest she might have pleaded independency; but made her afterwards out of the man, which showed her dependency on him, and she was made for his use as a helpmeet for him. The apostle argues the authority of the man over the woman from his being first created (1 Tim. ii. 12, 13).

Mr. Locke laughs at this argument, which, having been urged by Sir Robert Filmer, he answers thus: "This argument will make the lion have as good a title to government as Adam, and certainly the ancienter." Could this pass from a schoolboy? It is answered like a merry-andrew, besides the utter contempt of and burlesquing the Holy Scriptures. But we must suppose Mr. Locke (like the rest of the Commonwealth men) little conversant with those sacred oracles, otherwise he, who pretended to sobriety and a character, would not have attacked the argument of the apostle in the person of Sir R. Filmer. God did not leave it wholly to nature, but added His positive command and instruction for government between Adam and Eve (Gen. iii. 16; 1 Cor. xiv. 34). Otherwise Eve might have disputed it with Adam, as some of her daughters have done since. Honour and obedience are due from children to their mothers as well as to their fathers, but insubordination to him, if their commands should interfere with his, must take place. The supreme power is only in the Father. Therefore, when He asserts His supreme authority over us, He calls Himself our Father and never our mother. The common way of all the earth from Adam to this day has been that the firstborn son should succeed in the power and government of the father upon his decease. The way of the whole earth is the surest rule we have to know what we call the law of nature. But it is a yet surer indication of matter of fact that this was the method from the beginning, when we see not its beginning or institution set up as a new thing in after or later ages, but to have come down in full currency from the beginning.

The first commonwealths that ever were in the world were those of Greece, which began by rebellions of soldiers. And the whole curse of them while they lasted was confusion and contest about their new schemes of government which they had invented. Before that time the way and manner of the whole earth, without any exception, was hereditary monarchy. This rule of hereditary succession was broken sometimes by the special command of God, who is Master of His own rules; but we are not. Christ is called our "Elder Brother;" and the Church triumphant "the Church of the Firstborn." Mr. Locke, the oracle of the Whigs, says that "the power of the husband is founded on contract." Suppose the husband should make a contract to obey, and the wife to command. Such promises are frequently made in wooing. Would that cancel the original institution? At this rate the duty of wives would be very different. Mr. Locke is so gracious indeed as to suppose that this contract did not begin till it could begin, and that age and reason loosen the bonds of this subjection as children grow up, and leave them at their own free disposal. These bonds are not temporary because they do not exist, if by that he meant any sense of duty towards our parents, for children in swaddling-clothes cannot have that sense. They could not come before age and reason, which wear them quite off; so they never were at all!

CHAPTER XI.

CATECHIZING IN CHURCH—CONDUCT OF "REHEARSAL"—CHANGE OF RESIDENCE—MEMORIAL OF THE CHURCH—VISIT TO OXFORD—WEATHERCOCK AT MERTON—ABRAHAM GILL—HAYMARKET THEATRE—LITERARY FORGERIES AND PIRACIES—TINDAL'S "RIGHTS OF THE CHRISTIAN CHURCH" ANSWERED—HEADSHIP OF THE CHURCH—THE ADMIRAL AND ALDERMAN—MEDITATED DISCONTINUANCE OF "REHEARSAL"—ASGILL'S BOOK—COWARD'S — EDWARDS — HOADLY —"OBSERVATOR'S" NEW EDITOR—MR. DODWELL'S BOOK—FALSE REPORTS—SCOTTISH CLERGY—SUPPLEMENT—EXTRACTS FROM "REHEARSAL."

A DEVOUT and estimable Parish Priest, who recently went to his rest,[1] was one of the first who revived the practice of public Catechizing in church after long abeyance in general, which at first met with much objection as an innovation. About five years after its successful establishment—for he was a man who could bide his time, and quietly persevered in whatever good work he commenced—an assistant Curate, in conversation with a parishioner, heard her express, to his surprise, great satisfaction at it. "Why, I thought," said he, "that though you generally attend you had a prejudice against Catechizing." To which the lady replied, "I had once, and told the Rector so; but have long changed my opinion." "And will you tell me why?" said the curate. "Yes," she answered; "for this reason. I like your

[1] Rev. R. W. Miles, Rector of Bingham, Notts, October 26, 1883.

sermons all well enough; but I learn much more from the Catechizing, and hear things explained I did not know without displaying my own ignorance." That was an excellent reason, and the best of all testimonies in favour of catechizing in church. A priest can convey information thereby in an easy, familiar way, and through questioning children correct prevailing misconceptions which would be deemed generally beneath the dignity of the pulpit; though this might be a little less strained than it is, with advantage to ordinary hearers. The anecdote here may serve to illustrate another matter. The *Rehearsal's* popularity had grown immensely among all classes within two years, so as to have nearly driven the *Review* of De Foe out of the field, and provoked from Tutchin's *Observator* complaints which plainly declared him on the losing side. Because a great many Dissenters had been favourably influenced, and persons in the highest ranks were known to approve of the paper, the cry was revived of its being in the pay of a party, and subscriptions solicited. Particular statements were even offered on this point, such as that one clergyman in Devonshire had collected a hundred pounds for the author. All of them were mere fabrications, as before; and those particulars of persons and places merely inserted to invest the stories with an air of probability. The real reason of success lay, like the catechizing, in furnishing information without exposing their ignorance to great numbers, who had but slight acquaintance with history and facts necessary to be known in order to a right judgment concerning disputed matters of Church and State. The *Rehearsal* supplied these, and set people thinking instead of hastily adopting opinions which first came to hand, or fell in with their inclinations. Nor did any more need instruction than those who called themselves the Upper classes; just as many parish priests could testify to be the case still from personal intercourse with candidates for confirmation, or as haphazard misquotations of Scripture and religious errors by aspiring politicians and statesmen abundantly declare. Another reason was that readers of the *Rehearsal* found no personalities nor scurrilous attacks made upon individuals, whether on one side or another, or in any rank, so that they could read with profit and without pain. No one could take up a *Review*, or *Flying Post*, or *Observator* without a dread of seeing himself or a friend lampooned in the most offensive manner, or an insinuation artfully conveyed, more cruel than an open libel. Whereas the Rehearser only alluded to persons to defend them, or where they had first forced themselves upon attention by some public act. What distressed them still more was their failure to discover the writer in his *incognito;* after many guesses and assumptions, every one of which he successfully parried, without denying any correct statement or making incautious admissions. And he continued to write anonymously, the better to escape being drawn into personal questions of any kind; for he had no apprehensions on his own account, because he had no reason to fear such opponents as his, however threatening their attitude, nor any intention of uttering statements offensive or improper against the Government. De Foe had scarcely been liberated from prison, and Tutchin eluded a conviction for libel, before both were risking fresh perils from authorities, some of whom had too much reason to be sensitive about their characters and proceedings; such as Harley, who yet did not hesitate to retain De Foe for the purpose of defaming others. Leslie, however, could neither have stooped to such acts, nor wanted discernment to see that an honourable conduct of his paper would probably prove safer as well as more creditable. What he did complain of was apathy on the part of some clergy, who seemed indifferent whether truth or falsehood should prevail, and of others who allowed themselves to be beguiled into the delusion that alliance with Whigs and Dissenters against their own brethren under the brand of High Church could ultimately issue in anything but their own ruin. Yet this was done in a strain of mild remonstrance, which was the furthest possible from censoriousness or appeal for sympathy for himself, with proofs from history how such policy had always failed before, and must in its very nature be a failure. It was their battle he was fighting, and the cause of the Church at large. Clergy have often thrown cold water upon those who have done so, or been jealous of their abilities; nevertheless this want of appreciation did not stand in the way of doing what he conceived his duty, and if he carried his cross bravely, so did he meekly at the same time.

For some five years he pinioned himself to a desk day after day, with but occasional intervals of rest and relaxation; whereas, if he had chosen to direct his talents into another channel, grasped at preferment within his reach, or studied the virtue of moderation at the expense of principle, concealing his convictions, he might have passed as men do now, by safe and silent courses, to the smiles of peers and prelates. They have their reward, and he had his. He had removed from lodgings under the roof of his friend the Quaker, still his friend as much as ever, to a house of his own for the convenience of his wife, whose health had begun to show symptoms of failing, which caused him much anxiety; a home indeed of very modest pretensions, and still within easy reach of business haunts. She was of a quiet and retiring disposition, so that restricted means were not a subject of much regret, and affection led her to find an interest in her husband's pursuits. Had they desired to mix more freely in society, his reputation was sufficiently established to have provided it; but they continued pretty much in that of the friends they had first known. And there is no trace of their absence from 1701 to 1706, except for two short visits to the Continent, the longer being spent in Holland just before the *Rehearsal* was opened. Frequent visits and secret interviews at the court of S. Germain, with which Leslie has been credited, had little existence except in the imagination of friendly or unfriendly biographers; and often, when he has been presumed busy in hatching plots over there, he was listening with an air of mere casual attention to conversation in a coffee-house about himself and his writings; or at home preparing another number for the press, when reported to be down in Suffolk or Devonshire canvassing or collecting; or at Swallowfield on a visit to Lord Clarendon, his esteemed and fastest friend, who had withdrawn from public life and was growing infirm, while report perhaps was busy with his appearance at the Old Bailey on a charge of libel.

Stories of this description were put into circulation at that date against various persons, and found ready credence without an iota of proof, which seems to show the thing itself was too probable. He therefore may have suffered little more annoyance than any other public man who happened to be obnoxious to a party or faction. But entries in several diaries of charges and convictions, summonses and bails, are more frequent than is consistent with even ordinary care on the part of the writers to ascertain the truth of what they left to posterity.[1] No less than three occasions are thus recorded of prosecutions against

E.g. Luttrell's "Diary."

him in the years 1705-6 when, so far from the Government having any design against him, his papers were very acceptable to a majority, and not even Harley could be supposed to have any animosity or excuse for proceedings against him. The most important of these was in connection with a publication entitled "The Memorial of the Church of England," which created a great deal of excitement in the year 1705, was animadverted upon in the House of Commons with much warmth and severity, and supposed to be glanced at unfavourably in the queen's speech. Its main purport was to represent the Church to be in danger from factious movements of Whigs and Dissenters, enforced by a variety of considerations, and severely commenting upon ministers of the Crown, their names being indicated in a form too slightly disguised to admit of doubt. All efforts to discover the author failed, and Parliament, though several persons were pitched upon or suggested for inquiry, had to be content with ordering the offensive pamphlet to be burned by the common hangman. Perhaps it is still a moot point who wrote it, for no one ever claimed or acknowledged the foundling; but the honour of parentage appears to lie between Mr. Hill, the Rector of Kilvington, and Dr. Drake; more likely the latter than the former, because it contains expressions which can hardly be reconciled with his known opinions. Some persons attributed it to Leslie, of which for a long time he took no notice, till directly accused of its authorship, and a warrant stated to have been issued for his apprehension. The Government never for a moment suspected him, nor did any search or examination point in his direction. However, then he came forward voluntarily with a disavowal of any acquaintance with the matter, but pointed out how impossible it was that he could have written it, for (on p. 45) towards the end were statements admitting the principle he had continually denied, of "power originating in the sovereignty of the people." He further affirmed that he had taken less notice of it for some time because he suspected it to be a repetition of De Foe's base hoax in the "Shortest Way" to bring odium on the Church. Still, however, it may be found labelled with his name among collections of old tracts in various public libraries. Those who have taken the trouble to read this "Memorial" will have scarcely thought their trouble repaid, or found in it sufficient to account for the excitement occasioned by its appearance, if flames had not been already kindled fiercely in angry breasts. About that time he and some members of his family happened to pay a brief visit to Oxford, when he walked with them through the Bodleian under the name of Mr. Smith. This little disguise occasionally was necessary to escape curiosity and compliments, freely tendered by undergraduates at the University, with whom his reputation had made him a favourite. But very naturally the excellent Mr. Hearn, misled by common report, imputed it to an intention of "fleeing from justice;" and though he would not for the world have hurt a hair of his—wig, immediately dotted down in his note-book a record of his penetration on September 15.

A letter published by a Mr. Stevens contributed to fan the flames and protract agitation, so that the "Memorial" had many recurring allusions in the *Rehearsal*, provoked by attacks of the *Observator;* but the subject may here end with clearance of Leslie's name from any connection with its elaborate censures and complaints.

At Oxford another mischievous piece of scandal was manufactured and reproduced in London to cause a ferment, originating doubtless from some misconception in the first instance, and exaggerated in its retail as gossip by De Foe. The *Observator* announced with a flourish of trumpets a discovery of iniquity at Merton College. A weathercock had been set up with a motto, "*Semper eadem*" and the queen's arms, which was immediately explained to have a mysterious signification, which wicked Tories had conceived and shrewd Whigs had discovered. The *Rehearsal* took pains to prove, by irresistible evidence, that nothing of the kind had been done or intended, but simply an old sign cleaned and repaired exactly as it had been before. Meanwhile offensive charges were flung indiscriminately at the Queen, the College authorities, and persons of distinction, and sinister designs whispered about, which caused simple folk to lie uneasy in their beds lest the Pretender might come in the night. When the invention was substantially refuted in every particular, they had to be content with De Foe's assertion that no one could prove such a thing had never been designed. Upon this graceless evasion he and his companions were not ashamed to ride off, rather than confess that their notorious appetite for slander had betrayed them into a base and wicked fabrication.

"A review of the times, their principles and their practices," was the purport of the *Rehearsal;* therefore it contained, among many thoughtful dissertations, allusions to wretched *canards* as bad as those which fill the columns of petty provincial papers of a later date. Such was the story about an Abraham Gill in the diocese of Ely, whose title to Orders was very questionable; but having obtained recognition as a clergyman of the Church of England took upon himself to discard her Liturgy and doctrines, and permit a Chapel-of-ease to be turned into a schismatical meeting-house. When this conduct called for the interference of the Rector, an outcry of cruel persecution was raised, and the High Church party, as usual, arraigned at the bar of public opinion, till the facts of the case were rightly stated, and the man's character and antecedents exposed; then, without apology or confession of error the Scandal Club simply dropped the subject. A performance of "Hamlet" was announced at the Haymarket in aid of a Chapel-of-ease to S. Martin's. Here was a splendid opportunity for De Foe to launch out into invective, with many repetitions of the names of Mr. Collier and Leslie, which he lost no time in utilizing. Indeed, he could hardly be expected altogether to refrain, had he been a man of more delicate and refined organization. For it was a foolish and unseemly undertaking, certain to provoke hostile criticism, to shock many pious persons, and likely to result in very slender assistance to the object in view. Our Rehearser evidently felt that his task of defence was an uncongenial one, and had to content himself with putting a few facts in the right light. Neither Mr. Collier nor himself had the remotest concern with the transaction. No clergyman at all was involved, but "an unwary churchwarden" had assented to a proposal from actors and others who were too poor to contribute money that their services in a performance should be accepted in aid of the building fund. A system of galling restrictions upon the press, together with infliction of barbarous punishments and ruinous fines for whatever judges and juries might denominate a libel at the instance of the court or Government often defeated the purpose for which it had been established. Naturally persons burning with indignation, or a mere desire to express opinions right or wrong, burned more fiercely for want of a free vent; so anonymous publications multiplied. This again worked disadvantageously for successful authors. Their own writings were unscrupulously pirated, and the profits misappropriated by inferior scribblers; while, on the other hand, any publication attracting attention was readily imputed, to promote its sale, to some well-known name. De Foe suffered much injustice in both these respects, and loudly complained; nor did his wrong less deserve sympathy because he was himself reckless in scattering groundless imputations against opponents. Leslie does not seem to have been injured in the former way; at least, he never complained of it. But he was a victim to the latter practice, as has been already observed in regard to the "Memorial." There were also several other instances. After his death catalogues were published of his works, containing pamphlets which he never owned, and of which no evidence beyond vague assertion or conjecture was produced. Only the bare names of several survive, without a possibility of test or scrutiny being applied to their contents. Even, however, in his lifetime, and more especially at this period, he found it necessary to disclaim four such forgeries. There was first a " Second Part of the Wolf Stript," a title which stamped the writer with an obvious intention of deceit. Then there appeared a " Letter " addressed to the author of a " Memorial on the State of England." This " Memorial," in opposition to the other about the Church, defended the Whigs and Dissenters with the Government in its recently altered form in favour of that party. It was deemed a very able pamphlet on their side, emanating from Matthew Tindal, the so-called historian, but an apostate of discreditable character, who, after going to Rome under King James, reverted under William, and was then a professed Deist. A more infamous book was his "Christianity as Old as the Creation," answered by many controversialists, including Dr. Waterland. The letter addressed to him was composed by a Mr. Stevens, rector of Sutton, in Surrey, really a Whig and a Low Churchman, but who, smarting under some personal offence, assumed the character for the nonce of a Tory, though not very cleverly. His meagre performance was burned by the hand of the hangman, and himself, upon conviction, sentenced to a fine and the pillory, the latter part being only formally put in execution. Meanwhile Leslie had the unpleasant necessity of disavowing any acquaintance with him or his work. The *Observator* also charged him with composing "three scandalous libels," naming two: (1) "Britain's Just Complaint; (2) that virulent libel on the good queen, called "God's Curse on the Sin of Disobedience, that they shall be taken off in the flower of their age." To this accusation he replied at once frankly. "For the first, I have always heard it attributed to Sir James Montgomery of Skelmerly. But I assure you it was none of mine. And for the second, I never saw it, nor heard of it, till I read this title of it in the *Observator*." Montgomery had aided in the Revolution, but returned to his allegiance and engaged in a plot for the restoration of King James. His name would not have been mentioned now, but that he was safe out of reach on the Continent.[1] Notwithstanding this, Tutchin had the effrontery to return to the charge a month after in these words concerning the "Sin of Disobedience"—"He says he did not write it, or ever heard of it, though it is evident he did write it, and that virulent libel was answered by the Bishop of Salisbury (Burnet) some months after the good queen died." Readers will hardly think the retort too severe or undeserved which this elicited. "Whether the bishop answered it or not, I know not, nor did I hear of it before. But is this a proof that I wrote it? I dare say the bishop would not charge it

[1] Who is said to be the author of "Declarations from St. Germain."

upon me; but I have inquired, and cannot find that ever such a book was printed. If so, this is pure invention. I quoted this to show an original of impudence and the obdurateness of a Whig hardened against shame and repentance.—Let him show his evidence. I provoke him to it, and when he can prove it, I'll be content to be thought as great a liar as he is."

Of course the challenge was not accepted, and as characteristically Tutchin neither retracted nor apologized to Leslie and the public for his fabrication.

During his stay at Oxford he had an opportunity of reading a letter from ministers of Geneva to the University, which he was able to turn to good account in connection with a fresh work from Tindal's pen, of a more important character than the previous one. Though entitled disingenuously "The Rights of the Christian Church," it was an elaborate and virulent attack upon the Christian Church, denying those rights. He betrayed in it some leaning to his old stepmother of Rome, but otherwise rank infidelity and accumulated hatred for the Church of England, such as only perverts feel in a general way. The book, however, on this account was highly extolled among Whigs and Dissenters, who could not see or care that if Christianity were proved an imposture their own position would be more unwarrantable than any other. Leslie, therefore, dissected this book completely, exposed its false assumptions and frivolous sophistry in the clearest manner, and then proceeded to demonstrate in opposition the divine rights and authority of the Christian Church. Tindal wrote a defence of his book, trying to shift his argument when it had been shown to be absurd as well as untenable; but he could not retrieve his ground. His whole case was built upon empty hypothesis and gross perversion of the plain words of Scripture. De Foe showed himself in high feather for a while at this support to his cause, and enlarged grandly upon what was termed the Horeb contract between God and the people of Israel, that He should be accepted as their chosen King. It appeared a fine corroboration of the Whig principle of government originating with the people, which had been overlooked strangely by all divines. But he had, after many flourishes, to relinquish Tindal as he had done Milton, Sidney, and Locke, one after the other. Upon this abandonment of successive positions, Leslie spoke in a triumphant tone perfectly justifiable; yet he disclaimed any praise to himself, for he did so only if possible to provoke his antagonists to further efforts, that the victory of truth might be rendered more complete and unquestionable. His prospect was with pity, not pride.[1]

Like Toland, Tindal met bland smiles and patronage, notwithstanding his antecedents and present attacks upon Christianity, from latitudinarian prelates who scowled at and scolded its defenders if only they were deemed high Tories. Therefore it was very desirable to strip off the sheep's clothing and show the wolf of infidelity, which multitudes of people could not detect for themselves, and expressed great surprise and gratification when this was done for them in the pages of the *Rehearsal*. But its author did not rest content with exposing fallacies and perversions of Scripture. His object was not only to destroy but build up, and in place of the errors which he refuted to supply positive doctrine and sound principles. A mere system of negatives and protests he deemed as bad, or worse, than falsehood. Accordingly he inculcated, with all the force and clearness of which he was capable, in plain popular language, the divine government, heredi-

[1] Bacon's Essays: "Of Truth."

tary right, the power of the priesthood, the visibility of the Church, and sin of schism—disbelief or denial of which engendered that revolutionary spirit which had overthrown Mitre and Crown in England once, and were working up to repeat the same experiment if possible again by the hands of an ignorant populace, under the sinister guidance of designing infidels and republicans. Happily he had discernment as well as ability to make their finest weapons recoil on themselves, and show the inconsistency and inconsiderateness with which these men seized upon any plausible pretence for defaming or damaging the Church of England. Nothing at that date was more common than to take exception to her as a Parliamentary institution, and established upon Erastian principles. Dissenters of all sorts flung this stigma in the face of her members, especially Presbyterians. Leslie therefore showed the charge to have no foundation; for the Act of Submission, generally urged to prove it, had been made to that infamous monster of sacrilege and blood Henry VIII. by Popish clergy; and the title, "Head of the Church" claimed by him, was repudiated by his daughter Elizabeth, never to be resumed by any succeeding Sovereign with consent of Church or State, nor is it recognized in a single Church Formulary. When this had been irrefragably established, what did the redoubted Tutchin do, but turn round and boldly exclaim that it was high time a new law should be passed to declare Queen Anne's headship, and prohibit, under penalties, its denial? He did not care about inconsistency or contradiction; but he had silently to beat retreat when Leslie pointed out how disastrously this new law might be enforced against English Presbyterians and other sectarians in separation from their Scotch brethren who denied the right of any sovereign to meddle in their religious affairs.

De Foe taunted him in the *Review* several times upon his silence concerning the projected Union between Scotland and England then busily agitated, and for promoting which he himself had a well-paid mission under Hartley and Godolphin, and had been permitted to kiss the queen's hand on appointment. Let De Foe have his due. If he had possessed the instincts and education of a gentleman he would have been a very great man, for it is wonderful how much he achieved in spite of his grievous faults of character, and what industry and talent he brought to bear upon any enterprise he took in hand. He made himself useful in this business to his employers, and earned whatever remuneration he received; nor did Leslie grudge it to him, but declined to occupy the *Rehearsal* with that subject, because, so far from wishing to oppose or delay the Union, he entirely approved of it. Indeed, he was ahead both of Whigs and Tories, for he expressed a desire that it should be extended to include Ireland; but as it was entirely a political measure not involving any definite principle, he had no intention of meddling with it one way or the other, and confined himself to his original plan. When he strayed from this, the fault lay with opponents themselves. Such an instance here occurs, of a grand encounter between an Admiral and an Alderman, who having no Homer to record their destroying wrath, and the mischief which ensued from what time these heroes, Dilks and Seager, were divided, the matter forced itself upon our Rehearser's notice. Sir Thomas Dilks was not a Whig, but a Tory; not a Dissenter or Deist, but Churchman by profession; not of low birth or condition, but a gentleman of aristocratic origin and connection, and a flag officer, therefore an object of aversion to Mr. Seager, a baker at Portsmouth, a member of its corporation, and an ardent Dissenter. Both were present at an entertainment given by the Mayor in his public capacity, on which occasion Sir Thomas, in conversation, made use of some profane words, as Seager asserted, but none of the rest of the company heard, so they could hardly have been uttered in a loud voice. Still, if used at all, the oaths were most improper, and at that time rendered persons liable to a penalty. What was strange on Seager's part, besides his acuteness of hearing, was his notion that the improper language was purposely intended to offend himself, though the speaker had not addressed him personally at all, but only the Mayor, and though many of the company might be supposed to disapprove of profane expressions quite as much as he. Nevertheless, he gave the Admiral into custody of a policeman for publicly breaking the law, who however on advice of a magistrate refused to act. Shortly afterwards the Admiral met the Alderman, and, having a cane in his hand, administered to him a castigation. Many said "it served him right;" others, more cautiously, "a man must not take the law into his own hands." Probably both were right. But such was the matter which two centuries ago was deemed sufficient to form a fresh apple of discord between rival parties from Portsmouth to London, because a Dilks then was a Tory, and Seager a Whig Dissenter. Except John Dyer's *News Letter*, which unfortunately did not stand high in public estimation, Tories had no other means of rectifying false or garbled statements than by an appeal to the *Rehearsal*. Leslie closed his account of the real facts of the case, which had been greatly distorted in the Whig papers, by an anecdote of the Lord Mayor of London at the same date, who, when a person uttered an oath at his table, laid a shilling down, saying, "Now, I pay this time for you, the next you must pay for yourself." At this time he had seriously meditated upon its discontinuance. He found its conduct a severe tax, and if he should look for the same success as hitherto he might be drawn deeper into the vortex of common politics. For both De Foe and Tutchin had received donations from the Kitcat Club, to encourage them in carrying on the war with fresh vigour against the Tories, and they had several friends in it who contributed the more useful aid of their pens. An explanation of its curious title may be interesting for those who have not met with it elsewhere. It was derived from Christopher Catt, abbreviated into Kit-Cat, who kept the Fountain Tavern in the Strand, where the lights of the Whig party delighted to assemble and regale themselves with mutton-pies, indigestible food which may account for the general dulness of their literary productions.

> "Hence did the assembly's title first arise,
> And Kitcat wits first spring from Kitcat pies."

Of course there were exceptions, and, *facile princeps*, the poet Dryden,[1] who, however, must have had a surfeit when he wrote some wretched lines to Tonson, the bookseller, secretary to this club, with an offensive addition: "Tell the dog that he who wrote them can write more." No more was needed to get his money. Leslie also conceived that he had fully redeemed his pledge to abase himself in his Divine Master's service by the variety and fulness with which he discussed religious topics. So the date, April 16th, 1702, was actually fixed for bowing his retreat from a stage on which he had entered reluctantly, when he was for the present diverted from his purpose by a necessity of entering the lists against two new combatants.

[1] Also Congreve, Lord Somers, Prior, who turned over to Bolingbroke's afterwards.

Mr. John Asgill was a briefless barrister who lodged near Moorfields, but had some property and a seat in the Irish House of Commons. His want of practice may have been either the cause or effect of his devoting attention to theological speculations, for which he was particularly ill qualified by a very slender acquaintance with even the English version of the Scriptures. No wonder, therefore, that he fell into absurd mistakes in trying to frame a theory about the mysterious subject of death, which had he kept to himself or his own circle of acquaintance need only have provoked a smile as an innocent craze. But he courted distinction, and resolved to enlighten the world by publication of a book propounding his system, the heart of which lay in an assertion that men only die for want of faith. Having such faith himself, a mortality should have been the reward and testimony of its possession. But alas! for the finest conceptions when subjected to the remorseless crucible of experience. The barrister himself one day disappeared from the stage of existence, and gave this emphatic denial to his own theory. Meanwhile, the few readers of his book up to this time—and they were very few—would have been well content to wait patiently the issue of events for clearing up in the same manner doubts about their own cases. Zealots in the Irish Parliament, however, could not brook so dilatory a process of determination. Asgill's book was formally brought before their assembly, and, a majority being Orange Tories of the first water, where faith and charity could not go beyond the tomb, it was condemned, and the author in his absence, for he had not the imprudence to appear, ignominiously expelled from membership. His book instead of himself gained a portion of immortality and, what was at any rate an immediate convenience thus acquired a sale and popularity hitherto unattainable. Some persons even suspected these proceedings in Parliament to have been a crafty device of his own, and that his book was forced on the notice of Parliament to acquire notoriety. The serious tone in which, however, he had written seemed inconsistent with such a view, and Leslie thought his design lay far deeper still, by professing to establish his theory upon the Holy Scriptures to bring them into discredit, since men could see for themselves the certainty and universality of death. He quoted many texts, but applied them in such a silly, senseless manner, and betrayed such general ignorance of all history and religion, that it is difficult now to deem him capable of this design—"to banter the authority of the Holy Scriptures and the whole Christian faith." But Leslie thought this; and he had seen another heresy Quakerism, like twitch shoot its fangs underground, and spread till it became the nucleus of an organized society, silent and destructive, simply from contemptuous neglect in its earliest stages of growth because it appeared ridiculous and unattractive. Therefore he took alarm at the notoriety and sympathy accorded to Asgill, and resolved to apply his "weed-killer" to the roots of this deadly nonsense till he had eradicated it, and at the same time plant instead the true doctrine on death and resurrection. In doing this he explained many texts often misunderstood, or passed over without any consideration of their meaning at all—a very useful work if an Asgill had never furnished the occasion, or been elevated to the position almost of a martyr and confessor among unbelievers and misbelievers of every description.

Asgill did not stand alone, for another volume had become prominent from the pen of a Dr. Coward, whose patients were as scanty as the "counsellor's" clients. His theory was that the soul is nothing but the life of the body, and is extinguished with it as the flame of a candle, but to be lighted again at the resurrection and burn for ever. This he also pretended to base upon Scripture, as Leslie suspected "for the same purpose to make men disbelieve them; and that himself believed in no resurrection, but having got the soul dead he intended to keep it so." He answered, if the soul be no more than the life, then at death of the body there must be an end of both. If at the resurrection the body live again, there must be a new soul; so one soul will suffer or be rewarded for another. It is no resurrection unless the same thing that died rise again. What is called one's person is chiefly denominated from the soul; for eating mutton does not make one a sheep, but flesh enlivened and acted upon by a human soul becomes human flesh. On the other hand, if a dog eat a man it does not make that dog a man; therefore the soul is the chief part of the person, who is composed of body and soul. There can be no such thing as a human body without a human soul. And as the particles are continually changing, it is a very needless question which of them shall be raised again. This will be enough for the philosophy of the subject as a specimen; but what he proceeded to say was the gist and drift of the *Rehearsal* reasoning, that though those who argued for the immateriality and immortality of the soul from nature had the best of it, yet the full proof could only come from revelation. Heathen philosophers, so far as they had inklings of truth on this subject, as upon sacrifice, priesthood, marriage, etc., got them from immemorial tradition. They did not institute these practices or doctrines, but found them in use, descended from Adam. In the text, S. Matt. x. 28, Coward explained soul to be no more than life, which is to make our Saviour say that a man may kill the body, yet not take away its life. In conclusion, it was shown that the doctor's claim to originality even had no foundation. He had been anticipated recently by seven other writers, if, indeed, he had not copied from them; and both he and Asgill had only revived old exploded heresies, the former of persons in Arabia, whom Origen was sent to dispute against, and condemned by a Council; the latter of Menander, a disciple of Simon Magus.

No sooner had this subject been dismissed from consideration, than the doctrines of Predestination and Election reappeared for agitation under the auspices of one Edwards, a Calvinistic doctor at Cambridge. These questions have been worn so threadbare by discussion in all times, that it is quite unnecessary to touch upon them here, or refer to him and his sermon for "re-establishing Calvinistic doctrines long stifled, and to extirpate Arminianism," further than to say that "if he had no free-will he could not help it, that may be his excuse," which Episcopalians in Scotland also could charitably apply to a book he published full of abuse of them. Leslie stated the Catholic doctrine with his usual force and clearness, showing at length how consistent the tenth and seventeenth Articles of the Church of England are with the teaching of S. Paul, whilst from their perversion most terrible consequences have resulted. But it was impossible for him then, as it is now, to put these points in a new or better light than it had been done often before; so that very brief notice of his argument must suffice at the close of this chapter.

Way must now be made for a more imposing preacher, with "a sermon of pomp" and a flourish of trumpets from a Grand Jury, reviving the old controversy upon Moderation, which had been for a considerable time left by the Whigs like a horse out at grass on the plains of Salisbury. This was Mr. John Hoadly, chaplain of Bishop Burnet, and by his favour made at an unusually early age Prebendary of Salisbury Cathedral; however, such dignities are not generally conferred only as the reward of learning or merit. He must not be confused with his brother Benjamin, a more notable man in controversy, Bishop of Bangor, then of Winchester. John indeed obtained high preferment, being advanced successively to the sees of Ferns, Dublin, and Armagh, in Ireland. Probably he became a sounder divine than Benjamin, after removal from the influences of earlier years at Salisbury; at any rate, he caused no such disturbance in the Irish as his brother did in the English Church. Yet his preferment to the Primacy was one of many instances how unscrupulously the Episcopate was abused to serve the purposes of political parties formerly in Ireland. When quite a novice he had published a letter in defence of the bishops, which he deemed worthy of reprinting at a later date, and it stated the case for Occasional Conformity with a fair amount of point and cogency, without running into dangerous admissions upon matters of doctrine and discipline. His other literary efforts were confined to some "Humorous Views of Bishop Beveridge's Works," the last subject an ordinary person would have selected as a proper one for the exercise of facetiousness. However, the wit speedily evaporated, leaving no trace behind, and happily the works remain unmethylated. This "sermon of pomp" bore on its title-page nineteen names of the Judge and Grand Jury at Salisbury Assizes, as though it needed Lay recommendation to back it up. So it did. For it contained little new, though obviously composed and corrected with much care. What was new was of course not true, and of a painful description from the effort to be striking and sententious. Mr. Hoadly trespassed very closely upon the borders of impiety. As, for instance, in the commencement, where he suggested "that if the Scriptures do not furnish a sufficient Rule of Faith, so that any honest man can find out the way of salvation for himself, it must be said that either God did not design to give us a clear revelation, or else that He could not so express Himself as to accomplish what He designed." What he intended to imply is clear enough and true enough to a certain extent. But his mode of expressing himself had a strong savour of profanity, and was very unseemly in the pulpit, for he "put upon God a dilemma which he meant for human creatures who ventured to disagree with himself." The reply in substance was: "I allow the Holy Scriptures to be a sufficient rule. But there are helps ordained of God towards our better understanding of them, of which, if we make not due use, we cannot plead the obscurity of the rule. It is written that the lips of the priest should preserve knowledge, and that the people should seek the law at his mouth.... I wonder that Mr. Hoadly, being a priest himself, forgot this help. To leave every man to himself is a dangerous thing. But to charge it upon God, and put that alternative upon Him, that He either did not design we should understand our duty, or that He could not express Himself, was a very bold and dangerous attempt." Again, Mr. Hoadly said, "Those disputes which vex Christianity, and have vexed it from the very beginning, on difficult and abstruse points, have been much more deplorable in their consequences than considerable in themselves. Such they are that men may be saved on both sides, yet such as a man would take some pains to convince men in." This followed after a passage alluding to early controversies concerning the Saviour's Divinity, the Incarnation, and

Trinity, therefore the inference appeared fair that he meant a man might be saved on both sides of these, and that they were not considerable in themselves, which involved a tremendous imputation upon the Church and General Councils. Further, his words were shown to have been taken from Toland's book, "Christianity not Mysterious," therefore rightly termed " stabs to Christianity in the dark," and couched in generals well enough to be understood by those whom he courted, a more effectual method to undermine Christianity than if he had made an open attack and declared himself. "S. John calls deniers of the divinity of our Saviour antichrists, but Mr. Hoadly's moderation would have given them a softer word, told them that they might be saved on both sides, and that the controversy was not worth the contest. He says, 'Christ came to turn men from their iniquities,' but there is not a word of His being the Propitiation and Atonement for them—not a syllable of the doctrine which distinguishes a Christian from a moral heathen. Again, he spoke of 'God not being so tied up to one form of government in the Church as to leave those who want it under condemnation'—turning religion into mechanism and a charm, and making his own sect a conjuror's circle, the only place of safety from the devil, chaining God down, as heathens their idols, to one's own house or city." Now, all this sort of language he could not fail to know would be popularly understood to imply that the Church might be no better than a conjuror's circle and sect, to which God's goodness was not confined or chained like a heathen idol. Otherwise it had no meaning at all, which alone would have been a great fault upon such an occasion, in a sermon prepared under the eye of a bishop suspected of Socinianism, and indebted for some of its most noticeable contents to the study of infidel publications, then printed with an unusual sort of recommendation. Criticism was thus plainly invited if not challenged, and to point out defects and faults was a duty and service to the Church. Leslie in discharging this had no personal motive whatever, for he had never seen Mr. Hoadly, nor had any knowledge of him till copies of the sermon were forwarded with request for a review in the *Rehearsal.* What he censured was, not the man, but the principles which he employed his position as a preacher and authorized teacher of the Church to promulgate; then proceeding in his characteristic way to construct as well as destroy, and upon the ruins of the demolished discourse to establish sound and edifying doctrines. The only pulpit which he could conscientiously occupy without being trammelled by political oaths, where he could be widely heard, and by larger audiences than even in Salisbury Cathedral at the Assizes, was the *Rehearsal*. There he spoke fearlessly, lifting up his voice like a trumpet, and giving no uncertain sound upon the need of Christian faith as well as morality. If he had not done his work effectually, to the comfort and encouragement of many members of the Church, and the conviction of many sceptics and unbelievers, he would never have provoked such virulent hostility and attempts at interference from Whig partisans and Dissenters as he did, though happily for a long time these were all abortive.

John Tutchin, born at Lymington, closed his ignoble and unfortunate career on September 23, 1707. His harsh treatment for engagement in Monmouth's rebellion had attracted to him more sympathy than his bravery, and this would have been turned to more profitable account in any other situation than that of journalist, where the temptations proved irresistible to personal abuse and libel of opponents. Though he and De Foe rowed in the same boat, they could not manage generally to keep stroke or pull together, which caused many awkward capsizes. And the reckless manner in which he put Machiavel's maxim on the art of throwing mud into execution frequently recoiled with most injurious effect upon both his party and himself.

Ridpath, his successor in the editorial chair, promised to conduct the *Observator* in a more prudent and decorous manner, which in itself conveyed a strong admission of the truth of charges in the *Rehearsal;* but either the recurring force of nature or external influences proved too potent for submission to such wholesome restraint, and after a few numbers the paper resumed its wonted style, commencing with a very far-fetched and wanton attack upon the gentle, retiring Mr. Dodwell, as well as upon Leslie, for which not the slightest provocation could be pretended against either, while calling for their "expulsion from the nation." Leslie readily advanced in defence of his friend, whom he termed "of the first if not the highest rank in the learned world, and as eminent for his piety as his learning, therefore for whose good company, if expelled, he would feel obliged to the new *Observator.*" What made him so angry with this good man? A book lately published concerning the Immortality of the Soul, which had made some noise in the world, and to which several answers had been written. These proceeded for the most part upon a thorough misconception of Mr. Dodwell's meaning—comparing him to Asgill, though they intended Coward; for they accused him of denying the immortality of the soul, which he did not, but drew a distinction between this as natural and actual. He argued for the latter as the gift of God conferred in the sacrament of holy baptism; and so it was represented as "a piece of Jacobitism levelled at the queen's title and the foundation of the Constitution," because he questioned the validity of Dissenting baptism. Leslie did not concur in Dodwell's theory, for reasons which need not be entered into here, because that would involve a lengthened statement rather concerning his book than its defence; but he showed very plainly that it was a gross misrepresentation to raise such issues at all, and that whether Mr. Dodwell's theory were right or wrong, there was no excuse for directing such a storm against him, because the same had been asserted by many persons before; in ancient days by Justin Martyr, more recently even by writers of their own party—Milton, Baxter, and Robert Fleming. Attacks upon Leslie himself, made up of wild gossip and old reports of being a turncoat priest, having been in three battles and fought at the battle of the Boyne, only evoked a smile and assurance that he had never been in battle in his life. The origin of these blunders have been already explained in confusing him first with the son of another bishop than his own father, then with his own brother, followed by additions and exaggerations incident to all such stories. Nor need their ready credence and circulation among opponents call for animadversion when friends and admirers, even descendants, quite as inconsiderately have adopted them from time to time. The immediate purpose in view was to damage the *Rehearsal*, because it cast such an inconvenient glare upon principles and practices of the times. These, with false reports of warrants and arrests, are still to be traced in Luttrell's "Diary" and other such remembrancers. They were the current topic of the day, taken from Whig papers, where the wish was father to the thought, and nothing of the kind had ever taken place. Leslie's first intelligence on several occasions of his giving bail or being imprisoned was on reading them. Here lay a difference. He confessed he would have stopped them if he could; not having the power, he answered them. They, not being able to answer him, tried or pretended to stop him. Whigs and Dissenters were much ruffled in temper at their discomfiture. He was reasonably elated with a success which enabled him to achieve still more.

Arrests and imprisonments had befallen Tutchin and De Foe, notwithstanding all the patronage of Ministers and subscriptions of clubs. He declined either subscriptions or patronage, yet had not been subjected to legal proceedings of any kind. If he had many political adversaries, the majority had no personal animosity against him, while they were equalled in number by both personal and political friends; moreover, multitudes at a distance, in various parts of this kingdom and of Scotland, heartily recognized the services he gratuitously performed for the Church at large. Nowhere did she need assistance more than in Scotland against the infamous cruelty of the Presbyterian body, never more unblushingly infamous and cruel than in Queen Anne's reign. Nowhere did he more desire to assist her or strive more earnestly, if to little purpose. Accordingly, it is gratifying to reflect that to this day his memory and services are affectionately treasured by some of the worthiest sons of that most faithful but suffering Branch of the True Vine.

It is evident, from several passages of his writings, that few things ever grieved Leslie so much as the conduct of the Presbyterian body in Scotland towards the Clergy there. After these had been mobbed and marauded, proscribed and plundered, till they had been reduced to a state bordering on starvation, the hireling Whig press was instigated by the General Assembly to hinder collections in England on their behalf. However, the motives were too transparent, and the characters and claims of the noble band of sufferers too unquestionable, for this scandalous conspiracy to succeed; so even the queen was persuaded by her ministry, the archbishop, and Bishop Burnet, to subscribe among great numbers of other influential persons. Nor is there any portion of the *Rehearsal* more deserving of admiration than that in which, single-handed, he contended for the sufferers against Calvin's ungenerous sect, and pleaded her wrongs. His heart may be heard beating in every line. So now the memory of the bishop and himself, though strangely slighted by the Church of Ireland which owed them most, nor ever has produced a worthier father or a worthier son, is still cherished by the more orthodox branch of Scotland.

Passages from the "Rehearsal."

7. The Sacrament of the Altar a True and Proper Sacrifice.—Must we now despise the most solemn and proper priesthood that God ever committed into the hands of men, to offer up the same sacrifice in figure which Christ in reality daily offers to His Father in heaven, the sacrifice of His own body and blood once offered upon the Cross? The priest at the Altar stands there representing the person of Christ our great High Priest, presenting himself in our flesh and blood to His Father as our High Priest, who, by the sacrifice of the Cross, has made full atonement and satisfaction for the sins of the whole world; to be applied to all who with true faith and sincere repentance lay hold of it. He has commanded the same thing to be done by His priests on earth in these symbols of it, which He blessed and called His own body and blood, to show the nearness of the relation between this sacrifice upon earth and that performed by Himself in heaven.

But the rage of these men against the priesthood upon earth will leave none in heaven. They will not let Christ be a priest now, though he is called "a Priest for ever." For if His offering His once crucified body in the presence of His Father, and, in virtue of that, making daily intercession for us, be not the proper act of a priest, and a true, real, though unbloody sacrifice (for He is not to be sacrificed again), then He is not now a priest. But if these are proper acts of priesthood, so they are when performed in symbol by His priests on earth. We offer the unbloody sacrifice as it is offered in heaven; but the Church of Rome offers a bloody sacrifice, which is abhorrent. For if it be a real blood as they say, then the sacrifice is really bloody, and the blood of Christ is poured out again in every sacrament. And this commemorative sacrifice of Christ already come and slain, and now our High Priest in heaven, is a more noble sacrifice, and as properly the act of a priest as the typical sacrifices under the law, which prefigured Christ to come. And if Christ is more properly a priest than Aaron, who was but a type of Him, so is the evangelical priesthood more properly priests than the Levitical. And if "no man taketh this honour to himself but he that is called of God as was Aaron;" and if "Christ glorified not Himself to be an High Priest, but He that said unto Him, Thou art a Priest for ever;" how monstrous does it look to have such notions set up among us, that every man, nay, and woman, is as much a priest as those whom Christ ordained and appointed to succeed Him in that office, nay, as Christ Himself, whom these men will not allow to be any priest at all, and overthrow our whole religion which is built upon it!

What Whigs call "the top of priestcraft" is Christ, our great High Priest, in heaven; who, by leaving behind Him a priesthood upon earth to celebrate the same worship and offer the same unbloody sacrifice of His body and blood for the people which He, in person, perpetually perform in heaven, has by this means united heaven and earth into one family. The same atonement and sacrifice for sin being offered up in both. In the one by Christ Himself in person; in the other by priests whom He sent, as His Father had sent Him; that is, with the same commission of binding and retaining sin, in subordination to Him and in His name; and to whom, at the institution of the holy sacrament of His body and blood, He said, "Do this," that you have seen Me do—in blessing the elements, etc.—"till My coming again." "And he that despises you despises Me." This torments the evil spirit out of all bounds. Here he sees his own ruin and eternal destruction aggravated by the redemption afforded mankind in the priesthood of Jesus Christ, making atonement for their sins. The devils know Christ to be their King, they feel His power to be superior to theirs, and have been forced to confess it. This they believe, and tremble. But they believe not Christ to be their Priest, that is, to make atonement for their sins, which is the proper office of the priesthood. Thence comes their despair, their rage and envy against mankind who have Christ for their Priest as well as for their King. First to redeem them and then give them the glories of His kingdom. But His kingdom is all terror to those who have Him not first to be their Priest. He is King in hell as well as in heaven; but he is only a Priest in heaven. And they who believe not in Him as their Priest in this world will not have Him King in the next. To confirm this the more to us, and that we might have it perpetually before our eyes, He has delegated His priesthood to earthen vessels, to men subject to like infirmities with ourselves, and gave them the glory which His Father had given Him; that is, to stand in the midst between God and men; to transact with them, and sign and seal His covenant with them in His name, as His attorneys or ambassadors; to remit and retain their sins according to the rules He has prescribed to them, and to offer up the sacrifice of His blessed body and blood. He commands them to let no man despise them, that is to keep up the dignity of their office. For by this an intercourse is opened between heaven and earth, and the angels ascend and descend. They who see Christ offer up this sacrifice are present in our assemblies, and behold the same thing performed by His priests on earth in those symbols He has commanded, and called His own body and blood for the remission of sins. As the priests and the people did eat of the sacrifice after it was offered, so here we eat and drink what Christ calls His body and blood. This provokes the rage of the devil above all things, to see a heaven thus instituted and set up on earth, answering each other like two indentures—the same worship, the same priesthood, the same sacrifice. And God has showed us no other way of going to heaven but by the ministry of His priests upon earth, to whom He has committed the word of reconciliation and the administration of His sacraments. He that will not hear the Church is to be reckoned as a heathen. But the devil would persuade us, as at the beginning, not to fear this threat, for that we shall not surely die, although we go out of the road which God has prescribed to us. No, but we shall be as gods, we shall be all priests, and offer up sacrifices every one for himself. And what signifies these outward institutions? They are all priestcraft! Do you think God would damn a man for eating an apple, though it were forbidden, or for not washing himself, or taking a little bread and wine, though it were commanded? And what are these priests that would arrogate this to themselves? Look upon them; what do you see in them more than other men? By this sort of argument the devil has seduced many. And in all ages his malice has been chiefly exerted against the clergy, for the institution of the priesthood is the destruction of his kingdom.

8. *Of Rebellion.*—There is no sin but has its subterfuges and excuses. The plainest sins have been distinguished into nothing, nay, turned into virtues by men of art and cunning. There may be some difficult cases, as is seen in our books of casuistry, but in the main and in the great duties of Christianity the rule is plain to any honest and well-designing mind. He will make a hedge about the law and refrain from every appearance of evil; he will fly from sin as from the face of a serpent. He that once comes to distinctions and salvos about his duty is weary of it, and would be glad to get rid of it, and he seldom misses to find out a means. He that would be secure must strengthen himself in the ways of the Lord, must hate and detest all sin, put on the armour of God and prepare himself against all temptation. But if he seeks to compound with sin, and wishes such a thing were not one, that he might comply with it—that man has sinned already, and will go on all the way, even to the excess of sin. Hence it comes likewise that men are furious against one sin and very gentle towards another. This does not come from the fear of God, but (it may always be observed) there is something of party and interest in the case, or of violent bent and inclination. There is no man given to all sins, but most men have some beloved sin which they

would excuse, and show their zeal in crying out against other sins. They

> "Compound for those they are inclined to,
> By damning those they have no mind to."

Rebellion is called witchcraft in the Holy Scriptures, and the common epithet of rebels is sons of Belial, which shows that this sin was learned from the devil, who was the first rebel, and it is of a much higher class in wickedness than the ordinary sins of the flesh. For the king having limited himself by the law, the law is the rule when this comes to be applied to any particular case, and the king has granted to us to plead the law with him in all such cases. But it allows of no coercion over the king in any case. The Whigs tell stories of kings that have been coerced, and particularly name King John. To which it is answered, that ten thousand instances might be given of the breach of other commands of God, for one instance of coercing kings, yet that did not abrogate any of these commands of God. It is particularly remarkable of Presbytery that it never yet came into any country upon the face of the earth but by rebellion. That mark lies upon it. A Whig is a Dissenter without his religion, but retains his principles as a government, therefore they are dear brethren. And the Dissenter overlooks the atheism and immorality of the Whig, because he is useful to him in carrying on his rebellion, yet rails at immorality in Churchmen.

9. *The Church a Society.*—The Church is a society in the great society of the world, and in the several kingdoms and societies of it. But every one of these societies has a chief governor or head within itself to regulate its affairs. Thus every Church has its bishop for its head and governor, and every kingdom has its

head. The head over all Churches is the Same, who is Head over all kingdoms; that is, none but God, whose kingdom ruleth over all. As all nations are one kingdom to God, so all Churches are one to Christ, the chief Bishop. And as God has made no universal deputy or monarch over the world, neither has Christ made any universal bishop over the Church. But what if these bishops differ among themselves, and so there be opposite Churches set up one against another, as we see it done, to the no small ruin of Christianity and the peace of the Church of Christ? What if kings differ among themselves, and kingdom rise up against kingdom, to the disturbance of the peace of the world? The case is the same; and though it be lamentable and a sad concomitance of our fallen and corrupted nature, yet it is better than if all the world were under one king, or all the Churches under one bishop. For, considering human frailty, there would be more rebellions and bloody wars under an universal monarch than as it is now. Thus, as to the Church, if the universal Church of Christ all depended upon one bishop, unless he were infallible and omnipotent, the whole Church must go to ruin, and there could be no remedy. With all the divisions of the Church, it is in a better condition than if under the absolute dominion and government of one poor fallible man, subject to errors and passions. Therefore let us not be wiser than God.

Church and State may part again, as several times they have done, and each stand upon its own foundation, which therefore they cannot lose by their union. This makes it rather a federal than an incorporating union, by which last all distinct and independent powers are for ever abolished and extinguished. The Church takes care of religion, and the State of civil concerns, and these are not contrary the one to the other. Nor can they ever interfere while each keeps within its own limits. For example, the State condemns a man for murder; the Church, upon his repentance, absolves him; yet this does not hinder the sentence of the law to pass upon him. So here is no interfering, because the censure of the Church does not cramp the sentence of the State, nor the sentence of the State the censure of the Church.

It is not to be supposed that any bishop would command one from his bounden duty and service to the king; or if he did, it would be an unlawful command, and he would be obliged to disobey it. Or if it happened by chance, the bishop, not knowing what command the king had given, would excuse attendance at the time and place.

10. *The Power of the Keys.*—There is a declaratory part, which is also judicial, as when a man, vested with authority and executing the office of a judge, declares the law. It is a sentence. When a herald reads a declaration of war with the solemnity appointed, it authorizes and begins the war. Another may read such a declaration as well and as loud, but it signifies nothing. Thus the clergy are heralds appointed and authorized by Christ to proclaim His peace to the world, or His wrath if they obey not. And He has promised to ratify in heaven what they thus declare in His name upon earth. But may they not exercise this power of the keys very unjustly? Can they save or damn at their pleasure? No doubt God will reverse any unjust sentence that they pass. He is King, they are but His ministers, and the King may pardon whom the judge has condemned. But this shows the sentence to be judicial, for nothing else is reversed or reversible. No court would reverse the sentence of a private person because it goes for nothing. But if a sentence pass by a lawful judge, though it be unjust, yet

it will take place unless reversed by a higher authority. And there needs no express reservation of this superior power in the king when he grants a commission, for it is implied. This obviates all the objections of the Church using the power of the keys unjustly. The supreme authority of Christ the King is still implied and supposed; who is not tied up by any unjust sentence—"*clave errante*," as the phrase of the schools is. For while the administration of government is committed into the hands of men, it is liable to mistakes and errors. Therefore when Christ promises to ratify in heaven the sentence the Church shall pass upon earth, it is still supposed that it be passed justly. Christ says that "God judgeth no man, but hath committed all judgment to the Son." And the reason is given: "Because He is the Son of man." It is not said because He is the Son of God; as if all God's judgments were to be dispensed by the hand of man. From the beginning of the world God has dispensed His blessings by the hands of men, sent men to be His prophets and priests, to intercede and make atonement for sins; the last judgment will be pronounced by the mouth of The Man; and God judges no man but mediately, by the intervention of man. A man cannot be said to be truly penitent, if he refuse to own his crime and submit himself to the censure of the Church. And God will not remit his crime, though he be sorry in his heart he has committed it; but will retain his sin and ratify the sentence of the Church, while he continues in his obstinacy against her. One cannot be reconciled to God while standing out in obstinacy to the Church, for He will maintain His own institutions; and he who expects to go to heaven any other way than that which God hath appointed makes himself wiser than God, and may find his folly when it will be too late. What allowances He will make for extreme ignorance I will not determine; "His mercy is over all His works." But for those who offend of malicious wickedness, who obstinately break off from the Church and despise her authority, who place themselves in the seat of the scorner and turn everything that is sacred into ridicule, these are in the gall of bitterness and their condition most desperate. Now one may plainly see that the power of the Keys is to open or shut the gates of heaven, and that there is no entrance thither to those who die in obstinate opposition to the Church, though they should repent of all their other errors except this. Therefore a man ought to be very sure that the censure of the Church is unjustly passed upon him before he ventures his soul on it. Those who go out of the Church excommunicate themselves, and with this aggravation, that it is their own act and deed; whereas a man may be excommunicated wrongfully. The separation of Dissenters from the Church of England is a schism; but not hers from the Church of Rome, because that Church imposed sinful conditions of communion. Some men think they are safe if they follow their conscience in anything; they forget the Holy Scriptures are given as a rule to our conscience, and we are obliged by the law of God, whether we think so or not; else we might harden our conscience, let passions and lusts blind the eye of reason, wink and shut our eyes and not see the way, and then say, "How can a blind man see?"

11. *Of Predestination.*—It is said that Predestination is a Scripture word, therefore no man ought to speak against it. Holy Scripture often speaks to us after the manner of men to our capacities, for otherwise we could not understand them. We have no words to express the infinite nature of God; therefore, whether fore or after is

attributed to God in Holy Scripture, we must take that word *ad captum*. Such is the word predestination, or fore-ordaining or fore-knowing. God knows all things, but He foreknows nothing, because all things are present to Him. He ordains, but He does not fore-ordain. Yet we must use these words because they are according to our capacities. If we argue strictly and properly from them, we shall fall not only into many absurdities, but even blasphemies. Perplexities have arisen from taking the word in a strict and literal sense, without any *as if* or comparison supposed in the case, or any allowance for a word *ad captum*; but downright supposing a time past in God, and a decree already past concerning things to come with God—which absurdity being granted, others follow inevitably on both sides. Such decree being supposed, it takes away free-will; else the will of man might disappoint the decree of God. On the other hand, without free-will supposed, it will be impossible to give an account of all the promises and threatenings in the Holy Scriptures, and the protestations of God that He delighteth not in the death of a sinner, and His earnest invitations to repentance. As this is the perplexity, so remove the first absurdity and all clears up on both sides. Let us understand God's predestination not strictly and philosophically, and consequences drawn from it, but in its general meaning and import; then we understand the firmness of God's promises, and of His covenant made with us in Christ impossible to be frustrated. The whole difficulty being as to time of fore and after, which we are sure is not nor can be in God. It is of God only we speak, when we speak of His eternal decrees before man was made; for man was not then in the case, otherwise than as all future things are present with God. But if we apply this to ourselves, then it will follow that I was born before I was born, even from eternity, because my birth was then present with God; and my death is now present with Him, therefore I am now dead. I am not dead, because all live unto Him. Thus we apply to ourselves what we call His fore-decrees, and say that the freedom of our will is now tied up by them. Therefore let us leave the word *fore* out, and say only that God ordains the punishment of wickedness and the reward of virtue. When we say that God fore-ordains, there comes in all the confusion. No Predestinarians can refute this, since they all allow that there is no fore or after in God. Therefore, if they will speak properly of Him, they must use words only of the present.

The rigid Calvinistic notion of the word predestination, and the inferences drawn from it, are not only most absurd but likewise blasphemous against God. And the effects of it seen among common Presbyterians are terrible. Their heads being perpetually filled with abstruse notions of predestination, election, reprobation, and secret decrees of God, and that they have no free-will or choice what to do, but must go on as it is secretly decreed, this makes men careless (for why should they struggle when there is no remedy, and their sentence is already past, and that irrevocably?); so it is observable that more of these die in despair than any other sort of people. On their death-bed they have cried out for "assurance." And when the merits and satisfaction of Christ has been preached to them, they would say, alas, "What is that to me, if I be not one of the elect; for Christ died only for the elect?" This is another of their doctrines pursuant to their notion of predestination, that the decrees of God may not be frustrated. When some have been asked why they doubted of their election, and bid look into their lives, which, bating human infimities, were good and virtuous, therefore they might take this as a mark of their election, they would answer that the good works of the reprobate were hateful to God, therefore this was no sure mark. The condition of such people is most lamentable. Election is with them a secret decree without any respect to our works, and they can have no other assurance of it but that of their own imaginations. They cannot, as the apostle requires, be always ready to render a reason of the hope that is in them. Nay, they speak against reason, and think it rather a hindrance to faith. Thank God, the faith learned in the Church of England is this, that Christ died for all mankind, and consequently for me in particular. And I have His promise, which is an infallible assurance, that if I believe and trust in that complete satisfaction He has made for all my sins, and truly repent of them, I shall be saved. Though my faith be weak and my repentance unworthy, and fit to be repented of, and all my righteousness as "filthy rags," yet I despair not, because the satisfaction made for my sins was performed by Christ in His own person, without me, in which I have no share at all. I did not and could not pay one penny of my debt, or make any satisfaction to infinite offended Justice; but my whole debt was paid by my Surety, and by Him who alone could make satisfaction it was made. My faith is a hand which reaches this medicine to me and applies it. The virtue is not in the hand, but in the medicine. The stronger the faith, the greater the comfort. Therefore, Lord, increase my faith, and I pray that it fail not. If it be well grounded, though weak, and my repentance be sincere, though unworthy, I am upon Jacob's ladder, and though upon the lowest step, yet on the road to heaven. Some are upon a higher step and some on a lower, but all are safe.

This is my faith and my assurance, this is the reason

and the rock upon which it is built. What reason can any man give for his being elected by a secret decree which he knows not? There can be no sure mark of it by the principles of predestinarians. It is but imagination. Impressions on the imagination may give great pleasure, and even raptures of joy. If these are built upon the true foundation, they are gold and precious stones; otherwise they are but hay and stubble, and will not endure the fire. We may know them also by their effects. If such transports leave us more humble in ourselves, and with more love and charity to others, they come from God. But if they fill us with spiritual pride they come, no doubt, from the spirit of pride. Nor is any so proud as he who is proud of his humility. Whatever are the decrees of God, they are not contrary to His revealed will. Therefore I may cheerfully set about my duty, and surely trust in His promises. . . .

There is one thing which predestinarians boast very much, that their doctrine is agreeable to the Thirty-nine Articles. Now, though this be no argument as to the doctrine itself, yet to the Church of England it is of very great consequence. The tenth Article is of free-will, which is not denied, but rather supposed and asserted. But it supposes the concurrence of the grace of God by Christ to be necessary to incline and guide our will, and to work with us when we have that good will. The seventeenth Article is of predestination, and keeps us to the Scripture phrase of God's ordaining before the world began, of calling whom He foreknew, etc., which is to be understood in the same and no other sense than as these words are used in Holy Scripture, namely, *ad captum*. Then they are full of sweet, pleasant, unspeakable comfort to godly persons. But the Article checks the curiosities of this dispute, which is what I have been blaming. Observe, further, that there is not a word of reprobation in this seventeenth Article, nothing of God's having fore-decreed any to misery, but it speaks only of those whom He has elected to salvation, so that Calvinists can find in it no colour or umbrage in their favour. And whatever the opinion of particular men might have been, this cannot be charged upon the Church of England.

12. *Of Universal Redemption.*—Predestinarians do not allow universal redemption, or that Christ died for all. Because, they say, that if He died for the reprobate, it was totally in vain, and the end of His sufferings must be frustrated as to them. Besides, that He could not intend to save those whom God has reprobated by an eternal decree. As to eternal decrees, enough has been said already. But now, the Scripture is plain which says that "Christ died for all," and "would have none to perish," and "as in Adam all die, even so in Christ shall all be made alive." He died even for those who perish. We may understand this by a familiar example. Suppose one came to a prison, and taking a list of all the debtors, should pay their debts, costs, and charges; and opening the doors, should tell them they were at liberty who would accept it, and go out in such a time. After which the doors should be locked again, and those there should be kept till they had paid the uttermost farthing. Some thankfully accept the offer; but others despise his mercy, or will not believe him, and prefer the sordid life of a prison, the pot and the pipe, and will not come out. This is the very condemnation our Saviour spoke of, when He said that men loved darkness rather than light. God will not save us against our will—free-will. But there is no merit in us when we accept of His salvation. He pays all the debt, and the thanks and glory are to Him. Otherwise, how could wicked men be blamed, if He shed no blood for them, nor gave them any saving grace? This

brings us to another point. From internal decrees it is inferred there can be no falling from grace, because this might defeat the decree; and, therefore, that men cannot finally resist this grace or fall from it. Dr. Bales was the physician called in the night that Oliver proved a "true deliverer of his country!" The Protector was in great agonies of mind; often started and asked those there if they saw ought. At length he called for his chaplains, and the first question he asked them was, "if there was any falling from grace?" To which, being answered in the negative, "Then," said he, "I am safe." For he supposed that some time or other in his life he might have had a little grace. Then this usurpation, with the murder of the king and devastation of three kingdoms, besides much bloodshed abroad, and the overthrow of the Church Establishment, could do him no harm! This is a short way of quieting conscience, and to lull men asleep in their sins. Thus poor souls are deluded by these doctrines of decrees. In consequence of which it is a maxim that God sees no sin in His elect; which is, indeed, that the elect cannot sin. Then it is all one whether we are good or wicked. These are monstrous principles, and make one not wonder at their preacher in London, who, being asked what progress he had made, said he had made many proselytes, but all the effects he found was that he had preached a congregation of Christians into a congregation of devils. Perhaps he did not know the cause, that it was the natural consequence of the doctrines he had preached. These are more fatal to the souls of men than idolatry, or the worst part of Popery, unhinging the whole of Christianity, taking away faith and repentance, and dissolving all obligation to a good life.

CHAPTER XII.

The Prince—Invasion—Benjamin Hoadly and Sermon of Pomp—Ill Health—Death of Prince George—Dr. Gregory—Giving Security—Sacheverell's Trial and Episcopal Appointments—"Best Answer"—"Best of All"—Mr. Higden—Tyrrel—Supplement—Extracts from "Rehearsal."

WHAT shall he be called? A man of many titles. Prince of Wales—the Pretended Prince of Wales—the Pretender—the Pretended Pretender—James III.—Chevalier S. George. It matters nothing now which of these any person deems the more appropriate to him, and more proper for one's self to adopt, and involves no question of hereditary or parliamentary right. Because both are combined in the title of the reigning sovereign in England. *De facto* has become also *de jure,* upon the principles advocated so consistently and persistently by Leslie himself; and if he were alive he would be foremost in acknowledging that the house of Stuart being extinct, there can be none to dispute the claims of the house of Hanover. Equally large and unqualified must be the admission due from those who trace the right of the Crown to the Revolution settlement and the Act of Succession, for those national engagements preclude them on their own principles from trying to alter the constitution of the country as then determined, whether for better or worse. A *plebiscitum* would not produce any material difference, if it were conducted in any fair and reasonable manner, whatever republicans and democrats may pretend upon occasions, or leaders of a party, who are notably of foreign extraction, try to persuade the people to believe. Such men who talk of a mere "titular sovereignty" in Great Britain,[1] are not only guilty of disloyalty, but their language is in direct contravention of the Revolution settlement, of the conditions made with the house of Hanover in accepting the succession, of Acts of Parliament unrepealed to this day, and of all the principles professed by the Whig party two centuries ago. Perhaps the reason lies in this fact, that candidates for popular leadership in the present day are most of them not of English, Irish, or Scotch descent, but imported from America, Germany, and Italy; therefore having no patriotic attachment to the Constitution either by inheritance, tradition, or conviction. Of course there are exceptions, but these are not men who have hitherto exhibited talents for statesmanship to qualify them for trust in the enormous venture of a fresh revolution, nor of courage requisite for the enterprise, because the English nation will probably never again be so blind as to engage in a civil war to feed the vanity and cupidity of individuals unprepared to take foremost posts of danger. It was not such stuff as modern demagogues are made of, that enabled a Cromwell or a Prince of Orange to filch a crown from the owner's brow, and terrify the House of Lords into treason or submission. Now loyal and patriotic people who wish for peace, but "peace with honour,"[2] at home as

---

[1] A speech at Birmingham, 1884.
[2] "Is not peace the end of arms? . . .
No. Let's use the peace of honour."
("Bonduca.")

well as abroad, are freed from that dilemma and conflict of conscience which painfully entangled those who lived in Leslie's time; when *de jure* and *de facto* titles stood in glaring opposition, and to support the one, even as an abstract principle incapable of further assertion, was to incur suspicion of active designs against the other. There was seated upon the throne one who, upon the *de jure* principle, had only a parliamentary title, and of might against right, almost as liable to the charge of usurpation as her predecessor. Across the Channel was a young man, the trumped-up accusation against whose birth had long since not only been disproved but abandoned by the very persons who first set it afloat; who could not be deemed guilty of charges laid against his parents; who had never injured his country and professed devotion to it, claiming allegiance by an hereditary title of the most unquestionable character; but of a religion hateful to the nation, and whose return, whatever pledges he might offer of relinquishing the arbitrary courses of his infatuated father, was naturally dreaded by that portion of his subjects who had driven him into exile. What was an honourable man to do? Silence was impossible, because an oath at any one's suggestion might be tendered, to say nothing of the pain of ignominious self-obliteration, which would compel a declaration and put an end to hedging and evasion. That exactly was the difficulty which Leslie foresaw must render life intolerable to one of his ardent nature and solemn convictions, if he had wished to adopt a neutral position even temporarily; therefore from the first he chose his side against his interests, and endured much suffering and loss in adhering to it openly, undisguisedly—not, however, hastily, for he declared that he had made the strictest inquiry into the question and examined all the objections which he could meet with from others or suggest to himself, but retained his conviction. "The flagrancy of fact from Scripture, as well as reason, determined me against all bias to that side of the question which lies furthest from the world as to me." He who would read this pathetic expression without respect and admiration would only be one deserving of neither himself. The sting consisted in this, that against the *de facto* sovereign he had not one hostile sentiment, while for the sovereign *de jure* he did not know what beyond that he had to say. He could only hope the best and wait. But the Pretended Pretender could not wait himself. He could not count upon his ebbing fortunes—as they drifted further into unreality upon a distant shore, growing itself colder in the lapse of time— returning at any high tide without some supreme effort on his own part. Therefore he determined to make one, and issued a declaration of war in February, 1707, which was to be published if supporters could be found in sufficient numbers to take the field when he should arrive in Scotland; trusting also that Marlborough and Godolphin were out of humour enough at last, under the direction of Sarah, to play the part of traitors openly once more and go over to the winning side. Marlborough kept out of the reach of Sarah; and her storms raged higher than ever upon discovering that the abigail, Hill, whom she had introduced as a poor kinswoman to the royal palace, used her position to supplant her. A sweeter temper, a nobler spirit, a more devout character, could scarcely have brooked such ingratitude and deception without indignant remonstrance, but within six months the web was woven too successfully to be undone. Harley had made the abigail his tool, though he had soon to give way before the influences of the duke and Prince George in fear of the Pretender.

She—as Mrs. Masham—had ousted Sarah, and the queen felt bound to stick by her new favourite, wearied of the old friendship which had become a burden. Had James come sooner, and stayed longer than he did, then the question what to call him had been settled undoubtedly in his favour, very differently from what results proved. He sailed from France upon March 17, 1708, for Scotland, with a force extorted from the French ministry, who had little mind for fulfilment of Louis's chivalrous engagement to James II. on his death-bed unless assured of success. Some thought that his own reluctance to start equalled theirs to hazard anything beyond courtesy and hospitality at S. Germain, and that secret orders were given to Fourbin, commander of the expedition, not to land. At any rate he did not; and brought the young heir safely back, after hovering near the coast of Scotland for some time without accomplishing anything, upon the plea of difficulty. The value of this plea need not be narrowly scrutinized, since one ship and four thousand men were lost, which was at least on the surface some testimony to sincerity of purpose if combined with safety. What appears more probable from all accounts on both sides, and an impartial consideration of actual circumstances, is that if the attempted invasion had been followed up strenuously and energetically it would have been crowned with success. For the Union project had been so mismanaged in Scotland as to alienate both Presbyterians and Jacobites. Lowlanders would soon have joined James's standard. From thence insurrection would have passed by rapid strides from north to south of England, where many things had combined to detach from Queen Anne the good will of a large proportion of the people, especially her own uninteresting want of character and vacillation between Whigs and Tories, weariness of war, and the violence of the Whig press against the Church Establishment, which had given rise to the cry that it was in danger. But the French fleet returned to Dunkirk; discontented Scotchmen returned to their homes; discontented Englishmen had no necessity to run the risk of leaving theirs, and the queen and her Government were relieved from great panic and peril. All ended, therefore, in a mere flash of the pan; the scare for revolutionists, trimmers, and Tom Doubles soon passed; and as they breathed freely again they talked loudly of what they would have done, and what now should be done to prevent the Pretender.

He had fain to content himself with a conviction of failure, not being attributable to any want of courage on his own part, and of writing another letter to his adherents, deploring the disappointment of their mutual hopes, and pledging himself never to cease his efforts to recover his crown. About this time he assumed the title Chevalier de S. George, which must have been deemed a fortunate circumstance by those who wished to be safe on both sides. "Pretender" had been adopted at first as a title of dubious signification, and only gradually came to bear its more unfavourable sense. What a pity that these waverers did not bethink them of the still more indefinite term "Claimant"—not yet polluted by a gross imposter—as a safe and convenient cloak which committed a speaker irrecoverably to neither side!

Meanwhile the paper war continued to reflect the vehement passions and interests which stirred the public mind. Ridpath had even less ability than Tutchin, with all his coarseness. De Foe's promises of amendment always ended in the same way, and his well-paid services in Scotland as spy upon the Jacobites and scout for the Kirk, whetted his appetite for fresh onslaughts on the Church of England, under cover of protesting against Jacobites, Nonjurors, High-Flyers, and Tantivy men—this latter a euphemism to denote the boot-whip-and-spur-policy of postillions as adopted by Tories. John Hoadly had acquitted himself to the satisfaction of the grand jury at Salisbury in commending moderation towards Dissenters in immoderate terms; but Leslie had ventured to impugn the one-sidedness of his liberality, and question the propriety of his language. Now his brother Benjamin came to the rescue, among a fresh batch of pamphleteers and sermon publishers, whose sermons and books had somehow hitherto fallen flat, though undoubtedly he was an abler man. He could hardly have been jealous of his brother's success, though it looked like it, but it may be supposed was simply animated by an earnest desire to stamp his opinions with higher authority; and it is a curious thing physiologists have not accounted for, how opinions, even new ones, run in families. Accordingly he preached and published a "sermon of pomp," heralded by the tin trumpets, and endorsed by judge and jury at Hertford. Hoadly ostentatiously professed to scorn penny papers like the *Rehearsal*, yet he attacked Leslie's principles and very words so closely there, that he said "he might bet him a penny he had read the penny paper, which, though so beneath his notice, he answered in a penny sermon."[1] Its subject was the blessing of liberty, distinguished from anarchy or lawless confusion on one hand, on the other from slavery or an absolute subjection to the will of another not bounded by any wholesome and good laws. What he wanted was "a liberty or property such as cannot be shaken by any

[1] Like John Knox's disclaimer concerning Aylmer's book, "I have not read him."

humour or arbitrary will of one man or society of men." This is exactly what everybody has always wanted, but how to secure it has been the difficulty, because it can be shaken both by a single man and a company over and over again. If the people may take arms to resist what they deem slavery, then comes in lawless confusion. If the question be, whether Government act justly in depriving subjects of liberty or property, who is the judge? Hoadly intended his auditory to understand himself to be the advocate of liberty, and others whom he indicated not indistinctly to be the advocates of slavery, which accordingly he painted in the blackest colours, very easy to do with a little rhetoric. His examples from Scripture were not happily selected; for instance, when he pointed out the "Israelites refusing God to be their King, because they were so little sensible of the difference between slavery and liberty." For it showed that the notion of a commonwealth did not then exist; and that when the people would choose for themselves they chose wrongly, but still a king instead of a God; so they are not the best judges of what is right or good for themselves. Again, it was said the miracles of Moses distinguished his government from others. To which it was replied in the *Rehearsal* most acutely, "This, instead of a salvo, pins the basket faster upon the orators for resistance; for if pretences could be made against a governor of God's own appointment, with such mighty works in attestation of it, how much more might they be made against an ordinary governor, who managed by his own skill and wisdom?" And further, who were the people? Some were for Moses in the right; the major part against him, in the wrong; therefore a majority is not always right, nor *vox populi vox Dei*. Mr. Hoadly spoke of the two Houses of Parliament as "co-ordinate legislative powers with the crown." But this was to repeat and assume the old notion of rebels and regicides, already confuted in the *Rehearsal*, and at variance with his own Prayer-book. If he did not read the former, he ought to have been better acquainted with the latter—specially a service for November 5, then interpolated by authority only of his own revolutionary party. Lest he should take amiss the freedom with which his opinions were corrected and shown to be mere mob-notions of government, though he had attacked Leslie frequently in print before receiving any reply, he assured him it was not with himself but those notions he quarrelled, and that, on the contrary, with some of his works he had been very well pleased. Assistance from the *Review* could hardly have seemed a valuable compliment to Mr. Hoadly in any case, and De Foe's banter, as usual, betrayed his superficial acquaintance with Scripture, as much as his irreverence in handling sacred topics. Shortly after this controversy and the failure of the Chevalier's expedition, it was said that Leslie had gone to S. Germain engaged in preparation of some new plans. But there is ample proof that as he had not been consulted or concerned in that enterprise, so he was not in any new one meditated. On the contrary, by express desire of the Chevalier, his communications to him were confined at that time to mere reports of public events, doubtless with a view to his own security; nor had he any inclination to embarrass the present Government. Early in 1707 he had an attack of gout, which compelled him to seek change of air for a month in the country, during which he heard nothing of what went on in the world, beyond common reports about the Duke of Marlborough's grand schemes, and the demands of Dissenters, announced by their fugleman, De Foe. Letters after that prove he remained almost continuously at home in London till late in the summer of the next year, with the exception, apparently, of a brief visit to an old friend in Suffolk, which was entirely of a private character. Then he had another severe attack of illness which threatened his life, and it was gravely doubted by himself that he could possibly recover. During it he did not fail to review his past life, nor neglect to seek those spiritual remedies the need and benefit of which he had so often urgently recommended to others. And it was well this should be known, for the privacy in which a clergyman's sickness has frequently been enveloped, has created an impression that he did not desire or receive the ministrations of another priest. Nothing could seem more effectually to promote disbelief in such ministrations themselves on the part of the laity. Who, rather for his own sake, should put himself in the hands of a spiritual adviser able to point out faithfully and kindly flaws and failings unknown to himself, which have hindered his usefulness, as well as administer to him absolution and the Holy Eucharist, than a clergyman? For this reason it was that Leslie took an early opportunity, when the danger had passed and he was able to resume to some extent his ordinary occupations, of testifying publicly in the *Rehearsal* that he had not been negligent in his sickness of the proper ordinances of religion; and that his very connection with this paper had occupied his serious concern. Its publication had for some time past been increased to nearly twice a week, but was now intermitted for ten days, which of course led to another report of prosecution, and also helped to identify him more clearly as the editor. His "sick-bed thoughts" were of too strong a nature to be digested easily by readers of the *Observator*, who did not want to think there could be any necessity for a priest's interference. Ridpath's remarks, therefore, which could be readily anticipated, afforded a convenient opportunity for reiterating the doctrines he had already inculcated concerning the Power of the Keys and the Blessed Sacrament of the Altar. This he did, moreover, the more distinctly to challenge attention to them as no novelties of a Nonjuror, or remnants of Romish superstition, but the positive teaching of the Church of England in her Book of Common Prayer. And how had they come to be thus regarded, or lost sight of, but because so generally slurred over, or omitted, or acknowledged with "whispering humbleness and bated breath," by clergy themselves, while pulpits were resounding continually with declamation upon moderation, toleration, liberty, government, and other political topics, deemed likely to be more interesting than purely spiritual matters, to mixed and not very religious audiences. So it came to pass, he observed, in reply to complaints, "the religion of some men consists all in negatives, and they think nothing is meant by the word "Protestant" but protesting against the pope, which whoever does, Pagan, Turk, or Socinian, they think him a good Protestant, and in this fury have run themselves out of all Christianity, who will allow neither Church nor priesthood, and for fear of the sacrifice of the mass will own no sacrifice at all."

Prince George of Denmark died in October, after suffering much from dropsy and asthma, nursed during his illness most tenderly and devotedly by the queen herself. If he was not a noble character, nor behaved well to his father-in-law, yet he was an amiable man, who made no enemies nor interfered improperly with State affairs, for which he had little capacity. Leslie could reflect with satisfaction that none of those darts often directed against him in public prints had ever been feathered by his pen, but that, on the contrary, even when the Prince sided with the ministry against the Church party, he invariably spoke of him with the utmost kindness and respect. Another death soon followed, which he felt more deeply. It was that of a very dear and esteemed friend, Dr. Gregory, the learned Professor of Astronomy at Oxford. They were very intimately acquainted, and agreed upon most matters of religion and politics. The doctor had a large circle of admirers for his learning, among whom was another eminent man, a mutual friend, Dr. Smalridge, who rose afterwards to be Bishop of Bristol, and celebrated among contemporaries as much for his peculiar sweetness of temper and integrity as for his learning. In announcing to Dr. Charlett the death of Dr. Gregory and his burial at Maidenhead, with his desire to have seen him, Dr. Smalridge mentioned that "Mr. Leslie accompanied him from Bath, and assisted him in his sickness and *in extremis.*"

If mathematicians are prone to push their modes of investigation beyond the limits of science into the domain of faith, learned and pious persons are also sometimes too credulous and impressionable. And in connection with Dr. Gregory's name may be mentioned the subject of Second Sight, in which he was a believer, and to the time of his death engaged in collecting instances of it, which appeared well authenticated, as had been Samuel Pepys. What became of that work, or if it was ever published, cannot be stated; but he stood by no means alone in his belief among notable persons of that time, to mention no more than Boyle, Lord Clarendon, Dr. Hickes, Lords Reay and Tarbut, who bestowed a great deal of attention upon the inquiry. At one of their social meetings Leslie contributed an anecdote of an elf arrow shot by a demon at his father with a terrible noise, and said to be well attested,

Whether he believed it himself, or only told it as a good story, is a question, nor would it confirm the pretensions of visionaries, since they do not profess to be under the influence of evil spirits. It is curious also that this faculty, if of higher origin, should be chiefly confined to Scotch peasants! Happily the Bishop of Raphoe suffered no more than a fright from the designs of his enemy, when, if demons did not take human form, many human creatures acted like demons.

Misfortunes proverbially seldom come singly, but the next was one of a different kind and easier to bear. A scandalous story was spread abroad by the faction in their papers that Leslie was threatened with arrest for debt, which caused him publicly to state the simple facts of the case, and put a different face upon the matter. Twenty years ago he had given security for a person, which, as usual, resulted ultimately in his being called upon to pay when he had not the means—"losing both his friend and loan." If there had been a Statute of Limitations he would not have taken advantage of it, and the only reason of difficulty was the losses sustained in consequence of the Revolution, so that no imputation could possibly lie against his honour. But he abided by the engagement of "good-natured folly," and made arrangement for redeeming the bond to the perfect satisfaction of the creditors, nor had they ever threatened to molest him in any way. Shortly afterwards the claim was discharged; meanwhile he had to be content with feeling no scar upon his conscience, and learning by sharp experience the wisdom of Solomon's warning, "He that is surety for a stranger shall smart for it, and he that hateth suretyship is sure." Yet the philosophy of the Old Testament must be interpreted in the warm light of the Gospel: "From him that would borrow of thee turn not away." The world is deceitful enough to force upon Christians the necessity of prudence; but how much worse it would be if they had always to be cold and hard, "only lending to receive as much again"?

Sacheverell's trial, and the tremendous excitement attendant upon it, are matters so fully narrated by several historians, that it may be presumed no one wishes for any addition to the heap of accounts, nor do they admit of much variation; if the majority are highly coloured by party bias, this is more or less a result of that reaction sure to follow upon every movement in which passions and sentiments have been overstrained to a high degree. Tories were inordinately excited, and carried the populace with them for a champion and a cause, which the indiscretion of their opponents, rather than anything in him or it seasonably presented. When agitation had subsided, having run its natural course, and Sacheverell had no resources for its continuance or revival, the usual consequence ensued—that he sank into obscurity, and the cause lost ground together with the waning of its popularity. High Churchmen would have acted more prudently if they had foreseen this certainty of a reaction, and declined to identify themselves too closely with either Dr. Sacheverell or the Tory party, which really had very little sympathy with them. Their objects were selfish and political; only to use the cry of "The Church in danger!" to defeat the Whigs, and install themselves in office. But the same game has been played many times since then, and with much the same result. It will be repeated till Churchmen learn to separate principles from party, and rely upon her inherent character and authority for support against all opposition. Then the cry will cease, "The Church is in danger!" and its establishment perhaps rest on a firmer basis than ever, though that should be to them of inferior concern compared with her spiritual integrity and freedom. It has been the fashion among Whig historians to cover Sacheverell with ridicule, in order thereby the more effectually to damage the cause with which he was so unfortunately associated. But no one who candidly examines the subsequent sermons which brought him into prominence a second time, and were made rather than gave occasion for disturbance, will deny that, like the first, they were of more than average merit, considered as pieces of sermon composition. As for the opinions expressed in them, they were just what it was very well known and expected that clergymen should say; nor half so strong and offensively put—as those of Whig candidates for notoriety upon any special occasion throughout the year. If he became intoxicated by the flattery accorded to him, it was no more than most persons might fear they would become themselves under any similar circumstances. But it is satisfactory also to remember that after his substantial victory, and when excitement cooled down, he brought no scandal upon the clergy by his life or ministry, nor sought to trumpet himself into fame by political publications, as did so many on the other side; but devoted himself henceforth quietly to the duties of his country parish during the period of his suspension.

The *Rehearsal* continued to be published, with few interruptions, till the end of March, 1709. Its last half-year's numbers were mainly occupied with theological subjects, and restatements of some already considered. Then it was abruptly brought to a conclusion. For a long time the strongest pressure had been brought to bear upon the Government, and influences exerted at court to stop it, but hitherto in vain; because no plausible ground could be pleaded for such a step, as it had never exceeded the limits allowed by law. While it was notorious the *Observator* and *Review* had violated these by scandalous attacks upon the Throne, the Government, and almost every personage of authority in Church or State supposed to sympathize with the Tory party. Continual dropping will wear away a stone, and this was not forgotten by Burnet and his friends when admitted to secret conference with the queen. The law itself also for regulating the press had been altered, as a convenient handle for suppressing publications deemed obnoxious by the ministry, among whom Leslie could no longer number any personal friends. Therefore the blow was struck beneath which the *Rehearsal* expired, after a brief life of three years and eight months, in its 408th number, to the deep regret of a large circle of friends and admirers, and the equal gratification of the opposite faction. This partial and high-handed proceeding made a great disturbance; and if there had been a disposition to contest its legality, funds would have been freely supplied for resistance, which the Government would have found a more difficult and unfortunate enterprise than even getting a conviction against Dr. Sacheverell. They did not, however, venture upon any of the harsh proceedings reported in the Whig papers against Leslie personally, and he had no desire to become either a hero or a martyr in such a matter. Reluctantly commenced, it was with no reluctance discontinued, for he had been over-persuaded to go on from time to time long after he was wearied with the conduct of the paper, and shackled more than he liked or approved by his publisher; which is not surprising, because legal proceedings were formally instituted against him, which, however, went no further. Therefore the Rehearser bade farewell to the public with a short enumeration of the works he had answered, and the motives which had animated him in undertaking and discharging a disagreeable duty. How well he did it must be left to the judgment of readers who will take the trouble of considering carefully the specimens furnished in this biography, or, still better, the original papers of the *Rehearsal* in their integrity, wherein the man himself and his opinions may be seen more clearly in some respects than any account could convey. For his honesty and earnestness, stability of purpose and kindness of heart, his extensive acquaintance with theology in all its branches, reasoning powers, and inexhaustible wit, are as perceptible there as they are to those who met him in society, or at that celebrated and charming rendezvous, Child's Coffee-house. If the *Rehearsal* has fallen out of notice, even more than the rest of his works, owing to its inclusion of so much matter the interest of which has entirely evaporated, yet it contains finer passages than can be found in them, and treats in a masterly manner other subjects of first and last importance to all times. Its dross was an admixture and accretion from the world where his lot was cast, and the purer metal entirely his own.

Before its conclusion Benjamin Hoadly, whose book on "Measures of Submission" occupied much of the latter portion, published some more sermons of pomp.

The last of these formed a noticeable feature in a curious controversy. Through Godolphin's influence Bishop Trelawney had been promoted to the valuable see of Winchester. He and Compton of London had been the two prelates who were understood to have invited the Prince of Orange over, though the fact was never admitted formally; and since then they had reverted to their old party, apparently because their services had not met the rewards expected.[1] Trelawney's advance-

[1] Trelawney is not so generally accused, but William boasted of more than one.

ment, therefore, brought much odium upon Godolphin among the Whigs, when he was most anxious to cultivate their support—the more so because the bishop had never anything to recommend him but his birth and connections; so Godolphin engaged for the future to consider party interests more carefully in such appointments. The queen, however, did not consider herself bound by this engagement, and when two other sees became vacant, without consulting the treasurer or the general, nominated Mr. Offspring Blackall to Exeter, and Sir William Dawes to Chester. This produced a violent storm in the cabinet and the party. But remonstrance was useless, for the queen pleaded promises and would not cancel the appointment; but to soothe the irritation of her ministers pledged herself henceforth not to act without their advice; and shortly afterwards, to rectify the balance in favour of the Whigs, Dr. More was promoted to Ely, Dr. Trimnell to Norwich, and Dr. Potter appointed Regius Professor of Divinity at Oxford. Sir W. Dawes is spoken of by Burnet as an aspiring man, anxious to be at the head of his party; but other accounts show him, on the contrary, to have been rather of a retiring and modest disposition, who got this preferment, and subsequently the archbishopric of York, without any desire on his own part. Blackall, of Puritan antecedents, had held different preferments in London, and as well as Dawes was a chaplain to William; but, like him, had never cordially approved the Revolution, or changed his opinion upon further consideration. Among other writings which brought him into notice, was one in defence of King Charles's authorship of "Eikon Basilike" against Toland, who supported Bishop Gauden's claim, an imposition now generally discredited.

In 1708 Bishop Blackall preached before the queen a

sermon, which by her command was published, upholding "the powers that be," but upon the ground of divine right, not an authority derived from the people. Hoadly fished up another of his lordship's discourses preached four years previously, and upon a comparison between them charged him publicly with flagrant contradiction, and asserting that her title was only that of a successful usurpation. Now, it appears plain enough these two charges had a good deal of foundation in fact, whatever the bishop himself intended, or failed to discern in his desire to justify his own position as well as the queen's; for her title to the throne in opposition to her brother could not possibly depend upon divine right, as hereditary, or upon anything but the Revolution basis. Leslie, however, might fairly undertake the bishop's defence, because he thus rudely attacked was a personal friend of his own, a man of exceptionable character, one whose worth even Burnet did not question, and because this sermon was made a pretext for reiterating those doctrines which Leslie abhorred with all his soul. A letter appeared thus lengthily entitled, "The Best Answer ever was made, and to which no Answer ever will be made" (not to be behind Mr. Hoadly in assurance); but this "vapouring title" was only intended as an oblique reflection upon him for his self-confidence and practice of indirectly and covertly glancing in his sermons at the arguments of opponents, instead of boldly and fairly meeting them. First the writer, by way of preface, complained of the bishop's treatment, that he was held up in opprobrium before the world, while pretending to venerate his character and station, for a mere change of opinion, to avow which, if sincere, was creditable to him rather than otherwise; such, too, as Hoadly himself had been guilty of, for he had gained preferment in London upon the supposition of believing what he now condemned. "If the bishop had been in error and gone along with the stream in some things—as who has not?—there can be nothing more glorious to mortal man than to return from it, and to preach up the contrary doctrine. And to insult a man for this is the work of the devil, who is tormented at that which gives joy to the angels of heaven. S. Augustin thought it no dishonour to him to write a book of Retractations." The more delicate point could not be so easily handled, so it had to be explained with a "good night to you, and a fresh appetite" for the letter in this manner: His lordship, in his sermon, 1704, says that "though God appointed government, He did not name the persons who should govern." And in his sermon, 1708, he makes the person of the king to be sacred and inviolable as being the minister of God. His lordship might mean only that God does not name every king that reigns, as in hereditary monarchies, yet the same right descends that at first was given. Thus God did not name Joash, but his right is thus set forth by the high priest. "Behold, the king's son shall reign, as the Lord hath said of the sons of David." "Though Athaliah called this treason, because it was against *de facto*." Now, there is no clear proof that this Answer, still less the preface, ever was written by Leslie, and there are some things in it difficult to reconcile with his well-authenticated works, both of style and sentiment. Yet it has been so universally attributed to him; it contains so much which he would probably have said; and the differences are not so palpable as in the case of the "Memorial," "Wolf Stript," and other publications; nor did he deny it when it would have been possible in some way, though the *Rehearsal* had stopped; that he must presumably be accepted as the author. But this involves another question, whether the "Best Answer" ought to be considered by itself as a *bonâ fide* defence of Bishop Blackall's sermon, or in connection with a later publication, "Best of All," which has also been commonly attributed to Leslie. If the latter be the case, then the reference to Athaliah was a trap laid for Hoadly. If the former, then its special pleading could hardly have been welcome to the queen, or even the bishop, for it implied an imputation upon her understanding or his prudence—the same which he put upon Hoadly as a blunder in supposing some resemblance to have been insinuated between her position and that of the Old Testament usurper. In any case the lawyer is more apparent than the divine, and it was properly signed by a student of the Temple. At the same time, Hoadly was shown to have hazarded some equally rash assertions. He had subscribed to the Book of Homilies, which affirmed the doctrine of non-resistance, which now he denied. He placed the queen's title and the Revolution upon the foot of resistance now, whereas that had been expressly disowned by William and the Convention. He said the resistance against King James was the contrivance of all ranks, including bishops, to their immortal honour, and "if a guilt, more so than the murder of King Charles I." Facts of history contradict him here, for the whole nation let that murder go by default, since none appeared to give a negative, though the few miscreants who perpetrated it did not represent the secret feeling of a majority; whereas no opportunity was afforded of appealing to the nation in King James's case. He disbanded the army and withdrew, overawed by the Prince of Orange's force, who pretended not to come for the crown; and the bishops, whether falsely or truly, all denied any invitation from themselves. Hoadly, therefore, had no standing-ground in court against the queen and bishop, nor the person whom he called a pretended son; because, if only pretended and not a son, there could be no need to say anything about him.

When the argument assumed a more general form the divine may be supposed to supersede the lawyer, because it was returning to the old subject on which Hoadly, with the *Observator* and *Reviews*, had been completely defeated in the *Rehearsal*, and most of his fresh considerations were borrowed from Toland and Hobbs.

A supreme contempt for the Lower House of Convocation, which had condemned his book, was couched in language savouring much more of violent indignation; and his charge of disrespectful demeanour towards the bishops, jarred with his present complaint against one of their lordships. "That's my man! Let not your noble courage be cast down," said Charon to his pupil Achilles. . . . "Though you will be censured by none, you here show that the highest are not free from your censure."

As to the difference between their two schemes of government, it came to this: " If appeals are to everybody, this is anarchy; if not, the people's chosen governor is as absolute as any other. If the last resort be to the king, there is an end of controversy; and though an unjust decree may be given in some cases, yet in the main it is for the good and benefit of the people, and peace and order are preserved. If the last resort be in the people, there is no end of controversy at all, but endless confusion."

Here was the other letter, which appeared in the following year, strangely entitled "Best of All: being the Student's thanks to Mr. Hoadly, wherein the second part of his Measures of Submission which he intends soon to publish, is fully answered. If this does not stop it." Hoadly had caught at or been caught by the reference in the "Best

Answer" to Athaliah, and indignantly volunteered a defence of the queen, thereby falling into a trap designedly laid in it, to be exposed in "Best of All"—unless this were only an ingenious after-thought of some one else than Leslie, remembering how such traps in the *Rehearsal* had often ensnared Tutchin. At any rate, said its author, "who applies a scandal is the one who makes it." Here is a strange thing. If one tell a story as far off as Adam or Noah, or name any one that was not very good in all the Bible, some will presently cry, " Oh, this is certainly meant of —— and ——, who I think are not much obliged to such vindicators. . . . As for what you assert, that paternal right cannot descend to a daughter, you cannot turn it upon me. I never said or thought it—the treason comes home to your own door." Hoadly had complained that, " if his principles were as destructive as represented by the Nonjuror he should not be attacked, for so was he doing real service to his master," by whom was meant the Chevalier. On the contrary, it was because they were destructive of all government whatever. He promised a second part to his book, in which the original of civil authority should be largely discussed ; meanwhile he advocated the principle of resistance upon authority of the Convention, which expressly disowned it for the plea of an abdication. "You call me a Nonjuror who has given very just grounds of loud complaints," said Leslie. "I know my own innocence in this matter, and it does not at all affect me. But what is this to the argument ? This is calling for help. Would not a little sober reasoning have done better for the honour of the Revolution, not to say your own ? Keep close to the point. I am as willing to be in the wrong as in the right, and if I am wrong I will own him my benefactor who shall set me right. The common saying of kings being made for the subjects, and not subjects for kings, was not so from the beginning, for the first subjects were made for the use and benefit of the king, and it was for the benefit of the subjects too, as it is still, to be obedient to their governors. What our Lord argued against divorce is what we say to the Commonwealth frame, that from the beginning it was not so. It began among heathen Greeks, and shall we prefer that to the institution of God in Holy Scripture? If you will paint a king like a monster or mad, then think on the other side of the madness of the people. If you put extreme cases, put them on both sides. There is another consideration—make a difference between errors in administration and constitution, much more fatal and harder to be remedied. There can be none in the constitutional monarchy. If in your second part you still pursue your former principles, I have ventured to call this an answer beforehand, because it is impossible to find any other original government than what I have set down, unless you have a fancy for the pre-Adamites."

Such are the more salient passages of the two letters, omitting the argument upon the origin of government, to which, if Hoadly could only reply by repeating objections which were not arguments, it was no wonder, for abler men than himself had failed in the same attempt. But if some persons who then applauded him enthusiastically as a divine and politician, and menacingly uttered now loud complaints against Leslie to frighten him, could have foreseen how Hoadly's views in religion would carry him on to the very verge of deism and denial of Christianity, they would have started back with affright. And if Bishop Blackall's sermon was so difficult to defend, why was it but because it virtually involved the hopeless task of reconciling sound doctrine with a false position? There could be no bridging over the chasm between *de jure* and *de facto* possession of the throne, or exempting Queen Anne from the charge of usurpation any more than her predecessor, except upon presumption of her brother's consent for the time, which had not been asked though it might have been obtained. Therefore, those who vainly tried to reconcile these opposite positions exposed themselves to painful rebuffs such as Hoadly gave to Blackall, and Burnet to Compton, when he told him that he was treading on very tender ground in proposing severe measures for repressing any opposition to the Government. The only two consistent parties were the extreme Revolutionists and Nonjurors.

While these letters were being digested by the latitudinarian divine, Leslie left London, and no trace of him has been found for some months. That he had not gone to S. Germain is certain, because Lord Middleton, writing from thence, was unacquainted with his place of retirement, for the interpretation put upon expressions and names in Macpherson's, the Stuart and Hanover Papers cannot be fully relied upon, because they are not always consistent with each other, nor with facts otherwise ascertained. Thus "Lamb," presumed to mean Leslie, is spoken of as dead in one letter, but very shortly afterwards as alive.[1] His residence then in the country may be inferred from a statement of his own, that being at a distance from libraries he could not verify a reference. No clue to the particular locality is afforded; nor is it necessary to presume any very special reason for absence from London, beyond such simple circumstances as health, a holiday, or visits to friends. In his case, however, with any of these may have probably concurred a desire of avoiding either the possibility of the oath of abjuration being tendered to him at some officious

[1] Of course it is possible the term was metaphorical.

or ill-natured person's suggestion, or of conversation respecting the *Rehearsal* just starting again under new direction, with which he had no concern. Whatever amount of leisure he enjoyed during this period, he had also plenty of employment, both at hand and in prospect, similar to that just completed. The first portion consisted in a letter to another clergyman, Mr. William Higden, up to now a Nonjuror, who had published a "View of the English Constitution," in vindication of himself for taking the oaths, the nature of which can be inferred from the answer of Leslie. The terror of the Abjuration Act had worked upon his mind to induce a compliance which conviction had not suggested. But when reasons were announced he could not complain if they were very closely scrutinized by former confederates. So Mr. Higden's book naturally incurred analysis at the hands of one little disposed to look too leniently upon his defection, even though he had bespoken great charity and moderation on the part of any one undertaking to answer it. Leslie complained in the first place that one who had pronounced the Government "a wickedness and usurpation" should now profess to comply, not because he had altered his mind, but only for reasons of prudence and fear which would justify compliance with any other government set up in its place, and be morally worse than adoption of revolutionary principles. In the second place he rebuked him for boasting that his manuscript had been so much admired by readers, that he thought its publication would bring over many other Nonjurors. At least, before repeating arguments which had already been urged, he should have read the answers to them. He had no new ground to rest upon, only pleading for submission to iniquity established by law, and possession without right and against right. If Mr. Higden had not been a person of consequence or credit, whose abandonment of principle Nonjurors felt to be a blow to their cause, or his book of more merit than appears from the review of it, one can hardly think he would have been honoured with particular notice. And it may be here mentioned that though nothing more has been ascertained respecting himself, many years afterwards a brother of his came forward to testify his esteem for Leslie, and contributed towards the publication of his works, when he could not but have anticipated this letter might be included among them. Its chief value consists in a full and clear account of what is called commonly the Constitution, and as commonly misunderstood. "In England by Constitution is generally understood legislative authority residing in the Sovereigns and three Estates, but it was not so from the beginning. God made kings, and kings made parliaments. These are very good things, for in the multitude of counsellors is safety, but when they degenerated became authors of great mischief, as dear-bought experience testifies. In Saxon and Norman times parliaments had no place; nor till Henry III. had the Commons any share or vote in the government of the kingdom. Even then this was not a settled thing, for the king named who were to be returned; nor was their consent necessary to the raising of money or making of laws. After this every order taxed themselves separately—Spiritualty in Convocation, Lords Temporal and the Commons in their Houses. And when at the Restoration the clergy submitted to be taxed in common with the rest of the nation, there was an express salvo made of their right, and that this submission was on account of present necessity. Only facts have been taken to make precedents.

"Again, kings have granted limitations or concessions of authority, but any coercion against them is of necessity void. If mere possession of a throne or exercise of sovereign authority make a king, then Oliver was as good as any other, for sailing west brings one to the east at last. Possession implies right, where no better right remains. When Henry VI. was on the throne Richard set forth his title by proximity of blood, and Parliament declared it could not be defeated. The York and Lancaster disputes every one turned upon this point of *de jure* against *de facto*. And why were usurpers anxious to obtain resignation from the deposed monarchs but on this account? Even Richard III. pretended the children of Edward IV. to be illegitimate, or he would not have murdered his nephews.

"So Queen Jane was denounced and deposed by Queen Mary. Thirty-eight sovereigns in England all claimed the throne upon the *de jure* principle. Magna Charta, the foundation of Acts of Parliament, is a charta from the king. If laws have been allowed which were passed in the reigns of usurpers, it has been simply for the sake of convenience." In conclusion, after an admirable and exhaustive summary of history in support of his principles, Leslie showed that a Mr. Tyrrel, author of a General History, had set up again a system which stood condemned by law, Scripture, and Church authority, without even the air of novelty to recommend it. Both Mr. Higden and Mr. Tyrrel did no more than repeat "Sherlock's old case of Might against Right with its weathercock pleas, which no one would admit to be sound in regard to private property exercised against himself. In fact, he who has no right but possession, loses his right with possession. It is Mahometan, not Christian right."

Quite apart from the controversial use for which it was first employed, this whole letter's contents are of the utmost value, because they prove by an historical induction of particulars upon what foundation the constitution of England rests, and that if, as proverbially said, possession be nine points of the law in practice, yet the remaining point, if it be *de jure*, is that which the law itself alone recognizes as right. It would be well if those who venture to write and speak upon constitutional questions would first make themselves acquainted with the essential facts of history here lucidly stated and arranged.

13. *Of Charity.*—1 Cor. xiii. 13. The charity here spoken of is commonly understood to mean giving to the poor, whereby the sense of the chapter is lost. It signifies love, and to what it is to be extended the apostle has showed, exemplifying the limits of the Church by the unity of a natural body. Every word refers in the chapter to this, and to that breach of it which was made at Corinth by men vaunting themselves in the spiritual gifts then liberally bestowed, and refusing on this account to submit themselves to their ordinary superiors in the Church who perhaps had not those gifts. There will be an end of all such gifts; but charity will go with us to heaven, where are no poor to be relieved, but there is perfect unity and the love of it. Heaven is unity, and hell discord; as we promote the one or the other here, we shall have our portion with it there. This is a terrible consideration for those who make little of the unity of the Church upon earth. He has a strange opinion of his own gifts who thinks them so necessary as that the Church and religion should fall without them; or that it is worth dividing the Church and causing a schism on account of them. It is left to the freedom of our will to make an ill use of, and to abuse even miraculous gifts as well as natural. Bearing and

believing all things was meant of what the members of the Church should bear for her, and believe of her; that is, put the best construction possible upon her commands and institutions rather than break her unity. And there is a lenity and condescension likewise to be used towards Dissenters, that all fair methods of conviction should be used before she proceed to severity. An heretic is to be twice admonished before he is rejected. This is a matter of discipline and prudence to be used by the Church, or varied according to times and circumstances; as the serpent is not to swallow the dove, so neither must the dove blind the serpent. Men must be wise as well as harmless; especially the governors of the Church ought to watch, to have their eyes in their head, lest the wolf get in among the sheep. If the sheep perish through their negligence or cowardice, the blood of those sheep will be required at the hands of the shepherds. As we must give no offence to those who are without, so neither to the Church of God; and if both these cannot be, surely the Church is to have the preference.

14. *The Danger of Schism.*—If Christ delegated His power to apostles, and they to others to continue to the end of the world and if no historian of those times makes the least mention of any change of government, but all with one voice speak of episcopacy and the succession of bishops in all the Churches from the days of the apostles, and in those ages of zeal when the Christians were so forward to sacrifice their lives in opposition to any error or deviation from the truth; if no one takes any notice of episcopacy as being an encroachment upon the rights of presbyters or the people, or a deviation from the apostolical institution; if these things are not possible to any thinking man, then episcopacy must be the apostolical and

primitive institution, and it is as impossible to be otherwise, as to suppose that all the great monarchies in the world should be turned into commonwealths all at one instant, and yet that nobody should know it. Such revolutions could not happen, but they would have set the world in a flame. And if presbytery or any other form of government except episcopacy had been the primitive institution, the bishops could never have stolen themselves into possession and usurped upon all Churches without any notice, and without vast struggling and contests. If bishops then were constituted as governors of Churches, he that disowns the governor of any society or corporation disowns the government of it, and cannot be called a member of such a society, and consequently has no title or right to the privileges of it. Then their ordinations in opposition to episcopacy are invalid, and sacrilege and rebellion against Christ who instituted this society, and gave to it its character; and if their ordinations be null, then their baptism is so too, and all their ordinances. They are out of the visible Church, and have no right to any of the promises of the Gospel, all made to the Church and to none other. Nay, baptism by a layman or a midwife in case of necessity is more excusable than by those who have no authority, or worse than none. If we cannot have the ordinances as Christ commanded them, it is more dutiful to God and expresses greater humility in ourselves to pray Him not to impute the want to us, than to take upon us to institute new ordinances, or set up a new priesthood of our own heads as Jeroboam and Micah did. Certainly it is less culpable for a layman to do some one priestly act, as to baptize upon necessity, than if he should set up false Orders and pretend to the office. With Christian concern Dissenters are asked to consider that what they receive in their congregations are not the Sacrament. The ministrations are null and void for want of lawful authority, but sacrilegious like the offerings of Korah; while themselves do not deny the validity of episcopal ordinations.

It is said the word bishop sometimes signifies a presbyter, and therefore that they mean the same thing. The word emperor sometimes signifies commander; suppose, therefore, any one should deny that there ever was an emperor at Rome, we should think him a madman. Such trifling from the etymology of words would not have been endured in former times. The word bishop signifies an overseer, and presbyter elder, or alderman, to express authority, and not only age; but that every elder was an overseer is such poor stuff as to fret one's patience. Again, they say that episcopacy encroached by degrees. Let them show when it began, and we can reckon the encroachments afterwards. Erroneous opinions may be instilled from one to another, and nobody may be able to tell who was the first broacher; but government is always public and before every man's face, and no history of those times can mistake in notice of it. No man can tell the beginning of episcopacy at any time since the apostles; but we all know that there was no Presbyterian "Church" in the world before John Calvin. Now, suppose we come to the Sacrament, and have a doubt whether the man be lawfully ordained and can consecrate and administer, will not the text Rom. xiv. 23 come into one's mind? What a condition, then, are Dissenters in, who cannot eat in faith? They may shut their eyes wilfully, but this is fresh aggravation of their sin. What compassion can they have for their tender infants to carry them to disputed baptism, when they have that which is clear and undisputed offered to them? Will they present the provocation of their offerings, and pawn their souls upon the greatest uncertainty? Will they say it is not an uncertainty, when they cannot answer for themselves? Is not this to be self-condemned? "To put the stumbling-block of their iniquity before their faces, and then come to inquire of the Lord?"

How can he who has put himself out of the Church admit another to be member of it? Can one who is not free himself make another free of any corporation? No. If one is baptized by a schismatic, he is baptized into his schism and made a member of it, and not of the Church. And what is a man's duty if he is verily persuaded that this is the case? Shall he be silent and let them go on in their sin, rather than be at the pains to convince them, and displease them at all hazards? Or, if such silence would be guilty and argue self-love rather than the love of our neighbour, shall he mince the matter and alleviate or excuse the sin? This would be to "sew pillows," to hate our neighbour and suffer sin upon him. The preservation of the faith and doctrine of the Church depends, under God, most chiefly in the support of the Government as a society, whence she is called in Scripture the pillar and ground of the truth.

To bring a long dispute to a short issue—there is in every question what is called the root or heart of the cause; but lopping off branches is tedious work. What jangling has there been about the etymology of the words bishops and presbyters! What sort of bishops, what powers they had, and whether they were diocesan bishops like ours. Let these objectors show any bishop since the apostles who was not a diocesan bishop. S. Ignatius of Antioch, S. Polycarp of Smyrna, Irenæus of Lyons, etc.; and so it was of all the rest. Let presbyterians show one instance to the contrary. S. Jerome of all the Fathers they quote most, because of two or three mistaken expressions, and his epistle "Ad Evagr.," for the sake of that in it, "What does a bishop that a presbyter does not?" But they wisely drop the very next words, part of the same sentence, "except ordination." That is, the presbyters preach, baptize, and consecrate the Holy Sacrament; but the power of ordination S. Jerome here excepts from them, and makes it peculiar to the bishop. He closes that same epistle with these words: "That we may know the apostolical constitution to be taken from that of the law, what Aaron and his sons were in the Temple, that same are the bishops, presbyters, and deacons in the church." And in his epistle against Montanus he says, "With us the bishops hold the place of the apostles." And "be subject to your bishop, and receive him as the father of your soul."

15. *The Church the Pillar and Ground of the Truth.*— 1 Tim. iii. 15. Is the Church so the pillar and ground of the truth as to be the author of it, and that the truth of the gospel depends upon the authority of the Church? No; the gospel is the revelation which Christ gave to the Church. He is the Author of it, and it stands upon His authority. But He has left this sacred deposit with the Church to keep. The Church is to keep the truth and to preach it; to watch against errors and heresies which are contrary to it and to confute them; and when necessary to restrain them with the spiritual sword of discipline and that authority which Christ has left with her, to cut off rotten members from the body that the infection spread no further, and to graft them in again upon their repentance and amendment. This is what we call the power of the Keys to open and to shut, to admit into the society and to exclude out of it. Forasmuch as heaven and earth are one family, and the Church the same in both under the same Head, which is Christ, He calls this

power which He has left to His Church upon earth, the keys of the kingdom of heaven, that they who are justly excluded from His Church upon earth stand likewise excluded in heaven, as He has expressly promised. Thus the Church is the pillar and ground of the truth, not only as teaching it but supporting and preserving it by that authority with which Christ has invested her. Therefore the Apostle S. Paul directs the bishops of the Church "to speak and exhort and rebuke with all authority, and to let no man despise them." Not to prostitute their authority or to give it up to any, for Christ gave them no more than he saw was needful for the government of His Church and the support of the truth. Therefore, if they part with any of it or compromise it away upon any pretence whatever, they betray their trust, and render themselves incapable to preserve the truth which will be required at their hands. This made S. Cyprian, say "How dangerous it was in divine things, that any should recede from his full right and authority!" Therefore the apostle exhorts to "put on the whole armour of God. . . . against wicked spirits in high places." These are potent enemies, and shall the Church lessen her authority with which to fight against them? Shall she deliver up her power into their hands, and surrender to them the sword of the Spirit which was committed to her to defend the truth? Wherever this has been done, wherever the power of the Church has been lessened or transferred, there the truth has suffered proportionably. Thus, when the pope would transfer to himself the power of the whole Catholic Church, and reduce all bishops under him as his deputies and subjects, and transferred the Episcopate into the Pontificate, what errors in doctrines and heresies ensued, even to idolatry! And when the Episcopate was overthrown in England, and transferred into the hands of the people, what swarms of heresies arose like locusts out of the pit, and darkened the whole face of the land, of which the names are transmitted in the books "Heresiography" and "Gangræna"![1]

If priests preach up this doctrine and insist upon the authority given them, they may be called ambitious and proud; but they will not be contemptible. It is their not asserting their just rights which Christ has given them that makes them contemptible, as the prophet tells them: "Ye have corrupted the covenant of Levi, saith the Lord of hosts, therefore have I made you contemptible and base before all the people." Who will obey any authority that does not exert itself, but is ashamed and afraid of its own power? The Church has lost her authority for not asserting it, and in a great measure has the sins of her rebellious children to answer for in not teaching them better, but suffering them to despise her. And the way to retrieve it is to let them know the high dignity which Christ has placed upon His Church, to teach even principalities and powers in heavenly places. We allow it to be the best interpreter of Scripture; that is, the Church from the beginning. But it is a great fallacy to apply to the Church of Rome whatever is said of the Church in general, either in the Scriptures or the primitive Fathers. And, in short, we are willing to put the issue with Romanists upon the current sense of the Scriptures in all ages, and appeal to it in all disputes. Because the judgment which the Church of Rome claims in matters of faith is a judgment of authority, that such things must be believed to be matters of faith because she delivers them as such, which is no less than blasphemy. And if it will not hold in the first article of

---

[1] Echard's "Hist.," iii. 45; Dryden, "Absalom and Ahithophel," 151-247.

the Creed, the belief of a God, neither will it in the rest. These articles of faith are of too high authority to be subjected to any human authority. It is only of smaller matters and of less consequence that the question can be asked, "Who shall judge?" The works of creation demonstrate a God. For nothing can make itself, and it is purely from one's own reason that he believes a God. The Church has taught belief in Christ, but not by way of authority, for one could not believe a Christian Church without first believing a Christ; and she pretends to no authority other than what she has received from Him. We receive the belief of God and Christ upon her evidence, though not her authority. The sacred oracles of the Scriptures were deposited with her to be kept, to be preached, and propagated. This makes her the pillar, and only pillar upon earth, of this grand deposition.

The Church has very great authority, though not over God, or Christ, or Holy Scripture. Her authority is over her flock, who are commanded by Christ to be subject to her. She has authority to preach the Word to them, to sign and seal the covenant of God with them in the Holy Sacraments, and in the remitting or retaining of their sins. In this sense also she may be called the pillar of the truth, not only as the keeper of this sacred deposition, but the administrator and dispenser of it; to offer up the incense of the prayers of the saints, and to bless them in the name of the Lord. Thus standing in the midst between God and the people in the person of their great Mediator, whose sacrifice her priests offer up continually for the people, in representation and in conjunction with what Christ in person offers to His Father in heaven. This power and authority is indeed very great, and reaches even to heaven, and has its effect to all eternity. Therefore, those who are justly thrown out of her communion, or unjustly separate themselves, are cut off from the communion of God, and have forfeited their rights to all the promises in the Gospel, which are every one made to the Church and none other.

What allowances God will make for ignorances, the prejudices of education, or other unmalicious causes of their separation, in His extraordinary and uncovenanted mercies, we must not determine. This we are sure of, that they who have left the covenant cannot plead by it. They may say God is merciful, but they cannot say He is faithful and just to forgive their sins, for that can be said only on account of the covenant, which, being made with His Church alone, they who are out of that are out of the covenant. "The Son of man hath power on earth to forgive sins." God hath given such power unto men. It is not to one man, but to men. And Christ gave the same power in express words to other men, and He sent these "as His Father had sent Him."

16. *The Solemn League and Covenant.*—This Covenant swore to preserve and defend the king's Majesty, person, and authority (Charles I.), yet cut him out of all authority, and at last cut off his head, and was framed for that very purpose. It is word for word the "Holy League" in France, changing names only, and was sent into Scotland by Cardinal Richelieu, who was the constant correspondent and aider of these covenanters he had made, and their recourse was to him, whom they solicited for a French power to invade the kingdom (for the preservation of the Protestant religion against King Charles I.), and wrote a letter to the French king to put themselves under his protection! They reserved their allegiance to the French king according to their bargain with Cardinal

Richelieu, yet swore it to King Charles I., and obtained his favour while they were conspiring to depose him. They were protected by the very government they abhorred, they were cherished by the Church they disowned, they ate the bread of the nation they betrayed, and were entertained by the silly creatures they debauched, and who in their hearts abhorred their designs. Mr. De Foe's rhetoric thus agrees to a T with the covenanters, and they sat for the picture which he has drawn of them to the life! These were the loyal men who invited over a foreign prince against their own natural sovereign, while they were swearing fidelity to him, and calling God to witness the sincerity of their hearts. Their letters to the French king were taken with a Covenanting lord in London, who was sent to the Tower, but pardoned by the king after his usual clemency, and made chief minister of the kingdom.

CHAPTER XIII.

DEATH OF LORD CLARENDON—MARLBOROUGH'S VICTORIES—
LETTER TO M.P.—COMMENTARY AND EVENTS IN TEN YEARS'
WAR—THE CHEVALIER AND QUEEN ANNE—POSITION OF
NONJURORS—MRS. LESLIE'S HEALTH—GOOD OLD CAUSE—
WARRANT—OUTLAWED—MR. CHERRY.

DURING that exciting and memorable period from the peace of Ryswick to that of Utrecht, or the opening twelve years of the eighteenth century, the hand of death had been busy as ever. And many friends and opponents of Leslie had been numbered among the lost—Nonjurors and Tories, as well as Whigs and Revolutionists. Conspicuous among the former was Henry, second Lord Clarendon, who died October 20, 1709. A more generous, high-minded, and conscientious statesman has never existed, who with integrity combined talents of a very superior order, and great industry in the discharge of whatever public duties he undertook. These qualifications were clearly exhibited during his government of Ireland, when he had such a difficult task to perform, of trying to satisfy King James without doing violence to the constitution, and either complying with, or coming into open collision with the incendiary Tyrconnel, who did as much as his master for his ruin. If Lord Clarendon lost his balance for a little while when the Prince of Orange first arrived in England, it was no wonder, considering the agitation produced by his son's defection, and the fatuity of the King's conduct, which made it doubtful what was the duty of subjects whom he appeared to have deserted without a sufficient cause. But he soon recovered his equilibrium, and returned at the gravest risk to his allegiance, when he found that James with the memory of his father's fate before him had retired under threats of personal violence. After that he took no further active part in public affairs, and ceased to contend against the inevitable, though he could not be induced, like his brother the Earl of Rochester, to accept a settlement professedly which at heart he secretly disavowed. To him the title and estates passed, because Lord Cornbury had died before his father. What a difference the turn of events had made to Leslie as his chaplain; for in the earl's prosperity he could have surely read his own, united to him as he was also by ties of personal affection and esteem. In misfortune, however, these suffered no relaxation, but proved a source of mutual consolation; and it was in Lord Clarendon's society more than any other living person perhaps beyond his immediate family, that he most delighted. Not only had other esteemed friends been removed by death, but some had succumbed in order to escape it, to the next necessity and alternative of taking the oaths for the sake of bread. Revolutionists who spoke warmly about tenderness towards Dissenters felt no compassion for Nonjurors, nor would allow them a conscience. Those, therefore, who had no kind patrons like Ken, nor admirers like Hickes, nor could turn to another profession like Wagstaffe, nor gain a scanty subsistence by their pens as the learned Collier, nor had some private resources unexhausted like Leslie, were reduced to very terrible straits indeed. Thus it is related of one that a gentleman, meeting him in a new cassock and gown, asked if he had swallowed the oaths? To which he replied, with what anguish of spirit may readily be understood, "Yes, I have; but I stayed till I had nothing else to swallow." For assistance of such cruelly distressed Nonjurors, Leslie had been forward to collect and contribute even beyond his ability, nor did he ever utter one word of reproach against those who yielded to the pressure, except when any, not to escape starvation but to obtain lucrative appointments, deserted their colours, or like Higden affected a change of convictions, and challenged public criticism by writing in support of their new alliances.

In order to appreciate the next productions of his pen which call for notice, it is necessary to bear in mind the general history of that period; whereas he wrote to throw light upon public affairs, and unveil the motives of actors both in and behind the scenes. These were "Natural Reflections upon the Present Debates about Peace and War, in Two Letters to a Member of Parliament, from his Steward in the Country," dated December, 1711, and March, 1711–12. It is of no consequence whether the member of Parliament was a real person or an imaginary one like the steward; though it is not impossible that he might have undertaken some secular business, such as this of collecting rents and looking after property. He returned to London only for a short time, and never again continuously resided there for more than some weeks at a time, owing to various circumstances which will be mentioned in due course. Therefore he had leisure for this occupation; his former experience at Glaslough and legal knowledge eminently qualified him for it; nor could any landlord have better provided for his own interests, while conferring a favour without wounding the most delicate sensibility. If some passages be read side by side with a relation of the more important or interesting events which occurred, they will serve mutually to illustrate each other, and give sufficient idea of the pamphlet as a whole, which when published attracted very general attention, and contributed in no inconsiderable degree to hasten that which was its main drift and purpose, the composition of a European peace upon just and honourable terms.

Marlborough had pursued his amazing career of conquest almost without a single check or reverse, scarcely delay, nor this last, ever attributable to any want of enterprise or foresight on his part. From Ramillies in 1706, May 12, to Malplaquet or Blareignes, September 11, 1709, and then on to Douay, including Oudenarde, Louvain, Brussels, Ghent, Bruges, Ostend, Lisle, Mons, and other battles and sieges in which his own life was freely, almost too freely, risked, but the most miserable mismanagement occurred. Only such a commander could have exercised the influence he possessed over soldiers, who went into battle on some occasions at his desire saying prayers, but without either bread or water having been tasted for hours. All obeyed cheerfully; and no one ever conquered him but his wife. The fight at Ramillies only occupied two hours, while that at Blenheim had taken seven; yet victory was no less hardly gained, or more splendid in the one than the other. At Douay he confessed to a doubt about success which he had never felt before. Proposals of peace made once and again he was instrumental in causing to be rejected, though he constantly affirmed that complaints against him of desiring to prolong the war were unjust. Certainly his conduct gave too much occasion for this suspicion, and if he was not guilty, his relations in the Ministry and others in high offices were to a large degree. Those who bore the burden and longed for peace formed a far larger portion of the nation, but were often affrighted into suffering silence by fear of being called Jacobites or Frenchified. To this refer these observations in the letter: "Except some who are visibly gainers by the war, and a few bitter Whigs whom we know to be their tools, there is not one countryman I believe in England who is not weary and does not wish for peace. The country is exhausted, and the poor increase so fast upon us, that if no remedy be applied they must in time eat us up. Good substantial tradesmen and many thousand hands employed in manufactures who were able to contribute towards the poor, are now grown so themselves, and put upon the parishes.... Conjurors who would enchant us out of our senses are only such as having great employments in the war, and vast sums in the funds, which pay no taxes charge in armour, and feel nothing of the burden. The general (Marlborough) and the ministry (Whig), having refused to accept very advantageous offers of peace after the battle of Ramillies, were forced to take in a set of men with a previous bargain to screen them from their miscarriages (in Spain and by sea). We have nothing but a decayed trade to trust to, and our credit is crazy, without any projects for restoring it. A merchant would stand ill upon the Exchange if there were such disputes about his credit.... If we cannot force otherwise than by defending a town which shall cost us a campaign, when will the war end at this rate? It is the just terror of inspectors.... As to the disposal of public moneys, which is the true cause of all opposition to peace, £35,302,107 up to 1710, unaccounted for in grants to Parliament, is a heavy charge which must light somewhere, and is a substantial reason why some men should be afraid of peace, as night-birds of the day. As also why the old preliminaries were not accepted by some, who made not so little as £100,100 a year by the war." The frightful revelations made in Parliament, despite the strongest efforts to screen several persons including Marlborough, more than corroborated this severe reflection, and the next about the unreasonable manner in which the King of France was dealt with, who had offered most honourable conditions of peace. "They stood out upon one article, which I dare say not one of themselves would have submitted to if he had been in the King of France's place. They will be content to wait like a Welshman, who, to be tried for his life, had the choice of the twelve honestest men he knew for his jury, and named the twelve apostles; but being told that they were not here, and it would be a great while before they arrived, replied he was in no hurry, but could stay till then."

Allusion was made in the letter to Dr. Charlett of the "great things Marlborough was reported to be about to do with the King of Sweden;" and he did effect them. For Charles XII., whom Louis had in vain made the greatest efforts to win over to his side, was charmed by Marlborough's happy manner and speeches into the interest of the allies. But his grand successes in Poland lured him on to his ruin. He was bent upon a wild scheme of conquering the Czar, so invaded Muscovy; but the issue of his ambition was a terrible defeat at Pultowa, and he fled into Turkey, there to plot and stir up strife between the Sultan and the Czar. Herein lay a warning which the letter well pointed out ought to be taken to heart by other sovereigns, conquerors, and nations. "The Czar courted that king for peace, and but a few hours before the battle of Pultowa offered him safe and honourable terms, such as we may suppose the King of France willing to grant; but his heart was lifted up. Secure of victory from his many successes, but not that the Almighty would not turn against him, he did not see that when reasonable satisfaction is refused, from that time forth right and wrong change sides; and God, who had so wonderfully asserted his right against such an unequal force, now forsook him. He was struck as 'it were with a thunderbolt in a moment, and remains an instance to all Christian princes not to lose the opportunity of giving peace owing to selfish views, or trusting to their own strength and conduct."

Bishops, clergy, and dissenting ministers were concerned in urging on demands for war, and discouraging all proposals for peace, therefore it was a most seasonable and proper thing that religious people should be reminded of the responsibility incurred by acquiescence in this policy. "The blood and desolation of war is so terrible a remedy that nothing but the utmost necessity can excuse it. God will require a severe account of those princes and powers of the earth, to whom He has committed this sword of vengeance for every life unnecessarily lost, and it will be reckoned murder in His sight if the war be not just, or a reasonable peace refused. When the bias of the mind is for peace, difficulties lessen, and men inherit the blessing of peacemakers, which they are not capable of who delight in war."

The Emperor of Austria and the States had both opposed a peace whenever proposed, but the pretence of withstanding the ambition of the King of France could no longer be sustained, when he submitted to fair conditions, and his country was evidently exhausted by war and famine. Nor had either fulfilled their engagements in regard to expenses. Besides, if Austria were allowed to annex Spain, and had already made short work of the pope's interference, it might become as dangerous as ever France had been.

But now this emperor was dead of small-pox, which almost simultaneously carried off the dauphin; therefore his resentments, whatever justifications they had afforded for commencement of the war, could not be pleaded rightly in support of its continuance with his successor. It was urged by a pamphleteer on the other side, first as an excuse for the emperor's failure to contribute his share of expenses, "Has not the house of Austria been exhausted by continual wars for thirty years past, and its weakness discovered by inability to compel the princes of the empire to do their parts?" Then within a few pages the writer sets himself to magnify the new emperor's resources. Which elicitated this retort, "If the emperor cannot make such efforts he is a poor ally, and we have no reason to continue the war, or hopes to be better used than we have been. On the other hand, if he is able to make such efforts as will recover Spain, etc., we have reason to look about us lest we breed up an eagle to pick out our own eyes. What if, as King of Spain, he should revive his claim upon the States? . . . Who knows not that the Dutch were in all the management of the "good old cause" against King Charles I.; and acted the second part in the reign of Charles II.? But it seems not the last, for they are pursuing Queen Anne with their memorials prompted by agents from the discontented party here. . . . Our allies can give us no more promises than they have done, but they never kept them in any one campaign, either as to their quota of men or money, or the time of taking the field. And we were forced to make good all their deficiencies every year. Do we expect anything else from them if we should continue the war twenty years longer? It is generous to help a neighbour in distress, but not over prudent to do it without all regard to our own interest. Charity begins at home, and I would not take a thorn out of another man's foot to put it in my own."

England was at war in Spain, but it was said by the Whigs, not against Spain. This was like the bombardment of Alexandria in 1883, "a warlike operation," but not war in Egypt; or in 1884, the French expedition against Foochow in China, "anticipating a declaration of war" in a practical manner. England was only engaged in forcing upon them King Charles from Austria, whom the nation did not want, to prevent the French keeping there another King Philip, whom a majority at least liked better. And what had been done by ten years' war? Little or nothing of any use, at an enormous cost and many failures; notwithstanding all the splendid courage of the gallant but eccentric Peterborough, or the efforts of Stanhope, who was doubtless brave but neither skilful nor successful with a single exception, the capture of Portmahon in a poor little island. In Spain, since the siege of Gibraltar, nothing had been effected at all, and the people deeply embittered against England. So the letter declared, "They tell us we must have no peace till all Spain be reduced, but they tell us not when that shall be, or that it is ever likely. We must fight on, and tax on, till the Greek Calends. They were invited to join us as their friends, and have told us to our cost that we quite mistook their inclinations, must guess again, and that another ten years' war would not make them abandon their king or his son, to whom they have sworn."

The Protestant interest had once been put forward as a ground of war on the Continent. It was a curious reason to assign in the first instance for alliance with the emperor, a more bigoted Papist than Louis; but since that it had been more curious still, for some of the allied princes had renounced Protestantism for Popery, and in none of the treaties for peace had this interest ever been mentioned either by the agents of England or the States, therefore it was answered now. "Have not the Austrians always persecuted Protestants most cruelly? Will not what was done in Hungary and Bohemia at least equal the severities to Huguenots in France? And yet there was not one article in favour of the Protestants of any country whatever in the grand alliance for this present war, or in the former preliminaries offered by all these powers. By what the Protestant interest abroad has gained, or is likely to gain by the war, the sooner it is ended the better."

Upon the sea no more had been gained, but a sad series of losses and disasters entailed. A grand enterprise had been designed in 1707, which was to be very secretly and suddenly accomplished. First Calais was to be taken, and then Toulon. The former was abandoned, and the latter failed completely; nor was that the worst. In returning, Sir Cloudesley Shovel's vessel, the *Association*, with two others of the fleet, ran too near the Scilly Isles, then called the "Bishop and his Clerks" or the Dog Isles, struck upon the Gillston rock, and sank in a very few minutes with some three thousand souls on board. Lord Dursley managed to steer his vessel more safely, and carried home the grievous tidings of the fate of his superior officer and comrades. How far any blame was due to want of caution on Sir Cloudesley's part was of course a disputed point among experienced naval men, though beyond all doubt he was a brave commander, who from a cabin-boy had risen to the highest post by dint of his own great talents; so his loss was an aggravation of the terrible calamity. One single feature of the story had a painless aspect. The only survivor from the three ships of war was the chaplain, who had gone from his own vessel to administer the last Sacrament to a dying man in another, and was saved by being cast by the waves upon a reef. After this, the country rang with complaints from the merchants of there being no convoys for their ships, or these being intercepted by the French, so that commerce was at a standstill. It could not, therefore, be in the interests of trade that war was continued, any more than in the landed interest or religion. And still less for the sake of posterity, for which an enormous heap of debt was being laid up with the most lavish recklessness, as the present day can testify. Revolutionary Whigs were the first who introduced the practice of going to war at the expense of descendants, and leaving to future generations as their only legacy a national debt; but once begun, it found such favour that at last multitudes of good simple folk have been persuaded that in it lies the chief safety of the nation. What if an idea here foreshadowed be already on the eve of accomplishment? "Posterity may not think fit to be undone because their fathers were madmen. They may either cancel these debts or tax the funds till they make them pay themselves. Nor can Whigs take this ill, for it is their current doctrine that we are not bound by the rules and laws of their forefathers, but that every man is born free, and to consult his own preservation." "The wit of man cannot find out ways and means to oblige posterity; no, not themselves neither further than they have a mind to. How many laws of our forefathers and Acts of Parliament have Whigs broke through to carry on their designs? Necessity with them answers all arguments, and this necessity has no law." Chancellors of the Exchequer have more than once acted upon these suggestions, perhaps they may further improve upon them. Whatever was the ten years' war about? What was it for? Historians do not agree, nor speak positively upon the point; nor need they, since contemporaries in its favour were as little agreed or decided. William began it, but that seemed no reason by itself for continuing to play a desperate game. He had not the experience of those ten years to satisfy him of the unreasonableness of his undertaking. The letter concluded with some excellent remarks, as pertinent now as ever, upon that old stalking-horse of ambitious and meddlesome politicians, the balance of power. "That is, a new partition of the world, that no one nation may be an overbalance to another in riches or power, of which we have had several schemes, no two of which agree together; and this is thought the only method to procure a firm and lasting peace, without regard of taking from any by violence what is truly and justly their own. It is impossible to bring nations to an equal balance of power or riches. Or if it were done, if all the nations were reduced to an equal balance even of a grain weight, then a grain on any side would cast the balance. This ten thousand accidents every day would produce. So that we must balance the wisdom, the industry, and courage of men as well as their honesty and conscience, and likewise to secure Providence not to favour one more than another. It is indeed no other than to take the judgment of the world out of the hands of Providence and entrust it to our own skill and management. Instead of '*Dieu et mon Droit*,' it is '*Je maintiendray*.'" "God has divided the world into nations greater and lesser as He has thought fit. And He keeps the balance of power in His own hands; but men would fain have it in their own. We must be content when we do otherwise. He often lets us see our folly as well as irreligion by suffering many years of war to leave us nothing but repentance for all the blood and treasure we have expended."

What much aggravated discontent in England as well as distress, was the influx of foreigners. Some Protestant refugees had been settled in different parts of the kingdom, and collections made for their relief under the queen's authority; others sent to Ireland and North America at the public expense. This generosity naturally induced numbers more to swarm over, till their support became a serious blunder; and what was worse, they were not content with toleration and maintenance in England, but soon began a work of proselytizing, and joined with Dissenters in opposition to the Church, till many both poor and rich cried out for their removal. This was alluded to in the following terms:—"Our Popish allies grant us nothing in favour of Protestants at their court, and we have seen them fall a sacrifice to the Jesuit interest at Vienna. . . . Which, if not the design of some half-faced Protestants whose religion was subservient to their ambition, was certainly the effect of this confederated war, and laid the axe to the root of Reformation abroad—also filled us with a fresh set of refugees, their prince being willing to part with his Protestant subjects. As the cry is on one side, 'No peace without Spain,' may we not on the other side honestly say, 'No more war till the Churches in the Palatinate taken since it began be restored, and Protestants in Hungary and Silesia restored to their liberties'?"

The "Letter" has thus been reviewed at length in consideration of the great importance and variety of the subjects included in it, also in order to exhibit at a glance both the events which took place, and the feeling produced in the heart of the English nation, which by no means beat in unison with their will who had the direction of affairs, and of which Leslie had good opportunities of judging by his independent position in politics, if he was not quite a disinterested spectator of the game beween the two parties, Whig and Tory.

Nothing has been said of the Chevalier, because he did not count as a figure nominally on the board, nor was therefore mentioned in the letter; but that he was to direct some of the moves became clear enough when his removal from France to Lorraine was actually stipulated for in the conditions of peace at Utrecht. This one was most painful to the chivalrous King of France; to Austria any treaty would have been distasteful by which no longer war should be carried on at England's expense for their security and aggrandizement. Now, then, some account of the Chevalier is due, and the more necessary because the time had come when Leslie's personal relations with him became intimate, and of the most paramount and perilous concern to himself and his family. While the dissatisfaction caused in Scotland by the Union was at its height, his adherents there thought he ought to make another effort to recover his crown; but any such effort, however ready he was, remained impracticable, because the French king pleaded inability to afford assistance, and the French Government was secretly resolved it should not be given. He had, therefore, to seek laurels of a much humbler kind by volunteering in the ranks of Vendome, the French commander, who if in private character base beyond description showed a genius in military affairs by no means inferior to any one's but that of Marlborough, though Leslie spoke of him slightingly.[1] So the Chevalier after all must be counted a pawn on the board between the players in the game itself. Queen Anne had been very indignant at the descent upon Scotland, and then first applied to him the word "Pretender" in a speech to Parliament, though he

[1] See Burnet, vol. iv. pp. 14, 74, 121, 192.

had often been termed "pretended prince" before. No actual compact was ever made between him and her, such as he proposed. But her private inclination may have reverted in his direction to some extent the more just, because that project of bringing over one of the house of Hanover was being persistently pressed upon her; though she had to preserve an impenetrable silence on the subject in private, and in public say what her ministers advised. Her feelings must have alternated from time to time between the Chevalier and the Hanoverian family, with little love for the one and none for the other, according to circumstances and the conduct of their avowed or supposed adherents, till she hardly knew what to think, nor dared to move. That Marlborough was in a similar dilemma of feeling and opinion for several years, needs no further proof than his own letters; but the stain upon his memory is ineffacable of having been ready at any moment to betray either as he had betrayed King James, affording a most melancholy reflection. Incomparably brave, clever, graceful, kind, and tender, he was also incomparably false. When, therefore, dismissed from his employments, none could help feeling that whatever ungenerous influences had been at work for his fall, that fall had been richly merited. Other men called traitors and more loudly condemned than he, were very far from deserving any such opprobrium. They simply refused to forsake the cause they had once sworn to serve, or to shackle their consciences with new and contrary oaths. None could have been more free from all taint of treachery or falsehood, even if their judgment were at fault. Of course the death of King James II. and of William made some change in the position of individuals and parties; and if Whig governments had been wise, they would have left this change to do its natural work. But they were no more wise than just, so Jacobites and Nonjurors were tempted and forced into a decisive attitude they might never have assumed, especially when the right was claimed of tendering to any person the oath of abjuration at the peril of his freedom or even life. The majority in England of Jacobites or Nonjurors were well content to yield a passive obedience, and even more to Queen Anne, if the Government could only have been content to let them alone and leave the future to Providence. One exception to the general tenor of legislation was the Act of Grace, in 1709; but as none had more need of such oblivion than Marlborough and Godolphin themselves, they might well have given it a very cordial support.

Acting upon the suggestion conveyed in the titles of some contemporary pamphlets, the "Wisdom of looking Forward," and the "Case in View," political affairs have been anticipated for a few years in order to render intelligible Leslie's own position and prospects in regard to them. Yet to do so more clearly the precepts shall be reversed, and the titles of other pamphlets acted upon, the "Wisdom of looking Backwards," and the "Case in Fact," by a survey of the history of Nonjurors considered as such rather than as Jacobites, which many were only in a very passive sense. Leslie was both; actively engaging in politics, yet, how moderate his resistance to the *de facto* possession was may be inferred from these words: "It is the concern of every true son of the Church of England to pray for the queen's life and a happy and speedy peace." If similar moderation had been exhibited on the other side, and the disposal of events left to Providence instead of attempting to forestall the future by provisions and securities for the Hanover succession of the most unreasonable and vexatious description, the probability is, not that the nation would have decided to return to the house of Stuart, though the apprehensions of revolutionists on this score betray the unreality of their pretensions to represent its sentiments, but that enthusiasm for the latter would have been greatly diminished.

Leslie continued to be the chief medium of communication between the court of S. Germain and the Nonjurors as an ecclesiastical body, from the time of the first consecrations till the peace of Utrecht or the queen's death. But of course this position neither entitled him to assume any authority over Nonjurors, nor brought him into conflict with their bishops, Hickes and Wagstaffe. No occasion for jealousy of any kind ever arose, and their cordial relations with each other prevented any temptation to it. He did not even officiate usually in their congregations, which met with little disturbance after the first fever of the Revolution, because any regular practice of ministration would have probably provoked further measures of repression like that on his preaching at Ely House, and furnished fresh fuel for *Observators* and *Reviews*. Though, therefore, he had leisure to devote himself to more general work of a political character, none the less he remained heartily devoted to their community. The death of Dr. Lloyd, April, 1709, deprived-bishop of Norwich, occasioned that crisis which Dodwell's "Case in View" had premonished them to prepare for. Bishop Ken only remained now of the former canonical succession, and he had voluntarily, after being offered the see of Wells from Queen Anne, ceded his right in favour of Dr. Hooper. Poor Kidder, who with his wife perished in the miserable storm of 1703, had been "the stranger" who "led astray his lambs and sheep, to break from Catholic and hallow'd bounds, contracting latitudinarian taint." But when "that tremendous stroke freed the flock from uncanonic yoke"—and Heaven, through Queen Anne, in Hooper "sent a successor to his mind," the saintly prelate not only waived his own claim in order to the other's acceptance of the queen's offer, but supported him in whatever ways he conscientiously could. He had taken no part in the consecrations, even objected to them. Dodwell professed ignorance and refused to be hampered by recognition of them, when the "Case in Fact" was realized. He, with Nelson and some others, thought the schism in the Church ought now to close, the blame of which hitherto lay at the door of the Establishment, but henceforth would lie at that of the Nonjurors if it were continued. He argued very forcibly in favour of his position in both pamphlets and a "Further Prospect," 1707; but his earnestness led him to overweight his case by statements which are clearly untenable upon canonical and ecclesiastical grounds. His objections to the jurisdiction of Hickes and Wagstaffe would nullify all episcopal authority whatever in times of persecution. He stood on much safer ground when he insisted upon the original cause of separation being at an end, and the Christian duty of union superseding all minor scruples. However, it is not necessary to rediscuss the question at length on his side or the opponents', but confine attention to the fact that now there had occurred a schism in the Nonjuring community itself, or rather a re-absorption in the other portion of the Church of England of many of its most influential and prominent members. Leslie sided with the party who stood out against reconciliation; but he has nowhere in his writings treated of the subject directly, so that his opinions can only be inferred from his conduct. On March 17, 1711, the last of the deprived prelates was relieved from all his sufferings, at Longleat, and buried at Frome Selwood;

where since then a beautiful church has been erected by a faithful priest, not unworthy of being remembered with him.[1] And on June 6 Dodwell went to rest, only preceded a few months by another friend and associate, the learned Thomas Smith.[2] Dr. Hickes was at that time very ill, but lived on for some years longer. Under these circumstances Leslie might well have felt reluctant to say anything beyond the necessities of the occasion, or run the risk of infusing any element of bitterness into the dispute, which might give pain to old and valued friends.

He had some other serious matters on hand at this time sufficient to occupy his undivided attention. Burnet had made a violent speech in the House of Lords, assailing him with more than ordinary bitterness and disregard for facts. This was followed up by a sermon in Salisbury Cathedral on the anniversary of the Restoration, when he did not deem it unbecoming the sacredness of the place his own office or the occasion, to indulge in personalities scarcely less inaccurate or acrimonious. So pleased was he, further, with his performances, as to secure their immediate publication. Here he was more careful, for the sermon and the speech were reproduced so exactly as delivered, that it showed his boast of extempore speaking and preaching meant only what it still may be presumed to do on the lips of those who most ostentatiously make it. He must have desired that Leslie should know how he had attacked him; that posterity also might have the benefit, he secretly committed at the same time to the "History of his Own Times" a digest of his utterances on these occasions, when the victim of his malice might be no longer alive to confute them.[3] Probably he reckoned upon

---

[1] Rev. J. W. Bennet.   [2] Edited Ep. Ignatius and Ap. Ep.
[3] iv. 277–279.

immunity then, for he knew too well by experience the force of Leslie's pen—this was, indeed, the cause of his wrath—because the *Rehearsal* had been stopped by the Whig Government under urgent pressure of himself and his associates. However, he was soon convinced of his mistake by a reply beneath which he writhed bitterly, and though he found his revenge in a prosecution which caused Leslie much trouble and inconvenience, this could not heal the wound, or take away the shame of the castigation he had wantonly provoked. It consisted in a pamphlet entitled "The Good Old Cause, or Lying in Truth," by one "Misodolus" (hater of deceit) professing to defend the bishop from a speech palmed upon him by some impostor, and to dissect a sermon as falsely attributed to him. Speeches in Parliament, where then the daily press had no access, were a matter of privilege dangerous to touch, and those reported generally came from the authors themselves, so that what have been thus preserved were not those most worthy in other people's opinion. When, therefore, the Bishop of Sarum's speech came forth to the public, it was evident by what means, and what importance he attributed to his attack upon Leslie, at which in its original form during delivery many peers were known to have expressed great disgust. One allusion in it will illustrate his recklessness of speech in general. He referred to some proceedings in Convocation, where he had persuaded the Upper House to reject a proposal of the Lower to censure some books, on the authority of Chief Justice Holt, that without a royal licence it would render them liable to a *præmunire*—a terrible instrument of royalty which Whig statesmen have so often since threatened clergy with, that it has come to be like the boy's cry of "Wolf!" in the fable. When inquiry was made, the Chief Justice denied he had expressed or held such an opinion, or had spoken upon the subject at all![1] In order to reply at length to the sermon, Leslie adopted this ingenious plan, which in itself conveyed a moral, of treating it as a forgery, from the discredit of which he ought to be relieved. The substance was as follows: "'The notion of kings having their power from God came in with the Reformation in opposition to Popery.' It is scandalous to put this on the Bishop, for none knows better that all the ancient Fathers have it, who took it from Holy Scripture. 'The Scriptures did only establish the several constitutions and government, that were in the world.' What before there were any? Did kings derive authority from laws which derived theirs from them? By what authority, then, did kings make those laws? When I go before you, and you go before me, which goes first? 'S. Paul's doctrine against resistance was meant only for the Jews.' Then he mistook his direction. Did he mean nothing for the Gentiles, who wrote to them? 'Apostles did not determine how much was due to the emperor and how much to the senate.' It is a pity, indeed. S. Paul commands to submit to the king as supreme, and takes not the least notice of the senate, not being skilled in the doctrine of co-ordinate powers, which were impossible had he been a Whig. He finds the Apocrypha more to his purpose; but the only book in it (Maccabees) which he quotes is not allowed to be read in church. 'Mattathias, a private priest, began the resistance against the Syrians.' This is far from the case of natural born subjects, for after the death of Alexander the Jews were free, and Syrians were not then lawful sovereigns. The sixth Article would have cut the throat of this speech, so he left out its words, that 'the Church doth not accept the Apocrypha to estab-

[1] Repeated in "History of his Own Times," iv. 188.

lish any doctrine.' 'Queen Elizabeth assisted the Lords of the Congregation in Scotland against Queen Mary, and rebels in France and Holland against their natural princes.' If he had inferred from that her subjects might rebel against her, she would have made it a wry-faced argument. But did Queen Elizabeth do well? They in their turns abetted rebellion in England; for you know one good turn deserves another, and the one precedent is as good as the other. But let us look at her thoughts of resisting supreme powers in her own words to the Scots: 'If they shall determine anything to the deprivation of their sovereign of her royal estate, we will make ourselves a plain party against them to her revenge, for example to all posterity; for we do not think it consonant in nature that the head should be subject to the foot.' He instances Charles I. giving aid to the Rochellers. Richelieu made sufficient reprisal, who said he would find the king work at home, and sent the covenant into Scotland transcribed from the Holy League in France. 'It was no wonder if, after such a war, the doctrine of non-resistance was preached with more than ordinary warmth, yet some kept these in view, though they did not think it necessary to mention them.' Not necessary? To preach the Word by halves, and speak only smooth things! Then why, if he did not think fit to tell all in a published sermon, enjoin 'an entire obedience and an absolute submission to that supreme power God hath put in our sovereign's hands,' if he thought it only limited and conditional? 'I told King James it was impossible for him to reign in quiet, being of the Romish religion. He answered me quick, Does not the Church of England maintain the doctrine of passive obedience? I told him not to depend on that, for there was a distinction which would be found out when men should think they needed it.' Why did you not tell him your own distinction? It might have saved that unfortunate prince. No, that was none of your design, but you kept it till he should be effectually ruined, and then you would tell it to justify all your treachery to him. They say his Confessor was a Jesuit, but you outdid him at mental reservation, equivocation, and hidden distinction. To tell him that nature might rebel against principle had been honest advice; but to say that you dodged in your principles and in your preaching was to call yourself a devil. After that the bishop preached his sermon for absolute submission! You complain very much of a distinction some have in taking the Abjuration Oath, still saving their allegiance to the Pretender. Why, sir, would you have none use distinctions but yourself? If a man may preach and pray with distinctions, why not swear? Maybe you may put it on the bishop that he had some reserve when he prayed for the Prince of Wales at the Hague. We are now come to the head of slander and innuendoes against particular persons. He says, 'Towards the end of the last reign a bold attempt was made on the king's supremacy by an incendiary, who is supposed to have no small share in this matter now before your lordships.' We must not guess whom he means. Must any one, who wrote as himself did, for the non-dependency of the Church upon the State as to her purely spiritual authority, be called an incendiary, and supposed to have no small share in the matter before their lordships? If that was true, you do that person a great deal of honour to make him instrumental in reviving that true Christian doctrine essential to the being of a Church as a society distinct from others and under a government of her own. 'Since resistance was used in the Revolution and invited by King William, and the limitation of our obedience if the king turn Papist, this puts an end to the notion.' Yes! But another than you possibly imagine! If a prince should turn Papist and you take arms, I doubt you would find judges, and law too, to end the dispute in another manner than you please. For hereditary right and natural allegiance are stubborn things which will not bend to an Act of Parliament, nor to a thousand usurpations. You told King James not to trust to passive obedience, for there was a distinction. And distinctions are dangerous things about one's neck to draw it into a noose, which sometimes prove too narrow to get one's head through.

"The sham sermon dissected! When will the persecution of this good bishop cease? Out comes another scandal upon him. A sermon on May 29. The subject of sermons on this day used to be a detection of those wicked principles and pretences which brought on that fatal Revolution. On the contrary, this is a downright vindication and recommendation of them to posterity. He fathers all this upon Christ, and makes Him patron of the "good old cause." This was preaching directly against the intendment of the day, as if old Bradshaw had come back by transmigration into this fouler body, and the spirit of rebellion by this second distillation. His principle is that possession gives right, which justifies Oliver. . . . But Oliver had a young Pretender against him, who at last prevailed. This is a full answer to all the sermon. The reader cannot miss applying it. There was none against the Roman emperor in our Saviour's time, therefore the text, 'Render to Cæsar,' was applicable to him, but not to that Oliver to whom it was here applied. 'A good government, settled in a long possession, is to be submitted to. Those who let claims sleep may well be supposed to relinquish them.' How long? The usurpations of our three Henrys lasted above three-score years, yet this did not determine the claim of the house of York. But can a claim be said to sleep while it is continually kept up and asserted? For the consequences drawn from our Lord's words are quite foreign to His design, and show the sadness of this cause of resistance, which is forced to seek refuge in strained constructions. And as he has dressed our constitution, we may well say there is not the like upon earth. He has made it up of three co-ordinate powers—all opposition, contradiction, and nonsense. The right of the crown is made not only a part, but in a manner the whole of a constitution. How wildly have we reckoned who put its total subversion upon the tyranny of princes, for then that can never be! 'I have gone further into this matter' (the birth of the Prince of Wales, called a secret fact by him) 'than I have ever done formerly, but the day and the present temper——' Why? What had this to do with the day? And what is the temper? Is it to draw a parallel? Thistles again! Very hard that you cannot speak a word without trapping yourself. I think you should never speak more. There may come a time when you may—repent. 'We do now celebrate the happy conclusion of a long and fatal series of confusions and wars, after we had gone from our ancient establishment of law and government.' The nation saw no way to recover itself but by returning to its ancient constitution, all in one voice concurring to call the king home from a long unhappy wandering. 'The royal family owed the Restoration wholly to the duty and affection of subjects, without any obligation to foreigners.' That was *àpropos*, and may serve for a thanksgiving the next 29th May. It is good to have a sermon beforehand. This was spoken like an oracle. Keep out foreigners, for they are merciless and there is no way to do that but by returning to our duty. In cases of competition for the crown, they will put in their oar. I fancy, sir, that you and I begin to agree pretty well. Our squabble now is but the falling out of lovers, and you know 'an inconstant lover is worse than a thief.' Return from wherein you are fallen, and you shall find me—there. Till then, adieu."

Nonjurors, Jacobites, Tories, Church-people, not only high but low, were transported with delight at this exposure and rebuke, because the coarse and cowardly thrusts of the unscrupulous prelate behind his screens at Leslie were appreciated very differently from his expectation, and caused unbounded indignation. Though he had spent his life in treason, gossip, and arts of popularity, no man was more distrusted by persons in high station, or more intensely detested by the populace, who nicknamed him "Gibby." It is a significant fact that, whereas Leslie, who adopted what was not deemed the popular cause, had scarcely any but political opponents and personal friends among them, Burnet and Hoadly both were mobbed once or twice, and even an outrage committed at the burial of the former, some four years after this affair. However, he still had his Whig friends in power, and the queen afraid to strike. Moreover, she did not like the allusions to young Pretenders. Burnet, therefore, who was infuriated beyond description, went with tears and gnashing of teeth to her and her ministers. Both were disposed to assist in the work of revenge, the latter little guessing that their own contemptuous dismissal should follow next. Upon July 24, 1710, a warrant was issued against Leslie, to which he put in no appearance. On August 8 he was outlawed, and on September 9 a proclamation for his apprehension, on account of some "positions tending to bring in the Pretender." In another statement it was said that he had "represented all the laws for twenty years to be no good." If he had said so, however imprudent, it would have been very nearly the exact state of the case, and what many people were thinking. But no such representation could have been tortured, even by lawyers, out of his words. Nor were there any positions which could justly bear such a construction about the Pretender as was put upon them. He was condemned in his absence for what enemies chose to think he meant. Under the Revolution thoughts and meanings were not so safe as under hereditary rule, or else Burnet had been beheaded many a time before he was invested with Scotch cambric. Yet how poor a compliment these proceedings conveyed to him! Not a word in them of any libel or wrong done him, because every word was so severely true and capable of proof, but only " positions tending "—the tendency being according to the interpreters, not the author—in the direction of a person never once mentioned. It was a curious circumstance that Middleton, at S. Germain, had presumed to find fault with Leslie on exactly opposite grounds,[1] that he had used unguarded language too favourable to Queen Anne. He did not specify, but no doubt referred to, closing numbers of the *Rehearsal*, or the letters upon the war. No notice was taken of this; and before long Middleton, with others at the court of S. Germain, became importunate for his arrival there. He went instead to a house provided by the kindness of Mr. Cherry, and remained there for nearly six months— partly because Mrs. Leslie was out of health so much that a long journey was not deemed safe. It is also said he was disguised in regimentals. Mr. Secretan is mistaken in adding that it was " at Mr. Cherry's expense and by his advice that he afterwards went to Bar-le-Duc;"[2] for such an obligation had no need to be incurred at that time, and the

---

[1] Hanover and Stuart Papers.   [2] Life of Nelson.

visit was subsequently from the Chevalier's own earnest entreaty, backed by a request from his Protestant attendants. None the less is Mr. Cherry's hospitality deserving of warm acknowledgment, and his name to be gratefully entwined with remembrance of Charles Leslie. Retirement to S. Germain might appear to have been an easy escape from the difficulties of his situation at this period. But reluctance to adopt that course can be well explained by remembrance of the queen-mother's inveterate hostility against the Church of England, with ceaseless efforts of her priests to proselytize any and every body whose importunities and shallow arguments could only annoy him. Then, moreover, political factions and jealousies were rife there incessantly, each enthusiastic about plans and projects with which the wisest and bravest friends of the Stuart cause could have no sympathy.

CHAPTER XIV.

Lord Rochester—Jacobites at Waltham—"Truth of Christianity"—Abbé S. Real—Death of Princess Elizabeth—Illness of Chevalier—Descriptions of him—New Consecrations—Nonjurors—Mrs. Leslie's Illness and Death—Chaplaincy at Bar-le-Duc—Conversions—Supplements—"Truth of Christianity," etc.

A TORY Government succeeded to office, but their measures need not be discussed, having no bearing upon the history of Leslie; nor, as far as the real spiritual character of the Church was concerned, had the new ministry any better ideas than the Whigs. But it should be recorded that at length the Bill against occasional conformity was carried under their auspices, only to reappear at a later date for fresh contention. Leslie wrote a letter to the Chevalier upon this subject, which also may be omitted. Were he alive at the present day, his own principles of the Church's independence of the State would probably incline him to a different field of action, and he would be found contending, not for imposition of tests of any description upon Dissenters, but her emancipation from Erastian fetters. Marlborough had finished his last siege of Bouchain to find a cold welcome at home, even dismissal from all his offices. He had asked for the governorship of the Low Countries, which once before he declined, but was refused. Since then he had applied for the permanent commandership of the British army, to be still more peremptorily refused by the queen, who took alarm at the request; and well she might, if only she had known for certain what was too truly whispered and suspected, but only revealed when he had long gone to his great account. Who, however, would not prefer the retirement of Leslie under the same royal displeasure to Marlborough's inglorious ease on return, when the characters and conduct of both in their respective spheres are considered? How could he have enjoyed such a splendid fortune as he had accumulated, when accompanied with a conviction of being at any moment liable to detection? Who not rather, with a stainless, unsullied conscience, be driven forth by legal tyranny an outlaw and exile from his native land? Leslie's residence at Waltham was a very perilous undertaking, which, if no domestic affairs had urged, his friends should hardly have encouraged; for such disguises and secrecy have an air of mystery about them, which provokes inquiry. However, there he remained securely till, his wife being somewhat recovered, they were able to accept the invitation to S. Germain, where they arrived on April 17, 1711. During his stay he committed to paper in French an account of the state of affairs as they appeared to him in England, but which very few readers would care to peruse as altered by translation into English; for it was mainly a recapitulation of facts and circumstances already noticed in these pages. Moreover, in the translation by another hand it must have undergone considerable modification, for it bears no traces of his general style, and contains some statements at variance with his undoubted wishes and opinions. A French priest took the liberty to carry this plan of alteration still further, so as to involve some unpleasantness at the French court, and when discovered, a severe reprimand to himself; but the details are not interesting enough for repetition.

In May of this year the Earl of Rochester died very suddenly, so he had not long enjoyed the title and property to which he had succeeded on the death of his brother. He was perhaps equal in ability and more of an orator, but his temper so violent as to make many enemies, and though a Tory in politics, a man of little principle or religion. Some people supposed that he often shielded Leslie, but there is no evidence of the kind, and there was so very little sympathy between them in disposition or opinions, that nothing can be justly deemed less probable; though the old friendship between him and the family might have inclined him to discourage any interference which his own political interests did not seem to require. During the visit to S. Germain, Leslie steadily adhered to the policy he had long recommended of abstaining from attempts to disturb Queen Anne; rather endeavouring conciliation and negotiation with her in securing her consent for reversion of the crown to her brother after her death, in lieu of the house of Hanover; meanwhile making preparations as complete as possible, in order to act immediately upon tidings of that event. This was not the advice palatable to many adherents either there or in Scotland, who wanted another effort at invasion without delay; but he knew well that the same chances of success no longer remained as attended the first if they had only been properly used, and that no support could be expected at the present in England, whereas the feeling had increased of late years in favour of the prince's recall when the throne should be vacant. And he had better opportunities than most people of knowing that such an event might not be deemed improbable at any time from the queen's evidently failing health. Had he deemed any more immediate action prudent in the Chevalier's interest, no one could reasonably have complained of his concurrence in the scheme, because his allegiance had been formally repudiated by her and her Government, and he put beyond the pale of law on a groundless pretence of disobedience to it.

It is time to return to a long-neglected subject. While these various events occurred, the literary world had submitted to their consideration two fresh publications, which formed a closing chapter to Leslie's earlier controversies on theological topics. The house at White Waltham he termed "my Tusculum," probably in playful allusion to Cicero's country seat near Rome. Yet two men, alike in the variety and extent of their intellectual attainments, and the fact of adversity at the hands of opponents, never resembled each other less in their manner of meeting a crisis, or in general character. The great Roman orator was utterly cast down, bemoaning bitterly his proscription to his brother Quintius. Leslie and his wife bore up cheerfully against misfortune, and upon arrival there he sat himself at once to prosecute the work which came to his hand, so that by November the task had been completed, and both Treatises were ready for the press long before their departure for the Continent. The first of these was the "Truth of Christianity demonstrated," and the second "A Dissertation concerning Judgment and Authority, with a Vindication of the Short and Easy Method with the Deists." This last was added particularly in a reply to a book entitled "A Detection of the Four Marks, being the Marks of the Beast calculated for the Cause and Service of Popery." But the former had evidently long occupied his attention, only withheld till leisure permitted their satisfactory conclusion, and time had been afforded for any reply which Deists or Socinians could produce to the "Short and Easy Methods" after their long silence. Anxious rather to hear what they could say against his arguments than himself, personally he might well feel at once relieved and disappointed at this solitary and miserable result; the malicious intention of which appeared by its title, whilst the contents were of the weakest, most impoverished description. He felt more than disappointment—"horror and amazement to see Christ not only blasphemed, but ridiculed by reduction to a level with senseless legends. Here the cloven foot appeared, and showed out of what quiver this envenomed arrow came—even of an inveterate and malicious Deist." So poor and mean the performance appeared as to the reasoning, that Leslie said he thought to neglect it, and let it sink under its own weight of nonsense and contradiction, till he heard that among some even of better capacity than the unthinking multitude, "whose prejudices inclined them to accept anything of this sort, it was boasted of as a shrewd and unanswerable piece against priestcraft and all the *fourbe* of revelation." This determined him upon writing an answer, confining himself in it to the four marks originally laid down, but in the "Truth of Christianity" adding four more to distinguish it from all false religions. His statement of only four religions in the world has been cavilled at by a modern sceptic. No doubt the enumeration is insufficient for embracing the swarm of heresies and sects which existed even two centuries ago; but it fairly included all the great species and systems of error under which the smaller ones can be classified at pleasure. What is insisted upon is the essential features of antagonism to the gospel in their fourfold form, and in this respect the division holds good to the present day. A more complete and accurate distribution, which should range all the varieties of disbelief and misbelief, from rank atheism to the newest and nearest imitation of orthodoxy, under their proper heads, would require several volumes instead of pages, and be a work of sacred zoology rather than theology. An epitome as usual will furnish what seems sufficient for readers, in order to estimate fairly the general character of the author's reasoning; and it may be the shorter, because a great portion of his treatise necessarily was occupied with repetitions of former arguments. A beautiful passage upon the English version of the Bible is a piece of simple and unadorned eloquence, which will not unfavourably compare with Cardinal Newman's striking eulogy of a later date, and find an echo in many hearts. Archbishop Whately owed some of his best ideas to Leslie, and another eminent writer has been similarly indebted; yet, strange to say, has never mentioned his name even in a passage where it is evident that he had his words in view. This consideration leads naturally to a matter seriously affecting Leslie's own literary reputation. Long after his decease an anonymous writer insinuated a charge of plagiarism in regard to the "Truth of Christianity," which if true would be as surprising as painful a discovery. Such things, indeed, have been done even by distinguished men. Living persons can remember a brilliant speech, delivered on a memorable occasion before an overflowing assemblage of great personages in England, borrowed wholesale from a French orator.[1] And the lame apology offered by a friend, of unconscious repetition, was as damaging as the silence of the great speaker himself, who could only have resorted to this expedient for meeting an immediate and imperative obligation from a stress of work and want of time, because

[1] Disraeli on death of Wellington, and Mr. Thomas Duncombe.

he showed himself on many other occasions capable of far grander efforts. But the instances of literary piracy are far too numerous to permit of particular mention, nor would they justify Leslie in the least if guilty. The charge then was this, that his work was only a reproduction in an English dress of one by the Abbé S. Real. Mr. Gleig so effectively vindicated Leslie in a most generous and appreciative article in the *British Critic*,[1] that nothing can be required further, nor any improvement made upon his defence. It would be an injustice to him, therefore, not to say that here simply the main points of that argument are restated. The remarkable similarity between the French and English treatise does not admit of the explanation that two authors conceived the same mode of reasoning against infidelity at almost the same time. Currents of thought do seem to flow in various directions simultaneously, and ideas float in the air like infectious disorders, but they are not generally of the best and purest description. One or other of these works must have been a copy, but by no means therefore a forgery, or made with any purpose of deception at all. The Abbé died in 1692, leaving behind several manuscripts which were published, including this disputed treatise. But in his own lifetime had appeared an edition of his works which did not contain it. What is the fair inference, but that he did not lay claim to its authorship while alive? And could it have escaped the vigilance of a learned man like Burnet, always in quest of information or been passed over in silence by him, if such a charge had been capable of substantiation at the time? Now for the explanation. It does not appear necessary to adopt in full Mr. Gleig's suggestion, that a French editor, knowing the real author's obnoxiousness to the English Government,

[1] xxiv., 1838.

might have deemed it a favourable opportunity of appropriating merit to a countryman of his own. That removes the piracy from the Abbé some two doors off. But as he certainly never pretended to its authorship, nor, was the manuscript proved to have been in his handwriting, nor produced for a long time after his death, it seems sufficient to suppose that an error was innocently committed in attributing to him the French translation. Leslie's treatise had been published anonymously, and many copies were circulated among friends and acquaintances abroad familiar with both languages. Nothing, therefore, was more probable than its translation as an exercise by some admiring reader, or for the purpose of convincing a disbeliever. Then internal evidence amounts to a demonstration that Leslie was the author. So very different from the case of Gordon's claim to the "Eikon Basilike" and other impostures, it bears all the characteristic marks of authenticity, being neither inferior nor superior in style or ability to most of his undoubted writings. Further, let it be asked, *Cui bono?*—To whose interest? The question can be answered safely in his case; he had no need to surreptitiously appropriate another man's labours, who had established a reputation by abundant and successful labours of his own. Whether the Abbé and Leslie ever interchanged communications upon the subject of the treatise, or had any acquaintance with each other, is not known; but nothing is more probable, and then the mystery would admit of a very easy solution honourable to both persons.

Although Queen Anne preserved inscrutable silence concerning her brother's letter, she urgently insisted upon his removal from France in the preliminaries for peace. Secrets were ill kept at S. Germain, for in addition to gossip and indiscretion bribes were lavishly bestowed to procure information for the English. But scarcely was it one that there a peace would no longer be unfavourably regarded, if this condition should not be too rigidly interpreted, and if the arrears of the queen-mother's dowry, so long withheld upon false and frivolous pretences, should be paid, amounting to about a million of pounds sterling. The Chevalier objected to go to Rome or Avignon, lest it might be attributed by Protestants to an overweening attachment to Popery, at a time when that alone seemed to stand in the way of reconcilement with his country.

After their visit to S. Germain, Mr. and Mrs. Leslie went to reside in Holland, but had not been there more than a few months when the latter had another attack of illness more alarming than the preceding, and very slowly regained her health. During this time several letters were despatched from S. Germain to which no answer was received, perhaps on this account, or some delay in delivery. In one of these from the Chevalier himself, he complained of "the difficulty in dark times of discerning friends from foes, and distinguishing false from true appearances." A study of the correspondence carried on between England and the two courts of S. Germain and Hanover which has come to light affords a sad commentary on this complaint; since it remains still a matter of dispute in the interest of which royal family several eminent persons were concerned, for they solemnly pledged their devotion to both. One point stands out clearly from the mass of hypocrisy and falsehood in these letters, that Lords Bolingbroke and Oxford wished to provide for themselves above all things security in any emergency, without the slightest regard to principle. Another inference may be drawn with almost equal certainty, that in whichever direction their personal predilections ran, their dependence rather lay on the prospects of

Hanover than S. Germain; but they detested each other so cordially, that a distinct assurance of the one being committed to any course would have proved a strong inducement to the other to embrace the opposite, irrespective of other considerations. "*Idem sentire de republica*" has never been a distinguishing feature of English Cabinets; so open questions now are those of religion, instead of trivial matters as formerly. But then the spectacle was presented of men in the Cabinet, who quarrelled in the presence of the Sovereign, and whose points of difference were more numerous than of agreement upon all subjects of policy. In the opening of 1712, the Chevalier and his sister were both attacked with small-pox, and the latter, just when good hopes were entertained of recovery, had a relapse, and sank beneath the fatal malady. Even political opponents in England were shocked to hear of the loss of this princess, whose amiability and superior intelligence were widely appreciated. The Chevalier happily soon regained his health, without a trace of the disease, though he was of a delicate constitution; but as yet had shown no symptoms of those vicious habits which, in later years, injured it and his character so seriously. Here will be a fitting opportunity to speak of him as he then appeared to his friends and adherents.

Leslie's description naturally claims attention first, because of his intimate acquaintance; and given in a letter to a member of Parliament, with a view of removing impediments to the Stuart line, was reprinted in a public letter in 1715, which will require observation in its place. "Concerning the person of the Pretender you desire to know. He is tall, straight, and clean limbed; slender, yet his bones pretty large. He has a very graceful mien, walks fast, and in his gait has a great resemblance to his uncle, Charles II. He uses exercise more for health than diversion, is seldom merry, thoughtful but not dejected. Gives great application to business, writes much, and no man more distinctly, also shows much criticalness in the use of words. He is a Stuart perfect in your language, and though driven by you into another nation, yet his and his father's court was still English, and his education the same." This letter was handed about among Tories in England, where it underwent many transformations, till the author would have been puzzled to find, beyond this picture, his own words or sentiments. How little credit can be attached to stories from spies may be easily seen by comparing different passages in the Stuart and Hanover Papers, where his name also is made a key for three different locks, but seldom fits any. He is called Leighton, Hannah, Lamb, pretty much at random, and even the brother of the Chevalier's physician, the excellent Mr. Kenyon! With the above description of the prince's personal characteristics it is interesting, however, to compare others of a later date. Walpole wrote thus: "The chevalier has the strong lines and fatality of air peculiar to them all," which corresponds with "the plaintive look" spoken of by many persons. Another writer, who obviously could not have been Nairn, as represented by Macpherson, wrote: "I should be glad to know what my lord (Bolingbroke) says of that knight, and whether he likes him; for they tell me he is a tall, proper, well-shaped young gentleman, that he has an air of greatness mixed with mildness and good nature, and that his countenance is not spoiled with the small-pox, but on the contrary that he looks now more manly than he did, and is really healthier than he was before; they say he goes to Chalons." The brave and unfortunate Balberino pronounced this eulogium upon him on the scaffold: "I am at a loss when I come to speak of the prince. I am not a fit hand to draw his character. I shall leave that to others. But I must beg leave to tell you that the incomparable sweetness of his nature, his affability, his compassion, his justice, his temperance, his patience, and his courage, are virtues seldom all to be found in one person. In short, he wants no qualification requisite to make him a great man.[1] In 1714 a proposal was made and favourably entertained for his marriage with a daughter of the Emperor of Austria, but it fell through; and in 1718 he married the Princess Clementina, daughter of Sobieski—King of Poland certainly not *de jure*. She was an amiable and attractive person, and brought the Chevalier a large fortune; but from that time his character began sensibly to deteriorate, with all the promises of his youth one by one destroyed. He treated her very cruelly, so that she died literally of a broken heart, which lost to him the attachment and sympathy of his best friends. Therefore, with a view of retaining a hold upon the English nation, it was deemed necessary to propose that his claim to the crown should be resigned in favour of his eldest son. This melancholy downfall will account for the very different picture from Leslie's drawn by Keysler in 1756. "The figure made by the Pretender is in every way mean and unbecoming. The pope has issued orders that all his subjects should call him King of England, but the Italians make a joke of this; for they term him the local king, or king here, while the real possessor is termed the king there. . . . He is fond of seeing his image struck on medals. His pusillanimity and licentiousness have lessened every one's esteem." Misfortunes are a poor excuse for any vices, but his have been somewhat exaggerated by unfriendly critics like Thackeray. "He never dared to draw his sword,

[1] Jesse's "Memoirs," vol. i. p. 223.

though he had it. He let his chances slip by as he lay in the lap of opera-girls, or snivelled at the knees of priests asking pardon."[1] It was owing to no lack of courage or promptitude on his part that the first attempt at invasion had failed and not been renewed. It will presently appear that upon the next more memorable occasion, at least he exhibited no reluctance to risk his own person in a far greater enterprise. For several years his infirmities compelled him to remain in great retirement, yet he lived to see George III. for some time upon the throne, dying at last at the age of seventy-eight, on January 12, 1766.

About this time which Leslie described Dr. Wagstaffe died, so that Dr. Hickes was left alone; the question, therefore, came up in a new form concerning the continuance of separation in the Church of England. Application was made to the Chevalier for his sanction to consecrate new bishops. His opinion was very unfavourable to the proposal as unreasonable at the present juncture of affairs, but he added that no new authority was required beyond what he had conveyed to them by Leslie upon the first occasion. The latter seems to have differed from him on this point, concurring with Dr. Hickes and the party who desired new consecrations. No words, indeed, of his to this effect have been found, but the general presumption seems a fair one from want of evidence to the contrary, and his continuing to act in accord with them. It was a great pity that such a happy opportunity was omitted of separating politics from religion, and practising passive obedience under circumstances greatly altered from those which had justified separation at the first, remaining content with a protest against what they deemed unconstitutional in government. In order to effect their purpose canonically

[1] Esmond, 305.

recourse was had to the bishops in Scotland; and Spinkes and Collins were selected for consecration—estimable and suitable men for the office, since the step was determined upon.

Another important question now arose, in consequence of fresh and urgent insistance from the queen and Government in England for her brother's immediate removal from France as an essential condition of peace, to which Louis XIV. could no longer object. The prince, seeing it to be inevitable, by anticipation fixed his own departure to take place so soon as securities for his safety should be obtained from the different states and rulers in Europe, with whose united consent Lorraine was chosen for his future residence. Some thought Queen Anne secretly thus intended to provide for his easier return to England; but they were those Jacobites who interpreted every event favourably to their own wishes. The Duke of Lorraine offered a cordial welcome, the more readily because, in seeming anxious to oblige her, he had stronger ground for demanding support to his own claim for redress from the King of France, who had almost of necessity for his own protection taken possession of the other's territory. To smooth matters still further for himself, whatever the Chevalier or his friends said was immediately reported by the Duke, with copies of letters to Bolingbroke in England, although he at the same time wished to treat his guest, not only hospitably, but with such kindness and friendship as his own interests permitted. Subsequently also he showed no little spirit in honourably refusing to withdraw this shelter when the English Government, upon a change of opinion, sent an order to this effect. Jacobites and Nonjurors began now to pick up courage and expectation under the Tory Government beyond anything known for a long time, and revolutionists to feel proportionately depressed or infuriated. Intrigues for a restoration of the hereditary right were a staple topic of conversation at home and abroad; nor were reports of a fresh invasion altogether without foundation, if premature and exaggerated. While Tories wished the Chevalier to be brought over, for the queen's failing health could no longer be concealed, Whigs clamoured yet more vehemently for the Elector or Electoral Prince to be fetched. Proposals and warnings on both sides still failed to elicit any definite intimation of her secret wishes from her lips. She would only reply to Argyle's remonstrances, "How can they say such things?" And to Burnet's prosy lectures—nothing at all. The Whigs went beyond remonstrance, inviting the Elector to invade England with an army while the queen still lived, and promising large subscriptions towards its support. Nor did he reject their proposal with indignation, but preferred for a while longer a more peaceable method of making his footing sure. Here was a strange exhibition of Whig loyalty to their own principle of obedience to the *de facto* possessor, while complaining of treason in those who wanted to bring over the rival candidate. Jealousy, not without reason, prevented the Electoral prince being sent instead of his father, though it was defiantly stated that, having been created a peer by the queen's pleasure, he did not longer need her invitation or even permission for arrival at any time. Meanwhile, to strengthen the family interest in this nation, De Foe and Ridpath received retaining fees to write it up in their papers.[1] If the Chevalier adopted no such mean artifices to obtain popularity, many of his supporters were very indiscreet and troublesome, not only in England but on the Continent in various places, with their ceaseless reports,

[1] Hanover Papers.

recommendations, and applications for pecuniary assistance or employment. Such was their number and importunity that "dear Mat," as the poet and treaty-maker, Matthew Prior, was unceremoniously styled by his friends in the cabinet, complained "that Jacobites were waiting before he was awake in the morning, and tall Irishmen put into bed with him." Among other English visitors in Holland at this time were the Duke and Duchess of Marlborough, the very mention of whose names the queen could no longer bear. To be as magnanimous in resentment, when her birthday came round, their two daughters sat before an open window in dressing-gowns as the carriages passed to the *levée*, and two more drove in Hyde Park among the crowd in similar *déshabillé!* When the Chevalier at length departed for Bar-le-Duc, with a view of satisfying the prejudices of English people, he took with him only Protestant servants, some of whom were very hard to satisfy. They thought his only hope of recovering his throne lay in abjuring the Roman Catholic religion, therefore proposed that if he could not conscientiously do that, he should temporarily simulate a conversion, the mask to be thrown off when the prize should be won. A baser and more unwise piece of policy never was propounded, or less likely to prove ultimately successful in this country, even though recent instances could be adduced in its favour among continental sovereigns. From the prince it met a firm and dignified rejection, with a touching appeal for the same generous allowance as he pledged himself prepared to extend to all his subjects. Other persons less unreasonably suggested that a grand controversial discussion should be held in his presence, upon the issue of which his faith in the future should depend, reckoning confidently upon the certain triumph of their own advocate. At the same time

Lord Middleton united with some other attendants in urging that Leslie should be summoned to supersede Mr. West, Protestant chaplain in the royal household. To this latter part of the proposal no objection was made, because it accorded with his own views and inclinations, but some delay occurred in consequence of Mrs. Leslie's illness. She had another attack of her complaint, and as her name does not occur again in any of the papers which have been discovered, and henceforth he and his son are always mentioned alone, the presumption must be that her illness ended fatally upon this occasion. Little has been said in these pages of their domestic life, because so little has been ascertained of its details through private sources, and he was so eminently a public character. But every one can feel that, owing to external circumstances, and the thorny paths in which their lot was cast, her life must have been for the most part a sad one; somewhat closely resembling that of the bishop's wife. For however warmly she sympathized with her husband in his trials, and whatever gratification his celebrity afforded her, any woman must have been sorely tried by the perils and persecutions to which his faithful attachment to the exiled family exposed them, with frequent removals from place to place. Happily their family was small, or such trials would have proved even heavier; and these were now all grown up to maturity. The second son, Henry, married a Spanish lady, of whom no particulars are recorded which need be repeated. A daughter married Mr. Hamilton, an estimable clergyman in Ireland, some time afterwards; and the eldest son, Robert, after receiving a good education from his father, finished on the Continent, now resided with him generally and accompanied him on his travels. He had the credit of assisting in the *Rehearsal;* nor is it improbable, as he fully shared his father's political and religious sentiments, with considerable intellectual powers; but, of course, that was a subject not prudent to disclose. Since he could not swallow the oaths, no profession was open to him; or else there need be little doubt, from the testimony of Dean Swift, Mr. Carte, and others, that he might have distinguished himself in several capacities.[1]

A pamphlet entitled "Hereditary Right," etc., in reply to another from the revolutionary point of view, provoked a great deal of angry criticism against Jacobites at this time, while really containing little which had not been said frequently before and as forcibly. But Whigs were in a more than usually disagreeable humour; and the Government desired no attention directed to their own projects or purposes, whatever they were. Therefore a warrant was issued for apprehension of the publisher and author. As usual, Leslie incurred suspicion, whereas he had no part in its composition. The publisher gave up the name at last of a Mr. Bedford as having brought it to him, who bore the penalty inflicted of fine and imprisonment. It was, in fact, a joint production between him and Mr. Harbin, another Nonjuring clergyman; and probably the exposure of his share would not have relieved Mr. Bedford, or else he was far too honourable a man to make a scapegoat of his brother-priest.

Now at last, on August 3, 1713, Leslie made his long-expected arrival at Bar-le-Duc, where he experienced a very gracious reception from the Chevalier, with a warm welcome from his fellow-countrymen. What had he come for? Simply, in the first place, to exercise his ministerial office without hindrance where it was wanted. That was the immediate and main purpose of his attendance, to which

[1] Swift's Works, vol. vii. 136; Carte, vol. iv. 413; Burnet, iv. 290.

any others were secondary and subordinate. He might be the friend, the confidant, the guest, or even spiritual adviser ultimately, of the prince, but his business was to act as chaplain to the members in the household of his own communion. The invitation offered and accepted was for this purpose upon an understanding honourable to both, but rather implied than expressed, that he should be unrestricted in performance of his sacred duties, and on the other hand not trespass beyond his province. At the same time, the Chevalier professed his readiness to listen to any arguments he might think proper to address in private to himself in favour of the Church of England. Nothing more could have been properly requested or granted. To have come there as an avowed proselytizer and propagandist would have been as injudicious and unbecoming a proceeding as can well be imagined, and the only result have been to fan flames of discord in the whole country as well as the court, thus most certainly rendering it too hot for him to stay. Yet this was what many foolish people thought and wished, not seeing that their speeches and reports were calculated to prevent the very object they professed to cherish, and mar at the outset the whole of Leslie's influence for good there. He never gave any sanction or encouragement to these schemes. He had no design or desire to take advantage of the prince's misfortunes, or hurry him into a premature or dishonest abandonment of his religion. Such an intention on his part would have been more guilty than the apostasy of his victim. To leave a Church is a leap of far too tremendous consequences to be taken or advised lightly and in the dark. How few so-called converts or perverts have realized the extent and importance of the step! Personal experience can testify the worthlessness of motives and reasons assigned for such changes. Here are a few instances. A priest left the Roman Communion some years ago who had held high office therein, upon the ground of religious scruples which had long troubled his mind after conversation with an English clergyman, into whose communion he was received, with a flourish of trumpets announcing the fact of his conversion in the newspaper. Yet that wicked man had recently committed a most terrible crime in Ireland, and while meditating it and his change of religion, had used all his sophistry to pervert to the Romish Church, perhaps as some compensation, a young undergraduate preparing for Holy Orders. The rest of his career was of a piece with this new departure.—A young lad besought a clergyman to take pity on him as an orphan, alleging that he was exposed to bitter persecution on account of his attachment to Protestant opinions. The clergyman took him under his protection, sent him to a first-rate school, and provided for him in every way till eighteen years of age; when suddenly, without the slightest explanation, one Sunday evening he decamped never to return. It was reported that he had been threatened and kidnapped, but what only could be ascertained further with certainty was, that he had returned to the Roman Communion, and engaged himself in public attacks upon the Church of England. These are on one side; now a few on the other, also selected as samples of the mode in which proselytism is conducted in modern days. A gentleman, who left the Church of England after the rest of his family had done the same, in conversation with an English priest who entertained for them a very affectionate regard, assigned as the chief ground of his defection the discovery that "there are seven Sacraments, whereas the Church of England teaches that there are only two, and denies Absolution and Penance," etc. When it was pointed out to him in reply that the Church of England makes no such statement or denial, and that he ought, before putting himself into the hands of a Romish priest for direction, to have applied to his natural and proper spiritual adviser for an explanation of the Catechism, which had been thus misrepresented, he could only say, "Well, that is what I always heard." Unhappily, many parents and teachers are as ignorant as his were of the meaning of this Exposition of doctrine, and need something more plain and simple for their guidance; for if the blind lead the blind, no wonder that they fall.—A young man had scraped through the university and examinations for Holy Orders, though the bishop expressed great doubts afterwards if he ought to have let him pass. He did so because he came highly recommended for unblemished character and devotion. After a few years this priest found time, amid parochial work, not for study of divinity under his authorized Leaders, but surreptitious visits to a Roman chapel; then shortly afterwards, without consultation or communication with his bishop or any English priest, silently transferred himself into the opposite camp, from whence he has summoned courage, under careful direction, to issue darts of controversy tipped with a show of wisdom, which himself was quite incapable of ever making, against quondam friends and the Church whose bread he had eaten. Another person apostatized upon profession of disgust at hearing a priest speak in contemptuous terms of the Sacrament as "worshipping a bit of bread;" omitting to consider how directly opposite to the Church of England's teaching upon the subject are such wicked and foolish speeches of ignorant priests here or there, and how shocking to the minds of thousands who know better.—One instance more. A clergyman who had come over to the Church of England from the ranks of Dissent, and became a popular preacher in a large town, delivered a series of controversial lectures against Rome, spiced with more than ordinary vehemence. What was the result, for he had crowded audiences? Not a single Romanist was converted, but several of his own congregation lapsed to Rome ; one of whom, a most respectable and intelligent tradesman, declared that "he never had a doubt till these lectures suggested many, and he thought, if no better answer could be given than he had heard, it was full time to inquire elsewhere." He went, and took his family with him. Priests most fond of controversial sermons and lectures, where they cannot be answered, are seldom those best qualified for the task, either morally or intellectually ; but whatever may be their merits or good intentions, it would be well if they considered the possibility of suggesting painful doubts and suspicions to less sophisticated intelligence by the practice of disclaiming against priesthood, which themselves have sworn to bear, and the doctrines of their own Prayer-book.

Transition indeed from one Church to another is a tremendous assertion of private judgment and authority in matters of faith, for which comparatively few individuals can show call or capacity, because it involves not merely adoption of a new Church and articles of belief, but condemnation of their own spiritual mother in the past. Leaving any of the multitudinous sects implies nothing of the kind ; though even so it ought not to be done lightly or unadvisedly. At most it is only leaving a bundle of opinions, and an unauthorized system, more or less erroneous, for admission into the Church which is the pillar and ground of the truth ; when also security ought to be given that those errroneous opinions are really renounced, not only transferred. But to leave the Church of Rome for the Church of England, or the Church of England for the other, is a step of such vast meaning and importance that to take it or recommend it hastily, and without most earnest conviction of necessity, is to load one's conscience with a very great weight. None felt this more sincerely than Leslie, and he repudiated distinctly the notion of trying to reconcile the Chevalier to the English Church upon any other terms than those which his own conscience, aided by all the helps his ordinary guides could give, should approve after full consideration. That he should lay before him this case was a duty; and he might, without a particle of vanity, presume his own experience and ability entitled him to undertake it more than most persons. But there he stopped. He failed where no one else would have succeeded; which disappointed numbers of eager friends of all sorts who mainly wanted a change of religion as removing a barrier to the succession. But now that these serious matters can be considered with sobriety and calmness becoming their solemnity, nothing ought to be deemed more honourable and worthy on the prince's part than his conscientious adherence to the faith of his parents, since arguments to the contrary could not convince him. He acted as every sincere and pious person ought to act, and would wish his friends to act, even when his own religious opinions lie in an opposite direction. Half-hearted or double-minded persons talk of "verts" and "versions," without the prefix which candour, the basis of true politeness, suggest; but their faltering inexpressiveness is a testimony how little their hesitation need be regarded. If the rightful, legitimate heir could not regain his crown without sacrificing his sincerity, or making a false profession of conversion—that is, apostasy and perversion—he did well in the sight of

God to refuse it. Had he been convinced, what had been the consequence it is utterly useless to conjecture; because so many other considerations were involved for deciding the question of succession between him and his rival, apart from religion; because, also, it is impossible to say what effect restoration might have produced upon his conduct. If the first two Georges were as sorry Protestants as he turned out a Romanist, yet old George III., with all his prejudices, would have been a great loss to England in exchange for such as he, whose only virtue seemed to be religious sincerity. He who said that "no gentleman would change his religion," was a statesman with very little religion to change. Middleton, who now laid down the seals of office to the Chevalier, after apostatizing to obtain them from his father, was little more than a Deist at heart; and thus spoke contemptuously, but not far wide of the mark, concerning perverts in general, that "a new light seldom comes into the house but through a crack in the tiling." Some great lights might profitably reflect upon this candid admission of their predecessor in the journey from England to Rome. The other promise, of allowing Leslie's ministrations to the members of the Church of England, forthwith was put into execution, and a room fitted up in the court for performance of daily Prayers, with administration of the Sacraments and other Rites as he should deem expedient; nor did he complain of any deviation from this pledge at a subsequent date. But this point will call for further notice in the last chapter.

Abridgment of "The Truth of Christianity Demonstrated."

A Deist's whole wit and skill are employed in working in himself a disbelief of any future rewards and punishments, only to live easy in this world, while yet not undisturbed by fear of an event which he cannot be sure about; for the utmost that he can propose to himself is doubt, therefore his is rather a disbelief than belief of anything. Christians believe; Deists only disbelieve. The Deist replies, "I believe a God as well as you; but for what you call the Holy Scriptures, I may think they were wrote by pious and good men who might take this method of speaking in God's name, as supposing their good thoughts came from Him, and have thus a greater effect upon the people." This is to make the penmen of the Scriptures far from good; not only cheats and impostors, but blasphemers and an abomination before God, such as the law condemned to be stoned. Heathen philosophers and moralists did not believe in their fables of the gods as matters of facts, nor preface them with the favourite expression of inspired writers, "Thus saith the Lord." To distinguish true from false revelations the four marks are set down already explained, and then four others are added as peculiar to our Bible, distinguishing it from all other histories. That the book relating the facts contains likewise the law of the people to be their statute-book. This fifth mark prevents the possibility of forgery. It is stronger to the Gospel than even to the Law of Moses, for no forgery could pass undiscovered without a concert of all Christian nations and peoples. Various lections are objected, but it is much more wonderful there are no more, than that there are so many, considering the multitudes of translations; nor is there one of them which alters the facts or the doctrines. The sixth mark is the topic of prophecy. No other fact ever had such evidence as that of our Saviour's first advent, from the beginning to the end of the Old Testament, on which was founded the general expectation of the Jews, especially at the time in which He did come. Nor only so. He was equally expected among the Gentiles at the same time, as, for instance, is proved by the Magi coming from the east to worship Him, according to Isaiah's prophecy. S. Matthew wrote the first Gospel in the same age when this fact was said to have been done, and is it possible, if false, it could have passed without contradiction when unbelievers, Jews, elders, and priests so much desired to expose Christianity? Then Tacitus, Suetonius, Cicero, and others confirm the general expectation; and the Sybils, whatever source be attributed to their prophecies. If it proceeded from the Jewish tradition, the Holy Scriptures are confirmed, and the miracle is only greater if we suppose God did send such a notion into the minds of men all over the world, strangely to chime in with the facts of the case. Again, beside greater prophecies of the Saviour's birth, death, and resurrection, there are others, reaching to minute circumstances, which, inapplicable to any other event, could only have been foreseen by God, nor were known by the actors, or else they would not have done them. To which ought to be added prophecies in our Bible of things yet to come. We may believe what is to come by fulfilment of the past, and there is no other law or history in the world which so much as pretends to this; it is peculiar to the Bible as being written from the mouth of God. There is one more evidence yet more peculiar than prophecy, which is, types or resemblances and exhibitions of the fact in outward institutions, ordained as laws from the beginning, to continue till the fact they prefigured should come to pass. Such, first, were the sacrifices instituted by God immediately upon the Fall, as types of that great and only propitiatory sacrifice for sin which was to come. These were continued in the heathen posterities of Adam by immemorial tradition from the beginning. Though they had forgotten the origin, they retained the reason so far as universally to have the notion of a vicarious atonement. Beside sacrifices in general, there were afterwards some particular ones, more nearly expressive of our redemption by Christ as the Passover. The double exhibition of Christ on the great day of expiation once a year, when the high priest entered into the holy of holies with the blood of the sacrifice whose body was burnt without the camp, and the other living representation of the scapegoat. Another was the brazen serpent in the wilderness. Another the manna, the rock, the cloud of glory in the temple. The sabbath is called "a shadow of Christ," a figure of the eternal rest He procured for us. Such a sign was the temple at Jerusalem, at which place and none other sacrifices were to be offered; and so great stress was laid upon this, that no sin of the Jews is oftener remembered than their breach of this covenant. A further design of Providence in limiting their sacrifices to Jerusalem was, that after the great propitiatory sacrifice of the Cross, the Jews removed from Jerusalem might have no sacrifice at all, and force them to look back upon that. Their present state of desolation was foretold in several places of Scripture. It is a living prophecy which we see fulfilling at this day. As the door was kept open to Christ before He came by the many and flagrant prophecies of Him, and by the types representing Him, so was the door shut after Him for ever by those prophecies being fulfilled in Him, and all the types ceasing, the shadows vanishing, when the substance was come.

Compare these evidences for Christianity with those preached for any other religion. There are but four in the world. Christianity was the first, for from the promise made to Adam all was Christianity in type, during the patriarchal and legal dispensations. First, then, as to Moses and the Law. The Jews can give no evidence for that which will not equally establish the truth of Christ and the Gospel. So that they are hedged in on every side either to renounce Moses or to acknowledge Christ. Moses and the Law have the first five evidences, but they have not the sixth and the seventh, which are the strongest; and Judaism, as it now stands in opposition to Christianity, has none at all. Secondly, for heathenism some of the facts recorded of their gods have the first and second evidences, and some the third, but not one of them the fourth or any of the other evidences. Thirdly, as to the Mahometan religion it wants them all, for there was no miracle said to be done by Mahomet publicly, save conquering by the sword. His Alcoran is a rhapsody of stuff without head or tail. Compared with our Holy Scriptures no argument is needed to show the difference. Heathen orators have admired their sublimity of style. No writing in the world comes near it, even with all the disadvantage of translation. The plainness and succinctness of the historical part, the melody of the Psalms, the instruction of the Proverbs, the majesty of the Prophets, and above all, that easy sweetness in the New Testament where the glory of heaven is set forth in a grave and moving expression; not like the flights of rhetoric, which set out small matters in great words; but the Holy Scriptures touch the heart, raise expectation, confirm our hope, strengthen our faith, give peace of conscience and joy in the Holy Ghost which is inexpressible. If there be truth in the Alcoran, then are the Holy Scriptures the Word of God; for the Alcoran says so, and that it was sent to confirm them, and expressly owns our Jesus to be the Messiah. How then, it is asked, came the false prophet to set up his religion against the Gospel, and to reckon Christians among unbelievers? No less than as other heretics who called themselves the only true Christians, and invented new interpretations of the Scriptures. The Alcoran is but a system of old Arianism, ill digested and worse put together, with a mixture of some heathenism and Judaism. For Mahomet's father was a heathen, his mother a Jewess, and his tutor a Nestorian monk, which sect was a branch of Arianism. So that in strictness Mahometanism is only one of the heresies of Christianity. . . . Deists profess to go upon bare nature and reason against revelation; but it is a natural notion that there should be a necessity for revelation in religion. For when man had fallen and his reason become corrupted, as we feel to this day, was it not highly reasonable God should give us a law and directions how to serve and worship Him? Plato concluded it to be necessary for a lawgiver to be sent from heaven to instruct us, and said, no doubt from perusal of the Scriptures and the primitive tradition, "Oh, how greatly do I desire to see that man, and who He is!" Again, he said, as if he had copied the fifty-third chapter of Isaiah, "That this person must be poor and void of all recommendations but of virtue alone; that a wicked world would not bear His instructions and reproof; and, therefore, within three or four years, He should be persecuted, imprisoned, scourged, and put to death, His word be cut to pieces as a sacrifice." There is one point remaining—that is, how to distinguish between true and false miracles. I confess I do not know the power of spirits, nor how they work upon bodies. By the same reason that a spirit can lift a straw, he may a mountain, and do many things which would appear true miracles, and so deceive me. All I have to trust to in this case is the restraining power of God, which is the strongest consideration in the world to keep us in dependence upon Him. Herein His great power and goodness are manifest, that He never yet has permitted Satan to work miracles in opposition to any whom He has sent, except when the remedy was at hand, and to show His power the more.

CHAPTER XV.

Bolingbroke's Complaint—Letter to Bishop of Meaux—Bishop Bull—Letter on Usages—Other Pamphlets—Death of Queen Anne—Projected Invasion—Robert Leslie's Advice—"Church of England's Advice to her Children"—Chevalier—George I.—Jacobites—Return—An Informer—Supplement—Case between Churches of England and Rome—Letter to Bishop of Meaux concerning the English Church.

A REPORT reached England that the Prince had been reconciled to the English Church, and received the Holy Eucharist at the hands of Leslie on New Year's Day, which awakened emotions of the highest gratification among Tories and Jacobites. But, after what has been already stated, it is almost superfluous to add that like so many previous stories it was devoid of any foundation in fact. He occasionally attended in a private capacity at daily service in the temporary chapel, perhaps even witnessed a Celebration, but beyond that made no advance in the desired direction. Leslie continued his ordinary ministrations among the household, with free access to his presence for conversation upon religion, but of course this was gradually discontinued when it became apparent that it could prove of no avail. On the other hand, Bolingbroke had no authority for his statement that "the Pretender treated

Leslie very badly," whether he referred to a subsequent period in Italy, or more particularly to their connection at Bar-le-Duc. No such complaint ever fell from his own lips, nor does there appear any reason for it. But if there had been, the painful secret would not have been imparted to Bolingbroke of all men in the world. He was already suspected of having designed to betray the prince, and that suspicion was afterwards fully confirmed; while his notorious indifference to religion would have been sufficient to prevent any confidential communications between Leslie and him on the subject. What is more, no interruption of friendly relations with the Chevalier took place at any time. Their intercourse remained on the same footing as before; which could hardly have been the case if any sense of unhandsome treatment had been experienced in that matter which lay nearest to his chaplain's heart, and for the sake of which he went to Bar-le-Duc. That he felt disappointment at his failure can too easily be imagined. It must have been so, but that was better than an organized hypocrisy such as would have satisfied a majority of political adherents to his cause.

With a view of facilitating his object, Leslie at this time produced another treatise, in accordance with his established principle of conducting arguments upon paper rather than by conversation, in which people are apt to become heated and obstinate; and as affording better opportunities for study and reflection. Under any circumstances, however, this work would have been sure to be written, and the substance had long previously been prepared, for it was necessary to complete the plan originally formed of furnishing English Church-people with a full system of defence against all adversaries. Its title was the "Case Stated between the Churches of England and

Rome," and took the form of a dialogue between members of the two communions, in which all the main points at issue between them were brought out to be freely canvassed. Since publication of this work the state of the case has very materially altered, and the gulf of separation been seriously widened by the Church of Rome's action in imposing fresh terms of communion. Members of the Church of England in this sad fact have yet a source of much consolation, knowing that the awful responsibility of division cannot possibly be charged upon them. Their doctrinal standard remains unaltered from two or eight centuries ago; and that is the same as the English Church held twelve centuries ago; that also identical in all essential respects with what S. Augustine introduced; the faith once delivered to the saints derived from apostles. Many controversialist, have found in Leslie's treatise all the materials they required most lucidly and skilfully arranged; and if the amount of obligation has not been always so fully and gratefully acknowledged as was proper, yet himself would scarcely have wished it otherwise, so as the purpose were served for which they were accumulated. He proceeded invariably upon the maxim, "*Magna est veritas, et prævalebit,*" therefore would have made all comers welcome to enter into his labours for the truth's sake. But of necessity the value of his work is diminished now, because the Church of Rome has shifted her ground so considerably; as well as that weapons from his armoury have been so extensively borrowed for fabrication of new ones. Therefore the selection of passages appended here may be smaller than otherwise would be desirable; while those who wish to know more upon this subject can be confidently recommended to peruse the original; which up to a certain date will hold its place in comparison of all the most masterly statements which have emanated from any quarter. A reply, subscribed "A. C.," very shortly appeared, called the "Case Restated," the authorship of which has not been ascertained. It must in fairness be admitted to be written with considerable ability, and some points effectively and ingeniously urged in defence of the Church of Rome, especially in the former part; but mere verbal criticism is largely employed to evade and obscure the real question in dispute. Probably Leslie never saw this reply himself.[1]

A publication of much earlier date has been reserved for notice here, because virtually dealing with the same subject. In the year 1694 the learned and pious Dr. Bull, afterwards Bishop of S. David's, published his masterly defence of the doctrine of the Trinity, a copy of which Nelson presented to the famous Bishop of Meaux, who was so delighted with its perusal as to lay it before an assembly of divines of the Gallican Church. They were equally pleased as his lordship, and unanimously accorded a vote of thanks to the author. In conveying this honourable tribute, the bishop went further to express his surprise and desire for explanation concerning Dr. Bull's use of the term Catholic Church. He made a reply fully justifying the claim and character of the English branch, but other engagements caused considerable delay in its appearance. Leslie, therefore, to whom Nelson had communicated the correspondence, meanwhile accepted the implied challenge and answered his inquiry in a public letter. When, however, it reached that eloquent prelate he was dying, so that it is impossible to say what impression might have been produced. Now, it may advantageously be considered in connection with

[1] Perhaps Sutton. "A. C." standing for "a Catholic." Another answer by a Jesuit has not been seen.

the "Case Stated," by any one desiring to form an accurate conception of the Church of England's position between Rome on one hand and Geneva on the other.

> " Est modus in rebus, sunt certi denique fines,
> Ultra citraque nequit consistere rectum."

His stand is upon the old ways between superstition and schism.

One other publication demands special notice — " A Letter to Mr. B(? owyer) concerning the New Separation." Revival of what are termed the Usages, the use of unleavened bread, mixed chalice, and lights at celebration of the Holy Communion, had caused a fresh disturbance among Nonjurors; and he was formally appealed to for his opinion upon the subject. They were a gradually decaying community. The eminent Dr. Hickes, Bishop of Thetford, died in 1715, so incomparably superior to all others in learning, or else his decision should have been final. Leslie argued strongly, it will be seen, against introduction of these Usages, not as wrong in themselves, or superstitious in their nature, or unwarranted by the practice of the primitive Church, but as having become obsolete, therefore not absolutely necessary, and their revival unseasonable in regard to the position of the Nonjuring community at that period of depression.[1] His advice was sound, but cannot be fairly pushed beyond the present necessity to which it referred. Expediency is a relative term. What was inexpedient and inopportune for Nonjurors in their peculiar circumstances need be no longer so, when the Church is not antagonistic to the Crown or Government, nor includes separate encampments; and when a breath of Heaven-sent

[1] See on this subject, Rev. Dr. Gordon's "Eccles. Chron. Scot." vol. ii., 118-152.

vigour has descended upon the valley of dry bones of the last century, and beats in every pulse and limb of her living, growing body. The usages still remain a question of expediency and discretion in regard to circumstances; for they are neither enjoined nor prohibited in Holy Scripture nor by General Councils; neither enjoined nor prohibited by any formulary or authorized formulary of the English Church, but having the sanction and recommendation of primitive anti-papal practice. At least, therefore, they have a claim of preference to innovations and new-fangled schemes, and associations of questionable origin and without a vestige of authority. If they had not been suffered to fall into disuse owing to a sordid economy, Puritan tendencies, and slovenly neglect, much of the difficulty now experienced in keeping alive a spirit of devotion and piety had never been incurred—nor crude and precarious amalgamations with sectarianism adopted to recover the lost tribes of our Israel. When foundations are cast down, what shall the righteous do? Daubing with untempered mortar and restoring breaches with incongruous mixtures of style and material is sorry work, and cannot last. Where ceremonies, however, old and new, serve to gender strife instead of godly union and concord, their introduction is to be deprecated. There is a time for everything, and to be premature is as injurious often as being too late. A chief purpose is edification of the faithful, and when this is not attained Leslie's principle is as applicable as ever. But none can plead his authority in support of outside agitation, or obstinate prejudice against priests and communicants, who wish to worship with holy worship and present a pure offering to the Lord.

Some minor pamphlets, said to have proceeded from

Leslie's pen, are left without examination for various reasons. Of one or two no copies are known to be extant still, if ever indeed they existed at all. Others he certainly did not compose, and their imputation to him was mere guess-work or imposture. Others, again, are doubtful, such as the "Mitre and the Crown," a concise and closely reasoned little production, on a subject sufficiently indicated by its title, but which is extremely unlike his other writings. And, again, others are nothing else but pamphlets, either whole or in part already mentioned under different titles, suggested by some salient expressions of his—such as "Salt for the Leech," "The Finishing Stroke," "Delenda est Carthago," "The Principles of Dissenters." Two letters were written by him, particularly upon the subject of Convocation, the latter, in 1717, being the one better known. But it is not necessary to quote any portion of the contents, because to do them any justice would involve a lengthened explanation, whereas enough has been said upon that subject; and the new heats and contentions which led to the arbitrary and unconstitutional silencing of Convocation for upwards of a century belong more properly to what is called the Bangorian Controversy. Those who wish to know whether Hoadley as a bishop showed any better spirit or held sounder opinions than as a priest at S. Peter-le-Port, will find ample materials for a judgment in other works.[1] When his more famous letter was written he was staying for a while at Chatillon; nor did he return to reside at Bar-le-Duc, for the Chevalier had broken up his establishment there, owing to the grave crisis in his affairs which occurred in 1714. Queen Anne, who during the last two years had suffered several alarming attacks from gout, combined with other disorders, breathed her last somewhat

---

[1] As Overton's "Life and Writings of William Law."

suddenly, owing to an internal rupture on July 31—August 1st. One of the last acts of her reign was said to be the fixing a price upon her brother's head of £100,000, which more certainly was one of the first acts under the new reign. And the order to the Duke of Lorraine for his dismissal, which Leslie said was "forced upon her," though magnanimously rejected at the time, inevitably portended his departure, voluntarily or involuntarily, at an early date. Moreover his own constitution was too delicate to stand the climate there, so that his absences were frequent. Now, however, the queen's death rendered departure imperative and immediate. Her general character, conduct, and conflicting emotions about a successor need not be further enlarged upon. Her attachment to the Church of England, as she understood the term, under Bishop Compton's teaching, is unquestionable, and this would have qualified greatly any leaning to her brother's cause, if there had appeared a prospect of its accomplishment without loss to herself or a bloody revolution. The story of a death-bed confession to the Bishop of London[1] eliciting the reply, "Madam, I shall obey, but it will cost me my head," appears worthy of little attention. At any rate he kept his secret and his head, upon reflection, and was solicitous early to instruct a young princess from Hanover in the doctrine of the Church of England; which with scant ceremony she declined, preferring to take her divinity from the pages of the Socinian writer, Dr. Clarke. That Anne had "a heart entirely English" may be also readily admitted without Bolingbroke's commentary—"that is, extremely dull." It was a sad pity, if Church of England teachers could not sway her judgment upon politics, that they had no stronger influence of a moral kind; or that

[1] Robinson, successor of Compton.

the angry Duchess Sarah's reproachful present of the "Whole Duty of Man" and a Prayer-book exercised no wholesome restraint over intemperate habits, which were so notorious as to be the subject of coarse sneers in the German ambassador's correspondence, and ribald songs in the streets.[1] Some load of anguish or remorse lay heavy upon her heart, vainly and sadly sought to be drowned in this deplorable way. Her sudden death fell like a thunderbolt upon her divided cabinet; and if the crisis had produced any temporary concert, they were prevented from adopting measures on behalf of James III. by the regency, with admirable promptitude anticipating this supposed design, and proclaiming George III. Dr. Atterbury was ready in his episcopal habit to make a counter-proclamation; but ministers had not the nerve if the will to authorize so bold and hazardous a proceeding till they should see more clearly which way the tide would flow. A commotion ensued throughout the kingdom, the thrill of which was quickly felt upon the Continent, and multitudes stood on the tiptoe of expectation for the consequences to follow. But neither of the rival candidates for the crown of Great Britain and Ireland seemed in any great hurry to imperil his life in grasping it. Each waited as if for his adversary to strike the first blow for a full month, while streets, coffee-houses, and clubs resounded with cries on one side—

> "King George our Defender
> From Pope and Pretender!"

On the other—

> "The king shall have his own again!"

and—

> "Young Jemmy is a lad right royally descended,
> With every virtue clad, by every tongue commended."

---

[1] Hanover Papers.

At length the Elector, tired of waiting, or impressed with the danger of further delay, arrived amid acclamations from his party the bolder and more numerous in appearance, if not yet awhile demonstrated to be the stronger. He succeeded, and shortly afterwards was publicly crowned, with all the time-honoured ceremonials and solemnity, as peaceably and easily as his predecessor, or any sovereign before. His demeanour towards the late ministry, or such of them as ventured into his presence, significantly intimated, without the need of words, what favour they might expect at his hands. Accordingly Bolingbroke slipped off in disguise across the Channel, while announced to patronize a new theatrical entertainment. The Duke of Ormond and Sir William Wyndham as quietly, but in a less undignified manner, followed his example. Lord-treasurer Harley (Oxford) was slower in his movements, or deemed himself safer, only to be lodged in the Tower on a charge of treason. Marlborough hastened back from the Continent with his freshest smiles; but they did not clear the brow of George, who had studied him long. Where was the Chevalier? and why did he not come? were questions asked with the utmost eagerness and impatience from the Land's End to Inverness and Cromarty. The only answer was, "He is coming;" but none could say when, while the stream flowed on in the contrary direction. First he had deemed it advisable to repair to Paris, that he might ascertain what assistance could be procured from Louis XIV. The gallant, grand old monarch was then at his last gasp, but signified a will to lend his aid if first the prince would see what he could do by reliance on his own friends in Scotland. So much the Duke of Orleans as Regent admitted had been promised when interrogated by the English ambassador in an unofficial conversation; while Abbé Dubois disclaimed any acquaintance with the matter on the part of the Government. Therefore, if an invasion was to be made, it came to this, that the Chevalier must go attended only by the Duke of Berwick and a few friends, a venture disapproved of by the queen-mother. It required, unfortunately, serious consideration when time was precious, and adherents of the cause were becoming dispirited, or clamouring that he should come as he was and at once or never.

Robert Leslie was at S. Germain at this time with his father. Now they were termed "old and young Mr. Leslie" by Lord Cardigan and others who met them there; so had time set its mark upon the controversialist in its silent but not imperceptible progress when distinctions and comparisons come to be made. He was, too, "in the sere and yellow leaf," prematurely enfeebled with care, toil, and sickness, as well as age, then in his sixty-fifth year. Robert was honoured with a particular inquiry of his opinion, when he warmly seconded the call from Scotland for an immediate effort, but with an air of deferential apology, if his words be rightly reported, which at this distance seems to imply some consciousness of delay or reluctance to start, more than befitted the occasion.[1] His father contributed assistance in a more congenial and serviceable manner than if he had exchanged for a sword the pen, his trusty well-tried weapon which had won many victories. He drew up a letter of very considerable length, copies of which were to be distributed in England, together with a declaration from the prince. It was entitled "The Church of England's Advice to her Children, and to all Kings, Princes and Potentates." Here are a few extracts: "My most dear children, it is now twenty-seven years that I have been seeking you whom my soul loves. I sought you, but I found you not;

[1] Stuart Papers. Macpherson and Carte, vol. iv. p. 349.

and to which way soever I turned myself, I saw nothing but desolation. I see the hand of the adversary upon all my pleasant things, and the heathen within the walls of my sanctuary. Every day, my dear children, adds to these calamities, and your next care should be how to extricate yourselves from present difficulties, and to ward off those which are rolling towards you with every tide of time To this end receive the instruction of your unfortunate mother; for I speak not to reproach, but to the furtherance of your temporal and eternal happiness. . . . The picking out of a stone from an arch renders it easy to sink the whole fabric. As a decoy to you, revolutionary leaders pretend the greatest regard to my preservation; but you already see in their practices, and may perceive in their principles, that which in a very little while, humanly speaking, will be my death. For there is a royalty in the Church as well as in the State, and the hand that will destroy the one will never be stretched out in vindication of the other. It may be a standing rule to you that the enemies of monarchy will never be very good friends to episcopacy. . . . Lord Sunderland advised King James in his own vindication, as he artfully termed it, to send the seven bishops to the Tower. The king consented; but he who never could do a severe thing recalled it, by offering them their liberty upon each other's bail. They, being better divines than politicians, were persuaded to decline the king's favour. The repentance of the greatest ecclesiastic in England shortened his days, and he never forgave himself his mistake in going to the Tower.[1] . . . The Prince of Orange was so regardless of his future state as to sign the Abjuration Act in the very hour of his death;

[1] A very different view from that of Whig historians, by one intimate with both.

and after it an instrument was found in his strong box, by which it appeared, if he had lived three weeks longer, the late queen had been committed to the Tower and her life taken from her. The present John How, Esq., particularly affirmed having seen the instrument. Parliament required him to prove his assertion or take the consequences; but the proceedings were dropped, and the queen persuaded to smother the matter.[1] Dr. Sacheverell had the courage to revive the ancient and apostolic doctrine of passive obedience, and in fact they brought me to trial in person of the doctor. There never was any law pretended in England to cut off an heir before the usurpation of the Prince of Orange, unless of Oliver Cromwell, whose acts have never been numbered with the laws of the land. . . . The Elector was proclaimed, contrary to all the fundamental laws of England, and by his coming will either prove himself very wise, or extremely other-wise. If he be wise, he must know that his makers are very well acquainted with the way by which a crowned head may be brought to the block, and by a strange paradox affirm that they are the rulers of him whom they shall elect to rule over them. If he believe he can support the crown upon their ticklish terms during the course of his natural life, it will be a reason why he should not be numbered among the wise for thinking that he came into the world with that infirmity which his reputation is known to labour under. . . . His parting with a religion that he knew, for one he knows not, is a standard by which his devotion is to be measured. It was said that the treasures of Hanover were to pay the debts of the English nation; but all you have seen of that was what entered the city of London with him in a cart, mop-brooms, brickets, tubs, and earthenware pots, etc. . . . The religion

[1] See p. 238; and Burnet, iii. 435.

he has sworn to maintain is the only one discountenanced by him. The love of your lawful king for his country has been sufficiently attested by many marks of affection to English officers and soldiers taken to France in the late war. He has promised to make the laws of the land the rule of his government, and to hear what I have to say in the business of religion when it may be done with conveniency."

This last observation was generally interpreted into a willingness to listen to Leslie himself; but that is a very narrow and forced construction for language supposed to come from the lips of the Church of England to her children, engaging an impartial hearing to all in future. The date affixed to the end of this letter, April 26, show what a long time was suffered to elapse before the Chevalier had made up his mind or completed his preparations, so that King George had not only got the start of him by a twelvemonth, but been able to ingratiate himself with the populace of London, which he did in a most sensible and manly manner; he and his family walking unattended in public places and freely mixing in amusements. Never was a golden opportunity more completely lost, either under ill advice, or a mistaken view of his best interests. Leslie knew the peril he incurred, but did not shrink from the bold step of going himself to London with the manuscripts of this Letter and the Declaration. He succeeded in having them printed and placed in safe hands for distribution, returning in safety almost before his absence had been noted by many friends; and this was done when his health was in a very unsatisfactory state.

On September 13, the prince set out to take ship for Scotland, but the carriage conveying him overturned, so that he was carried back much bruised and shaken. An ill omen, but a true one for his project. Meanwhile, the Government in England laid hands upon every important person suspected of sympathy with it, and put them in prison. Active preparations also were made to resist the invader whenever or wherever he should attempt to land. This vigilance and severity did not deter Jacobites and Tories from avowing themselves in favour of hereditary right, in language sometimes of cautious innuendo, sometimes without any figure or caution at all. Carte, the well-known historian, thus, when a cabman hailed him during a shower, merrily replied, "he could not afford to hire a carriage in *this reign*." Later, an officiating clergyman in a church at Edinburgh asked the prayers of the congregation " for a young gentleman who was, or shortly would be, at sea." Pulpits rang again with the old style of declamation on both sides, and foremost among the preachers was Sacheverell again! After his three years' honourable exile in Wales, he had been summoned back to preach before the House of Commons, and take charge of the valuable living of S. Andrew, Holborn. He delivered two or three stirring discourses, and then—what would Leslie have thought if he had seen it?—one morning walked quietly arm-in-arm with a friend to an office and took the oath of fealty to the new sovereign! Perhaps his judgment was affected by overhearing a stout Whig express a desire to "lay a horsewhip across his shoulders" on account of his last sermon. In the early spring died Burnet. And a far worthier, more honest, and kindly natured man, William Penn, true to his errors and to the cause of hereditary right to the last.

Most extraordinary phenomena and portents were reported in various places this year. Meteors falling, fiery squadrons and strange figures in the sky, accompanied by voices and sounds, and an eclipse on December 27, which filled multitudes of people with alarm. The prince landed with a few followers at Peterhead, but only to find himself too late. He made, indeed, a vain pilgrimage for many miles to rally scattered forces to his standard, and went through the empty mockery of a coronation at Scone, but all was over and all was lost before he came; at Sherriffmuir and Preston. Had he come sooner it might have been different; he had to be content with hoping it might still be so on another occasion; then on February 9 slipped back secretly to S. Germains. What Robert Leslie thought then he did not say; but if the prince was wanting to himself in some degree, many were still more wanting to the professions and promises on which he had too confidently relied. Those who proved faithful sealed their loyalty in blood, either in battle or the frightful scenes of slaughter which followed what has been named the Rebellion of 1715, because it failed; but had it succeeded would have been termed another glorious Revolution.

Leslie had gone to Italy before this disastrous conclusion of an enterprise on which he had too sanguinely built the very greatest expectations. And after that his history is almost a blank. The Chevalier followed, with whom he remained on terms of favour and friendship; as also with other members of the Stuart royal family, paying visits from time to time to them at S. Germain while the queen-mother lived, who invariably treated him with a condescension and consideration she never showed to any other priest, or even lay member of the Church of England. That she hated with all her heart. Many more notices of his name have been traced in the correspondence of various persons, who met with him in Italy, at S. Germain, and other places, which are not worth recording; but they afford strong confirmatory evidence of the high esteem entertained for his character and abilities among all classes. He did not reside continually in any one place during the closing years of his life, nor mix much in general society even where English visitors were numerous. This was in some measure owing to habits of selusion and study acquired in the earlier portion of his life, though he was very far from a recluse at any period by nature. Still more, it was occasioned by increasing infirmities and ill health, with restricted means. He had never been dependent upon any one, nor accepted remuneration for any of his works, theological or political, beyond the ordinary profits accruing from the sale of some pamphlets in great demand. Or else he could at various periods have acquired considerable sums of money by the hire of his pen to the service of party interests. The same high-minded independence made him unwilling to accept assistance at the hands of relatives who had compounded with the Government, though he evinced no personal animosity either to them or any others who did so. He never visited Ireland after the year 1691; but this was rather in the interest of the family at Glaslough than for his own sake, because he had nothing to apprehend till the last, and was very well known to numbers of persons by sight in London. But visits there would have been certain to be misrepresented as having some political design, and exposed them to suspicion of disaffection to the Government; or might even have led to some disturbance unintentionally, because Roman Catholics as well as Protestants greatly loved and esteemed his memory throughout the north of Ireland.

The Irish are an emotional and excitable nation, too much devoted to political and religious agitation for their own happiness or temporal prosperity. But they have seldom ill-treated open adversaries of their opinions, who have fearlessly trusted them and refrained from interference in disputed questions about the possession of land; the one thing to which they cling with a desperate tenacity often beyond reason and justice as well as law, because they have nothing else. Besides, his adherence to James II. was an additional claim to regard among the great mass of the people. In Italy he found himself, as in Lorraine and at S. Germain, isolated from the natives by his religion. He, who in England had suffered from very erroneous imputations of inclination to Romanism, there was eschewed as a champion of Protestantism, and priests were on the alert to whisper designs of proselytizing. So that he was out of harmony with the world in general as much abroad as at home. After the marriage of the Chevalier it necessarily happened that influence over him or the closeness of their former intercourse decreased. And he could not fail to feel pained at the deterioration of character observable in him; the more keenly because he had in his "Letter to a Member of Parliament" affirmed with great gratification the prince's exemption from " those vices incident to youth." All these circumstances combined to render his life miserable for the most part on the Continent, relieved and cheered, however, by the noble consciousness that he " had always followed truth as closely as he could without straying after worldly interests." Had those been his object, no man could have made a more advantageous bargain with secular powers, and he might have passed Burnet and Hoadly far on the road of ambition and preferment. Since he was, "through the providence of God infinitely wise and righteous, excluded for the greater part of his life from the public exercise of that sacred office to which he had been called, yet had he the comfort of having endeavoured in some degree to serve against its various adversaries the cause of God, religion, and of that Church into which was baptized, educated, and received into Holy Orders, and in which he resolved to die." This was not the language of a boastful, contentious, or dissatisfied spirit; but of one who valued truth above all things, and humbly submitted to the will of God.

In the year 1719 he felt that the shadows of eternity were gathering round him, and he should prepare to bid the world farewell—the world which had dealt hardly with him; yet he made no complaint of its treatment, or recurred to unkindly remembrances of the past. He had two great desires. One that his theological works might be collected and published for the good of the Church of England in future. Nothing was said about political writings—a silence significant of his desire to let controversy die with him, till it could no longer cause heat and distractions. The other wish was to return home to his own country, and be buried in the grave of his father and his mother. These wishes were communicated in the first instance to his beloved friend, the good physician at S. Germain, Mr. Roger Kenyon, who immediately set about securing their accomplishment with disinterested warmth and earnestness. He wrote to friends in England, who with equal promptitude and kindness took the matter up. Mr. Bowyer, the publisher, gladly promised his assistance; and at a meeting of those interested in the undertaking, it was resolved to print the theological works of Leslie in two folio volumes, a larger and smaller edition, at the price of two and one guineas each to subscribers. Conspicuous among those who exerted themselves was a barrister, Mr. George Bishop, of Gray's Inn, who collected a very large sum of money—no less than £750—in a short time, and wrote a great number of letters recommending the work and its author to persons whom he deemed likely to take an interest in both. These letters were as creditable to Mr. Bishop as to Leslie, for nothing could exceed the enthusiasm which he displayed, mingled with much delicacy and tenderness. Leslie was "in low circumstances" owing to the constant drain upon his resources, without any means of replenishment. But this was only cautiously disclosed to those who were thought proper to be entrusted with the secret.

Strange to say, the only reluctance and opposition to the business was encountered in the University of Oxford, once the stronghold of Toryism, where his name had been a watchword, and among some with whom he had always cultivated friendly relations! This vexed Mr. Bishop very much, and he complained in strong terms of this apathy, saying that the "very stones would cry out." The ostensible reason, or that assigned by Dr. Charlett, was objection to his mode of procedure being somewhat secret, which had been adopted to avoid the possibility of hindrance to publication on the part of the Government at the instance of Whigs and Dissenters. But it is tolerably clear that under this more honourable pretext was veiled an unwillingness to incur suspicion to themselves under the new dynasty. "*Tempora mutantur et nos mutamur in illis.*" There were some bright exceptions at least among authorities at Oxford. The vice-chancellor, the president of Trinity, Dr. Barnes, Drs. Bourne and Taylor. Some slight reparation was made at a later date by publication of a new edition in the Clarendon Press at the instance of Leslie's lineal descendant, the Rev. Edward Leslie, Rector and Treasurer of Dromore in Ireland, himself a learned man, and who twice refused the Deanery from conscientious motives, offered through Sir R. Peel.

No less than five hundred members in the two Houses of Parliament subscribed, some much beyond the price of the work; nor were they all persons of the same political sympathies, but who with honour to themselves generously combined to honour an opponent who had never used any but honourable modes of warfare. Leslie did not know of this noble conduct, or even of all that friends had done on his behalf, till too late to express his own gratitude. Mr. Higden, brother of the clergyman to whom the letter had been addressed concerning "the English Constitution," subscribed £400, and many hundreds of people besides, including "farmers and tradesmen in many country towns."[1] What could be a more striking testimony of the universal esteem in which his name was held? Leslie wrote strongly, severely, but seldom with any tinge of personal bitterness towards individuals. He often in the *Rehearsal* declared that his combat was with their opinions, not themselves, and excluded matters which would have increased its popularity to avoid personalities. If he censured Burnet and Hoadly in scathing terms somewhat imprudent, yet it was not unjust; for the offensive and libellous terms in which they spoke of him, even in the pulpit, would be beyond belief in the present day, if there did not remain several records which are not deemed worthy of citation here. Yet one can wish he had believed in this respect what they preached, if not practised towards him, that "moderation is a virtue." Of the writers in scurrilous papers he might well have taken no notice, had it not been that silence would have been misunderstood by readers, and that they were hirelings of more considerable persons. Against these upon principle he directed no attacks; never even against Godolphin, Harley, or Marlborough, whom he knew

[1] MSS. Bodleian Library.

to be amongst his most dangerous and deceitful enemies. One thing he probably regretted upon reflection, and in that he erred greatly—his attack upon King George I.; because therein he swerved from his own principle. The house of Hanover had not injured or offended him personally, and therefore deserved no wounding remarks at his hand. This must be candidly and sorrowfully acknowledged by those who cherish his memory with affection. But King George had a noble revenge, in which Lord Sunderland concurred. When it was intimated that Leslie had resolved at all hazards to return, for he could not conscientiously retract what he had written or swear allegiance, his Majesty in a very kindly and generous manner declared that "the old man should come home and die in peace." And when some malignant person—it was generally believed and reported Burnet's son—hastened to inform against him upon arrival, Lord Sunderland, with a look of immeasurable scorn, simply showed him the door.

The wanderer came back, the exile returned, in the autumn of 1721. His "heart untravelled" fondly turned to the home of early happy days, before ever he had become entangled in the meshes of controversy, or been buffeted by the winds of political agitation. His father led a stormy life; still more stormy was his. Which was intellectually the abler man cannot unfortunately be determined, owing to the losses by fire of all the former's, and many of his own, manuscripts.

The Dean of Dromore and his wife had shortly before left all their property to Robert, because legally it could not have been left to the father, still under the ban of outlawry; who submitted, it may be presumed, from a conscientious change of opinions, not the mere desire of a fine estate. He certainly had taken as active and decided a part in behalf of the Stuart cause, if he had not become so prominent and distinguished. Yet attachment to his father, and knowing how it would grieve him, may have induced him to coincide with his views so long as he possibly could, and till the critical moment came for choosing between perpetual exile and want in behalf of a hopeless cause, or reluctant submission when he had thereby no oath of allegiance to break.

His father lingered on for several months, utterly shattered in health and exhausted in spirit, and breathed his last on April 13, 1722, at three o'clock in the afternoon. His mortal remains were interred in the churchyard of Glaslough. His soul went back to Him who gave it, and rests in Abraham's bosom in the beautiful abodes of Paradise. There are no conflicts nor questions concerning *de jure* and *de facto*. No right of possession is claimed; all plead only the merits and satisfaction of the Saviour.

And here upon earth in these three kingdoms old causes and dissensions have become extinct. The house of Hanover has no rival with a better title. May the nation never again invite foreign interference with its affairs on any pretence whatever, or risk the certain blessings of peace and order for the miseries and uncertainties of another Civil War or Revolution!

Abridgment of "The Case Stated between the Church of Rome and the Church of England."

What is there in the communion of the Church of England that should make one think one's soul in any danger? Would there be any hazard if there were no invocation of saints that are dead in the public offices of the Church; no pictures or images of God to be seen there;

no elevation of the host, which was but of late years brought into the Church; no prayers for souls out of purgatory; if the public prayers were in the vulgar tongue; and if the Sacrament were given in both kinds; for these are all the differences you will find between your public Offices and ours?

It is certain that Jerusalem was the mother Church where Christ first planted the gospel, and commanded that it should be thence propagated to all other nations as Himself said, "beginning at Jerusalem;" and till after the vision of the sheet, no Gentile was admitted. So that the Jewish Christian was the only Church for some time, and she it was who converted the Gentile nations, and therefore was the mother Church to them all. . . . And Rome was not the first Gentile Church, for "the disciples were called Christians first at Antioch." And the Greek Church was before the Latin; the New Testament was written in Greek for their use, therefore the Greek Church could not be the daughter of the Latin, which was born after her.

"S. Peter having been Bishop of Rome, and Christ having constituted him to be the head of the Catholic Church"—this will not make her the mother Church. In the conversion of the Gentiles to Christianity, one man and one nation must receive the faith before another; but it gives no one superiority over the other except that of gratitude and esteem, but nothing of authority. Whatever the privilege of the mother Church may be, if it can be translated from one to another, from Jerusalem to Antioch and thence to Rome, then it may be translated from Rome also to some other Church, unless some positive command of Christ can be produced first to fix it at Rome, and then a promise that it shall never be removed. But the Church of Rome is not once named in all the New Testament, unless she is meant by "the Church at Babylon." Nor is there any promise whatsoever made to her, or the least intimation of her being the head of the Church, the standard and centre of unity to them all. Strange, if that be, as Bellarmine calls it, the sum and foundation of the Christian religion. As silent are the Scriptures concerning a supposed universal supremacy of S. Peter, or that he ever was at Rome or Bishop of Rome. Some after-writers have mentioned it; but that is far from such a universal tradition as is sufficient for the mighty superstructure which is raised upon it. Let it be granted; it signifies nothing, because all is founded upon some words said to S. Peter, as, "Thou art Peter," etc., "Feed My sheep," etc., which cannot be strained to such a universal supremacy as the popes have claimed, nor were so understood in the primitive Church. That the rock upon which Christ said He would build His Church was not Peter, but the faith which Peter then confessed. See S. Augustine (Sermon xiii.), S. Cyril, S. Chrysostom, S. Ambrose, S. Hilary, and many others. S. Peter was the apostle of the Jews, they were his particular charge; himself allowed that the gospel of the uncircumcision was committed to S. Paul; accordingly, he wrote not to the Gentiles, particularly not to Rome, which would seem strange if he had been bishop and that had been his principal charge.

S. Paul withstood him to the face before the whole Church of Antioch in behalf of the Gentiles whom he had misled; a behaviour not very suitable to the supreme head of the Church, if S. Paul had known anything of his being so constituted by Christ. As little had it become the other apostles to send their sovereign upon business, as they sent S. Peter to Samaria.

If, as some say, S. Peter was bishop of the Jewish converts at Rome, and S. Paul of the Gentiles there, S. Paul would have had a much greater flock than S. Peter, and the successors of S. Paul, not S. Peter, been the bishops there. The surest way to find out the truth is by fact, and not straining expressions which may have several meanings. In the history of the Acts, S. Peter has a great share, though not so much as S. Paul; and there is a council mentioned wherein both were present, and there is not a title of any superiority of S. Peter over S. Paul, or any other of the apostles. If the supremacy of S. Peter be so essential a point upon which the unity of the Church depends, it is inconceivable the Scriptures should be wholly silent on it— nay, showing the very contrary, in fact; and that our blessed Saviour should not have determined the question among apostles "which of them should be the greatest," but left them all upon a level.

Christ has but one Church on earth and in heaven, of which He is the Head; one part militant, the other triumphant, which makes not two Churches, but two states of the same. All the nations are one kingdom to Him; but He has appointed no universal monarch as His deputy. The pretence in the Church of Rome has been the great cause of divisions. For which reason God has appointed no universal monarch in the Church more than in the State. This was the frame of the Church in S. Cyprian's days, and before, from the apostles; the apostolate was given to each in partnership or in common with the rest.

As all nations are one kingdom, so all Christian Churches are one to Christ; and as the unity of the world consists in the law of nations common to all, so the unity of the Church consists in the common Christianity wherein all agree. There is not one word in Scripture appointing a universal head in the Christian Church, or of altering this common sentiment of mankind as to the meaning of the word Church, or taking it in any other sense than commonly understood by all the world. There were some before that of Rome; and bishops and fathers knew nothing of its supremacy, far less of its infallibility, nor ever appealed to it in their disputes with heretics, which had been the shortest and surest way, and impossible to have been forgotten, had it been received as the current faith or even opinion. On the contrary, other Churches have contended with that of Rome, and asserted their independence when encroachments began to arise and disturb the peace and unity of the Church. Unity was understood, not as being under one supreme bishop, but in the common faith, described by all having one Lord, one Baptism, one Faith, and one Spirit, from which they are called one Body. All Churches agree in that summary of faith called the Apostles' Creed. The twelve new articles which the Council of Trent has added to the twelve of the apostles, which we call the Creed of Pope Pius, is required to be professed by converts, and has made many contests and divisions in the Church. Sacraments are signs and seals of our faith, but not the faith itself, and therefore not put into the Apostles' Creed. They are "generally necessary to salvation," as our Catechism words it; but of five, one cannot say they are so much as generally necessary, because none can partake of them all. If a Church be answerable for all that break off from her, then the Roman Church has all our sects to answer for, and us too, which is one more. The Greek Church is an elder one than she is. And since the Reformation, the Roman communion is now reduced to a very small part of the Christian Church in comparison with those who differ from her. . . . Old and new Popery are very different things; Rome itself has in some measure been reformed by our Reformation. There never was a general or Œcumenical Council, where all Churches meet; no more than the Roman empire was all the world. Romanists are not agreed among themselves concerning general councils. Some are partly confirmed and partly reprobated; and one neither manifestly approved nor rejected; this is going through all the degrees of uncertainty. And what a thing it is to say that a council is partly right and partly wrong! We must have an infallible method, too, to preserve the acts of these councils, that they be not adulterated, as Bellarmine says they have been So that the scheme of infallibility of councils stands thus: the Church of Rome makes herself the Catholic Church and little party councils under the direction of the pope are universal and infallible. If infallibility be neither in pope nor council, where do we place it? Nowhere: nor can it be among men who are all fallible.

The Church is compared to a city set upon a hill. To a candle. Likewise to a woman persecuted in the wilderness. To a lodge in a garden of cucumbers. To a besieged city; and, lastly, that she will be so little visible as that faith shall hardly be found upon the earth. This is not to be reconciled but of different states of the Church and at different times. . . . The Church is called holy and beloved because of God's covenant with her to be His holy and beloved, which will be hereafter in those that are perfected, when the tares and the wheat shall be separated; but they must grow together till then. Then, and not till then, will the Church be "all glorious, without spot or wrinkle." She is still in her cleansing state, but not thoroughly cleansed. And the Scripture speaks of both these states of the Church, which, when we distinguish not, but apply what is said of the most glorious to the most corrupt, we must needs fall into many errors and mistakes.

The pretence of miracles, legends, and shops of relics which are bought and sold, instead of a proof, are the greatest prejudice to men of sense against the Roman Church. And it is the sorest blow which Christianity has received, while common people put these legends on a level with the Holy Scriptures as having the same authority, whence Atheists and Deists take a handle to render both alike fabulous.

Believing the Scriptures upon the authority of the Church, as the Church because the Scriptures bid, is the old circle running round and proving a thing by itself. What is it, then? We believe a God purely upon our own reason. And if God has given us no other guide but that, with the assistance of His grace, to believe in Himself, what further do we require for those of less consequence than the first and main article of our Creed? As Fermilian said to Stephen, Bishop of Rome, "Do not deceive yourself . . . while you think you can excommunicate all other Churches, you have only excommunicated yourself." If the Christian sacrifice of the body and blood of Christ, the most solemn worship of God, were confined to S. Peter's Church at Rome, as the legal sacrifices were confined to the temple, and if the Church of Rome, like that of the Jews, were the old Church in the world, yet the Roman would have no more pretence to perpetuity and infallibility than the other. As to Apocryphal books, we received the canon of the Old Testament from the Church of the Jews, which never admitted them. Again, we are sure they were not in the Christian Canon in the days of S. Jerome. The canon of the New Testament was established not at all upon authority, but plainly by evidence.

Precedence of bishops is not a matter of that consequence as to break the peace of the Church, and we should not trouble the world about any such thing. What the Pope claims is no less than absolute sovereignty over all the Churches and kingdoms of the earth by a divine and indefeasible right as heir of S. Peter, and the promises made to him. Behold the machine which God never thought of, of climbing to heaven upon a ladder of popes, cardinals, councils, etc.; and we must give no obstruction, because it would break the machine of their being our infallible guides to heaven. An infallible guide would not be an infallible assurance to us, unless we were infallible too; for besides our not knowing him or mistaking another for him, we might misunderstand his doctrine, and turn it to quite contrary purposes from what he intended. No man knows where this Church is to which the infallibility is annexed. Choose which we will, there are three to one against it; and what difference is there between having no guide, or one we cannot find? You must apply to every man's private judgment when you would make him a convert, else why do you argue or reason with him? Since this notion of infallibility came into the Church of Rome it has rooted out all charity, and her religion has chiefly been employed in cursing all the world but herself. Her canons are bagged with anathemas, and one hears little who shall be saved, but every page is full of who must be damned. The *bulla in cæna* pins the basket, and leaves very few to escape even of the Roman communion itself.

Now, it is the undoubted right of every national Church to reform, alter, and model their Liturgy as shall be most convenient, provided there be nothing put into it that is contrary to the faith, which is not so much as alleged against our public offices. They have a Breviary at Milan and in other places different from that at Rome. And in England, before the Reformation, there were divers in several dioceses. But these differences did not break communion, nor did the alteration at the Reformation, till the pope by the plenitude of his supremacy, and to be revenged upon Queen Elizabeth, took upon him to do so.

We call ourselves Catholics, and pray for the Catholic Church. Every bishop, every Church, and every member of it may be called Catholic, as being included in the general notion of the Catholic Church.

Confession is a good thing rightly used, but not in the sense of the Roman Catechism, that such a repentance as God will not accept is made sufficient by the Sacrament of Penance; and that very few can be saved without it. God has given us Christ as the one Mediator; but Romanists have multiplied saints to themselves without number, like heathen deities. And they pray to them jointly with God. "God and S. John help us," etc. The blessed Virgin Mary, if not preferred, is put on a level with her Son. Epiphanius reckons the worship of the Virgin, not then so rank among heresies, under the name of Collyridians; and he observes that our blessed Lord, foreseeing this superstition, never once called her mother. An extraordinary honour is paid to her in the Roman Mass, where the elements are offered up for her honour. This looks like putting her nearly on a level with the Almighty.

Transubstantiation is a mere school nicety which no man understands, and yet was transformed into an article of faith by the Council of Trent. Christ said, "This is My Body," but as to the manner or means how it was so He said not a word, whether sacramentally, figuratively, or symbolically; or, on the other hand, whether substantially, consubstantially, or transubstantially. These are inventions of our own from our poor philosophy; and yet about these is our whole dispute, which has tormented the Christian Church in our later age more than all the other mysteries of religion. When the substance of bread and wine in the Sacrament is gone, then their accidents are no more; that is, they are accidents and no accidents. And if the accidents, roundness, taste, liquidness, stand by themselves, why are they not substances? Who cannot see that what are called accidents then, are nothing at all in nature but abstracted notions of our own heads, yet disputed about as if real things and made articles of faith?

There is another error of subtracting from the institutions of Christ and the means of grace which He has appointed, in taking away the cup from the laity in the Holy Sacrament. That they might not think themselves deprived of this so beneficial means of the greatest grace, the schools have invented a distinction they call concomitancy, which is, that in all flesh there is some blood goes along or is concomitant with it, so that whoever eats the flesh partakes also of the blood. It is a nicety. Flesh may be so dried that no blood shall appear in it; and in a wafer there can be none without having recourse to miracle. I think it is too bold to throw off the institution of Christ upon such imaginations of our own, which imply that there was no need of the institution of the Cup; for if it be not necessary now, it was not then. But this Sacrament was ordained not only to express the death of Christ, but also the manner of it by the shedding of blood. It was therefore necessary, says the apostle (Heb. ix. 22). The Church may as well take away the bread and leave only the cup, and say that the flesh is contained in the blood. The Council of Trent makes it a heresy to say that the whole Christ is not under each species. But since the Body and

Blood of Christ were separated at His death, He ordained them to be so separated in the Sacrament.

The vow of single life was not imposed till Pope Hildebrand; and it was, says Sigebert, "without precedent, and, as many thought, of indiscreet zeal contrary to the opinion of the holy Fathers." Hildebrand was not obeyed in England for above a hundred years after.

We have not a word in Scripture of any such state of the dead as purgatory, where souls are put under pains equal to those of hell except for the duration. Souls are not said to be made better in purgatory; if not purified, why are they punished? The vindicative justice of God is satisfied before they are forgiven. God says, "He will not remember our sins," etc. How is that consistent with enduring the pains of hell for a hundred or a thousand years? And how do we know what souls go to purgatory? how long they remain there? and who of them are released? Can prayers, then, be made for their releasement in faith, otherwise they are sin? We have not seen any revelation for purgatory; and as for "the tradition of the Church," there are good and bad traditions. But the rule of Vincentius Lirinensis was, that what "was always received everywhere and by all universal tradition," we are willing to join issue upon as to purgatory.

How is it to be imagined that God should keep so many souls for years or ages in extreme torments without necessity? And if the pope has power to release, he must be a very cruel father who keeps one soul there an hour longer. How will poor souls there be deluded if the stock of supererogation should fail them! Can a creature merit at the hands of God for ever so great endowments bestowed upon him? And was there ever a man who did all his duty? We find the greatest saints applying to the mercy of God, and not pleading their own merits. Then, surely, they will disown all who do so.

Prayers for the dead among the Fathers were few, and for those supposed to be in peace to receive increase of happiness before the resurrection. We also pray for the dead, that it would "please God shortly to accomplish the number of the elect, and to hasten His kingdom, that we, with all those," etc. And we bless Him "for all His servants departed this life in His faith and fear," etc.; so that we pray for them as well as for ourselves. But neither these prayers of ours nor those of the ancients have any relation to purgatory. Some of the ancients had a notion of a purging fire at the last day, which does not come up to purgatory.

The public worship is not in a language understood of the people, as the apostle requires. The greatest number of the people cannot carry books of devotion with them, though if they did it would not be common prayer nor joining with the priest. The article in the Creed, "the Holy Catholic Church," was but late put in, on occasion of divisions, to mind people that they were all members of the same body. The next article explains this, and may be called a part of it, namely, "the communion of saints," who are the elect not visible upon earth. The archetypal and truly Catholic Church in heaven is that which is chiefly and principally meant by "the Holy Catholic Church," and "the communion of saints," in the Creed; and there only is perfect unity. It is rather exclusive of any particular Church, and extends to all Christian Churches, which make up the Catholic Church upon earth in such unity as our fallen state will bear.

AN ABRIDGMENT OF THE "TRUE NOTION OF THE CATHOLIC CHURCH," IN ANSWER TO THE BISHOP OF MEAUX'S LETTER TO MR. NELSON.

We esteem every bishop with his college of presbyters and deacons and the laity of his district to be a particular Church, wherein the bishop presides as representing the person of Christ, and to be the principle of unity in his Church as S. Ignatius speaks. And we think with S. Cyprian in his sixty-eighth Epistle to Pope Stephen), "there is a very large body of bishops joined together in the cement of mutual concord in the bond of unity, that if any of our college attempt to make a schism, and to rend and destroy the flock of Christ, the rest should assist, and, like good and merciful pastors, reduce the Lord's sheep into the flock." Hence all particular Churches, that is, every bishop with his proper flock, make up the whole, which is the Catholic Church. And all these are one flock, one Church of Christ, as S. Cyprian speaks in Ep. 55: "As there is one Church of Christ, distinguished into many members through the whole world, so there is one episcopacy of a great united number of many bishops diffused." And again, concerning the unity of the Church: "There is one episcopacy, of which part is committed to every bishop in full." "In full," is a law phrase, and signifies that part of this one episcopacy is so committed to every single bishop, that he is nevertheless charged with taking care of the whole Church. The learned Church of France always contested their liberties against the plenitude of papal supremacy. And we think it incumbent upon every bishop of the Church to assert his own inherent power given by our Lord, as S. Cyprian says: "How dangerous it is in divine things for any to relinquish his proper right and power!" Our blessed Saviour has told us that there will be divisions in His Church; and the experience of all ages has made it good. How many schisms have been in the Church of Rome—popes and anti-popes set up one against another, and some of them lasting for many years together? If those did not divide the Church of Rome, then we are cleared as to any schisms among us. Upon the pretended sovereignty of the pope, we charge the schism of those who have broken off subjection to their proper bishops. And others have proceeded to throw off episcopacy itself. What we plead for is the restoration of its original rights in the Roman communion, where, though the name is retained, the power is swallowed up in one.

Concerning the infallible assistance of the Holy Ghost in the Council of Nice, we know of no promise of such to councils or any particular Church. We doubt not the assistance of God's Holy Spirit to every man and assemblies of men who seek His glory; but this grace may be resisted by assemblies as well as by private men. The Church bears witness to the truth, and preaches and preserves that "faith which was once delivered to the saints," and in this sense is "the pillar and ground of the truth;" as the supporters and propagators of it, not the authors, or having dominion over it.

It cannot be strange that we should be at a loss about infallibility when there is variety and contradiction among those who assert it. But we have an infallible assurance of the faith, in its being delivered down to us by a universal consent of all ages and Churches. The rise of heresies does rather confirm it, because such were found to be novelties. And we rest assured of Christ's promise always to preserve a Church to Himself upon earth, though there is no promise to Rome, England, or any particular Church.

ABRIDGMENT OF "CONCERNING THE USAGES," ETC.

We must first find our Rule of Faith before we apply anything to it, or it to anything If it be Scripture, we know where we are ; but if it be tradition, we launch into an ocean which has neither shore nor bottom, nor we any compass to steer by, where we must be driven about with every wind of doctrine. Different Churches have different usages, and we may like one better than another ; but shall we make a schism for this? Our Saviour, who left us a form of prayer, left no form for the consecration of the elements, though He did for baptism. But the words that Christ spoke are spirit ; and therein consists the life of all outward institutions, and not in the *opus operatum* of the letter, and a form of words of human invention to work like charms.

Suppose any priest now should revive the love-feasts and holy kiss at the Sacrament, and administer it after supper, and not in the morning ; and give it to infants and even to the dead, which was forbidden in the Third Council of Carthage, canon 6?

The late Dean Hickes, at Barking, found the use of mixing water with the wine in the vestry, not at the Altar, to be the usage there ; but this made no noise, not making it a term of communion.

Some always use unleavened bread at the Sacrament. And it has more foundation in the Passover and institution of the Sacrament, than mixing water with the wine. Old Mr. E. Stevens I took to be an honest, well-meaning man of great zeal but weak judgment ; some thought him mad. He is the father of the new separation. And his fate may be a warning, for he had a mind to be of some Church or communion besides his own, and for that purpose he went to the chaplains of a Popish ambassador in London and desired to be admitted into the communion of Rome, but they would not receive him; unless he would come up to their terms, they would not go down to his, thinking him an enthusiast. He told me with joy, when a Grecian archbishop of Philippopoli was in England, that he would try to be admitted by him into the communion of the Greek Church; but was refused there also. And so lived a seeker. And his disciples of the new separation are seeking still.

If God has ordained outward things as means whereby we receive spiritual benefits, then ought they with reverence to be attended, and not laid aside, nay, vilified and spurned. God will not suffer His own institutions to be despised. The new separation make the water so absolutely and essentially necessary, that without it there is no Sacrament at all, and so we have had none ever since the Reformation. If so, they are greater enemies to the Church of England and at a greater distance from it than Rome itself, and have need to be reformed back again to Popery! They make more things necessary to salvation than God has made, which has been the great disturbance of the Church in all ages; while fanciful men, who are fond of their own imaginations, or of others before them, and proud of their discoveries, are not afraid, rather than they should fail, to mend and reform, not only our Liturgy, but the Scripture itself, and deny it to be a certain rule to us. They have also shown a disposition to revive the old tradition of communicating infants in the Eucharist; and then they can easily make it necessary. And send us new cargoes from time to time, which we have warning to expect, and we shall never have done, for tradition is a bottomless well.

INDEX.

A.

Abbé S. Real, 465
Admiral and alderman, 246
A letter to a gentleman, first cause, 25
Anne, wife of Richard II., 249; Queen, 238, 316, 317; bounty, 248; historians of, 316; bishops, 410; death, 495, 496
Apollonius, 107
Arius—Arianism, 147, 184, 190
Asgill's theory and confutation, 366, 367
Astell, Mrs., 291
Atterbury, Dr., 123, 497

B

Baxter and his saints, 341
Bentinck, 240
Best Answer, 411
Biddle, 214; exposition, 208
Blackall's, Dr., sermon and preferment, 410, 411
Blount, Charles, 87, 93
Bolingbroke's complaint, 489; character, 467, 490; flight, 498
Bourignon, Madame, 173, 184
Boyne, battle of, 94
Bull, Dr., on Trinity, 492

Burnet, Bishop, 10, 58, 135, 147, 160; enmity at the Hague, 58; antecedents, 135; history of "Regale," 147; discourses, 160-163; lectures to Queen Anne, 473; lying in truth, 451-457; death, 503

C

Calves'-head feasts, 293, 333
Carte in a shower, 503
Case of "Regale and Pontificate," 140
Catechizing, public, 349
Charity, 421
Cherry, Mr. Francis, 457, 458
Chevalier, small-pox, 468; sister dies, 468; Chevalier too late, retires back, 504
Church, head of, 362; pillar and ground of truth, 362; church, high and low, 295-297; mother of churches, 274, 426, 512; establishment, 338; infallibility, 29; a society, 382; communion, 338; terms, 338
Clarendon, 38, 41, 83, 433; his letter, 21; death, 432
Clerical magistrates, etc., 15, 16
Clogher, Bishop of, 12

Collier, Jeremy, 257
Commonwealth, 348
Comprehension scheme, 256
Compton, Bishop, 35, 58, 409, 496
Connor diocese, 40; Ichabod, 62
Controversy, 43; Bangorian, 495; results, 43
Conversion, 447; Mr. J. Stewart, 43
Convocation, 226-249
Covenant and solemn league, 430
Cowards, theory and confutation, 367, 368

D

Davenant, Dr. Charles, 301
De facto and *de jure*, 420
Deists, 88
Denmark, Prince George of, 403; death and character, 403
Drake, Dr., 336
Dodwell, Henry, 75, 77, 374, 375
Dromore, Dean, 14; defends house, 68; property, 242

E

Ecclesiastical history, abridgment, 276, 277
Electress of Hanover, 237; elector, 502, 504; generosity, 510
Ely, Bishop of (Turner), House, 83, 117
Episcopacy, divine, 424; rule, 30; in Scotland, 290
Erastianism, 126, 143

F

Foe, De, 263, 376
Fox, George, 179, 193

G

Gaffney, 131; Glencoe, 137, 140
"Gallienus Redivivus," 129, 137, 140
Gildon, Charles, 88
Glaslough, 14, 242, 510, 543
Gloucester, Duke of, 232

H

Hacket, Bishop, 40
Hallam, 6
Heresies, 184
Hickes, Dr., 74, 117, 126, 433, 471; death, 493
Higden, 418; brother, 509
High sheriffs, 41, 44
Hoadly, Dr. John, 399, 411, 412; Benjamin, 369
Hody, Dr., 77
Holy Scripture, 486
Huntingdon, Bishop, 244

I

Indulgence, 50-52
Irish, Ireland, 12, 65, 370, 377, 502

J

James II., early career and accession, 31, 33; first proceedings 35; at Oxford, 52; the bishops, 54, 59, 69; S. Germain, 234; death, 236
Jews, doctrines, 113; "Easy Method With," 107
Justification, 182, 183

K

Keightley, Lady F., 20, 24
Kennet, Dr., 122, 169
Kennion, Roger, 507
Kettlewell, John, 78
King, Archbishop, 10, 67, 95
Kitcat Club, 333

Index. 531

L

Leslie, birth, etc., 9; education, 11; at Temple, 12, 13; holy orders, 14; magistrate, 15; marriage, 18; chancellorship, 38; disputation, 45; removal to London, 63, 80; escape, 84; order of writings, 164; S. Germain, 235; "Rehearsal," 323, 337; illness of wife, 352; illness, 401; Nonjurors, 448; outlawed, 457; at Mr. Cherry's, 457, 458; S. Germain, 460; Bar-le-Duc, 475; in Italy, 504; return, death, 510, 512

Leslie, Edward, 508
Leslie, Robert, 242, 499
Locke, 329; treatises, 341, 344
Lorraine, Duke of, 472

M

Macaulay, historian, 6, 118, 119
Magdalen College, Cambridge, 47; Oxford, 48; Merton College, 356
Mahomet, 185, 487; "New Associations" and "Cassandra," 291, 305
Marlborough, 10, 322, 396, 401, 435-437, 498
Mary of Orange, 136

N

Nelson, Robert, 77
Nonconformist, term, 297, 298
Nonjurors, 2, 3, 8, 70, 81, 126, 434

O

Oaths, occasional conformity, 72, 249, 261, 312, 328
"Observator," 90, 324, 373, 374, 398, 402

Oliver's porter, 176
Origin of government, 246, 414, 415

P

Parker, Bishop, 259; Mr., 259, 425
Parliamentary title, 5
Penn, William, 169, 170, 193, 197, 202; death, 503
Predestination, 386
Presbyterians, 309, 376, 424
Priesthood, 148, 150, 216, 222, 374, 377, 379, 384
Private judgment, 272

Q

Quakers, 165, 193

R

"Regale," etc., 143
"Rehearsal," 290, 328, 330, 337, 350, 356, 373, 377, 408
Rooke, Sir George, 255, 327

S

Sacheverell trial, 406, 503
Sancroft, Archbishop, 53, 116-118
Satisfaction, doctrine of, 28, 213
Seven Bishops, 49, 54
Sharpe, 35; archbishop, 308
Sherlock, Dr., 71
"Short and Easy Methods," 87-89
"Snake in Grass," 192, 200
Socinianism, 28, 185, 202
Stillingfleet, Dr., 73, 214
Swift, 242, 296

T

Test Act, 320
Tillotson, Dr., 70, 132, 153
Tindal, Toland, 360, 361

Tithes, 182, 199, 220, 228
"Truth of Christianity Demonstrated,' 483–488
Types, 484
Tyrconnel, 38, 66

U

Usages, 493

V

Vox populi, 344, 345

W

Wagstaffe, 117, 118, 433, 449, 471
Wake, Archbishop, 122
War, France, 253; Spain, 240
Wesley, Samuel, 304
Whigs, etc., 283, 286, 382
William of Orange, invasion, 59; policy, 65; no title in Ireland, 98; massacre of Glencoe, 128; death, 240
"Wolf Stript," 305, 310–314
Wrongs of authors, 358

Y

York and Lancaster contests, 307

Z

Zadok and Eli 145

THE END.

www.ingramcontent.com/pod-product-compliance
Lightning Source LLC
Chambersburg PA
CBHW062123160426
43191CB00013B/2180